CRITICAL ACCLAIM
FOR *TRAVELERS' TALES*

"The *Travelers' Tales* series is quite remarkable."
— Jan Morris, author of *Journeys*, *Locations*, and *Hong Kong*

"For the thoughtful traveler, these books are an invaluable resource. There's nothing like them on the market."
— Pico Iyer, author of *Video Night in Kathmandu*

"This is the stuff memories can be duplicated from."
— Karen Krebsbach, *Foreign Service Journal*

"I can't think of a better way to get comfortable with a destination than by delving into *Travelers' Tales*...before reading a guidebook, before seeing a travel agent. The series helps visitors refine their interests and readies them to communicate with the peoples they come in contact with...."
— Paul Glassman, Society of American Travel Writers

"...*Travelers' Tales* is a valuable addition to any pre-departure reading list."
— Tony Wheeler, publisher, Lonely Planet Publications

"*Travelers' Tales* delivers something most guidebooks only promise: a real sense of what a country is all about...."
— Steve Silk, *Hartford Courant*

"These anthologies seem destined to be a success...*Travelers' Tales* promises to be a useful and enlightening addition to the travel bookshelves. By collecting and organizing such a wide range of literature, O'Reilly and Habegger are providing a real service for those who enjoy reading first-person accounts of a destination before seeing it for themselves."
— Bill Newlin, publisher, Moon Publications

"The *Travelers Tales* series should become required reading for anyone visiting a foreign country who wants to truly step off the tourist track and experience another culture, another place, first hand."
— Nancy Paradis, *St. Petersburg Times*

"Like having been there, done it, seen it. If there's one thing traditional guidebooks lack, it's the really juicy travel information, the personal stories about back alleys and brief encounters. The *Travelers' Tales* series fills this gap with an approach that's all anecdotes, no directions."
— Jim Gullo, *Diversion*

NEPAL

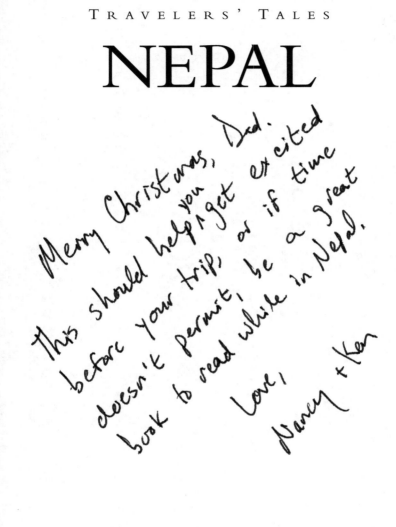

Merry Christmas, Dad.
This should help you get excited
before your trip, or if time
doesn't permit, be a great
book to read while in Nepal.

Love,
Nancy + Ken

JOURNEY WITH THE WORLD'S BEST TRAVEL WRITERS

Fill in this card and we'll let you know about the best travel stories we've found.

Which book did this card come from? _____

Name _____

Company (optional) _____

Mailing Address _____

City/State _____

Zip/Country _____

Telephone _____

Email address _____

We have other Travelers' Tales in the works. What other countries, regions, or topics interest you?

_____

Did you buy this book to:
- ☐ Prepare for a trip ☐ Class/Seminar ☐ Armchair Travel
- ☐ Interest in a specific region or topic ☐ Gift

Where did you purchase your copy?
☐ Bookstore ☐ Direct from O'Reilly ☐ Received as gift ☐ Online ☐ Other

☐ Please send me the Travelers' Tales Catalog
☐ I do not want my name given to outside mailing lists

Give us three names and addresses of people you think would like Travelers' Tales and we will enter your name in our monthly drawing to receive one free Travelers' Tales book of your choice!

Name _____
Address _____
City/State/Zip _____

Name _____
Address _____
City/State/Zip _____

Name _____
Address _____
City/State/Zip _____

TRAVELERS' TALES

"Like gourmet chefs sampling the produce in an overstocked French market, the editors of Travelers' Tales pick, sift, and prod their way through the weighty shelves of contemporary travel writing, rejecting the second rate and creaming off the very best. They have impeccable taste—a very welcome addition to the genre."

—William Dalrymple, author of
City of Djinns and In Xanadu

BUSINESS REPLY MAIL
FIRST CLASS MAIL   PERMIT NO. 80   SEBASTOPOL, CA

Postage will be paid by addressee

TRAVELERS' TALES
c/o O'Reilly & Associates, Inc.
101 Morris Street
Sebastopol, CA 95472-9902

TRAVELERS' TALES

NEPAL

✦ ✦ ✦

Collected and Edited by

RAJENDRA S. KHADKA

Series Editors
JAMES O'REILLY AND LARRY HABEGGER

TRAVELERS' TALES, INC.
SAN FRANCISCO, CALIFORNIA

Distributed by
O'REILLY AND ASSOCIATES, INC.
101 MORRIS STREET
SEBASTOPOL, CALIFORNIA 95472

Travelers' Tales Nepal

Collected and Edited by Rajendra S. Khadka

Cover and interior design by Judy Anderson
Cover Stamp by Edie Freedman
Cover photograph: © 1992 by Alison Wright. Costumed children view the Kumari, the
 living goddess, during the Indra Jatra festival.
Illustrations by Nina Stewart
Map by Keith Granger
Page Layout by Cynthia Lamb, using the fonts Bembo and Boulevard

Printing History

August 1997:   First Edition

ISBN: 1-885211-14-7

सुन्नेलाई सुनको माला
भन्नेलाई फूलको माला
यो कथा बैकुण्ठ जाला
भन्ने बेला सुरुक्क आई जाला

A garland of gold to you, the listener.
A garland of flowers to you, the storyteller.

Now may these stories go to heaven,
and when it's time to retell them,
come back immediately again.

—TRADITIONAL CLOSE TO A NEPALI STORY

*Dedicated to the loving
memory of my father,
Vishnu Bahadur Singh
(1932–1997)*

Table of Contents

Part Four
IN THE SHADOWS

Part Five
THE LAST WORD

Preface

TRAVELERS' TALES

We are all outsiders when we travel. Whether we go abroad or roam about our own city or country, we often enter territory so unfamiliar that our frames of reference become inadequate. We need advice not just to avoid offense and danger, but to make our experiences richer, deeper, and more fun.

Traditionally, travel guides have answered the basic questions: what, when, where, how, and how much. A good guidebook is indispensable for all the practical matters that demand attention. More recently, many guidebooks have added bits of experiential insight to their standard fare, but something important is still missing: guidebooks don't really prepare *you*, the individual with feelings and fears, hopes and dreams, goals.

This kind of preparation is best achieved through travelers' tales, for we get our inner landmarks more from anecdote than information. Nothing can replace listening to the experience of others, to the war stories that come out after a few drinks, to the memories that linger and beguile. For millennia it's been this way: at watering holes and wayside inns, the experienced traveler tells those nearby what lies ahead on the ever-mysterious road. Stories stoke the imagination, inspire, frighten, and teach. In stories we see more clearly the urges that bring us to wander, whether it's hunger for change, adventure, self-knowledge, love, curiosity, sorrow, or even something as prosaic as a job assignment or two weeks off.

But travelers' accounts, while profuse, can be hard to track down. Many are simply doomed in a throwaway publishing world. And few of us have the time anyway to read more than one or two books, or the odd pearl found by chance in the Sunday travel section. Wanderers for years, we've often faced this issue. We've always told ourselves when we got home that we would prepare better for the next trip—read more, study more, talk to more people—but life always seems to interfere and we've rarely managed to do so to our satisfaction. That is one reason for this series. We needed a kind of experiential primer that guidebooks don't offer.

Another path that led us to *Travelers' Tales* has been seeing the enormous changes in travel and communications over the last two decades. It is no longer unusual to have ridden a pony across Mongolia, to have celebrated an auspicious birthday on Mt. Kilimanjaro, or honeymooned on the Loire. The one-world monoculture has risen with daunting swiftness, weaving a new cross-cultural rug: no longer is it surprising to encounter former headhunters watching *All-Star Wrestling* on their satellite feed, no longer is it shocking to find the last guy at the end of the earth wearing a Harvard t-shirt and asking if you know Michael Jordan. The global village exists in a rudimentary fashion, but it is real.

In 1980, Paul Fussell wrote in *Abroad: British Literary Traveling Between the Wars* a cranky but wonderful epitaph for travel as it was once known, in which he concluded that "we are all tourists now, and there is no escape." It has been projected by some analysts that by the year 2000, tourism will be the world's largest industry; others say it already is. In either case, this is a horrifying prospect—hordes of us hunting for places that have not been trod on by the rest of us!

Fussell's words have the painful ring of truth, but this is still our world, and it is worth seeing and will be worth seeing next year, or in 50 years, simply because it will always be worth meeting others who continue to see life in different terms than we do despite the best efforts of telecommunication and advertising talents. No amount of creeping homogeneity can quell the endless variation of humanity, and travel in the end is about people, not places. Places only provide different venues, as it were, for life, in which we are all pilgrims who need to talk to each other.

There are also many places around the world where intercultural friction and outright xenophobia are increasing. And the very fact that travel endangers cultures and pristine places more quickly than it used to calls for extraordinary care on the part of today's traveler, a keener sense of personal responsibility. The world is not our private zoo or theme park; we need to be better prepared before we go, so that we might become honored guests and not vilified intruders.

In *Travelers' Tales,* we collect useful and memorable anecdotes to produce the kind of sampler we've always wanted to read before setting out. These stories will show you some of the spectrum of experiences to be had or avoided in each country. The authors come from many walks of life: some are teachers, some are musicians, some are entrepreneurs, all are wanderers with a tale to tell. Their stories will help you to deepen and enrich your experience as a traveler. Where we've excerpted books, we urge you to go out and read the full work, because no selection can ever do an author justice.

Each *Travelers' Tales* is organized into five simple parts. In the first, we've chosen stories that reflect the ephemeral yet pervasive essence of a country. Part Two contains stories about places and activities that others have found worthwhile. In Part Three, we've chosen stories by people who have made a special connection between their lives and interests and the people and places they visited. Part Four shows some of the struggles and challenges facing a region and its people, and Part Five, "The Last Word," is just that, something of a grace note or harmonic to remind you of the book as a whole.

Our selection of stories in each *Travelers' Tales* is by no means comprehensive, but we are confident it will prime your pump. *Travelers' Tales* are not meant to replace other guides, but to accompany them. No longer will you have to go to dozens of sources to map the personal side of your journey. You'll be able to reach for *Travelers' Tales,* and truly prepare yourself before you go.

—JAMES O'REILLY AND LARRY HABEGGER
Series Editors

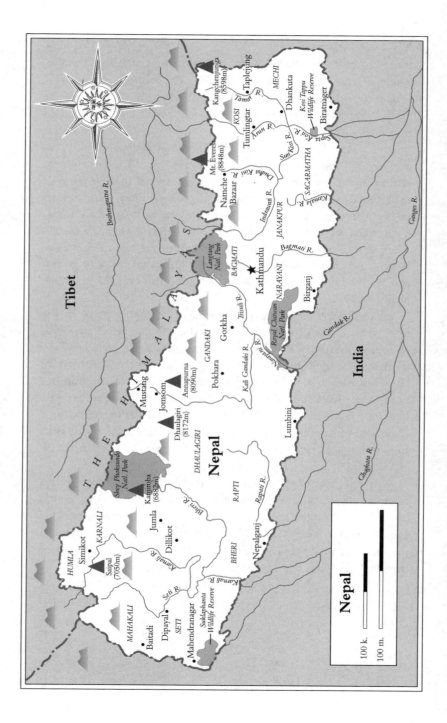

Nepal: An Introduction

Nepal has always been magical and mysterious, stirring the longings and fantasies of travelers of every stripe—spiritual seekers, mountaineers, hippies, yuppies, and backpackers young and old. Even the origin of its name remains elusive. As school children, we were taught that it was derived from a hermit called "Ne" who meditated on the banks of the Bagmati River in Kathmandu. Others have argued that Nepal was named after the Newars, the original inhabitants of Kathmandu. Recent research suggests that there was a non-Aryan tribe called "Nepa" (or "Nipa") who lived along the Himalayan foothills and that "Nepa-al" means "land of the Nepa people." Nepal once referred exclusively to the Kathmandu Valley, and even today, some people who live beyond the hills surrounding the capital city of Kathmandu will say "I'm going to Nepal" when they mean they are going to visit the Valley.

Nepal remained shrouded in a Shangrilaesque mystery until the early 1950s, forbidding entry to all but a few invited foreigners. Despite its political and geographical barriers (snowy Himalayan peaks to the north, disease-ridden *tarai* jungles to the south), for millennia Nepal has been luring outsiders as diverse as the 3rd century B.C. Indian Emperor Ashoka, 7th century A.D. Chinese pilgrim Hiuen Tsiang, and the inevitable, ubiquitous Jesuits—two of whom are presumed to have been the first Europeans to enter Kathmandu in the late 16th century. Many travelers come to Nepal today for some of the same reasons that attracted travelers of yore: pilgrimage to holy sites, view of the mighty Himalaya (the abode of the gods) and the possibility of solace, if not spiritual transformation.

Nepal is at the confluence of two mighty Asian civilizations: highland-Buddhist Tibet and lowland-Hindu India. The result is a fascinating blend of cultures, traditions, peoples, and languages that remains maddeningly elusive but quintessentially Nepali. Despite its strategic position, Nepal was never colonized by any foreign power, a unique feature of the country that is easy to overlook when you notice that Kathmandu's well-stocked shops and lodges along popular trek routes can provide almost anything that the sophisticated traveler desires.

Nepal is renowned for its temples and shrines, palaces and courtyards, and raucous, colorful festivals. It is not an exaggeration to say that there are not enough days in the year if the devout were to worship, pray, fast, or celebrate the mind-numbing array of Hindu-Buddhist-Animist gods and goddesses that reside in roadside temples, hilltop shrines, and mountain *gompas.* The faithful seldom care whether they are praying to Shiva or Sakyamuni, a rock or a river. As children, we sang songs glorifying the spiritual perfection of Siddartha Gautam the Buddha, the martial bravery as well as the suffering and loss of our foreign-bound *lahures* (men who joined the British Gorkha army), and "our Tenzing Sherpa" who reached the top of Mt. Everest. Such all-encompassing veneration mystifies the tourist and frustrates the academic. Finicky Western *dharma* bums soon discover that there are more temples, *gompas,* gurus, *sadhus,* and *rinpoches* to choose from than toothpaste brands in a Western supermarket.

The collision of the continental plates also produced a most breathtaking—and heartbreaking—landscape. There are still places in Nepal where you can observe in one single sweep the geographical range from the subtropics to the arctic, which the eminent Nepali geographer, Harka Gurung, has described as "a giant staircase ascending from the low-lying *tarai* plain to the culminating heights of the Himalayas." Although Nepal is one of the smallest countries in the world, no larger than Tennessee or Austria, its geographical diversity rivals those of much larger nations. The indefatigable visitor can trek across valleys and hills, summit a snow-capped Himalayan peak, raft down swift, frothy rivers that have cut some of the deepest canyons in the world, and explore the jungles of the *tarai* atop an elephant where one can encounter tigers, rhinos, deer, crocodiles, snakes and other wild creatures. More species of birds have been recorded in Nepal than in the USA and Canada combined.

I always ask those who have visited Nepal what is it about the country that they found most memorable. After the usual superlatives about the stunning natural beauty, their excitement is checked, and they linger over the memory of encounters with the people. They recall the Nepali people's genuine openness; their friendliness, charm and grace; and their simple, courteous hospitality. They are impressed by our desire to please and pamper them because it is done with dignity and without a trace of fawning servility. But this is not surprising. For us Nepalis, unlike some others, Westerners are not a reminder of oppression and exploitation. On the contrary, they are seen as messengers from the world beyond the mountains and across the "black waters" of the seven seas, and because we were excluded from that exotic world for such a long time, our hunger to know about the Others is probably more voracious than visitors suspect. So we treat them like long-lost meandering family members who have returned to tell us all about their adventures abroad.

Nepal has now been welcoming tourists for just over 40 years, and it seems every decade the tourist-oriented Nepal reinvents itself. The trickle of almost "accidental" tourists who first ventured into this roadless nation began to swell when Kathmandu was "discovered" by the hippies in the late 1960s, many of whom traded their hash pipes and secret mantras for Wall Street suits and stocks by the mid 1980s. Even as the "flower children" faded, yuppies began to sprout. Consequently, laid-back, passive tourism turned into "adventure" travel. Few "toked," many trekked. But the trickle and swell of tourism has now become a deluge, and Nepal in the 1990s, especially Kathmandu, finds itself high on the list of environmentally-degraded nations. "*Ke garne?*" (What to do?) Well, as we say in Nepal, "No problem." Ecotourism is being thrust forward as a possible solution to some of the problems spawned by "adventure" travel. Trekkers are now told to bring their trash back and to leave nothing behind except footprints.

It is Nepal's capacity to absorb, adapt, and transform that continues to fascinate and attract the visitor—whether an absolute god-king is replaced by a chaotic democracy, traditional dress by blue jeans and t-shirts, the arranged marriage by "love" marriage, or the family farm by business and trade. Often, in the inimitable Nepali style, the contradictory elements coexist. And as the alien, technological world demands faster and more complex adaptations in the traditional cultures of Nepal, what appears to remain constant is the open-heartedness of the people.

Not too long ago, I was showing Kathmandu to an Australian woman who was a first-time visitor. Secretly, I was a little unsure about being her guide. The city had become uglier; the pollution from the gridlocked traffic was especially noxious and obscured the mountains even on a crisp November day, thus eliminating one of the supreme reasons to visit and live in Kathmandu. Much of the terraced farmland in the undulating landscape was now covered with the new homes of the expanding population that poured into the city. The streets were littered with rotting trash.

As a special treat, I decided to take her to a village a few miles outside of the city where we could spend the night at a friend's house. We soon left behind the squalor of the city and were in the midst of comparatively tranquil traditional rural life that for many remains unchanged. Unfortunately, my friend was not there. We were told that something had come up unexpectedly and he had gone to Kathmandu. It was dark and getting chilly. We quickly found a spacious roadside tea shop that actually boasted of being a "restaurant & bar" and ordered tea and biscuits. At another tea shop diagonally across were a group of young men drinking beer and talking loudly. As I sipped my sweet, hot tea I noticed that there was an inner room, the "bar" as it turned out, which could accommodate the two of us for the night. We had our sleeping bags. I asked our tea shop owner if he would let us sleep in the inner room. He hesitated. This was not a hotel, he said. I replied I knew that, but it was dark and cold and I preferred not to go back to

Kathmandu that evening because it would be a long bicycle ride in the dark. The owner remained uneasy, then he disappeared into the back of the house. I heard him consulting with his wife. He reappeared and agreed to let us stay for a price. As I prepared to bring my sleeping bags inside, he motioned to me to stop. He explained quietly, "The young men across the street, I don't want them to know you are staying here with your friend tonight. They could make trouble. They belong to one of the political parties. They have lots of money and power—and they like to make trouble when they have nothing to do. Please wait until they leave, and tell your friend so she understands."

I was touched and grateful for his concern. I was also pleased that this man, so near to the big city, had honored the ancient tradition of offering *baas,* shelter, to weary travelers. It was a perfect example why Nepali people everywhere continue to capture the hearts and minds of strangers far and near.

PART ONE

ESSENCE OF NEPAL

KAREN SWENSON

✦ ✦ ✦

A Sensuous Stroll

*A kaleidoscopic world reveals itself
in the streets of Kathmandu.*

THE WALK FROM DURBAR SQUARE, THE OLDEST PART OF TOWN, TO Thamel, the backpacker's section of Kathmandu, presents me with two problems: sensory overload and the relative certainty of getting lost, not because there isn't a simple route, but because I find the temptations of detours impossible to resist.

I crossed Durbar Square, passing the lovely carved statues of Shiva and Parvati leaning out of a window to watch the passing parade, and exited from the square by a row of *thanka* shops, with their paintings of unfamiliar iconography of dancing, grimacing figures. I turned a deaf ear to the invitations, "Just come in and look," as I went past.

It was late afternoon as I went by the spice merchants sitting cross-legged among bags and bins heaped with red, yellow, and brown powders whose subtle aromas drifted into the street from the low-ceilinged shops where brass scales gleamed in the light from a single bulb. These were followed by the sari shops, where fabrics are opulently gilded and sequined and shop boys came out to seduce me in with "Sari, Madam, first quality, very cheap," or "Bedspread, Madam. See, beautiful design," spreading it open to the danger of other pedestrians and traffic in the narrow street.

Next door the gold and silver merchants, their windows glittering, keep their doors invitingly open so that you can glimpse women trying on earrings and exquisitely dainty necklaces. I passed the arcade whose entrance is decorated by a pair of carved dragons flanking a Garuda, the half-man, half-bird deity, with a snake in his mouth. Just before Indra Chowk's busy square I stopped at a Ganesh figure, his elephant body almost indistinguishable under his coating of orange paste, surrounded by figures, including a skeleton with a penis, a true example of wishful thinking by the sculptor.

The square houses the Akash Bhairab Temple, adorned with its odd combination of red, green, white, and flowered tiles plus four rearing metal lions, or are they dragons? Here people clustered around an inner square made of benches. In the center, on top of a pyramid of food surrounded by pompons of marigolds, was a fish with an egg in its open mouth. Everyone was throwing money into a pot before it and then anointing their foreheads with the red powder that had been set out for that purpose. As is often true for me in Kathmandu, I had no idea what this mini festival was about, and I never did find out.

There are many things one "should see" in this valley, but I secretly resent being bossed by guidebooks and am therefore a slipshod tourist. To me the little statue that one unexpectedly discovers down an alleyway, and impulsively responds to, means much more than the temple one had been instructed to admire for erudite and probably incomprehensible reasons.

—Dervla Murphy, *The Waiting Land: A Spell in Nepal*

Just out of Indra Chowk is a tiny street that glitters with glass and plastic bangles. Women come here to buy them by the dozens and to gossip as they choose the bracelets that will match their new saris. Here are also sold "jeweled" *tikas*, plastic red Hindu ornaments to be pasted on your forehead.

Leaving the square I passed a boy of twelve carrying a load on his back that would have burdened two donkeys. The Mahadev Temple's ledges were piled with Nepali *pashmina* shawls, blankets, and scarves in blue, beige, green, violet, and black. The

Shiva Temple next to it, with trees sprouting green out of its crown, was also cocooned with shawls and blankets so soft that just looking at them made me want to nuzzle in among them and sleep.

I frequently choose the wrong street when leaving Indra Chowk, but there is no wrong street when shops spill brass, gleaming in the evening light, into the street, or corners are piled with copper cauldrons above head height. Though it is precarious, because of traffic and potholes, those who take the risk are rewarded by houses built in European style with little balconies and plaster ornamentation over arched windows and doors, or the traditional Newari houses with lacy wood carving edging narrow balconies or magnificently framing windows. Brass oil lamps with rampant dragons dangle from carved struts which hold up eaves. Also when you look up you see wares hanging from first-floor windows: sweaters, masks, bedspreads, clothing of every sort from stern nightdresses to baggy pants for tourists.

And all the time that you are looking at saris, kettles, shawls, beads, you are being jostled and honked at. Rickshaws with scenes painted on the backs of their buggies practically push you into shops while they tinkle their bells furiously. They in turn are harried by motorcycles with clamorous horns. Cars crawl along trying not to crush either pedestrians or rickshaws while the mad *tempos*, three-wheeled vehicles, weave in and out among it all, spouting black fumes that cause women to pull their saris across their noses and Westerners to mutter about global warming. Simultaneously you are being importuned to change money, buy carpets, Tiger Balm, saris. No wonder travelers look as though they've been stunned by a cattle prod.

To escape for a moment I stepped into the Seto Machhendranath Temple on Kel Tole where, in the evenings, local musicians come to play. Immediately inside the door there is a scantily-clad European lady in bronze

Due to increasing theft of religious icons, the inner sanctum of shrines and temples are nowadays often locked up. Sometimes, the entire temple building is caged in an ugly metal frame to prevent theft and vandalism.

—RK

surrounded by oil-lamp saucers. Local wisdom has accepted her into some pantheon of deities. The temple court was filled with dogs, some of which it would be a great comfort to put out of their misery, ducks, shops, women winnowing rice, women resting against the mini temples called *chaityas*, smoking and talking, children throwing marigold petals at sleeping dogs. Inside the main shrine is a god with a face as white as a geisha's, almost smothered under mounds of marigold leis.

I passed shops that sell sweets in such garish colors that my stomach churned when I looked at them. These were interspersed with taped-music shops, electronics shops selling audio equipment, an old woman with her begging bowl before her, and other shops with hand-carved local instruments. I walked through Jana Bahal, where clay pots of all sizes are sold, as well as peas, peppers, tomatoes, ginger, potatoes, and mammoth lemons.

The tree trunk that is covered with nails and nailed coins at Bangemudha square is now so crowded that it seems impossible that anyone else with a toothache will be able to get a nail in to cure it, as is the belief. Farther down the street I passed the dentist's shops grinning with their wares.

Again dodging out of the stream of pedestrian and strident vehicular traffic, I went into the court of Yitum Bahal. It was full of children. Pairs of girls imaginatively played badminton with a knot of rubber bands, using the tops of shoe boxes as rackets. In an inside court there are two, not three as some guidebooks say, bronze plaques above a school. In the one on the far left Guru Marpa, a monster who eats bad children, is being fed a child by a phlegmatic mother. On the far right he is eating from a pot, one hopes, a vegetable stew. In the center of the court, around which the children chase each other, is a little shrine hung with laundry.

As the sun went down I knew I had reached the Thamel section because men, drifting like dandelion down, whispered as they passed, "Heroin, opium, hashish, marijuana." They apparently hawk their wares indiscriminately, since I am, to anyone of a noticing sort, blatantly a non-prospect.

Light spilled out of shop doorways illuminating the narrow streets as I tried to decide which of the tourist restaurants, with which Thamel abounds, I should choose for dinner. I have an old favorite started many years ago by its eponymous owner, a far-sighted Sherpa, KC's. In those days it was the only restaurant in Kathmandu where you dared to eat a salad. I was lucky, KC himself was there. We talked about the old days of the hippies in Kathmandu during the 1960s as I ate a bowl of his superb tomato soup with crunchy bread. Those days were gone and with them the sleepy small town quality the place used to have. Few cows sleep these days in the middle of Kathmandu's roads. But it has retained, despite huge influxes of tourists, its cultural identity and vitality. It remains, like the Himalayas themselves, a place I always will want to return to.

Karen Swenson is a poet and freelance writer who spends part of each year in Asia and part in New York City. She writes travel pieces for The Wall Street Journal *and* The New York Times *and practical pieces for* The New Leader. *Her latest book,* The Landlady in Bangkok, *won the National Poetry Series.*

✳

The energy of the place slams like a shock wave.... Kathmandu is so overwhelming, so packed with images, that succinct summaries seem almost impossible—certainly inadequate. I'm tempted to say "You'll understand when you get there...." It's a dream. I've never seen anything like it.

—David Yeadon, *The Back of Beyond: Travels to the Wild Places of the Earth*

BARBARA J. SCOT

✦

Women at the Tap

Entire worlds can be glimpsed through the prism
of the communal bath.

A SMALL SHIVA SHRINE STANDS WHERE THE LANE ON WHICH I LIVE joins the main road to Mahendra Pul. A grated gate keeps the goats from reaching in to eat the colored rice and flower petals placed there for the god. I can tell by a sideways glance through the grate that the light is a different color inside. I never lean down to look in directly, as I am shy of exhibiting such open curiosity, but I am aware of the stubby cylinder, Shiva's *lingam*, phallus, for which the offerings are brought to insure blessings for fertility and good fortune. Beside the shrine, next to the *chautara*, the resting platform built around a tree with gnarly roots, a water tap stands. This structure has none of the artistic beauty of Shiva's temple as it is set in a plain cement slab. Because of the old woman, however, this utilitarian faucet embodies for me all the symbolic magic of a sacred spring.

This tap, like all water sources in Nepal, supports a constant hum of activity even before daylight. In Mate Pani, the area of Pokhara where I live, many of the wealthy returning Gurkha soldiers bought land and built large cement-block houses with interior plumbing, but much of the population has no such amenities. A centralized water tap is to them as much a necessity as it is to the people in the hill villages. Now in the warm season, with my school on morning hours, I pass the cement platform before it is truly light. Always a line of women and children wait with water containers. People with small filled pitchers stand brushing their teeth and cleansing respiratory tracts with noisy expectorations. Saturday is the busiest day of all. I would like to sit all day by the *chautara* simply to record the stream of humanity, but it would be impolite to be fascinated with common things. I often go that way for errands anyway, so a collage of a day's libations at this humble brass shrine is not hard to construct.

Women, who arrive at the tap singly, group in clusters to scrub the dishes and pots in the sandy mud. The clean metal gleams while they stand and talk. Both women and men carry clothes to the water in silver basins. Each garment is subjected to a rigorous ritual of kneading, pounding, and wringing through several soaping sessions. Children come in twos and threes, the smallest entirely without clothes. The oldest, or an accompanying elder, administers the shampoo. The children submit to this foamy ordeal with patient resignation.

Young women often come alone. They bathe deftly, using their *lungis*, the all-purpose wide piece of material which is sewn in a tube. These girls accomplish their body cleansing and an entire change of clothes without revealing more than a few inches of skin. No man stares and even teenage boys do not sneak covert glances, for it is part of the code of such a crowded community that private rites performed in public command their own invisible shield.

> *Taking a bath is quite a procedure because you do it in public, using the* lungi *technique. You undress, wash, and dress again, all under the* lungi. *Needless to say this is a bit tricky, especially with all the villagers watching the best show of the year, as a bunch of pale Western amateurs struggle with wet* lungis.*
>
> —Preb Stritter,
> "A Bath for Christmas"

In earlier times, such complete coverings were not required of women. Once, it is said, a bevy of young cowherds were bathing naked in the river and throwing water at each other when the young god Krishna came upon them. He hid their clothes in the bushes, then called on them to rise from the water. They blushed red with shame. Then he commanded them to come from the river and one by one made love to them in the way each most desired. He bade them forever after to remain demurely dressed. And they have. Even while bathing in public.

But it is not necessarily so with old women. The first time I saw one naked to the waist washing her hair, I was shocked and asked the Nepali language trainer how this could be in a society that required the women to be so modest. She laughed. "Old women," she replied, smiling, "do as they will."

Barbara J. Scot is an avid climber, hiker, and naturalist. She lived and taught for a year in Nepal, and has returned twice for extended visits with husband and friends. She is the author of Prairie Reunion *and* The Violet Shyness of Their Eyes: Notes from Nepal, *from which this story was excerpted. The mother of two sons, she taught high school social studies for 25 years and lives in Portland, Oregon with her husband.*

★

Her hair is still black and almost every night her young granddaughter Alisha combs and oils it with a concentration she rarely shows in her more mischievous pursuits. On a sunny afternoon, Alisha massages her grandmother's bare back with oil and Aajima sits half naked in the warmth. There is no shame, no flaunting; she has been alive long enough to earn this careless repose.

—Elizabeth Baugh Staphit, "Journey to Impermanence"

* ✱ *

A Nosy Neighbor

The mysteries of the East are many.

ANXIOUS AND DISTRACTED, I GRIPPED THE TABLE LEG WHERE I SAT
in a tea stall pigeonholed in Kathmandu's noisy and crowded central bazaar. I tried to concentrate.

A boy wearing rags patched on rags stepped from behind the
counter and, balancing a trayload of tumblers of milk tea, set a glass
at an adjacent table. Then, he looked at me.

It was there. Something was crawling out of my nose.

The boy froze as if electrically shocked. Dropping the tray, he
ran from the tea shop, fleeing as from the curse of the Hindu goddess Kali, Shiva's wrathful manifestation, whose gaze alone can
mortify armies.

So, it was real, after all. Reflexively, I leaped up and over the
spilled and broken glasses, and found the boy half-crouched and
trembling against the wall of a nearby building, burying his head
into his folded arms.

"What did you see? What did you see?" I asked him intently in
Nepali, wanting to grab him and shake out an answer, or sympathy, perhaps. I felt as frightened as he. Shielding his eyes from mine,
he ran from my voice, head down, arms pumping, through the
alley and across the next street.

My thoughts raced, trying to piece together the chain of events. I prayed that the ordeal that had begun eighteen days earlier in the American Peace Corps office in Kathmandu might at last be nearing an end.

Recently graduated from college, I was a Peace Corps volunteer posted in Nepal, monsoon season, 1975. As I relaxed on the couch in the office lounge, reading my mail, a drop of blood splashed onto an aerogram from home. I looked up, unable to see where it came from. More drips appeared from my nose, bloodying my fingers. Not again, I thought—not an early symptom of yet another exotic Asian disorder.

I had recently returned from a trek to Mt. Everest base camp. In my mind I reviewed the trip—the 18,000-foot altitude, the thin, crystalline air, the simple meals of well-cooked, bullet-resistant buckwheat pancakes, and the cold, refreshing mountain spring water. At lower elevations, to drink untreated water, even if clear, would risk infection with hepatitis, typhoid fever, giardia, amoebae, and other parasites. But I disliked the taste of iodine pills, and a vigorous thirst could overcome my caution if the water looked as if it originated in a mountain spring. I had come to accept that, in Nepal, disease was an occupational hazard, and doctors, if available, often prescribed a shotgun treatment of broad-spectrum drugs. Risky place, this corner of Asia, I pondered while standing in the hallway, staring blankly at an outdated notice on the bulletin board.

Barney, the office doctor, stepped into the hallway. I said hello, but did not mention the brief nose bleed, afraid it might arouse too many questions. Barney was a pediatrician. Nepal, and tropical medicine, were new assignments for him. Each case he saw seemed to set off an imaginary beeper, allowing him to escape, scratching his head, to a medical text in his study. Generally, he would select an overweight volume, heft it onto the examining table, then read and re-read passages aloud to his patients, becoming more indecisive with each rendition. The volunteers referred to him by the nickname of *Ke Garne* (What To Do?) Barney.

Anyway, my nose had stopped bleeding. But when I bicycled through the bazaar to my apartment, it began leaking blood again, continuously, for twenty minutes. The next afternoon, I went to a tree farm to request seedlings for the village where I taught school. There, my nose dribbled again. Not knowing what to do, I held a handkerchief to my face like a shy, about-to-be-married Hindu woman hiding the terror and shame that she pictured awaiting her.

*W*henever Nepalis are confronted by what appears to be an intractable situation, their response is: "Ke Garne"—What to Do?

—RK

The following day, still bleeding, I saw Ke Garne Barney. He examined my nose with his nasoscope, and speculated that my nasal membranes might be weak, perhaps aggravated by the dryness and cold of high altitude. He gave me a bottle of Neo-Synephrine, a thumbs up, a good handshake, and a return appointment.

I gave the Neo-Synephrine a full trial, for three days, though from the first application my nose only seemed to bleed more. Each day, it bled in painless, erratic spells. It dripped in the evenings, but not while I slept or, unaccountably, until ten in the morning. I remained in Kathmandu, reluctant to return to the village where I was posted. Even without nose problems, to most villagers I was a strange enough apparition. I knew what they'd do with me: direct me to the shaman, who would likely deduce from a diagnostic trance that I had been infected by the hex of a witch with reversed feet, requiring that I shave my head and sacrifice a water buffalo to Narayan, an incarnation of Vishnu. Fine, but on my Peace Corps allowance I couldn't afford a water buffalo.

"Well, I might have to cauterize your nose," Barney suggested on the fourth day. "I can't think of what else to do." The Neo-Synephrine hadn't worked, and he could see no irritant.

"I'd like to wait," I told him, adding that I had heard that noses didn't smell as effectively after cauterizing.

"Well, yeah, I've heard the same thing," he shrugged in agreement.

Eight days of chronic bleeding. Rumors surfaced that Barney had misdiagnosed some patients, the positive side of which was that they got medically evacuated to Bangkok, a great place for overcoming homesickness. I needed another opinion, but during the monsoon Barney was the only Western-trained doctor in town. Perhaps Warren, a scholar friend who lived downstairs, would have an idea. Warren's guru was a Buddhist priest of the Newar ethnic group, and the man practiced traditional Asian medicine.

On our Chinese one-speed bicycles, Warren and I threaded through the bazaar to the pharmacy and clinic of Dr. Mana Bajra Bajracharya. Descended from a 700-year lineage of Royal Physicians, "Mana" practiced Ayurvedic medicine, an empirical science described in the Vedas. It works by treating fundamental imbalances, rather than symptoms, by realigning the body's complementary elements of nerve, mucous, and bile. Mana had earned a thick volume of testimonial letters from around the world—32 years' worth—extolling his cures for diabetes, hepatitis, arthritis, multiple sclerosis, sexual dysfunction, and cancer.

Sitting in the waiting room, Warren assured me that Mana would have a safe and ready treatment. Aging but animated, the doctor appeared in the vine-framed doorway. He summoned me into his examining room.

Dr. Mana performed a thorough Ayurvedic exam, which included reading my pulse and turning my eyelids inside out, presumably to search for clues in the sound and pattern of blood vessels. Mana's diagnosis was similar to Barney's, but he was puzzled by the duration of the bleeding. He prescribed aloe, an herbal astringent.

That didn't work either.

Fourteen days. The total loss of blood was not serious, but I began to question whether I would ever be normal again, as victims of chronic hiccoughs must feel, longing for rest. I wondered if I should have my nose cauterized, after all, or be evacuated to Bangkok or Atlanta's Centers for Disease Control. Perhaps the village shaman should be sent for. I couldn't concentrate, saw fewer friends, stammered slightly, and experienced jarring flashbacks of college psychology case studies of deviants, and of cautions from the U.S. Government shrink who screened me in the U.S. Long periods of isolation from familiar surroundings, they all said, could induce hallucinations, or worse.

On the eighteenth day after the first nose bleed, I bicycled down a cluttered, medieval side street of the central market. Thankfully, my nose hadn't dripped in several hours. But from the corner of my eye I thought I saw something emerge from my right nostril. I reached for my nose, which felt normal. I continued pedaling, presuming it to be a piece of coagulated blood.

There it is again. Then gone. *Yes, something is in there, and it's working its way out.* A panic flushed over me. My nose grew large in my field of view, and the world beyond my face diminished.

I needed to have this sighting confirmed by someone, by an earthling not yet infected. But if this thing was part of a widespread insidious infection, I feared people might not tell me the truth. I pulled over to a tea shop, ordered a glass of tea, and waited. Again I saw a blurred form, but felt nothing. That's when the boy in the tea shop saw it too, and at terrifyingly close range.

Dumbfounded, I stood in the alley beside the tea shop, watching the boy run off. I paid the startled shopkeeper for my tea, and the spilled tea, and biked back to my apartment. In the bedroom mirror I saw only a nose, a normal one. I drew up a chair and positioned myself squarely in front of the mirror, hands cupped on my knees, resolving to watch my nose until I saw it, the thing. For a quarter-hour, self-conscious but purposeful, I focused, a hunter stalking himself.

Then, as if trying to catch me unaware, a long, brown, eel-like creature slid out, silently, offering no physical sensation at all. Guardedly, it scanned the air and retracted, leaving no trace. The probing tentacle of a monster. Kali. A hallucination, a mirage. For a moment I felt non-human, an alien sent to earth on reconnais-

sance to test the spiritual or intestinal fortitude of those who dared
look at me. I would not last long in this incarnation. I would be
captured for dissection by the world's scientific community.

"*War-ren,*" I called haltingly. Warren ran up the stairs; from the
the sound of my voice, he perceived a turning point. We met in
the bathroom, where his initial skepticism turned to dread.

"Eee...*Yaah!*" Warren exclaimed gutturally. He held his hands
up, preparing to fend off the worm-like organism should it escape
and head in his direction.

Experimenting, I found that handfuls of water splashed up my
nose somehow drew out the animal a finger's length, weaving and
searching. I tried to grab it, but was unable to touch it before it
withdrew. Then Warren tried, his face distorted in trepidation and
disgust, betraying his stoic military school training.

We couldn't even touch it. Our index fingers and thumbs were
poised closely at my right nostril, but the slippery form retreated
before either of us could get it. Sensing any threat, the thing disappeared. So this was why I had found it strangely easier to inhale
than to exhale through that nostril: the thing had formed a kind of
a valve in there.

It was Sunday. Barney's day off. The American medical clinic
was closed except for emergencies, which were discouraged.

"Let's go see Mana," Warren proposed. He was confident that
Dr. Mana, though he missed the diagnosis, would at least recognize
the thing itself.

We bicycled through a bazaar teeming with busy, unconcerned
mortals. Like a Tibetan chanting his mantra, Warren rhythmically
intoned, "I don't believe it, I don't believe it," synchronizing the
don'ts to each pedal stroke. I repeated the familiar Buddhist mantra,
Om Mani Padme Hum, but it came out sounding more like "Oh
Mommy Take Me Home."

Mana motioned us into his study, an extension of his examining room. Demonic, cryptic charts peered from the tops of cabi-
nets overflowing with unbound ancient texts. Glass cases were
filled with odd-sized, murky bottles of tonics with Sanskrit names.

I thought I saw my name on one of the bottles. Mana said a few words in his tribal language to the gnomish compounder, who was wearing a smock caked with herbal and mineral—and what looked like animal—residue. He then turned to serve tea, assuming we had come to discuss a publishing project Warren had been helping him with. Warren stated that this meeting was of much greater urgency, then explained my situation. The thing was hiding. Perhaps it would burrow into my brain, or lay eggs. Ungraciously, Warren laughed.

"None of this is possible!" Mana interjected with customary confidence. "Thirty-two years I am a physician in Nepal, and I have *never* seen a worm in a patient's nose!"

I hadn't, either. "Watch this," I rejoined, equally confidently, though my voice was breaking. I asked Dr. Mana to call for some water, and we stepped into his courtyard, a square of buildings that housed his herb stores, compounding laboratory, and apartments of his extended family. His grandnephews and nieces ran about in carefree play until the compounder arrived with a glass. I squatted down. Mana and Warren followed. The children stopped playing.

I poured water into my hand and tossed it toward my nose. The thing came out on cue. Startling us, Mana jumped up, hands and fingers writhing, eyes rolling, face contorted.

"*Aaahhh!*" he cried, as if in anguish himself. "It's a *leech*!" A leech. A lurking, tenacious bloodsucker, evoking the quivering agony of Humphrey Bogart wading through a carnivorous, parasite-infested African river—an animal that had found its refuge, a human host, where it could develop, lay eggs, and finally emerge as an evolved, aggressive, and no doubt hungry, life form.

Villagers had told me that leeches are inauspicious even by themselves, but by manifesting one in my nose I had been transfigured into an evil spirit of semi-human form. Even the children recognized it. Panic propelled them from the courtyard, and they ran as if from a ravenous, multi-armed deity that subsists on small children. Women leaned from the courtyard's upper story windows and promptly latched the shutters, then climbed to the flat rooftops and called their neighbors to clamber over, across the roof—not at ground level—to see this from a safe distance. I felt a chill, and shivered uncontrollably.

By the time we enter the oak and rhododendron forests, the clouds move in. The buffaloes are single file, and disappear into the misty undergrowth. They wear straw slippers so their hoofs don't wear off while trekking up the stony trail. The rain comes down in fat drops, and that is when the leeches decide to ambush the convoy. Suddenly they are everywhere, dropping down from the lower branches, flailing their suckers from wet rocks, sucking the buffaloes without mercy. At the pass where we rest while the buffaloes straggle past, I pick out fifteen leeches from inside one of my shoes. The buffaloes are faring worse, there are hundreds of leeches hanging on to their flanks. They are bleeding from snouts and eyes, where leeches now gorged with buffalo blood peel off and drop by the roadside by the hundreds.

—Kunda Dixit,
"Nepali Monsoon"

Mana ordered tweezers, salt, and more water, figuring that the salt, a good leech repellent, might cause it to release. We squatted again. I splashed salt water into my nose. His tweezers could not touch the leech. He tried several times again. The salt water only caused it to retreat further inside.

"I don't know what to do," he confessed, frustrated that the case had seemed to defy his entire Ayurvedic medical tradition, and do so in front of his family. "I give up. Maybe your Western doctor has some kind of suction machine." Genial in defeat, Mana desired only that it be removed any way possible.

I called Ke Garne Barney at home from the phone in Mana's waiting room. Excitedly, I described the events, though perhaps not in the order they occurred. Yes, a leech stuck its head out when I splashed water up my nose, but it always disappeared before I could touch it. I asked Barney what he thought.

There was no response.

"Are you there?" I asked into the telephone. It was not uncommon for phone calls in Kathmandu to be disconnected.

"Yeah, yeah, I'm here." Barney didn't like surprises.

"Well, what do you think?"

"This is difficult. I don't know what to say, exactly, except that I...I'd like to make an appointment for you to see the Embassy psychiatrist."

I covered the receiver with my hand. Barney had decided that I was a drug- or culture-shocked deep end case—another not uncommon feature of Kathmandu. I needed someone to corroborate my story, a respectable witness. Mana was busy calming his extended family, who were peeking over the rooftops, worried about contagion; Barney would probably figure Mana as a quack, anyway. Warren, a long-haired, unemployed U.S. Air Force Academy dropout, might not qualify, but he occasionally did construction work under contract to a branch of the United Nations.

"I have a U.N. contractor here, his name is Mr. Warren Smithson, and I'm going to put him on," I said resolutely to Barney.

Warren was low on patience with any kind of authoritarian figure, which for him included American-trained professionals. He tried to turn the case around on Barney, asking if maybe *he* was nuts, reminding him that this was reality, that I had better get some respect, and that he had better know what to do about this, and do it soon. I reached for the receiver, fearing Barney might have us both carted off to the psych unit.

"Okay, okay," Barney relented. "So, what do you want me to do about it?"

"I want you to take it out," I tried to say calmly, though my tone was of exasperation and pleading.

"*How?*"

Barney knew of no precedent for a nose leech. Maybe his liability insurance wouldn't cover an untested leech removal procedure. I relayed Mana's suggestion about a suction apparatus.

"I'll think about it on my way down to open up the clinic," Barney offered. "But I can't promise anything.... I think the nurse should come, too, for this one," I could hear him add in an aside to himself.

Wearing the reluctant expressions of first-year anatomy students just introduced to their cadaver, Barney and the nurse greeted me with simple nods in the driveway of the American medical compound. Barney mumbled about not having been taught anything about this in medical school, of vacation time, and of his chances for getting transferred to a post in Europe or Polynesia. He kept glancing at his beeper hopefully.

The nurse and I helped him set up the naso-gastric suction pump, but the motor wouldn't operate: a burned fuse, with no replacement. Barney asked the two of us, for lack of specialists to confer with, if the pump would logically be the proper tool, and how he might use it if it did work. The nurse and I had no idea.

I sat on the examining table. Barney inserted the nasoscope but saw nothing, hoping out loud that maybe the leech had fallen out on my way to the clinic. He flicked his head as if shaking off a dream, then brushed his hair back slowly and tightly with both hands, momentarily smoothing the engraved worry lines of his forehead. He fished out a pair of hemostats, resigned to having a go at grabbing it, just as Warren, Mana, and I had tried.

I palmed water into my nose. I could tell that the leech appeared when Barney's body jerked. He hesitated, then bit his lower lip and approached, cautiously, as toward a dormant beast. Wait. Silently emerge. *Clamp.* Vanish. Wait. Emerge. *Clamp.* Missed again.

"Damn," Barney swore forcefully, as awed as the nurse and I by the lightning reactions of the primitive creature. Slowly, he backed away, as if trying to determine whether time was critical, or if he should stop right there and phone for advice, or perhaps step out for a cigarette.

Sweating, his hand unsteady, he advanced again and tried clamping—randomly—below my nostril. After several minutes, he nabbed the end of the leech, the head, on its way out for air. He cinched down the hemostats' miniature grippers, and the two of us paused, locked together in suspended animation. Then, with one palm on my forehead, he began to pull, slowly increasing the pressure. My focus narrowed and, cross-eyed, I watched the leech stretch outward. For the first time I could now feel the thing—pulling vaguely from the interior of my head, indeed as if from the back of my head. It wouldn't let go.

"Let me know if it hurts—otherwise, I'm...I'm just going to keep pulling until something happens," Barney stuttered, sounding unsure what that might be, or whether he was doing the right thing at all. He now needed two hands on the hemostats. I braced one foot and a hand against the side wall of the examining room, while my other hand gripped the back of the cushioned table to keep from being pulled forward. The leech was stretched out nearly a foot; again we hesitated in this position, braced. I could see Barney soberly trying to reckon. Under prolonged, static tension the leech might loosen and release, though his face was twisted in anticipation of a horrible accident.

My neck strained against the pull. I heard myself mouthing Warren's mantra. *I don't believe it. I don't believe it.* I realized that I might never again experience this, nor again see such an expression on a doctor's face. I had been told to expect the unusual in this country, but this was more like some altered, metaphysical dream. *I don't believe it.*

Something snapped. Barney hit the wall directly behind him, while I fell over backward across the examining table. I couldn't see where the leech went, if in fact it came out, or if it had taken part of me with it. I wasn't sure Barney knew, either, until, with deliberation, he held up the trophy—a fidgeting, clean, unattached leech, tightly seized in the clamps. Unstretched, it measured four inches long, was as thick as a pencil, and had a nickel-sized sucker on the host end. Barney's mouth hung open, grinning at the same time. As far as he could tell, he had done the right thing.

My nose dripped not a drop of blood. The leech, the hex, was gone. I said thanks and shook hands with Barney who was still speechless, and stepped from the clinic to again join the world of benign, unencumbered humans. I slowed as I passed a neighborhood shrine. A gathering of devout Hindus was chanting, conducting a propitiatory ritual. I wondered if they had seen visions as gripping as my real one.

Two days later I went to see Mana. He caught sight of me before I crossed the threshold of his clinic.

"I know how we could have gotten it out!" he declared buoy-antly from his waiting room. "If we had held a glass of water to your nose, and kept it there, it would have dropped off into the water on its own. Yak herders attract them from the nostrils of their yaks that way. Your leech had completed a stage of its life cycle—it was done living in the host, which is usually livestock, and was waiting for a stream to drop into and float down, to re-produce and continue its cycle! Ha! You must have picked up the leech by drinking water from a stream the way a cow does!" He laughed loudly. I could feel the people sitting in the waiting room gawking at me with open, uneasy concern.

Then I remembered the mountain spring water. I had inten-tionally drunk on hands and knees, face in the stream, thinking it more sanitary. Of course. Villagers drink spring water from cupped hands, I now realized, in order to look for and avoid leeches.

I returned to the American clinic to tell Barney. He was prepar-ing a small shipping box for the creature, which was now safely re-strained in a stoppered test tube. He was intrigued by Mana's explanation of the leech's life cycle, and said he would inquire about the removal technique in a cover letter to the Smithsonian Institution, where he was sending the specimen.

I expressed some apprehension. "But if our leech is lost in ship-ment, no one will believe the story."

"I don't think they'll believe it in any event," Barney responded as he carefully lettered a small label. I could see him grinning to himself, as if listening to his name being announced at a tropical medicine conference somewhere in France or the Caribbean. The label he prepared read simply, "Nose Leech. Nepal." I was grateful that my name, and I, were not attached to it.

Broughton Coburn worked and lived in Nepal and the Himalayas for over seventeen years. A graduate of Harvard, he is a native of Washington State currently living in Jackson, Wyoming. He is the author of Nepali Aama: Life Lessons of a Himalyan Woman; Aama in America: A Pilgrimage of the Heart; *and* Everest: Mountain without Mercy.

✳

When I walked in leech country, I worried about my most vulnerable area, only a part of which I could see. To pee outdoors, I had to squat perilously close to the grass where the leeches abounded. What if a leech attached itself to a sensitive spot and bored into a deep place I couldn't see?

And what about menstrual blood? A leech affixed in the appropriate cavity in a woman's body might even be useful when the flow is heavy. And it's possible the gentle, consistent sucking of a leech might even be pleasurable depending on the area of attachment.

—Marilyn Stablein, *The Census Taker*

✦ ✦ ✦

The Art of Walking

*Nepalis really know how to get
from here to there.*

BEFORE VISITING NEPAL, I DIDN'T THINK MUCH ABOUT WALKING—
I just walked, or so I thought. Now, having traveled in Nepal for
more than six months spread over three different trips done mostly
on foot, I recognize walking as an athletic endeavor to be done
poorly or well. Nepalis do it supremely well.

One day during a month-long trek around the Annapurna mas-
sif, I followed a Nepali porter on a day hike up thousands of feet
over rough terrain to a mountaineering base camp high on the
slopes of Dhaulagiri. As we walked, I became aware that I was following a true athlete, a master of movement on foot. Without his
normal load of trekkers' dufflebags, he covered ground like flowing water. He eased effortlessly from step to step, moving as
smoothly as if on an escalator. Like a good downhill skier, his
upper body was quiet and balanced; the work was all in his legs. I
clambered along and kept up, but I know for certain who ex-
pended less energy that day. And who got the style points too.

In the lower elevations of the Himalayas of Nepal—6,000 feet
to 13,000 feet, that is—Nepalis travel daily on trails so rugged that
our National Forests would have maintenance crews working on
them overtime. Children routinely walk several miles with hun-

dreds of feet of elevation change just getting to school each day. Villages are separated from major trading centers by deep river canyons and steep mountain ridges. A trip to the capital city of Kathmandu from a remote village is a walking journey of several weeks.

In the hills of Nepal, one of the ways to tell a distance is known as the rumali mil ("handkerchief mile"); it's the distance covered as a wet handkerchief dries when walking from point A to point B. Another method is the time required to smoke a hooka between two places.

—RK

In such a demanding environment, Nepalis early on acquire a graceful, efficient, and mindful walking style. Watch a cat and you'll see the same smooth, apparently effortless style. But try to imitate it and you'll learn that it's not so effortless. I studied and tried to mimic the Nepali walk, but found that I am handicapped by a lifetime of soft living which has left me with weaker muscles and less stability than any Nepali hill person. Even with a history of hiking and backpacking, I have neither the strength nor balance to sustain their "effortless" style.

Still, I learned skills from them that improved my walking. For example, in rugged terrain, Nepalis take small steps, so small that at times they walk almost toe to heel. A little practice illustrates why. Small steps uphill are less tiring—you take more, but the cumulative effect is less. Small steps downhill are more stable. You are less likely to miss your landing, jar a rock free, or slide on loose gravel. And as with going uphill, many small steps are cumulatively less tiring than fewer big ones.

Every step going downhill is onto the ball of the foot, with the muscles of the foot, ankle, lower and upper legs all acting as shock absorbers to catch and cushion the falling weight of the body. In contrast, I've seen Westerners walk as if on stilts, landing on the whole foot with the shock passed up through rigid joints to the body.

Nepalis also walk the trail-within-the-trail. On any trail several feet wide, you can see the inner trail the Nepalis have made, where the stones are shinier and the dirt is smoother. The inner trail winds around within the wider trail, always following the path of least resistance, seeking the solidest rocks, the levelest ground, and the steps spaced just right.

Nepalis seem to follow the inner trail naturally. During rest breaks I watched Nepalis walk at intervals along the same stretch of trail; successive walkers would almost without exception take the same sequence of steps, placing their feet on the same spots in the same sequence—left foot on one rock, right foot on another, left foot stepping up on a root, right foot on the level ground beyond.... Somehow they all arrived at this sequence on the correct foot, having earlier anticipated and measured their steps to pace themselves smoothly over the difficulties. A time-lapse photo from my vantage point would have revealed a smear of bodies passing above a set of superimposed feet, all carefully placed on the same spots on the trail.

Groaning with muscle aches after long days of hiking to Muktinath and returning along the Kali Gandaki River, I had the good fortune one day to fall in behind Kesang, the younger of our two Sherpa helpers. Feet clad in crumbling sneakers, he walked with a lantern swinging from one hand, at such an unvarying pace that we called him the "human metronome." I followed two feet behind him, and after an hour of unwittingly mirroring his rhythm, fell into timelessness. I lost all sense of physical discomfort, up became the same as down and was traversed at the same speed. I had nothing to do but enjoy the view, as though I was inside a well-muscled android.

—James O'Reilly, "Stairway to Heaven"

As if this artful, athletic pacing wasn't enough, Nepalis, especially porters, often are burdened by loads of 60 to 120 pounds. In the mountains, on all but the main trails where yaks and donkeys can be used, all trade goods and trekkers' baggage travel on the backs of the hardy hill people— both men and women. To maximize the economic value of their work, they carry mammoth loads every step. In the U. S., the back-packer's rule-of-thumb is that one's maximum load is one-third one's body weight, so my (theoretical) maximum load is 60 pounds, the lightest a Nepali porter normally carries. And these people are small—sinewy and tough, but small. It's a large Nepali who weighs in at 140.

A porter carries his or her load suspended from a tumpline—a continuous strap passed underneath the load and over the forehead. Holding the spine and neck perfectly straight, a porter walks slightly bent at the hips to rest the load on his or her flattened back. This arrangement makes ergonomic sense, but only for the practiced body. The load must stay absolutely balanced; allowing even a little sideways movement in the head poses great risk to the neck. More than one brawny but unpracticed Westerner has sprained his neck trying to heft a porter's load on a tumpline.

On rugged trails with crushing loads, walking barefoot or in simple thongs, Nepalis walk as far in a day as I can comfortably walk with a daypack. They stop frequently, resting their loads on trailside *chautaras* or on T-shaped walking sticks of just the right length.

Unburdened, Nepalis can walk leg-numbing, mind-bending distances. On one mountaineering trip I took, a Sherpa man covered, in one day, twice the distance our group had traveled in two-and-a-half days—from our base camp at 15,000 feet down to our previous camp at 12,000 feet, up a boulder-strewn river basin and over a 14,000-foot pass, down a steep, narrow ridge to the site of the next previous camp at 9,000 feet, and then several miles farther down another river. There he cut some bamboo wands for use at the base camp, and then he came back. In time for dinner.

While walking the steep and rugged trails of the Himalayas with their arduous loads, they smile, they laugh, and they sing. And, like their walking, their steadfast readiness to smile sets a difficult and admirable standard for us Westerners to emulate. We'd all do well to try.

I have heard stories of other fantastic foot travelers—Kenyan tribesmen who walk 60-mile round trips overnight to court their ladies, bushmen who run down wounded giraffes, and Tibetans who walk for weeks to reach a holy mountain which they then circumnavigate as homage. But I believe the hill people of Nepal are unmatched walkers. If the Olympics ever includes an event for

lugging horrible loads over high, harsh mountain passes, it will be
no contest. You'd hear the Nepali national anthem every time.

*Jack Bennett is a computer technician for the local hospital in Jackson,
Wyoming where he lives, but he gets out into the Tetons as much as possible for various self-propelled activities. He and his wife Linda also raise and
rent pack llamas for self-reliant back-country travelers. His favorite thing is
knocking around in places that require stamps in your passport. He consid-
ers himself lucky to have traveled in places such as Nepal, Tibet, Hong
Kong, China, Thailand, Britain, Turkey, Costa Rica, and other places near
and far.*

*

All day I have thought about the eerie trance state of these people as they
passed me in the ledge, and wonder if this might be a primitive form of
the Tantric discipline called *lung-gom*, which permits the adept to glide
along with uncanny swiftness and certainty, even at night. "The walker
must neither speak, nor look from side to side. He must keep his eyes
fixed on a single distant object and never allow his attention to be attracted by anything else. When the trance has been reached, though normal consciousness is for the greater part suppressed, it remains sufficiently
alive to keep the man aware of the obstacles in his way, and mindful of his
direction and goal." *Lung-gom* is, literally, wind-concentration, with
"wind" or "air" equivalent to the Sanskrit *prana*, the vital energy or breath
that animates all matter.

—Peter Matthiessen, *The Snow Leopard*

STEVE VAN BEEK

✦ ✦ ✦

Waiting for the Rains

Sometimes, to simply exist is a triumph.

THE BLOATED, FLY-BLOWN OX HAD LAIN IN THE FIELD FOR SEVERAL hours before the swarthy man dropped his soiled bag beside it. The clank of his tools broke the silence, a warning to the scavenger dogs and vultures gathered in two concentric arcs around the carcass.

High overhead, dozens of vultures wheeled in slow orbits about the ivory disk of the sun. At intervals, one would detach itself from the whirling mass and glide to an awkward collision with the earth where it would push its way among the scores of scrawny-necked, claw-billed birds squatting amidst the blanched rice stubble. Between the two rings, just out of range of canine teeth and avian beak, sleek black crows paced like cocky barristers. All the encircling eyes were on the corpse. Shiva's minions.

The sun's heat pounded flat the yellow paddy fields that ran ruler-straight to the sallow sky. The man wiped sweat from his face with the back of a blood-blotched hand. He was stocky for a *sarki*, the untouchable scavenger caste only one notch above the ninth circle occupied by the *dom* who toiled in human excrement. His caste status entitled him to render dead animals or cobble shoes from their skins. He was reviled for his trade, but when a fermenting cow, bullock, or water buffalo lay stinking in a village field,

29

Brahmans hurried to him, beseeching him to rid them of its presence, paying him a pittance or allowing him to keep the hide.

From his blood-rusted bag, he withdrew two knives, their blades dulled and blackened from inferior smelting. Grasping the small knife in his left hand and the scimitar in his right, he surveyed the throng of teeth and beaks. Shouting derisively, "Hey, you ugly beasts," he banged his tools together menacingly. The dogs shrank back, in turn snarling at the evil-tempered vultures to move away. Hierarchies of hunger.

He set to work separating the cadaver from its skin. There were no religious preliminaries; this was not a sacred cow but a lowly "*goru*," a bullock that had uncomplainingly pulled plows and carts for a decade. Its prominent ribs and slack skin said it had probably died of old age, although in a land of drought, it was hard to tell.

I often run into the gara, who transports his forge from one end of the village to the other. He repairs plowshares and spades, sharpens knives and sickles, and fills in holes in teakettles and pots. He is fed in every house and offered as many cups of chang *as he can drink and sometimes a bit of grain, which he takes home.*

Yet the garas, *always in contact with metal, are considered impure in the Tibetan culture and are the lowest on their social ladder. Until recently they could not enter the houses of other clans.*

—Eric Valli and Diane Summers,
Caravans of the Himalaya

The dogs shifted as the ripe scent bubbled out of the body. With teeth too dull to tear the thick hide, they had waited for human intervention. Now, they awaited the banquet, arrayed according to their own caste, lower-echelon dogs crouching, submissive tails between hunkering legs, wary that they might be savaged by a larger creature.

The *sarki* smiled wryly as he chased away the Brahman dogs and tossed slabs of raw meat to the inferiors. It was easier to identify with the bottom of the heap.

As the *sarki* worked, three Brahman men walked along the nearby road holding the corners of their pristine *dhotis* to their noses. It was hard to know if they were demonstrating distaste for the man's act or recoiling from the odor of putrefying flesh. The *sarki* ignored them.

When he was finished, he straightened up and wiped the knife across his *dhoti*. Daubing a rag at the gore on his arms, he watched the glowering dogs, savoring his command of the ground. Then he slipped his tools into his bag, he stepped back, and the dogs hurtled forward, a brown wave crested by the foam of snapping fangs. They swarmed over the ox, whose stiff legs vibrated like diving boards beneath their weight. The beasts screeched and screamed, teeth as often sinking into a neighbor's flank as into the carcass.

At first, the vultures hung back, but soon hunger sapped patience. Its vision blinkered to anything but the feast before it, a lone vulture waddled forward but was driven back by a wall of slavering fangs and menacing growls. Quicker than their rivals, the crows flitted in to perch on the ribcage just above the throng, tearing at the flesh with their hedge-shear bills. Other crows whiled their time by tormenting the vultures, pulling at their tail feathers or hopping up their backs to peck at their heads.

Eventually the tumult waned. Sated by the meal, the dogs slunk away, and the vultures strode in, ripping the flesh with hooked beaks, opening broad wings for balance like caped vampires. The man watched them, sucking blue smoke from a *bidi*. The dark, writhing mound of birds soon obscured the remains of the bullock, and black was the only color on the dun plain. A distant rice mill hooted a string of slow high notes like a toy train struggling up a hill.

This seared flatland is the *tarai*. Running along the upper edge of the Gangetic plain, it is a region of hell-heat and pestilence, dotted with villages like the one where I worked as a Peace Corps volunteer. Few hill Nepalis talked about the *tarai*, fewer wanted to know about it. To Westerners, "*tarai*" meant Chitwan province, a lush forest prowled by tigers and rhinos. But Chitwan is what all of the *tarai* used to look like: a thick jungle that ran from the Ganges River to the Himalaya foothills, from Kashmir to the Bay of Bengal. The upper *tarai* was the reputed home of the progeny of high-caste Rajput women sent to sanctuary along the foot of the mountains when the Moguls invaded northern India in the 16th century. Legend says that when the rajas perished in battle, their wives were obliged to bed their servants in order to preserve the race. Their children were known as *Tharus*, a hardy people said to be immune to malaria. The tale's authenticity is open to question but in its defense, Nepalis note that when a *Tharu* woman serves her husband dinner, she pushes the tray across the dirt floor with her foot. As the foot is the lowest, foulest part of the body, it is tantamount to the vilest insult.

The *tarai*'s thick forests were felled long ago, and the *Tharus* retreated to the lower Himalaya. Flowing into the void from the Gangetic Plain came the *madeshi*, sun bruised and rail thin. They came to farm the fertile plain on which rice grows profusely— when there is sufficient water. Burnt by a molten sun, it is a land as reviled by god as by the *pahari*, mountain Nepalis, who regard their hills as paradise and the *tarai* as perdition. Indians refer to Bihar, the state just south of the border, as "the nation's armpit." *Pahari* have scant more regard for their own "armpit" or its people. Yet, in truth, their dominant emotion is envy and resentment.

> *The tarai has been a warm and welcome refuge to those Nepalis who can afford to escape the bone-chilling winters of Kathmandu. Especially for the wealthy older folks, the tarai is the Florida of Nepal.*
>
> —RK

Perhaps the *pahari* are right. The *tarai* is hard to eulogize, much less to love. I lasted barely two years before I fled. Despite its 40-mile proximity to lofty Himalayan glaciers, it is a crucible. Its predominant color is the blinding ocher of the sun-baked adobe that clads its houses and ground. There isn't even enough vegetation for grazing. Trowel-wielding herders scalp grass from the hard earth, banging the turf tuft against the ground to loosen the root soil, then tossing it into a woven basket to feed bleating goats tethered to nearby posts. There is no other fodder for animals.

By March, temperatures reach 50 degrees Celsius (122 degrees

Fahrenheit). During the next three months, the *tarai* succumbs to the quiet cruelty of a tyrant who beats his subjects until they have no will to resist. With nothing to glue the soil to the earth, it soon swirls through the air. By April, the sky's breath blasts from a furnace mouth and the slightest breeze stirs dust devils. When the pre-monsoon winds blow in May, the landscape is shrouded by particle storms. Winds howl and fling the earth into the sky to blind and deafen. Shrieking gales reach sharp fingers into houses imperfectly sealed. Within hours everything inside is jaundiced by a yellow film and the dark interiors echo with hollow coughing.

The heat maddens everything it touches. A woman relieving herself in the fields at dawn is torn apart by rabid jackals. Another, reaching into a shrine, is bitten by a krait coiled behind the elephant god Ganesh. The air torments with scabies, shingles, bedbugs, and mosquitoes. Or spawns diseases from which one expires in the violent diarrhea of cholera, the freezing/scalding agony of malaria, or the fiery fever of cerebral malaria that turns brains to pudding, curdling them in a few short hours. And the *madeshi* smile through it all, quietly accepting what they cannot change, even when it kills them. Fatalistic fatalities.

In the *tarai*, I didn't so much live as exist. I was from the American Pacific Northwest, of lush valleys and endless rainfall. To me, the *tarai* was a barren cauldron. How could humans subsist here? Yet, they did, resigned to their karma, yet unbowed by it. The sun and their fellow man should have cauterized all humanity from them yet they embraced life, and eventually me. It was I, impatient with providence and accustomed to resolving difficulties with technology, who suffered noisily. I had been sent to help them improve their lives with the miracles of the Green Revolution—new varieties of high-yielding wheat and rice to combat starvation. They resisted, cocooned by comforting tradition, fearful of change. They had been doing things their way for 4,000 years, thank you, they had no need of my help. They were content merely to have me live among them, sleeping in a cattle shed, sharing their food and festivities.

I had rebelled against their servitude to providence. While the *sarki* labored, I had sat in the lee of a house, taking shelter from the desiccating heat. Beyond the bare house yard, the green rice beds were a shimmering mirage, the plants drying and dying.

"Do something!" I said to the others.

"Sit down *sahib*, there is nothing that can be done," they said.

"Draw water from the well," I said.

"And what will we drink?" an old man replied quietly. An earlier planting of seedlings had already wilted and died and the farmers had to replant, reaching for seed into the granaries reserved for food. Like the dogs, their ribs would protrude long before the rice was harvested four months later.

I had once asked a villager, "What is the worst thing that could happen to you?"

"That's a stupid question, *sahib*," he said softly.

"Why?"

"Because if it is going to happen, there's nothing we can do to prevent it. And if it isn't, why should we sit around worrying about it? Accept it. It is the only way to savor peace."

The attitude was anathema to me. To a Westerner taught that he could alter the course of his life through science and math, that he could overturn destiny and weather adversity, such acceptance of predestination seemed like mindless surrender. I soon saw the village ox as a metaphor for *tarai* life. The poor beast is beaten and mistreated, castrated even, and worked endlessly. When it dies, it is given no religious rites or thanks for its services. It is simply dragged into a field as the main course at a vulture banquet. I never was able to embrace their resignation, despite repeated evidence that they were right and I was wrong. It was these dichotomies more than anything that made me realize how different we were, and eventually, made me decide not to stay a third year.

By late afternoon, every beast has abandoned the ox. The bones, picked clean, are yellow as the cow–dust hour descends on the *tarai*. The air resonates with a high keening sound. In the village, an old blind begging troubadour crouches before a door. His high, reedy voice is accompanied by a mesmerizing drone rising from a wide, upturned brass tray wedged between his bony knees. On its center he has placed a vaneless vulture feather. He pinches it between gnarled fingers that slide down its rough shaft, its vibrations transferring to the brass pan, reverberating outwards in concentric rings of sound. In the far distance, thick clouds are moving out of the mountains. Soon, the singer's lament blends with the hum of a breath strained as though through wires, as if summoned by the blind man. Perhaps he is only the sounding board through which its fury is transmitted.

The suspended dust is suffused by the light of the dying sun, the cows are silhouetted against it as they move towards their byres. Darkness is slow in coming and when it descends, it is filled with menace. The breeze rises, the air cools. Over the weeks, in wisps, the clouds have traveled north from the Bay of Bengal, floated over the *tarai* and stacked against the high Himalaya that blocks their passage to Tibet. Now, chilled by the cold air, they reverse direction, moving into the void created by the thermals sucking heat from the land. The cloud wall halts a few miles north of the village, billowing Gibralters with bases floating like mirages a handsbreadth above the silent land.

By 8 p.m., they are beginning to growl. Lightning stutters deep inside them so they glow momentarily orange, first this one, then one farther west, then still another, pulsating along a broad horizon. The wind flees before them, sweeping through the village, furiously shaking the trees and scattering their leaves. Villagers bolt their doors. I stand at the northern entrance to the village, enthralled by the power I am witnessing. The lightning has seeped to the cloud exteriors. Embossed on the smoldering mounds, silvery filaments like tracery flit along the surface, thoughts on a gigantic brain. The wind rises to gale force. The lightning breaks free of the huddled clouds, striking the ground, momentarily bathing everything in searing light. Down the winding dirt road from the north, a woman in a white sari moves towards me, struggling to reach shelter. In the wind, the ends of her sari flap flaglike, etched momentarily in the magnesium strobe that illuminates her in freeze frames beside the skeletal tree reaching bleached-bone fingers into the sky. Dust devils appear in different places with each blinding flash. Mesmerized by the slide show playing before me, I am startled when the previously somnolent sky behind me cracks open, a deafening roar that begins far to the east. Like an endless Chinese firecracker, the crackling crawls across the back of my head and on to the west, its sound receding as it falls over the horizon in noisy pursuit of the dead sun. The woman reaches the village and enters her house.

I, too, hurry home, barring the door as the storm hammers at the house walls, thin barriers of wattle, mud, and cow dung. Powdered soil flows over the wide space between wall top and roof thatching. Borne on the wind is the sound of my friend Ramanand playing his harmonium and singing "*Hare Ram, hare hare Ram*" as he performs his evening devotionals, his only refuge from the raging gusts.

By midnight, the wind is dying. *Monsoon* means "wind" and this one bears no rain. It is a politician's storm; fury and din, with nothing of substance or sustenance. But my nose detects a hint of moisture in an atmosphere that seems charged with electrons, setting the cows stamping in their pens. Harbinger of the liquid violence waiting to pour down upon the land, this electric air hangs over the village throughout the night, the thunder rumbling across the sky at wide intervals, echoing against the mountains.

By evening, the air suddenly turns humid, a smell of warm wetness swells up from the valley below. A yellow moon rises from behind a range of billowing clouds to the east. The clouds glow in the moonlight, their insides incandescent with silent lightning. Then a sudden sharp coolness as the moisture turns into mist, and the mist, in turn, into a gauze of rain. The Nepali vocabulary has many onomatopoeic words to describe different kinds of rain: at midnight it turns from drizzly "sim-sime" to heavier "dar-keko" and by early morning it is torrential "musal-dhare."

—Kunda Dixit,
"Nepali Monsoon"

The sun rises but, for once, creates no heat. An ominous silence bereft of bird call or insect cry has descended on the land. The clouds waiting over the northern plain are now jet black as if still suffused by the night. By 10 a.m. they begin rolling south, charcoal masses filling a sulfurous sky. A roaring ocean moves slowly but inexorably towards me. Soon the neighboring village disappears behind a gray curtain. A tsunami of rain is moving towards India, blackening the ground as it advances, the wind icy where a moment before it was warm. The liquid wall beats a drum tattoo on the broad leaves of the banana trees. It enters the village like a black tarpaulin pulled across the pale earth, so slowly its progress can be measured in inches. Creeping towards me, turning the earth to glistening onyx, it reaches the house in torrents, pelting the roof thatching, the wind howling furiously. For moments, the rain is so thick I cannot breathe. I am drowning in air. There is no shelter because the wind drives the rain horizontally along the ground.

Then, it passes as suddenly as it came. In an instant, the sky is clear, prismatic water drips rainbows from the roof straws. As I look into the distance it is as if cataracts have been removed from my eyes. For the first time in months, I can discern individual leaves sharply etched on a tree. The ox bones have been washed clean, and the rice in the seedbeds glows a luxuriant green.

Although the storm has moved on to India, it will soon be followed by more black clouds, and more until the fields fill and the rice can be transplanted. In this realm of absolutes, it may continue to fall until the villages are islands in a vast sea, bringing a new kind of violence as the rats and snakes flee to high ground and invade the houses. With too little rain, the rice will scorch in the burning sun. Too much rain and it will drown. And all of this will be accepted with a shrug of the shoulders. It is the *tarai*. It is fate. Submit. *Hare Ram.*

Steve Van Beek spent two years as a Peace Corps agriculture extension volunteer in a small village in the tarai. *He has lived and worked in Asia as a writer/filmmaker since then. He is the author of many books about Asia, and he has a special interest in rivers. He has explored dozens of them, trying to understand how riparian people's perceptions of rivers affect the ways they use or abuse them. For his solo journeys, he was elected a Fellow of the Explorers Club.*

★

The Lama of the Crystal Monastery appears to be a very happy man, and yet I wonder how he feels about his isolation in the silences of Tsakang, which he has not left in eight years now and, because of his legs, may never leave again. Since Jang-bu seems uncomfortable with the Lama or with himself or perhaps with us, I tell him not to inquire on this point if it seems to him impertinent, but after a moment Jang-bu does so. And this holy man of great directness and simplicity, big white teeth shining, laughs out loud in an infectious way at Jang-bu's question. Indicating his twisted legs without a trace of self-pity or bitterness, as if they belonged to all of us, he casts his arms wide to the sky and the snow mountains, the high sun and dancing sheep, and cries, "Of course I am happy here! It's wonderful! *Especially* when I have no choice!"

—Peter Matthiessen, The Snow Leopard

IAN BAKER

✳

Jewel of the Nagas

Swine before pearls.

IN THE TIME BEFORE MANKIND, THE KATHMANDU VALLEY WAS covered by an immense primeval lake, ruled over by a class of serpentine water spirits called Nagas. In Buddhist legend, the more evolved of these serpent-like beings possessed *Manis*—lustrous, wish-fulfilling gems which they passed down through the ages to *rishis*, sages, and beneficent kings, those whose profoundest desires were to bring benefit to all living things.

According to Nepali legend, when the great Bodhisattva sage, Manjushri, gazed upon the watery depths of what was to become the Kathmandu Valley, he saw a radiant light emanating from beneath the lake's surface. Recognizing within this shadowy world of Nagas a sacred realm destined for human habitation, Manjushri drained the lake by cutting a cleft through the encircling hills with his magic sword. Deprived of their ancient territory, the displaced serpents found refuge in marshy ponds, rivers, and wells. From their hidden dwelling places beneath the Kathmandu Valley, these paranormal snakes maintain their authority over their original domain. When angered or ignored they can cause disease and calamities. When properly propitiated, however, the Nagas bring timely rains and bountiful harvests, peace, and revelations. Greatest of all their treasures, however, are their coveted wish-granting gems.

Yet the jewels of the Nagas are not simply matters of myth and ancient history, still less mere symbols of the equivocal bounty of the unconscious mind. Along with stolen temple art, *Banjhankri* bones, opium, and gold, *Nagmanis* have become the hottest, if most elusive, items on Kathmandu's infamous black market.

Several years ago, in the course of graduate research into Nepal's unique form of Vajrayana, or Tantric Buddhism, I sought out a revered priest who spent most of his days sitting on a velvet cushioned throne canopied by nine gold-plated Nagas. Mornings and evenings, the short, overweight priest would enter into trance, possessed, it was said, by one of the eight blood-drinking mother goddesses who protect the Kathmandu Valley. On certain days, long awaited by his devotees, it was not the mother goddesses who possessed him, but a powerful, high-ranking Naga. Invested with the spiritual authority of Kathmandu Valley's

> *There was a bungalow to one side of the hotel where I eventually took up residence. The path to it was through lush vegetation infested with snakes, but the snakes received their saucers of milk, and somehow I never felt any fear negotiating that path in the pitch dark after a late night out.*
>
> —Xenia Lisanevich,
> "The Fabled Exploits and Recipes of Boris of Kathmandu"

oldest gods, the "Guru" bestowed blessings on those who congregated in his small, low-ceilinged shrine room. Wreathed in the smoke of musty incense, the pot-bellied oracle gave advice to merchants and businessmen, attended to the sick, and prescribed rituals and offerings for those seeking spiritual or material advancement. (In Kathmandu, business success is often attributed less to hard work than favorable karma and well-exacted rites.)

The priest's disciples were eager to point out that even in ordinary circumstances, their Guru's eyes glittered and that when he walked his movements were lithe and sinuous, like a snake's. To communicate their desires and to bestow boons, Nepal's Nagas, it was believed, could take human form, and certain men and women could transform into Nagas.

Some years earlier, the Guru had unearthed a *Nagmani* from beneath the mud brick floor of a house belonging to his disciple Ram. Following the ancient custom, the *Mani* had been given to the Guru as a boon from a beneficent Naga, and with it he had healed Ram's wife of what appeared to be stomach cancer, an act which brought him much prestige in the local community. The disciples worshipped the luminescent gem, securing it in a silver urn kept secretly in the Guru's shrine room. Revering him as an emanation of the serpent king Vasuki Nag, the disciples made generous offerings to the Guru, hoping in turn to receive comparable blessings from the wealth-bestowing Nagas. Over time, however, the Guru's tastes became increasingly extravagant. As Bijaya, one of his chief disciples, confessed: "Our Guru eats as much as three men and he has become very sexy, sir. He has taken many wives!" Through the power of the *Nagmani*, Bijaya explained, the Guru could attract any woman he desired. His dedication to benefit all beings, I mused, had taken an unusual turn.

With full conviction that worship of the *Nagmani* would ultimately bring them all that they desired, many of the Guru's closest disciples gave up their jobs. Ram relinquished his faltering carpet factory and Bijaya left the responsibilities of his welding and auto repair shop to his younger brother. They took out bank loans to support the Guru and themselves, convinced that in the end they would be vastly prosperous. After several years, however, with nascent intimations of a less favorable outcome, the disciples—having heard of the incredible sums *Nagmanis* could fetch on the international market—began to pressure the Guru to sell his precious gem. After years of generous patronage and unabated devotion, it was time to cash in. With part of the money, they told him, they would build him a lavish ashram.

It was at this time that Bijaya first approached me: "Sir, you have many contacts in the West. Do you know someone who will buy this item? This one is not so expensive; only fifty *crore* rupees, about eight million dollars." Eager to learn more about this fabled jewel which had enraptured not only Bijaya and his fellow disciples, but the very soul of the nation, I agreed to a secret meeting with the Guru. When the Guru asked me if I had a genuine customer for his precious gem, in my eagerness not to displease him, I replied that it might be possible. There were other interested parties, Bijaya informed me, among them a Frenchman at the United Nations Development Project and an inevitable Japanese millionaire. When the Guru went into trance, however, the Nagas themselves determined that the jewel be passed on to me. Although I insisted that they should negotiate first with the other prospective buyers, Bijaya dismissed them, telling me that the mother goddesses who protect the vital interests of the Valley's residents had revealed them as "insincere." Disconcertingly, I alone had passed the test.

Before the *Nagmani* could even be shown to me, however, certain rituals had to be performed and religious penances duly observed. Under the Guru's guidance, Bijaya and the other disciples drew up an eight-page contract. The preface was worded as follows:

JAY SHRI GANESHAYANAMA

It is a matter of great pleasure to us that through the supreme grace of the all merciful lord and *nagas* we have been afforded this splendid opportunity to have great business of *Nagmani*.... The Nagas meet only the humblest saints who adore them without any selfish motive....

Accompanied by detailed drawings, the contract specified many of the *Nagmani's* visible properties:

1. Light of many colors emits continuously.

2. Two floating filaments can be seen in form of snakes.

3. Newspaper can be read at a distance of 3 to 3-1/2 feet from the source of light.

4. Maximum range of light about 8 feet.

As crucial, however, were the financial arrangements, as in point five:

> When it is confirmed that the item is a genuine one,
> buyer should make guarantee of buying that item within
> few hours or the following day...by depositing the earnest
> money as five percent of the total amount which equals to
> Nepali rupees 4,500,000 as cash on the same day....

Failure to show me the given item by a particular date would result in severe, self-inflicted penalties:

> If the seller won't be able to show the above mentioned
> item on the above date and time, he should pay Nepali ru-
> pees 5,000,000 to the buyer and middle man as a penalty
> on the same day in cash or fixed assets.

After I'd urged them to seek buyers elsewhere, the disciples—with distressing confidence—added the following addendum:

> If we become failure to do our program according to our
> promises, we are ready to obey any kind of punishment as
> you think.

The document concluded with the following invocation:

> May the Lord Buddha and Nagas bless the buyers and sell-
> ers alike for their prosperous and happiest long life.

A crudely typed lab report was attached to the contract indicating that the "concerned item" had the consistency of an eyeball and glowed, perhaps due to a high arsenic or phosphorus content. The report concluded by saying that the item was most likely highly toxic and by no means should it be touched. As Bijaya clarified, the *Mani* was the transmuted venom of the deadliest of Nagas, dangerous, no doubt, to the uninitiated, but infinitely powerful. Indeed, as stipulated in Article Nine of the contract:

If the buyer desires to keep this item in public exhibition, he should warn the exhibitors not to touch said item with the bare hands and [he should] instruct them to observe from a distance only. This item is very poisonous and in-halation over the rays can make instant death.

In preparation for the unveiling of this cabalistic gem which the Guru, for more than a year, had not shown even to his closest dis-ciples, I observed all of the "religious rules" prescribed in the con-tract. Such preparations, I was told, would protect us from all harmful side effects and enable us to experience the *Nagmani* as "Divine Power." I ate neither chicken nor eggs, avoided alco-hol and menstruating women, took purifying baths, and lit in-cense morning and evening in the four corners of my house to secure the blessings of Vasuki Nag. To inspect the *Nagmani* close up, Bijaya provided me with gloves and a magnifying glass, and after rejecting my Bollé glacier glasses, equipped me with a plate of welder's glass from his auto body shop. The light of the *Mani*, he insisted, could be blind-ing. In addition, a double-lock-ing safe was produced in which the *Nagmani* would be deposited along with my five percent "earnest money." When I calculated how I was supposed to pay the balance, I realized that, as the total was to be paid in Nepali rupees, it would fill the trunks of six or seven taxis.

The mother goddesses—or Matas, as Bijaya referred to them—dictated, through the Guru, the precise time that the *Nagmani*

J ust as men have three temperaments, so also their food.

He of the satva *temperament is pure and holy and takes food that is fresh, juicy, and pleasant. Such foods increase his energy, strength, and health.*

He of the rajas *temperament is sensual and lusts after the plea-sures of this world. Thus his foods are spicy, sour, hot, salty, bitter, and pungent. They harm the body and the mind.*

He of the tamas *temperament is ignorant and dull. He enjoys foods that are stale, rotten, tainted, and discarded by others. Such foods add to his bewilderment, delusion, and darkness.*

—The Bhagavad Gita: The Song of God

should be unveiled—3 a.m. on the night of the dark moon. Shortly before the appointed hour, it began to rain torrentially, a fact the Guru attributed to interference from the Nagas. The viewing had to be postponed. I began to seriously question the lengths I was going in my "field methods," but persisted nonetheless, despite a recurring pattern of cancellations and postponements. Although I observed all of the "religious rules," obstacles continued to arise at each scheduled viewing. On one occasion, the Guru insisted I had eaten one of the forbidden foods, thus making it unsafe to reveal the gem. Indeed, I confessed to having eaten egg noodles the previous evening, having failed to realize that eggs in any form or degree were totally taboo. On the next occasion, I got completely lost trying to find the house where the *Nagmani* was to be shown. When I regained my bearings, the auspicious time period had passed, and we had to reschedule. Despite the successive cancellations, the disciples remained strangely unperturbed. "This is the Nagas' work, sir. They are trying to block us. We must proceed patiently."

On the next occasion—also in the dead of night—freshly bathed and free of any leather, I entered the black-curtained room where the *Nagmani* was kept in its silver urn. A ring of honey had been drawn on the floor around a central table on the top of which was a locking briefcase. Bijaya whispered to me that the *Nagmani* and the urn were inside the case. We lit incense and invoked the protection of the Matas and the benediction of the Nagas. Just as the Guru was opening the Samsonite briefcase, a tall glass vase placed outside the mandala of honey shattered down the middle, spilling water across the floor. The water contained the accumulated mantras that the Guru had intoned in preparing for this event. That the vase broke at such an inauspicious moment indicated that the protective circle was no longer intact. According to the Guru, there was imminent danger that a jealous Naga intent on reclaiming the jewel would possess one of us and, with our unconscious complicity, cause us to swallow it whole. Once again, the *darshan*, or ritual viewing, had to be postponed. As we left the house, a huge bullfrog leapt out from behind the front door.

"That's a Naga, sir," Bijaya insisted, "They can take many forms. We have to be careful!"

Having failed to view the *Nagmani*, I considered dropping the whole affair, only to get pulled deeper into a strange world where the boundary between myth and reality blurred. My previous housekeeper, Sita—given to clairvoyance—began calling me, telling me she'd been seeing me in her dreams: a recurring image of a large black snake with open jaws, hovering over me as I slept. The dream was ominous, she insisted. I must perform the appropriate Naga-subduing rituals. Indeed, for several weeks, I had been having the kinds of problems Nepalis traditionally ascribe to disconsolate Nagas: financial arrangements had gone awry; my house had flooded three times during unseasonable rains. More to the point, an undiagnosable skin condition began to erupt on my hands and legs. The Nagas, it seemed, were less than pleased by my persistent attempts to experience their alluring gem, or, perhaps, were offended by my secretly harbored doubts about its reality. Presumably, they would be even more outraged by the disciples' display of overarching greed—negotiating the sale of what, by traditional accounts, was a physical manifestation of spiritual power.

Recognizing that it would be more to my advantage to accept the Nagas reality and be proved wrong than to deny them their due and suffer the consequences, I followed my housekeeper's recommendations. I called an exorcist to my house to perform rituals for subduing Nagas. (A section devoted to them can be found in Kathmandu's yellow pages.) Uncannily, within a few days all my skin afflictions disappeared. Eager now to further my dissociation from these temperamental snakes, I re-emphasized to Bijaya that as so much time had elapsed and the Guru still hadn't been able to show me the Nagas' illustrious gem, interest abroad was waning. I could offer no assurance that I could find a buyer. The disciples, however, were adamant; these obstacles were to be expected when dealing with esoteric matters. The Guru had "chosen" me to be the recipient of the *Mani*. Despite my protestations, they had no doubt that the outcome would be favorable.

A critical moment came a week later, an auspicious time the mother goddesses had chosen for the final viewing. Bijaya had watched through a keyhole as the Guru prepared for the unveiling. He watched the Guru remove a small vial of what he took to be chicken's blood, from beneath the folds of his red cotton tunic. The Guru swished it around in his mouth, letting some of it trickle down over his lips. He then lay down on the floor as if he had fainted. Pathak, the burly police inspector turned disciple, was calling the Guru from the next room. When he didn't answer, Pathak came in and saw him collapsed on the floor. The program was called off; the Guru, once roused, reported that the Nagas were creating serious impediments, and that to regain their favor, he would have to undertake a prolonged retreat. Bijaya, however, now suspected that the Guru had no intention of relinquishing the *Nagmani*. Indeed, in a desperate

An educated Nepali businessman, who also happened to be a naturalist, saw a snake outside his kitchen door. He knew that it was a harmless garden snake, but he killed it anyway. When he told his mother about it, she was alarmed. She insisted that it was not just an ordinary garden snake but a naga. She became afraid that misfortune would befall the family. Sure enough, within a few years, his wife and young daughter died. His business too faltered. Distraught, he sought advice and was told to do naga puja to appease the snake gods, which he did. Soon thereafter, things improved, and to this day he performs his naga puja *daily*. "The educated man in me says that it was pure coincidence that tragedy occurred in my life soon after I killed the snake, but I have not stopped performing my puja."

—RK

bid, he secretly broke into the cabinet where the *Nagmani* was supposedly kept, and found in the urn not the effulgent jewel, but a small black stone. Bijaya kept the secret to himself, but determined inwardly to find out where the Guru had hidden the real *Mani*. Despite their emerging doubts, he and the other disciples continued their patronage, conceiving it as the only means of maintaining their link to the "pearl without price."

One day, however, Bijaya arrived dejectedly at my home. "The Guru has cheated us, sir. He has disappeared from his house. We don't know where he has gone." A posse was sent out and two weeks later they found him, living in the village of Machagaon on the slopes of Champadevi—a thickly forested mountain to the south of Kathmandu. The Guru was ensconced there with his wife and his wife's sister, whom he had also taken as consort. Making some suitable excuse for his unannounced departure, the Guru agreed to return to Kathmandu and resume proceedings.

Things went from bad to worse, however. As the disciples pressed him to reveal the hiding place of the *Nagmani*, the Guru ran away again, and again a search committee was sent out to find him. They brought him back, but he continued to evade his captors, the last time, escaping through the bathroom window of the house in which they had interred him.

My interest in the *Nagmani* had begun as an exploration of the beliefs and practices surrounding a central icon of Nepali folk belief and progressed to a wary acceptance of realities which I could neither understand, nor convincingly dispel. The drama unfolding now, however, appeared more like a remake of *Monty Python and the Holy Grail*, the disciples' adventures having progressively less and less to do with the pursuit of spiritual illumination, let alone predictable business proceedings.

Bijaya appeared one afternoon, his usually fastidious appearance marred by grease stains. "I've been the whole morning at my machine shop, sir. I've been making shackles for the Guru. This time when we capture him, we will punish him badly." I reminded Bijaya of the last lines of the contract which he himself had composed: "Only those who have adopted the methods of adoration and meditation can receive this jewel of the Nagas.... No work should be undertaken which is found to be sinful..."

"That is true, sir," Bijaya said, "but in this case the Guru has taken all our money, he has deceived us. Our situation is quite desperate. He must receive a penalty."

Eventually the Guru was caught. As Bijaya recounted, they tied him to a chair and tortured him unsparingly. They kicked him and beat him with bamboo sticks, but as Bijaya explained, "The surprising thing is, sir, it doesn't affect him at all. No matter how much we beat him, his body shows no mark. In fact, he is *too* healthy. If you see his body, it is shining."

In the end the Guru and his disciples made peace, the Guru's insensitivity to pain somehow restoring the disciples' faith in his spiritual powers. Somewhat remorsefully, they rented him a new house and supplied him with every luxury. "The Guru is very mysterious, sir," Bijaya told me. "He's hidden the *Nagmani* somewhere, but to get it back we have no choice but to support him."

Despite the deceptions and endless charades, the *Nagmani* continued to haunt me. It had to be something more, I thought, than a total phantasm. Could belief alone explain the effect it had had on Bijaya and the other devotees? Had the Guru, through some arcane technology, created the *Nagmani*? Why then would he not show it, or if its powers had failed, why had he not simply explained that the Nagas had reclaimed it instead of subjecting himself to torture and harassment?

A t a popular level, even amongst illiterate people, any kind of work is equated with pain (dukkha) and people consider it an act of wisdom to avoid work. The opposite of dukkha is sukkha (bliss) which means living without having to work. People who can live without having to work are considered fortunate. As a career objective in modern Nepal, every Nepali tries to have a Jagir, a salaried job where one does not have to work but will receive a pay cheque at the end of each month. Candidates still show their zeal and enthusiasm for work at the time of applying for the job, because that is the rule one has to follow. But in such jobs one is not expected to actually work.

—Dor Bahadur Bista,
*Fatalism and Development:
Nepal's Struggle for Modernization*

I maintained regular contact with Bijaya who told me that the Guru had "vanished" once again, and even a month of searching had failed to reveal him. They'd gone to a rival Tantrika who'd told them that if the Guru gave up the *Nagmani*, he would lose his occult powers. "He'd become ordinary like you and me, sir," Bijaya explained. The Tantrika assured them, however, that through mantra, he himself could compel the Guru to turn over the sequestered gem. Though the disciples did not doubt the Tantrika's power, they rejected this approach as there would be no assurance that once the *Nagmani* fell into the hands of this compliant sorcerer that he would relinquish it to the rightful owners.

Bijaya had become morosely philosophic. "We have failed in our mission, sir. We have disappointed you. But, don't worry. Eventually the Guru will have to sell his *Mani*. He has no income source now, and no means even to buy rice for his many wives."

What kind of wish-fulfilling jewel could this be, I thought, that would allow its owner to go unfed?

Bijaya and his fellow disciples had largely abandoned their fruitless quest, convinced now that the Guru—even if found—would never reveal the *Nagmani's* hiding place.

Several months later Bijaya called excitedly to tell me he'd located another *Nagmani*. This one, he assured me, was already in the hands of his uncle. It emanated less light than the Guru's, but was more affordable—only four million dollars. Bijaya began to outline the procedure for the "viewing": security measures, "earnest money," etc. I interrupted him before he could continue. I'd spent enough time, I told him, chasing the Nagas' elusive jewel. If the serpent gods really wanted me to have it, they would have to bestow it without human intercessors, and without exacting a fee.

The day Bijaya told me about the new *Nagmani*, I drove into Kathmandu's surrounding hills, climbing sinuously on rutted tarmac past small hamlets and terraced slopes teeming with golden flowering mustard. When I reached the end of the road, I looked down on the improbable city of temples and half-built hotels. For ten years I'd been immersed in a complex culture that balances belief in Nagas with a growing addiction to cable TV; a city where the king is anointed yearly by a living goddess, and the staff of the national airlines sacrifices goats to their planes. A city where an ancient monarch once forced the Nagas to bring rain, and a talented auto mechanic trades in his career to pursue a mythical jewel. In this city of dreams, the lines between the spiritual and material worlds have never been definitively drawn. Gods can become peo-

ple and people gods. Of the diverse forces that compose the Nepali
world, none are more inscrutable than the Nagas. If their wish-
granting jewel is truly more than a metaphor for the mind's highest aspirations, only here in this shape-shifting city will it ever surface. For as a much-quoted poet once proclaimed: the strangest
dreams elsewhere on the planet are the abiding facts of
Kathmandu.

*Ian Baker is a writer, photographer, and explorer who has lived in India and
Nepal for the past fifteen years. He is the author of* The Tibetan Art of
Healing *and co-author of* Tibet: Reflections from the Wheel of Life *as
well as numerous articles on Himalayan anthropology and exploration. He
is the founding director of Red Panda Expeditions, a research-oriented adventure travel company committed to documenting and preserving the cultural
heritage of the most remote parts of the Himalayas.*

✳

If anything, Nepal is already becoming spoiled by success, Khenpo Rigzin
said, reflecting the burgeoning sense among some leading Buddhist lamas
that too much luxury is creeping into monastic life. In some cases, that is
already an understatement. A Kathmandu businessman told me how
when he tried to sell a Mercedes-Benz, he got no takers in the royal family or among the wealthy houses, but found a Tibetan *rimpoche* ready and
willing to pay cash for the car. One day, leaving a Kathmandu restaurant
after lunch, I saw two monks head toward a new Hyundai parked out
front. The older one got into the back; the younger one (wearing a cowboy hat) folded his robes, slid into the driver's seat, and sped away. The
ideal life of a monk, Khenpo Rigzin said, is to follow the Lord Buddha's
own advice to avoid cities, corrupting influences, distraction. He said that
only the greatest of lamas would be able to concentrate in the busy atmosphere of some *gompas* these days.
—Barbara Crossette, *So Close to Heaven: The Vanishing Buddhist Kingdoms
of the Himalayas*

✦ ✦ ✦

Behind the Scenes with Bertolucci

It should have been Fellini.

THE MAIN STREET LEADING TO THE ROYAL PALACE GATE WAS ABOUT twelve feet wide. Because it was an important day, all the young men and women of the city were in their best clothes. They stood on bamboo scaffolding and looked out the windows of their homes to have a glimpse of their beloved crown prince Siddartha Gautam, son of King Suddhodhan of Kapilvastu. Suddenly, there was the sound of drums, signaling the arrival of the prince. The big wooden gate swung open slowly, and Prince Siddartha appeared on a palanquin, borne by twenty men. The crowd, which had been waiting outside, loudly praised the prince, throwing flowers and red powder at him. The drums and people's voices grew louder.

In the midst of all this, hidden in a corner of a house, I was monitoring the crowd, carefully examining each person. Then suddenly, as I had anticipated, I noticed a young man, the kind that I had been worried about. He was on a bamboo scaffolding waiting to throw flowers at the prince. I noticed the danger and ran towards him, hiding myself within the crowd until I reached him. I grabbed him and pushed him inside a house. When he protested, I yelled at him, "*Bhai*! (brother) I told you all before that no one wore glasses in Buddha's time." Boy! Another close call. This tiny incident almost ruined the filming of that particular "take" of Bernardo Bertolucci's *Little Buddha* being filmed in Bhaktapur.

I had been hired as a local assistant director. My job was to work with the Western crew and find and direct Nepali extras. Such a big movie had never been filmed in Nepal. Over one hundred European crew and many tons of equipment had arrived in Kathmandu to film a story interweaving Buddha's life with the experiences of three present-day child reincarnations of a Tibetan Buddhist lama. The talk of the town was that "a Western Buddha is in Kathmandu." For the next four months I learned not only about movie making but also the absurd clash of cultures.

Since the film's plot revolved around identifying the true reincarnation of an important lama among the three child characters, our first task was to find two child actors. One was to play a rich Indian girl and the other a Tibetan street urchin. The American child actor had already been selected. We quickly located a girl who was indeed rich and Indian in real life, but finding a street-smart Tibetan kid proved more difficult. The Western crew did not realize that most Tibetans in Kathmandu are wealthy traders. Most of the Tibetan kids we found were well educated and would not pass for a poor kid. After an exhaustive search it became clear that it would be impossible to find a Tibetan street kid. The hunt now shifted to other ethnic groups. We finally did find a real street urchin—a shoe-shine boy, but he was a Hindu Indian, very different from the ethnic Tibetan the script demanded. But he was

A whole kind of folklore has grown up around the production: there is the tale of how the Italians found the perfect tree (for the Buddha to find enlightenment under), just next to the perfect river—but not, alas, at the perfect distance from the perfect river (so they raised the tree onto a platform and gave it plastic roots)....

Stories are told of how a farmer was asked to stop burning wood for a day, since his smoke showed up in the background of a shot. Sure, he said, if you give me 5,000 rupees. They did, and he received a whole year's wages for taking the whole day off.

—Pico Iyer, Tropical Classical: Essays from Several Directions

perfect for it so he got the role. I suggested that the name of the character should be changed because a typical Indian could never pass as a Tibetan kid. At first my suggestion was ignored, but finally the casting director was convinced of the vast difference between features of Tibetans and Indians and changed the character's name to Raju, which was in fact the boy's real name as well as my own.

Raju was a shoe-shine kid from Rajasthan, India. He was about thirteen years old but looked much younger. He hung around the Thamel district and had learned to speak some English and a few words of various European languages. He, along with twelve or thirteen family members, lived in the outskirts of Kathmandu in a tent made out of plastic sheets. After he was chosen for the film, Raju's life suddenly changed, at least as long as the film was being shot.

On the second or third day of shooting I had to pick him and his brother up early in the morning. I went to the field where Raju's family had their shelter. But I found out that they had been driven away by the local authorities for squatting. I was terrified that I would not be able to find him that day, and the shoot would be interrupted. Luckily, I located the family not far from Boudha, where our unit was filming. They had pitched their torn plastic tent in an open field. Because of the rain the night before the ground was muddy. Raju's father told me with a big smile that they hardly slept that night. This was not a complaint, but a way of making casual conversation. Later, Raju and his family were moved into an apartment. During the shoot, he was treated very nicely. Even the local Nepali crew started to show him respect, now that he was no ordinary shoe-shine boy, but an actor in a Western movie. Sometimes I felt quite frightened for him because of these changes. One day he whispered in my ear, "I know this is real (referring to his new existence) and it's not a dream, but it does not feel real." I wanted to tell him that in a way it was a dream and I just hoped that the dream would continue. But instead I told him that he was as lucky as his character, the reincarnated lama, reincarnating from shoe-shine boy to an actor. He smiled shyly.

One of the main locations for the movie was Bhaktapur, about twelve kilometers east of Kathmandu. It is an ancient city of fabulous temples and courtyards, the living examples of Newari artistic craftsmanship. It is a tightly-knit Newar community of farmers and artisans that is profoundly religious and very traditional. The Italian set designers worked for months with local craftsmen to turn the city into Bertolucci's imagined vision of Kapilvastu, the birthplace of Buddha. The set was breathtaking. Local people were amazed by the talent of the Italian set builders, especially when they learned that all those newly-added matching brick walls, carved wooden windows and doors, and large stone lions were made out of fiberglass. People were stunned when the fiberglass lions were easily lifted by a single person onto a truck at the end of the shooting. These foreigners could indeed fool you. A local potter laughingly told me one day, "If a white person could be Buddha (referring to Keanu Reeves), why can't fiberglass be stone?"

We were filming in Bhaktapur's old Durbar Square. The other Italian assistant directors and I were making sure that the camera would not pick up any unwanted events or modern objects like TV antennas or our Nepali extras wearing watches, eyeglasses or sneakers. When we were ready to film I got an urgent call on my walkie-talkie from one of the assistant directors. An old woman was on the roof of her house doing her *puja* and ignoring that filming was about to begin. "Raju, come here quickly and ask this lady to go inside the house. Our camera is pointing in that direction." I ran with my Newar assistant to that location and asked the old lady to go inside her house until filming was over. She paid no attention to me and continued what she was doing. My assistant asked her again. Finally she turned around and said, "I have been doing this *puja* for the last fifty years, always at this time and in this place. You come here

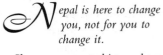

Nepal is here to change you, not for you to change it.

—Slogan seen on t-shirts and tea shops in Nepal

from outside and ask me not to do my *puja* in my own house." My assistant told the woman in Newari that everyone in the neighborhood had been paid for the use of this location. "Not me," she said, "and even if I had been offered money, I wouldn't have broken the rituals that I have been doing for such a long time. My *puja* is more important than these foreigners' movie." She slowly finished her *puja* in her own good time, and only then disappeared inside her home.

On another occasion, we had to find about 400 extras for one particular scene in Bhaktapur. According to the casting director, the extras had to be "Indian looking." We would be walking down a street when suddenly he would grab an Indian food vendor (there's quite a significant Indian migrant labor population) and tell me that this is the look he wanted. I told him that since Bhaktapur is predominantly Newar, a Mongoloid ethnic group, it would be difficult to find many "Indian looking" people here. "Then get them from outside," he answered.

I politely replied that this is not like filming in Hollywood where you can order up what you want from a casting agency. If we brought "Indian looking" extras from outside Bhaktapur, there could be a riot and perhaps even bloodshed. It would be like invading someone's house with strangers and throwing the owner out. I was greatly relieved when the producers decided to use local Newars as extras and avoid a local ethnic uprising.

Then the casting directors took Polaroid pictures of every possible extra. I realized that this was standard procedure in Western film-making, but I had strong doubts that it would be of much help to us in Nepal. Hundreds of photos were taken in the midst of chaos. People were pushing and shoving to get the chance to be an extra. One of the Italian assistant directors was assigned to write the bio-data of every potential extra:

"What is your name?"

"Ram Maharjan"

"How tall are you?"

"I don't know."

"What? OK, what is your address?"

"Moru Tole."

"House number?"

"What is that?" he giggled.

"You don't know what a house number is?"

I explained, "No, we don't have an organized system in Nepal."

He gave a loud, frustrated sigh. "OK, your telephone number?"

"I don't have one."

"No telephone? No house number? How are we ever going to contact these people?" he muttered to himself, and then handed an ID card to the person. "OK, when we call you next time you bring this card. And when I tell you to come at 7 a.m. you come at that time. Do you understand?"

I translated. The old man nodded his head indicating that he understood. But I remained doubtful.

The day of shooting arrived, and not surprisingly, everything went haywire. The Western-style selection system did not work. The photos didn't match the people and vice versa. I had to remind our Italians, "In Rome do as the Romans do," likewise "in Nepal do as the Nepalis do." But cultural collisions continued.

We were filming a scene where King Suddhodhan presents the infant Prince to his subjects. The location was a lush, green rice paddy just outside of Patan. We had selected about 1,000 extras, half men and half women. Our costume department had instructed the leaders of the five villages from which we had selected our extras that all 500 women extras should come in plain red saris, without any makeup or jewelry, especially no wrist watches. And men should wear white *dhotis*.

That evening I received a telephone call from one of the village leaders who was furious that we had asked male extras to wear *dhotis*. "What do they think we are? We are Nepali, not Indian. We don't wear *dhotis* here." I was a bit afraid, since I knew this particular area was highly charged politically.

I mentioned this to production. "Why should we worry? We are paying them for their services." Boy, it was much simpler to make my own people understand than these Westerners. I explained to the village leader that the scene we were going to film takes place in Buddha's time and in the *tarai* where some ethnic groups do wear *dhotis*. The production would provide the *dhotis*, so finally the villagers agreed to wear them.

On the day of the shooting, we arrived on location at 6:30 a.m. Amazingly our Italian crew had already established the set, even though we had shot on another location until quite late the night before. I was always amazed by their professionalism. Our extras were supposed to be on the set by 7 a.m., but I was very nervous because Nepalis are not known for their punctuality. Thankfully I was wrong. I saw hundreds of human figures emerging from all different directions. Our extras arrived right on time. But to my horror I only saw male extras and perhaps just a handful of women. What had happened to the rest of our female extras, around 500 of them? I asked our village leaders. "Oh! they have to prepare the morning meal for their families. Then they'll come."

Hearing that, the first assistant director, Fabrizio, could not control himself. He started to jump up and down, swearing in Italian. "Raju! Don't they understand that we are making a film?"

"Yes! But in Nepal!" I yelled back.

I tactfully told our village leaders that they should bring all female extras right away otherwise we will be shooting all night long without any breaks. That did the trick. They left immediately and returned with all the female extras. My relief was short-lived. Many of the women came dressed in their best clothes (luckily they all were wearing red saris as we wanted), but for this glamorous occasion they were wearing their best jewelry, including wrist watches. After all they were going to be in a movie. I was often implored by extras: "Raju *dai* (brother), can I wear my pants under my *dhoti*?" or "Can I leave my dark glasses on because the sun is too strong?" or "Is it OK to wear my sneakers?" "No, no, no. Nobody wore Levis or Nikes or Ray Bans in Buddha's time."

After four months of hectic shooting, one day the foreigners packed their belongings and headed home. For all those months Bhaktapur had been transformed. People were just getting used to being filmed in their courtyards, alleys, and houses. Now the invasion had ended. Some time later I went to Bhaktapur again just for a visit. I was happy to meet all those extras who had become friends. As I was walking in this town of pagodas and palaces, I saw in the distance the same old lady on her rooftop performing her *puja*. She looked calm and meditative, like Bhaktapur itself. I was glad to see that the ancient town had returned to its normal routine.

Raju Gurung is an independent documentary filmmaker and professional musician. A native Nepali living in both Nepal and the U.S., he makes documentary videos on arts and cultural traditions of Nepal. A graduate of Berkelee College of Music in Boston, he has released a solo album of contemporary Nepali music.

✳

Entering the old Palace Square of Bhaktapur, I was surprised to encounter an enormous mob. Standing on tiptoe, I heard muted drums and cymbals, followed by the unlikely bark of a bullhorn.

The man next to me, who had apparently been drawn into the crowd while heading home from both work and dinner shopping, hopped up and down for a better look. He was clutching a portable typewriter under one arm and a live chicken under the other. "Oh, *daju*," I asked. "*Kay bhayo*? What's happenin'?"

"*Movie gardaiccha*! Making a movie!"

Sure enough. The crowd was mesmerized by the filming of a made-for-television extravaganza, *Night Train to Kathmandu*. I waded into the crowd and got a look at the action: blonde American kid-actors in LaCoste t-shirts posed in saucer-eyed disbelief, surrounded by a troupe of ethnic dancers wearing papier-maché masks. A few steps away, barefoot local ragamuffins had abandoned their begging to gape at the Panavision cameras.

—Jeff Greenwald, *Shopping for Buddhas*

CYNTHIA KANETSUKA

* * *

Mortal Again

*What is life like for a former
living goddess?*

I<small>T IS AN EXTRAORDINARY FACE THAT PEEKS OUT FROM THE INTRI-</small>cately carved wooden windows. The face of a child, dressed like an elaborately made up doll in red. The heavy black kohl of her eyes extends to her temples, and an all-seeing silver third eye, or "fire eye," is painted in the middle of her forehead. She remains at the window for a few seconds, then mysteriously disappears. She is Kumari, the living goddess of Kathmandu.

Ever since my first visit to Nepal many years ago, I have been intrigued with this child, whose countless pictures on postcards and guidebooks have now made her a tourist attraction. These visitors congregate in the courtyard of her palace, the Kumari Bahal, hoping that the goddess will offer a glimpse of herself. If she doesn't, a male caretaker present in the courtyard accepts money, and perhaps will encourage the Kumari to peek at the expectant tourists.

I have returned to Kathmandu after many years. Keeping in mind the renewed interest in goddess worship in the Western world, I decide I want to discover as much as possible about the most famous living goddess in the world. I know that as a non-

Hindu I am forbidden from personally meeting the Royal Kumari, but I would be happy to meet an ex-Kumari.

Outside the Kumari Bahal I meet a shopkeeper who says he is a member of the family that looks after the current living goddess, but he refuses to give me any information unless I give him a thousand rupees. I realize that learning much about the current Kumari will be difficult and expensive. But it appears that the goddesses are smiling on me. Mr. Shrestha, who runs a lodge on "Freak Street," puts me in contact with Upendra, a young man who is related to Devi, an ex-living goddess. Upendra offers to show me where Devi lives, but refuses to work as a translator for me. He tells me that most ex-Kumaris do not like talking to foreigners. Instead, I arrange for a Nepali friend to help me in my quest.

Shy and reserved, as most former Kumaris are known to be, she tells me a sad story. "I was just a little girl. Once an old, sick man came to be blessed. He was so sick he coughed and a touch of spit landed on my toe. My attendants gasped. He died the next day. I felt very sad. I believed I was responsible for his death."

—Carroll Dunham, "Living Goddesses," *Marie Claire*

While wandering around Kumari Bahal, my Nepali friend and I step into a printing shop. Once again I am in luck. The friendly owner, Mr. Sakya, knows Devi's family and immediately offers to take us to visit her home which happens to be directly across from his shop.

Mr. Sakya leads us up a dark, dank stairwell, reminiscent of Dickensian London, to the family's quarters on the third floor. Devi herself opens the door and Mr. Sakya explains why we are there. Surprisingly, she agrees to be interviewed, but she will absolutely not let me use the small tape recorder I have with me.

To me, Devi is a classic Nepali beauty with doe-shaped eyes, high cheekbones, a long straight nose, full lips, and long, glossy black hair. She wears no make-up, and her beauty is not marred by the long, drab garment, like a Western nightdress, which she is wearing. Her room is small, and the windows look down onto a noisy lane. She sits on the bed facing the three of us. At the head of her bed is a glass cabinet with a sliding door. Inside, there are a cassette player, tapes, cosmetics, stuffed animals, and ornaments. On the wall above her bed is a picture of an Indian pin-up girl taken from a calendar. A framed certificate announces that Devi has passed a typing test. A denim jacket hangs on the door.

My questions are going through two translators; Devi speaks Newari (which is different from Nepali), which is translated into Nepali by Mr. Sakya, and my friend translates the Nepali into English. Devi's answers are simple and she does not respond to anything too personal. I wonder if the translators are screening some of my questions to protect her.

She tells me that she was chosen to be a Kumari when she was four but doesn't remember anything of the ceremony. As the living goddess she felt divine and particularly enjoyed the attention she got when she was taken out on her ornate palanquin during the special festivals. I ask if she regretted her loss of freedom as a child. "I was a goddess, and I never felt envious," she replies, "because I knew that when my time was over I could play and do what I liked." However, she admits that when she became an ordinary girl again, she had difficulty adapting to her family, particularly her younger brother, and she constantly yearned to return to the Kumari Bahal. It took her two years to adapt to the mundane, secular life.

I learned that Kumaris traditionally received no schooling. On losing their divinity, the government gives them a small monthly income, which generally goes towards formal education. Devi said she was studying at a local women's college and that her fellow students did not know that she was once a Kumari. She is reluctant to say if she has any boyfriends, but she does believe that she will get married. In the past ex-Kumaris often remained single as many men were terrified of marrying them. Since she was once a goddess, people believe that her husband will die early or misfortunes will fall upon the husband and his family. But apparently this attitude is changing and nowadays some men believe it is auspicious as well as prestigious to marry a former Kumari. Still, many Sakya mothers live in fear that their daughters will be chosen as a Kumari, and afterwards she will not be able to lead a normal life.

Throughout the interview, Devi avoids eye contact. Nevertheless, I am struck by the serenity that this 21-year-old possesses—a presence which I have not seen in other Nepali women of her age. After the interview is over, I make an appointment with Devi to come back a few days later to take some photographs. I am curious to see how she will dress and if she will wear make-up. She is the same age as Anna, my daughter, who was conceived in Nepal, whose first words were in Nepali, who left Kathmandu when she was 18 months old, and who even looks a little like a Nepali because she's half Japanese. She'll be arriving from Japan soon to spend her Christmas holidays with me, and I hope Anna will get an opportunity to meet Devi.

On the appointed day, I walk past two small temples near her house. I feel they make a perfect background for the photo session. But Devi refuses my suggestion to be photographed there. She insists that I take them in her house.

Devi is accompanied by her two three-year-old nieces, Usha and Mina. They are wearing glittery dresses and hats; it is obvious that I am going to take their pictures too. Devi is wearing a simple pale green *salwaar kameez;* her eyes are lightly made up with kohl and she is wearing just a touch of lipstick. During the entire photo session, Devi poses on the bed with her two nieces on either side of her.

Afterwards, I show Devi photographs of Anna. As soon as she

The Kumari is considered to be the incarnation of Taleju Bhawani, one of the Hindu goddesses. How the goddess became a Kumari is the subject of many legends. One of them recounts that when the goddess, in human form, was playing dice with a Malla king, he lusted after her. She became angry and said she would never return. The king pleaded with her, and in time she relented, finally promising to return as a young virgin from the Sakya clan of Kathmandu.

—Larry Habegger,
"Pilgrimage to Muktinath"

discovers that I am a mother, she becomes much more friendly. I tell her that Anna will be visiting from Tokyo and would she like a present from there? She asks for nothing. Since I have seen local cosmetics on the glass cabinet behind her bed, I know that she likes make-up. I decide to ask Anna to bring some cosmetics and other small gifts from Japan.

A few days later, Anna arrives full of smiles and bulging bags. The little lane near our guest house has been totally dug up. There are great holes and mountains of mud everywhere, making it difficult to carry her bags, but I'm pleased that she remains unperturbed and has a sense of coming home. On Christmas Eve we go to visit Devi, who is watching TV with her parents. We are ushered into her bedroom and Anna gives her the gifts she has brought, including a palette of heart-shaped lipsticks in different shades. I watch them together—and I find that it is impossible for me to comprehend their differences. Two young women of the same age. One a former living goddess, the other a liberated Western woman. But standing close together, both with long flowing hair, they appear as if they are friends who are posing for a snapshot. Suddenly I am transported to a time many years ago, when Anna was six, and I'd sent her a postcard of Devi as the Kumari. On it I wrote: "This little girl is a living goddess. She can't run and jump like you. One day I would like to bring you to Nepal to see her." Amazingly, all these years later, here we are.

Finally, on Christmas night, I get to see the Royal Kumari when she is brought out to witness the ritualistic cleansing of the Seto Machendranath, one of the valley's many gods. In that worthy Nepali tradition, the white or "*Seto*" Machendranath is worshipped by both Hindus and Buddhists.

Along with a few locals and photographers, I wait at the entrance to the Kumari Bahal. Shortly after dusk the Kumari is carried out in the arms of one of her four bearers and seated in a simple palanquin. She is an extraordinarily beautiful ten-year-old child who does not seem burdened with her heavy ornate jewelry and exotic make-up. I closely follow the palanquin as it wends its way through the narrow streets of Durbar Square towards the Seto

Machendranath temple, where people have already gathered for the ceremony.

The Kumari is lifted out of the palanquin and seated on a throne erected in an alcove facing the deity. She watches as the priests undress the Seto Machendranath and anoint him with sacred herbs, oil and milk. Meanwhile, a stream of people offers flowers and coins, and prostrate at the feet of the Kumari. Disregarding my non-Hindu status, I too approach the Kumari and offer some coins and touch my head to her red-painted feet. As I rise, I catch sight of her dark, intense eyes, shining from a small, round, perfect face. She appears to be in a deep meditative state, and I recall reading a description of her powers which said that through her "third eye" she can see miles away, to the other side of the earth—and beyond to other dimensions of time and space.

Whatever power this small being possesses, I too feel transported as I watch the rest of the ritual. As a final blessing the priest lifts the vessel containing the remainder of the sacred herbs, which sprinkle onto our heads as he scatters it over the crowd. Even as the crowd erupts into spontaneous cries of exaltation, the Kumari is lifted into the palanquin and carried back to her palace.

Filled with the energy of this ancient ritual, I visit Mr. Shrestha's lodge—smack into a Christmas party in full swing. The guests, mostly young Westerners, like their hippie predecessors, wear the best of their Nepali and Indian silk and velvet costumes: colourful hats, scarves, and long skirts. Some appear stoned, others are drinking, and all are intent on having a good time. Mr. Shrestha, the lodge owner, and his wife greet me and offer me a glass of *Khukuri* rum. As a Christmas treat, Mr. Shrestha has installed a large-screen TV and is playing a video of Brazilians dancing the *Lambada*. A few couples are moving to the fast sensual rhythm. As I quietly sip my rum, I reflect upon my interview with Devi, the ex-Kumari, my brief worship of the living goddess, and now a different celebration of yet another faith. All in a span of a couple of weeks in this unique city of Kathmandu which for me will always symbolize the eternal juxtaposition of the old and the new.

Cynthia Kanetsuka is a freelance writer and photographer who first went to Nepal on an overland trip from London to Kathmandu in 1966. She remains attached to that part of the world and is currently writing a book on her 30-year love affair with Nepal. She lives on a small island in British Columbia, Canada, and when not traveling she gardens.

★

Two American friends and I were in the courtyard of the Kumari's residence. It was early evening and we were deciding if there was enough light to take photographs. I looked up—and there was a child's impish face looking down at us from the top floor's carved window. The Kumari herself! At the same moment, my friends noticed her too. I was so flustered I did not know what to do. I had not expected to see her. Quickly, I bowed towards her with my folded palms as I would in a temple and murmured *namaste*; my friends followed suit. When I looked up, she gave the briefest flash of a smile, like a child happy to be acknowledged, and then disappeared. Just as quickly, a man whom I had only vaguely noticed loitering about the courtyard, put out his hand and demanded, "You give money. It's for the Kumari." That magical moment was instantly lost as I resentfully fumbled for some rupees. The sacred instantly became profane.

—RK

JEFFREY HEIMAN

✦ ✦ ✦

Observations from Mrigasthali

Life and death, the pure and the polluted,
mingle at Nepal's holiest Hindu temple.

"THEN YOU MUST ACCOMPANY ME TO THE TEMPLE AT Pashupatinath," Mr. Nair said as we moved toward the front of the plane bound for Kathmandu. I accepted and thanked him, having said a minute earlier that the temples of this country were my object, not really the mountains.

We had spoken briefly during the flight, mainly while I craned my neck to get a glimpse out of his window because mine was over the wing. When I apologized at one point for impinging upon his view, he invited me to the whole window; he'd taken this flight many times before but affairs in Delhi had kept him and his wife too long from doing *puja* at the holiest temple in Nepal.

Better to meet later in the week, he'd said, after business in Kathmandu. "Take a rickshaw to my hotel, ten rupees from Chhetrapati, where you will stay. Early morning best." We pressed our hands in *namaste*, and he and Mrs. Nair were gone. This was good. I had a plan, or had been given one.

Already an hour in the airport with a planeload ahead of me, I wondered if I'd get to town before dark.

"Gawr, look at the queue. Where you from, mate?" Warm, throaty vowels from the guy behind me. They were British, a cou-

ple, Hal and Sal; they'd flown in from Dubai where their trip began
with a visit to a friend, a consular official.

Once outside, Hal got us a cab for 30 rupees apiece to the hotel
we figured we'd book into together. It was about 5:30. Lowering
sky balanced on distant peaks. We kept quiet.

Over weighty breakfasts next morning at one of Kathmandu's
many bakeries, Hal announced they'd decided to start the day at
Pashupatinath and stroll onward, and I would be joining them. It
was not an interrogatory, and I submitted, glad for the company on
my first day in the country, hoping only that Mr. Nair wouldn't

just happen to slip in a visit to
the temple at the same time. I
didn't want him to think I'd
passed on his invitation.

We walked to the end of a
lane of whirring embroidery
machines and hailed a rickshaw.
After crossing many little hills,
we got out at the long approach
road to the Pashupatinath temple and wandered areas open to
non-Hindus. We found a 7th-
century Shiva laid horizontally
into a stone embankment,
crossed the river and "beghat-
ted" ourselves for fifteen minutes before walking on to the
huge pug stupa at Bodnath,
where we had Cokes and *momos*
under the omniscopic eyes of
the Buddha.

Wonderful. At this pace I'd
have "been there, done that" in a
day in a half. I looked for an excuse to spend the rest of the day
alone. "Listen, folks," was all I

*estivals at Boudha are
always major social
events; you run into everyone you
know. Or, if you stay in one spot
long enough, everyone you know
runs into you. Joel and I—joined
now by a dozen other expatriate
friends—decided to perform an ascending series of devotional koras.
And so, after lighting dozens of
candles, dispensing many rupees
and giving the gigantic prayer
wheel at the base of the steps a
good spin, we began.*

*We started at the stupa's lowest
level and spiraled our way up the
layer-cake stories of the white-
washed, mandala-shaped plinth.
At last we found ourselves on the
uppermost level, directly beneath
the all-seeing eyes of the Buddha,
circling alongside the 108 guardian
deities set into niches in the stupa
wall. And I could not help but feel
happy and confident.*

—Jeff Greenwald,
*The Size of the World: Once Around
Without Leaving the Ground*

could dream up, "I'm kind of tired. Think I'm going to head back."

"Wanker," Hal smiled. "Sleep in America."

And, as if the great contriver Dickens himself had penned this scene, just as I stood to bid my friends good-bye, I saw Mr. Nair and his wife strolling clockwise around the stupa. Had to be. They spotted me right away and came over to share their pleasure at the holiness of this site.

"You have come to visit the Buddha. You know this little country has thirty-thousand temples." Today Mr. Nair had changed his khakis and Madras shirt for thin gauzy whites and sandals. I wondered if he felt himself to be nearing the age when a life of productive extroversion must cede to prayer, contemplation, spiritual work, perhaps even mendicancy. Mrs. Nair, lipsticked, bespangled, *tikka*ed, hennaed, and beaming at her husband, said nothing, but didn't appear to think he was headed away from home.

"We liked Pashapu...pa...pa...ti," Hal said. Sal giggled.

Oh, God. I had been found out.

"I see," Mr. Nair said, trying not, I thought, to glare at me. "You have been to the temple."

"Very briefly," I admitted.

"Yes, well, short or long, this is not a problem, young man," he said. "Much to learn. You must always visit twice. To see if the experience sits in your mouth as a stone or a fruit. We will meet?"

"With pleasure."

"Good, tomorrow. And since you know where it is," he said dryly, "I shall see you at the gate at nine o'clock in the morning."

At 8:45 I was at the head of the approach road I'd walked the morning before. I understood why he wanted to meet so early. There were no tourists or pilgrims out yet, only a few families waking by the side of the road, young, shirtless boys picking up twigs in the sparse woods. One, when he saw me, dropped his load, held out his hand and sang through the saplings: "Rupees, one rupees." I walked on. I could smell fires and hear boiling tea but did not stare into anyone's camp. A bit farther downhill sellers unfolded bright cloths on which they arranged rows of Shiva *lingams*, tiny plaster casts of Buddha's footprints, "bone" Buddhas sitting, Shivas dancing the end of the world, incense to clear the air for meditation, strings of beads to aid in concentration—and everyone ready to stand if I slowed the pace of my walk.

At the bottom of the hill the road joined up with one leading into the temple. I bought a glass of tea and waited. Mr. Nair was right on time.

"Very good, you've come," he said.

I said it was good to meet again, and walked beside him into the part of the temple enclosure open to all. I wanted to ask about all the garlanded Shivas in a random stack of shrines, but Mr. Nair followed the path to a stone bridge over the river. He stopped in the middle, leaned against the ancient smoothed stone rail, and said, not to me but just beyond, perhaps to the array of Westerners he might have imagined coming to learn, "You see, here you are in the domain of Shiva, the protectorate, as it were. One of the holiest places a Shivaite can pray."

"How does Shiva come to be associated with this temple?" I asked.

"This is a matter of history and language. The site of this temple dates back to 5th century A.D., by your calendar. But I will tell you that stones were placed here one thousand years before that. When your Sophocles was putting out the eyes of Oedipus on stage, we were loving Shiva.

During the Neolithic Age and early part of the Old Bronze Age, the cult of Pashupati, the Lord of the Animals, and of Parvati, the Lady of the Mountains, became established amongst the Dravidian invaders. It involved a great philosophical and religious movement which under the name of Shivaism was superimposed on Animism, and became the principal source from which later religions have been drawn. The salient features of this religion are the cult of the phallus, the bull and the snake and, to a lesser extent, of the tiger and lion, the mounts of the goddess.

—Alain Daniélou,
Gods of Love and Ecstasy: The Traditions of Shiva and Dionysus

Well, some of us were more conniving than loving because they know Shiva does like flattery. Or, let's say prayer. He sees immediately, and is very quickly pleased to give." Mr. Nair looked at me directly, lips still creasing around words to be said though he had finished speaking.

"Does Shiva not destroy as well?"

"Yes, but not as you would think. Not individuals. Even if you are a thief and ask for bad help, Shiva will give it. It is Brahma who will take care of you later. Term for this is *Ashutosh*. Shiva who gives his blessings right away. Quick return on your investment of prayer."

I wondered at the image, at the efficacy of prayer when one's steps are already mapped. "Is this why there are so many temples to Shiva? Because he hears and responds to the wishes of humans."

"Perhaps this is true. Every king of Nepal, and in modern times every prime minister, has had his hand in the expansion of Pashupati. Even King Birendra at present. What you have here is not a single temple but a city. A city to Pashupati. With at least ten thousand figures cut of stone. Some very, very old. Even for us old Hindus." Now he smiled to the side, again forming inaudible phrases. I felt as if I were engaging only the part of him not used for prayer.

About 50 yards up river, under cover of overhanging trees, a man lifted his *lungi* to squat. His children splashed in the river nearby, unconcerned. This excited me. The sacred architecture. The profane shit. I could take in both without shifting focus.

"And Shiva of Pashupati?"

"Yes, yes, I am coming. First, this river, the Bagmati…" Here he seemed to drift, become wistful. "Sacred to Nepal as the Ganga to India. This water cleanses. Cannot become impure. Room for all of our misdeeds in this water. Though if you want to drink, perhaps go a little up. River is low now. You can see it holds our misdeeds too long this time of year."

Below us the water trickled through an eddy of trash, boxes, burnt material, orange peels, flowers, a long bone.

"Pashupati is Shiva, but in a special way," he resumed. "You see, these languages, Nepali, Hindi, Sanskrit, are very rich, very old. We combine words to make others. In English you have the word animal, and this name in Nepal is *pashu*. After *pashu* you have the word *pati*, which means husband or master. So Shiva of this temple is the husband of *pashu*. Not to say he copulates with animals, but he is the great caretaker, which is the meaning of *nath*. This is very good, I think, because the nature of his being is always present in the name. Perhaps like your English names Smith or Mason?" He chuckled at his witticism, leaving me uncertain as to whether he intended the comparison to be taken seriously. I learned later that Mr. Nair was not a university lecturer but a banker.

The need to know who is or is not a Hindu is taken to its logical and absurd limits by temple gatekeepers, such as at Kathmandu's Pashupatinath, where a sign warns off non-Hindus.

A young journalist, a Brahmin, was stopped from entering the temple, abode of Shiva. His only fault was that unlike an average Nepali, he was six feet tall and lighter-skinned than most. No amount of arguing in his native tongue, showing his Brahminical sacred thread, or even his identity card as a reporter for The Rising Nepal, *would convince the policeman that he was not an infidel. Sacred threads could be bought in any shop selling* prasad, *said the guard, and he had heard Peace Corps volunteers speak better Nepali.*

—Dipak Gyawali, "How Not to Recognise a Hindu," *Himal South Asia*

We leaned quietly against the wide railing. The sun was not yet high enough to burn but it did bring more of the sacred city out of shadow. To the left, I knew from the map, was the central complex, closed to non-Hindus, the huge two-tiered pagoda, and beside it Nandi the bull, Shiva's transport, whose golden butt could be seen from the high banks across the river. At the far end of the main complex was a boxy tumble-down building, not ornate like the religious structures. Contiguous but leaning away. Not sure it wanted its own inhabitants.

"Look below," Mr. Nair instructed. There was a raised darkened stone platform, eight or ten feet square, at the base of the wall up to Vishwarup, the main temple. "Aryaghat," he said. "Last lying down place for the great men of Kathmandu."

Common as it is to lie down one last time, I felt the breath in me singe when he said this. "Many people want to die here. Go over to the *ghat* opposite, now, and sit." He lifted his hand professorially to the high *ghat* across the bridge where I'd gabbed with the Brits about 24 hours ago. The wooded hill above the *ghat* is called *Mrigasthali*, the place of the deer. We thanked each other, not at any point touching hands but raising them in *namaste*, a gesture that had come to have so much more meaning for me here than ever in the ashrams of the new world. We had brushed shoulders, though, while leaning on the rail. Neither of us had flinched then.

He clasped his arms behind him and strolled back over the bridge, disappearing among the hawkers who had all come to life. In spite of deep religious feeling, a wife who followed him agreeably, vital work and vast knowledge, Mr. Nair seemed to be a solitary man. I had no way of really knowing this but I could not remember his eyes. Only the lips that seemed to wish me to understand more than I did.

I crossed the bridge, turned left onto the wide esplanade and walked along some steps at the back. Just above me were about a dozen open-sided little stone houses, each with a *lingam*, a stylized phallus, imbedded in the *yoni*, the stylized female vessel. I sat down on the steps.

Monkeys were clambering out of the river and up a hillside. They leapt from overhanging branches to the wall of that nondescript building at the right of the temple, up its rusted window gates to a rotting veranda, and hurled themselves back into the river shrieking like hyper children. With arms and legs splayed, they hit the water on furless rumps or stomachs, bounced back to the shore and pecked and chased each other up for another run. It was hot enough now for me to wish I too could swing down into the water. But what a river it was. A foot deep at most, clogged with everything inedible the temple discharged: sweepings off the floor, plastic boxes, soda bottles, shards of metal, pottery and brick. I had to accept that this water could purify, especially since a woman just to the right of Aryaghat was wringing it out of her shining black hair while another a few feet up was scrubbing her clothes against the silt-laden steps. Neither paid any mind to the people beginning to congregate on the landing above.

Beside me a *sadhu* rested his stick and sat. Flowered, solemn, a
gentle guardian of Shiva's way, wrapped in strips of saffron cloth
and someone's cast-off hiking
boots, dreadlocks to his waist,
seeds and beads and globs of
stone around his neck, bangles
up his arms, white streaks along
his forehead, and eyes so
rimmed in red from *ganja* that I
began to swirl. Whether the
costume was for effect or devotion, it didn't matter until he
touched my knee. He took a
pipe from a purse at his waist, filled the bowl, and held a wooden
match and sucked until the little nut of *ganja* had gone to ash.
Ahhh. Then nodded to me. But it was too early, or too late. I
waved it off, politely.

> *I*n an area frequented by
> Western tourists near the
> Pashupati temple, a well-known
> sadhu *has often startled unsuspect-*
> *ing tourists by exposing his "great-*
> *est human member." Among other*
> *displays, he can lift a ten-pound*
> *pile of bricks by his erect penis.*
>
> —Maureen DeCoursey,
> "Greatest Human Member"

Now there were many people across the river on Aryaghat, only
twenty or thirty feet away. An older woman in a white sari leaned
against the wall. All the rest were men, maybe fifteen of them.
Some carried armloads of logs, which they arranged in neat piles,
fuel to burn the body. Below the platform, at the water's edge, a
head-shaving was going on. The shavee, a man in his late 30s, sat
gazing down, elbows on raised knees. The shaver stood before him
in the water, dipping the blade into the river now and then but
using no soap. Never checking for balance, he worked mechani-
cally. He left a small tuft at the top and signaled the next to sit
down. There were three in all. Three sons of a dead man who was
about to be carried down the long flight of steps from the temple
above. Wide double doors opened. Two dogs ran out. On a bamboo pallet the dead man lay under a shroud of gold and saffron
cloth and marigolds. The shaved men and one other, the pall bearers, shouldered their father and walked without music or pomp
down the thirty or so steps. Children ran down beside them.
Frenzied dogs got underfoot and had to be kicked. When the bier
reached bottom, the woman in white began to keen and tremble.

Someone went over to talk but she couldn't bear her husband's leave-taking and cried out again, drawing the heads of tourists and locals crossing the bridge. The man who consoled her became impatient and ushered her sternly back up the stairs.

The dead man was laid on the ground while the pyre was built. His head from the eyebrows up was uncovered. Not much to see but a ring of white hair around a hard copper pate. Enough to know he had lived, had held the bodies of sons who now held him, and had the wealth to insure his cremation on the *ghat* at Pashupati. I had taken a book out of my small knapsack but could only hold my finger on the page to be read. Here was a being about to slip back to *samsara*. After this body, another, until, as Mr. Nair might have said, accounts are righted. Not death but the torrent of life that wins. Again and again one faces the challenge. The task of living, it seemed, carried hope. A dead man in the West may lie in state for a day but his destination is the dust, when there is no more balancing to be done. The living lose.

But this man waiting on the bamboo pallet didn't seem all that dead. Just lying there with his eyes closed, he still had bulk, color, and readiness. The courage to go forth? I was imagining too much. Can any funeral rites ever quiet the wrenching sadness of those left living?

The wife of the dead man peered down from the top of the temple steps, hands up to hide the sobs. The pyre was nearly done. Cross-hatches of logs the length of the body had been built about three feet high and filled in with twigs and straw. The pall bearers, uniformly shorn, in crisp light-colored clothes, carried their father to his point of departure and laid him on it as lightly as they would have put a baby to bed. One son drew the saffron shroud over the head, bringing all in attendance to silence. Another son cupped holy river water in his hands to sprinkle over the body, and the last poured on powder from a bag. Then the sons stepped back and another man took a match to a sheaf of straw and ignited kindling under the body. I had the idiotic notion that there was still time. He could wake up and get off. But the sons lit their own sheafs and walked around the body three or four times, stopping at each circuit to touch their flames to the thick mat of straw under the old man's head and feet. First smoke, then hissing steam, then flames rose from the gaps in the pyre. Dogs fought madly with each other on the steps, backing interlopers into the water. No one bothered with them now. The living had their prerogative. Or couldn't be controlled. Monkeys flew off the high veranda of that lone building at the far end of the temple, clumsy ones screeching down the cliff walls. Slapping water. The dead man burned. When the shroud began to curl away, a fire-bearer drew a bundle of straw through the river and laid it over the body, creating dense smoke. The sons stayed close, tempering the flames with water to insure complete cremation and perhaps to cloud the eyes of onlookers, a mix of Nepalis and tourists who lined the bridge now and the high *ghat* beside me.

The sons doted on their father, stopping only to splash river water into their own burning eyes. Otherwise, they circled the pyre and stoked the flames with a long stick, occasionally rapping on the skull.

When ash began to sail over, I got up to walk among the people on the bridge. Old locals, young unemployed, pilgrims, some jostling for a view, some rapt as children reading. A few Europeans stood ill at ease with their long lenses but many explored the macabre behind video cams. The dead man nestled into the coals. Smokeless flame left the head visible and more sheafs of straw were rushed to the river, then draped over the body.

There was a little commotion. Young men pushed through the crowd, holding up arms strung with silver chains and bracelets. One man raised his face to me. Before I could deflect his advance, he said, "No, I don't selling to you. I can see you not buying. These are for tourists."

The seller, Shambhu Pokharel, who carefully wrote his name in Nepali and English when we finally sat down, wanted out. "I know English, I have traveling all over Nepal and India, but I am selling this...this stuff. Very cheap, not even silver. Come with me."

We crossed to the other side of the bridge and walked along the embankment, away from the temple. I looked through breaches in a wall as we passed. Families lived in these unroofed enclosures. Lines were strung with clothes. Small fires glowed. Mothers sat with blank-eyed babies in their arms. Old men chewed bread. There was stillness in the air but not calm. We sat on a step by the river. "Making me mad, this work."

I accepted his tacit invitation to ask, "What kind of work would you like?"

"Anything, teacher maybe. You from USA? I want to come to America."

Shambhu could have been 25 or 40, with a face like a dry dirt road, hair not barbered but hacked, shirt split off from the collar. Missing half a thumb. Hid none of this. Eyes clean as eggs and as big.

"Do you have a way to do that?"

"Needing friend in America. Wanting to send my son to school but if I don't pay nine hundred rupees, they are not letting him stay." He took a crumpled piece of paper from his shirt. On it were two lines of Nepali with the amount he owed penned in a space.

"Money is hard." Between the pouch around my neck and the one in my pocket I figured I had around four thousand rupees.

"I don't asking you. I don't like this life."

"There are people everywhere who don't like life."

"This true? But here is too much hard. Look my hand."

"No one helps?"

"Who is helping is helping himself. I am not asking Shiva."

The sun had begun to set. I didn't want to leave him yet and asked if he'd walk with me. We crossed the bridge back to the *ghat* on which I'd spent most of the day. The crowd had thinned. The dead man was greatly reduced.

"He rich man, good man," Shambhu said with a wry smile, turning away from the cremation. "Now look this man." He raised an arm languorously toward one of the *sadhus* crouching not far down the *ghat*. "He eat milk, only milk. Very power. He give you anything. He have nothing but he give everything. Not like tourists. Giving one rupee. I don't like them but I have to like them. Today I make thirty rupees."

"What is that place?" I asked, pointing to the building from which monkeys had been leaping all day. The lonely, plain, grill-windowed barn.

"This...this the waiting to dying house." Uninterested, he stared beyond me toward the *sadhu*. I turned. The *sadhu* was giving *namaste* to a tourist. "Dying people living, coming, walking, sleeping, waiting to dying. Dying here good," Shambhu whispered. "Not for me. I die. I going other side of bridge. Few woods, fire, then push in river. Finish."

A few days later I ran into Mr. and Mrs. Nair at a tea shop in Bhaktapur. He told me they had witnessed the cremation from within the temple compound, and had been pleased to see that I had stayed for the length of the ritual. Just good fortune we could all be there on that day.

Jeffrey Heiman teaches in the English Department at the City College of New York. This story, in slightly altered form and under a different title, appeared in The Massachusetts Review.

★

Bouddanath at dusk is breathtaking. The courtyard entrance is filled with trays of lit butter lamps, trays of fire, gesture upon gesture of remembrance.

When you lose someone you love, someone who loved you, there is no consolation except the wheel of time, which continues to turn, carries you away from the moment of loss. Walking around a place like Bouddanath helps push the wheel forward a little. Which is why, when I learn of my mother's death, I come here in the softening light, to walk, and to light butter lamps.

A most auspicious number, some Buddhists say, is 108. So is 1 or 3 or 13. In the generosity of Buddhism, any number is in fact fine. She lived 83 years. I would light 83 lamps.

I merge with the crowd, walk three times around the outer wall of Bouddanath, spin the little quintets of wall-set prayer wheels. Near the Sakyapa temple, I find an upstairs room with wall-length windows. Walkers outside, whether on the ground or the stupa roof, can see the lamps burn. Wooden benches at the windows hold hundreds and hundreds of brass bowls. Each contains butter and a small wick. A few are already lit. Most are not.

With a slender wax taper the length of my forearm, I light the first lamp, the one for the year she was born. I hold the taper beside the wick for a long time.

This is a new ceremony for her spirit as well as mine, and there is hesitation in the room, a need for her agreement to this gift. When I pull the taper away, the lamp remains unlit. The seconds breathe by.

Then suddenly the lamp flames. Who is to say that her spirit came there then? Who is to say it did not?

I light the lamp for her second birthday. Its flame leaps at once like an opening eye. I bend my clumsy head and hand to attend these little lamps, to praise of her days, to the growth of light and warmth. One by one, each in its own way, each year of her life catches fire.

—Joan Zimmerman, "Walk the Walk, Light the Lamp"

JOHN FLINN

* * *

Season of Slaughter

*A trekker gets an unexpected glimpse
of one of Nepal's favorite festivals.*

TWO PEEVISH SNORTS AND A HALF-HEARTED BELLOW WOKE ME
from my sleep. Unzipping the door of the tent, I found my view
of the world outside framed by the muscular haunches and woolly
dreadlock underbelly of a loitering yak. Just beyond it I could see
another yak, and beyond that another and another and another.
The quiet field where we'd set up our camp had been transformed
overnight into a stockyard.

I pulled on some clothes and stepped out of the tent. Milling
about were more yaks than I'd ever seen in one place, maybe two
dozen in all. Standing among them were six men from the nearby
village of Manang. Dressed in Tibetan-style maroon robes, they
were shuffling their feet to ward off the morning chill. I waved,
and they waved back.

It was a glorious day. Our campsite was perched on a bluff
above the Marsyangdi River; above us the impossibly high summits of the Himalaya thrust into the sky, as elusive as apparitions.
Across the valley a massive blue glacier twisted and tumbled like
an icy dragon off the peak known as Gangapurna.

As I admired the view one of the Manang men reached into his
robe and pulled out a curved *khukuri* knife. Its polished blade

glinted in the morning sunlight. Then the man walked up to the nearest yak, grabbed a handful of hair on its neck and, with a casual manner that stunned me, slashed its throat.

Startled, the beast wobbled on its legs for several seconds before toppling over on its side with a loud thud. From where I stood I couldn't see whether the man had cut its windpipe or severed an artery. The yak lay there, gasping and twitching and spastically pawing at the dirt.

As the animal sprawled dying at their feet, the men from Manang laughed and joked among themselves. Amid the grandeur and beauty of the Himalayan backdrop, the cruelty of this scene was almost too much for me. I felt clammy and queasy. But the scene was morbidly compelling, like a bad car wreck. I didn't want to look but I had to.

My friend Surendra has invited me to a festival in Kirtipur where many animals will be sacrificed. I tell him I will be busy. In my country we eat meat but don't much enjoy watching animals die.

In our highly urbanized world, we like to hide from ourselves the fact that we, like all animals, kill to live. Whether it is plant or animal, we take another's life in order to preserve our own. Perhaps it is easier for us that the meat that arrives in our kitchens and is served on our tables is many steps removed from the living animal.

—Robert Peirce, "Death in the Afternoon, Kirtipur Style"

My mind flashed back to the day before. As we had walked through the village of Braga, several of us had made a detour up the hill to the *gompa*, or monastery. It looked like a whitewashed medieval fortress, festooned with strings of tattered, faded prayer flags.

Coming out of the doorway was the sound of chanting. We followed it inside, feeling our way through darkened corridors to a large central room. As my eyes adjusted to the ancient, smoky, candle-lit blackness, I could see four Buddhist monks. Their faces clearly showed concern. Three of them, their leathery brows deeply furrowed, were murmuring mournful-sounding prayers while a fourth fashioned little statuettes of yak butter.

"We are praying for the animals," one of the monks said. "Dasain is coming. There will be many killing. Many, many killing."

Suddenly the last few days had begun to make sense. As we'd walked up the valley of the Marsyangdi we'd encountered a mass movement of domestic animals in the other direction. Enormous, bleating flocks of sheep and goats, so many that they spilled out of the trail onto the hillsides, were being marched down-valley by their owners.

At the time I'd assumed they were simply being sent down to lower elevations for the winter. But now I understood: they were headed for what one Nepali friend of mine calls "the festival of slaughter."

It comes each fall toward the end of the fortnight of Dasain, a Hindu festival marking the triumph of good over evil. More precisely, the holiday is supposed to celebrate—and appease—the Mother Goddess Durga, the divine protectress who slew Mahisasura, the demon that terrorized the world in the form of a wild buffalo.

Like all gods and goddesses of Hinduism, Durga, the wife of Shiva, can take many forms. In one she's got eighteen hands holding eighteen weapons. In another she's the ferocious Kali, with a wickedly projecting tongue and a necklace of skulls. Or she can manifest herself as the Kumari, the gentle virgin living goddess.

Even in her most benign form, the Mother Durga is one bloodthirsty goddess. She will remain compassionate if treated to generous offerings of blood, but if neglected can turn vengeful. This is one reason Nepal's Hindus celebrate Dasain with such fervor. Even their Buddhist neighbors get caught up in it.

The killing begins on Kalratri, the Black Night, when hundreds of buffaloes, chickens, sheep, goats, and ducks are herded into Durga temples and slaughtered. Black buffaloes, representing the demon Ravana, are singled out for special ritualistic killing.

By dawn thousands of animals are being sacrificed in temples throughout Nepal, and blood runs through the streets. Once on this day I saw two young men, lacking a sharp knife, simply push a water buffalo off a cliff. The Newars, Kathmandu Valley's most prevalent ethnic group, call this day "*syako tyako*," which means "the more you kill, the more worldly goods you gain."

As the killing subsides, still-warm blood from the slain animals is scooped up and lovingly dappled on pictures of Mother Durga. More is spattered on cars, buses, motorcycles, rickshaws, even airplanes, to protect them from accidents in the coming year. Workers bring their tools—axes, shovels, plows—to receive a red coating of Durga's blessings. On this day, it is said, virtually every household in Nepal eats meat.

What puzzled me was that here in Manang, the people were clearly Buddhist. By slaughtering the yak, were they merely sending a supply of celebratory meat to Hindu villages down the valley? Or was this another example of how the two religions in Nepal have blended, overlapped, and intertwined with each other like fingers in a handshake?

In the field, the dying yak finally stopped shuddering. Wielding knives and hatchets, the men moved in on it like a pit crew at the Indianapolis 500. One slit open its belly so that its guts spilled on the ground, steaming in the morning chill. Someone else began slicing off the woolly hide.

A man moved in with a hatchet and began hacking off the yak's hind legs. When he'd gotten one haunch free he tied it to a young girl's back and she went running back to the village, trailing tendrils of blood and gristle. Soon there was nothing left of the yak but a pile of offal and a large red splotch in the dirt. Elsewhere in the pasture other teams of men from Manang were methodically felling the other yaks and carving them up. Our placid campsite had become a killing field.

The stone wall that lined the flagstone lane through Marpha was leaking blood. Through a narrow opening I saw men swinging khukuris *into huge animal carcasses. A short distance away men were washing long yellow intestines in the stream that flowed along the path. A crone carried a* doko *load past us and into a stone house, her back stained red, her calves streaked with blood.*

We'd come to Marpha looking forward to the local apple brandy, but we discovered we'd arrived on that day of the year when the people of Marpha cull their yak herds, storing meat for the winter and assuring the health of their remaining stock.

—Larry Habegger,
"Pilgrimage to Muktinath"

I'd always considered yaks to be ornery beasts, but these were just milling around docilely, as if to say, "Will you be slaughtering me next, or should I just hang tight for a while?" Perhaps they shared the Hindu belief that animals sacrificed for Dasain gain enough merit to be reincarnated as human beings.

Behind me I heard an awful screeching. I turned to see Ram, our cook, pulling on a leash attached to a protesting sheep. Its forelegs were braced against the dirt, and its face showed terror. Unlike the stupid yaks, it seemed to comprehend its fate. Outside his cooking tent Ram tied up the sheep's legs, laid it on its side and began shaving its neck as it panted rapidly. Tonight our Sherpas and porters would share in a Dasain feast. By noon the field was littered with offal piles and red splotches, and only a few yaks were left standing. We turned away to take care of our own business. This was our last stop before turning off the trail and heading up to base camp, and we needed to spend the afternoon conducting an inventory of our climbing gear and high-altitude rations.

We spread out a tarp, unzipped some duffel bags and began assessing the damage to our food. After traveling halfway around the world in the cargo hold of a jumbo jet, being jounced in buses and trucks and riding 80 miles on the back of a porter, some of the packaging had burst.

The duffels were coated with a multi-colored sawdust that was equal parts Swiss Miss cocoa powder, Pop Tart crumbs, freeze-dried turkey tetrazzini and Cup-a-Soup particles. I pulled out a big gooey clump that I eventually identified as half a dozen Fig Newtons, mushed and fused together.

One of the butchers from Manang, an old man in a fur cap, came over to have a look. His sleeves were rolled up and his arms were soaked in blood to his elbows. He squatted down next to our tarp and watched, fascinated, as we sorted our instant Cream of Wheat, mashed potato flakes, and dehydrated sweet-and-sour chicken.

The old man, looking puzzled, said something to Nima, our *sardar*.

"He wants to know what all this stuff is," Nima said.

"Tell him this is American food," I replied.

The man's face lit up in astonishment. I peeled open a PowerBar, tore off a piece and handed it to him. He held it in his hand and examined it closely, as if it had just arrived on a space ship from Mars. I gestured to him to put it in his mouth. He chewed on it thoughtfully for a moment before a look of disgust crossed his face. He swallowed hard and shuddered.

Then the old man turned his attention to the large Ziploc bag I was using to repackage some burst Swiss Miss packets. His eyes grew wide as I showed him how I could create an airtight seal by zipping the closure shut.

The man called Nima over and whispered in his ear.

"He wants to know if he can have some of these bags," Nima said.

I handed him three. Minutes later the old man was back out in the field among the steaming entrails, demonstrating to the other men how the Ziploc bag could hold a yak's liver. He zipped it shut, turned it over and shook it, just like they do in the television commercials.

A former mountaineer, John Flinn eventually discovered he enjoyed the long approach marches to Nepal's peaks more than he did the climbing. He is currently the travel editor of the San Francisco Examiner.

✳

"The yaks are our parents," says Tilen. "We could not survive here without them. There may be two thousand yaks. Like our children, each one has a different name." They are called *yak thabo* when they are black with white spots, *yak dongbo* when they have a white star on the forehead, *yak kawa* when they have a white head, *tsen yak* when they are golden, *yak ralden* when their horns are not symmetrical.

They are called *lha yak* when their fur is completely white. These are sacred and are never killed for their meat. Their fur is never cut. They will never carry loads that are considered impure—boots or clothes. Every year, a ceremony is given to honor them.

When they grow old, they are left in peace, and when they die, like the Dolpo people, their bodies are cut up and offered to the vultures.

The yaks give their strength to carry loads for man. They provide milk, meat, and leather. Their fur is used to make ropes, sacks, and is woven into tents. On the high plateau, "where there is not even a word to describe a tree," yaks furnish the only source of fuel: dried dung. In Dolpo, rare juniper bushes are used to light the fires, and yak dung is the only way to keep the fires going.

—Eric Valli and Diane Summers, *Caravans of the Himalaya*

✦ ✦ ✦

Flights of Fancy

There was a time in Nepal, not so long ago,
when there were more adventurers
than tourists.

"YOU BAAH-STAARDS!"

The expletive rose above the din and commotion of the tin-roofed building that served as Kathmandu's domestic air terminal in the spring of 1975. Some airline clerk was being loudly reprimanded for overloading an aircraft, not preparing a departure manifest on time, or creating some other obstruction to safe and efficient flight operations.

There was only one person in Kathmandu who swore that loudly. Hearing this familiar voice made me confident that today, on my easterly flight across Nepal into the high Himalaya, I could relax. Not only would I get there safely, I'd also enjoy tall tales of Himalayan folklore as in-flight entertainment. Piloting the single-engine Pilatus Porter to the remote mountain airport of Shyangboche was Captain Emil Wick, the Swiss pilot. He was the best mountain pilot in Nepal, and a great storyteller, a living legend.

Kathmandu used to attract larger-than-life characters, now gone. I knew many of them and remember them fondly: Russian ballet dancer-turned-Kathmandu-hotelier-restaurateur Boris Lissanevitch; Freddie Bowles, the poetry-writing-English-marine-turned-bartender who settled here and married a Nepali woman; Father Moran, whose radio call-sign, "9N1 Mickey Mouse," was familiar to ham radio operators worldwide.

uch loved and much written about, Boris was a key figure in the history of modern Nepal.

Those who knew him first hand—his family, the many people who worked for him, and the countless people he helped—encountered a boundless spirit of generosity and compassion, a person who gave as much attention to the troubles of those caught in unfortunate circumstances as he did to his meetings with the rich and famous. At the Royal Hotel, he was always taking in hard-luck cases, giving them jobs, and finding them a room to stay.

—Xenia Lisanevich, "The Fabled Exploits and Recipes of Boris of Kathmandu"

Captain Wick was a man made for, and happiest in, this romantic, swashbuckling era that has passed away and will soon be forgotten. Times change, modernity encroaches, and what was a life of adventure degenerates to the routine and technological. But in 1975, it was still a time of adventure, romance and an irresponsible attitude towards Nepal's unwieldy bureaucracy.

At 12,500 feet elevation, Shyangboche is a frighteningly short airstrip high above the Sherpa capital of Namche Bazaar. It's especially suited to, and virtually demands, the STOL (short takeoff and landing) capabilities of the Swiss-built Pilatus Porter. Emil Wick was deputed by the Pilatus factory to Royal Nepal Airlines in 1972 to train Nepali captains to fly this magnificent high-performance machine.

The Nepali pilots didn't like to be assigned to fly the Pilatus, mostly because there would be no subservient retinue of co-pilot and air hostess to follow the noble captain across the tarmac. Emil, however, *loved* to fly the Porter and had logged more than 14,000 hours in it. If he was flying, we'd take off on time and almost certainly land on time at our destination unless weather conditions were truly abominable.

At Shyangboche there was even a uniquely Nepali hazard of yaks grazing on the runway, but Emil always made an initial low pass over the field to chase off the furry beasts.

Emil first came to Nepal in 1960 to pilot the *Yeti*, a plane brought by the Polish-Austrian-Swiss expedition to Dhaulagiri. At that time, Nepal's hinterland was very much off-limits to foreigners. Non-Nepali passengers on domestic flights had their passports stamped, and planes even carried Nepali liaison officers. That is, they were *supposed* to. Emil found an easy way to avoid the omnipresence of officialdom. He told me how in his distinctive Swiss-German accent. "Once in the air, I'd discover a few bumps and those liaison officers were suddenly not so happy about flying any more. Many days I flew alone."

The *Yeti* played an important part in the successful Swiss ascent of Dhaulagiri. Because the chosen approach route crossed over high passes too dangerous for porters, the expedition stamped out a landing strip in the snow near the northeast col, at 19,200 feet elevation. The touchdown of the *Yeti* on Dhaulagiri remains in the *Guinness Book of Records* as the highest landing on earth of a fixed-wing aircraft.

Emil made many landings there himself on skis, ferrying expedition supplies. There was a return load also. "We were staying in Pokhara, but there was no electricity and no fridge. So we always carried a big drum up to the glacier, filled it with snow, flew it to Pokhara, and cooled our beer."

This particular morning Emil had only one paying customer—me. I was off to Shyangboche to supervise some electrical work at the Hotel Everest View. The back of the plane was loaded with two 55-gallon drums of kerosene. I climbed into the co-pilot's seat. Emil—short, stocky, always smiling—performed his exhaustive pre-flight walkaround and jumped in. He carefully ran down the checklist. He was absolutely methodical, never rushed through the list, and never seemed to skip an item.

Satisfied with the look and ground performance of the aircraft, Captain Wick hurled some abuse at the control tower, and soon we were airborne, heading out of the 4,200-foot-high Kathmandu Valley.

" *A Nepali pilot told me that he follows the I.F.R. system to navigate when flying.*"

"*And what does I.F.R. stand for?*"

"*I Follow Road.*"

—conversation overheard at a trekking agency in Kathmandu

After we leveled off, I asked Emil about the demise of the *Yeti*. "We crashed at Dhampus," he said. "I remember the day, May 25th, 1960. I wasn't flying; it was a Swiss military pilot. We were not so high, about 17,000 feet, but that was high enough for a crash. That crash place was not a glacier, just a snow field. Still now I can hear the 'brrr, brrr' of the crash. We went downhill onto the nose and onto the propeller. Then we hit a rock that turned us just 180 degrees and the airplane was nicely staying there. It is still there.

"We couldn't go down the mountain because the weather was bad, but we had food for two days, so we slept in the plane. Finally we walked down to Tukche, stopped for the night and then hired some porters and walked to Pokhara. We're the only people to walk down Dhaulagiri without climbing up first."

We crossed Lamjura Pass, at 11,750 feet, yaks scattering as we skimmed the prayer flags adorning the *chorten* that marks the entrance to the Khumbu region. "Beauty!" he cried as the plane suddenly dropped into the valley on the other side. "It's always windy like hell on this side of the pass; you get a nice ride." As the plane bumped around in the downdraft, I tried to hide my terror by probing Emil for more stories about Dhaulagiri.

In 1973 Emil again ferried expedition gear to Dhaulagiri, this time for an American team. Instead of landing on the glacier, he airdropped the supplies for this expedition. "I had to squeeze my ass out over the Annapurna range and cross the Kali Gandaki Valley at 25,000 feet. There are a hundred thousand ghosts flying in those Kali Gandaki winds.

"We had to do the drops from the west to the east, if possible. We went up, and if Dhampus Pass was clear, we crossed it and then went to French Col at 17,500 feet. We would turn and come from the west, fly past the spot where we landed in 1960, then come in low and slow and drop. Sometimes the boxes caught an updraft and went higher up before they dropped. The expedition would radio, 'You bastards, fly a little bit higher or you'll damage everything!'

"I had John, one of the expedition team, with me to push the boxes out. After the drop site, the icefall goes down, down, down; so he was a little bit afraid all the time he was sitting by that hole in the floor.

"One day, I told him, 'OK, you make two parachutes,' and I went and bought a chicken, a nice cock. Next morning I said to him, 'On the first flight when it's not yet really bumpy, we take that goddamn chicken. First we drop the whole lot and then we drop the chicken.'

"I put the chicken on the co-pilot's seat and tied a long streamer on it so we could watch it fall. We don't tell them anything on the radio. I told John, 'First of all you drop the cargo; then we will see if we are good or not.'

"We could see the snow was right, beautiful; so pop! out went the cargo. It all landed in the snow, no problem. Then they told us by radio, 'Thank you, thank you very much, wonderful.'

"Now, I said, 'we go again,' and out went the cock. And that goddamn cock he was not going straight at all; he circled round and round. He landed very close to the kitchen tent. They said over the radio: 'You bastards, what are you doing there?' The cock was alive and the cook said, 'OK, fine, we have two bottles of wine and a cock—we eat the bastard.' And they took the chicken into the kitchen. But the Sherpas said that no, you cannot cook it, it will upset the gods and spoil the expedition.

"So they brought the chicken back out of the kitchen, and that poor cock sat on the glacier and didn't even shit; it was too nervous. At 17,500 feet, that was the highest-landing chicken in the world. Finally, when the expedition was done, they took it down to Tukche and cooked it for dinner."

By this time we were passing high above Lukla, the notorious airstrip that serves the Everest region. It has a one-way runway, with a ten-degree uphill slope and a mountain wall at the end. Emil told me about the time he had landed at Lukla the other way, lining up with the runway just in front of the mountain and landing *downhill*. As he made his abbreviated final approach, the entire village came running out. "They thought I was going to crash, for sure."

Were getting close to Shyangboche. Emil lowered the powerful Pilatus flaps, and began our precipitous descent for the postage-stamp-sized runway above Namche Bazaar. We made the obligatory yak pass, barely clearing the trees and the huge rock at the end of the runway. The beasts lumbered off into the nearby potato fields. We turned in front of Kwangde Peak and landed gently, with plenty of runway to spare. The kerosene, my stomach and I were safe on the ground, on time, at our destination.

A year or so later, I was sitting at Lukla waiting for a flight. I didn't have a reservation; so in accordance with the Lukla rules, every day, as people who did have reservations arrived, I moved farther and farther *down* in the waiting list. The weather was lousy—rain at Lukla and snow in the high mountains and at Shyangboche airstrip.

Emil had slipped into Shyangboche a few days earlier and was trapped in the sudden storm. Every day, the Sherpas optimistically rolled up huge snowballs to clear the runway and every day before they finished, the snow started again. They succeeded only in creating a perimeter of solemn snowmen, silently guarding the desolate airstrip.

Helicopters, of course, are not necessarily stopped by snow. One chopper came to Lukla to evacuate a trekking group that was running late and another stopped by on its way to a rescue mission at Tengboche monastery. One chopper pilot reported that Captain Wick was sitting in the plane on the snowy Shyangboche runway, swearing into the radio.

About 4 p.m., in the last minutes of daylight, as I sat grimly contemplating my ever-descending status on the roster of would-be transients, I heard a plane overhead. On a hunch, I grabbed my rucksack and raced for the airport just in time to see the Pilatus Porter emerge from the clouds.

Soon I heard a familiar voice cheerfully call out: "Anybody for Kathmandu?"

In Nepal, in the winter, 4 p.m. is late in the day, almost dark. By then, anyone in Lukla with any sense is either in bed or drunk—or both. I was the only available candidate for departure, with or without a reservation. I was all too willing, even if the weather was less than perfect. And what's a little weather, after all, with Captain Wick flying the trusty Pilatus Porter?

Straightaway, I jumped into the plane as airport staff hollered from their beds that it was illegal for me to fly without a confirmed reservation. The weather was getting worse by the second. Billowing fog was now completely obscuring the end of the runway. We would depart immediately or not at all.

Emil took a look, shrugged, said, "Let's go," and off we sped, right into the soup.

Seconds later, when we were climbing through the whiteness, he was rather less sanguine. "Shit! There's mountains all around us and they are harder than the plane, so we better find a hole. Aha, there's one!" And we shot nearly straight up through a tiny opening in the overcast, emerging into the late afternoon sun.

Emil matter-of-factly radioed the controller in Kathmandu for airspace. "Reporting Alpha Bravo Charlie departed Lukla at sixteen-fifteen. Present level one-six-zero, estimate Kathmandu seventeen hundred."

"Ah, say again," came the quizzical reply.

"Flight level one-six-zero that's sixteen-thousand feet," radioed Emil.

"Negative, you cannot fly that high."

"Affirmative. Will report when we are over Jiri."

And click! off went the radio. He turned to me with a knowing grin. "They don't allow unpressurized planes to fly this high without oxygen," he said. "And the oxygen bottles from all the planes have already been borrowed by the hospital."

Before he came to Nepal, Emil was a test pilot and delivery pilot for Pilatus. He knows single-engine performance very well, having delivered single-engine planes to, among other places, Cambodia, Australia, and Africa.

He's also a certified sailplane pilot and figures that the Pilatus Porter does pretty well as a glider. "Once we had a test flight. On the checkout sheet, it said: 'STOP ENGINE, RELIGHT IT.' I called the tower and said, 'I am at ten thousand feet overhead. Any traffic?' The tower said no. So I switched off, gliding down—wonderful—to 8,000 feet. I look at the Director of Civil Aviation behind me and said, 'Look, so easy...STARTER ON.'

"Silence....

"I run the checklist again. Again nothing. So I told the tower, 'I am no more so high; so I am landing runway two.' From so far down I could only do that.

"She shouted, 'Negative, negative, use runway two-zero. *Two-zero!*'

"'Negative, I have no more engine.'

> "*When there is a plane crash in Nepal, the Civil Aviation department investigates it. But the sad part is that the investigation and its report remain secret. Even pilots can't read it. The report is not published, so we do not learn from the mistakes that may have caused that crash. Nothing is made public.*"
>
> —Captain Binod Puri
> of Everest Airways

"'What—you're crashing? You're crashing?'

"'Not yet, later maybe.'

"And then that director behind me asked, 'Are we crashing?'

"I said, 'No, we are flying.'

"The prop slowly turned, we landed easy, and then I had just nice speed and went off the runway onto the taxi way and stopped there.

"That Civil Aviation man said, 'With you never I again fly Inspector Pilot.'

"I said, 'It's not my fault, it was the goddamn starter switch.'"

Emil had yet another yarn for me. "Once the AID [American Agency for International Development] boss had three friends who wanted to go trekking in Langtang. He said, 'I come with you and come back with you.'

"But the weather was bad, so I said, 'Fine, we go fast, no stopping over there, just out we go, come back, and maybe we make it.'

"So we flew up and did take off from Langtang in a hurry and left the others to go trekking. As we came down that Trisuli Valley, it started to snow. I couldn't see nicely. I said to myself, be careful, flaps down slowly…s–l–o–w–l–y. I could open the window, but I couldn't put my head out. It hits like needles, that snow. So we went on.

"I heard on the radio: 'Airport is closed, all aircraft diverting, wind three-five, gusting up to four-zero knots.' I said to myself, that is something. It was like a dust storm below. Finally I could see the airport, and down there was the Thai International. It had crashed on the nose wheel and the ass of that DC-8 was sticking out in the sky.

"The wind was huge, the visibility nearly none, and I was starting to pick up some ice. I said, 'Jee-sus Christ, I'm the second one.' So now no bullshit.

"I told the tower, 'I cannot divert, I don't know where to go, and there's a thunderstorm. I have fuel for forty-five minutes left. So I am circling around and you give me all the time the wind. Once the wind is less than now, I'm landing *across* the airstrip.'

"When we got closer, I said, 'I am landing on the taxi way and I stop on the runway.'

"The lady in the tower yelled over the radio: 'Negative! Negative! No permission!'

"I said, 'Listen, I go twice around and you tell always the wind.'

"The plane was shaking; that director was white. He said 'Emil, you think we crash?'

"I said, 'Somehow we get down.'

"'Wind 35 knots…wind 25 knots…'

"I said, 'It's now or never.' I told the tower: 'I'm turning for approach.'

"'Negative! Negative! No permission!'

"I said 'I give the permission myself and I am now on approach and I'm landing on the runway.'

"'NEGATIVE!'"

"We went in…half flaps, maybe, not more. We went down like a helicopter. On the width of the runway we stopped.

"Now we are down, but because of the wind I could not turn; I could only go straight. I called the tower and told them to bring a tractor and four men for hanging on the struts.

"The first thing when we got to the domestic apron, the director of the airport came and said, 'Captain Wick, we must check the fuel.'

"I said, 'You can check the fuel.'

"'Now we must write the report: *Why you did land?*'

"I said, 'Now I must write the report, because you told me I cannot land. You want to kill me or what?'

"They did not write the report and I did not write the report. It was finished."

At the reporting point on our flight back to Kathmandu, Emil called the tower as he said he would. "Charlie reporting overhead Jiri, level niner-zero."

"That's Jiri down there," he said superfluously, motioning with his head, "the first big Swiss project in Nepal. Once they had rabies there. A small Lhasa Apso bit one of the old Swiss nurses; those bastards, they bite you like hell sometimes. So they called on the radio 'medicine, medicine, medicine!'

"So we had this medicine and I had the Swiss cheese maker with me. The weather was goddamn bad and I said, 'We put the medicine nicely into a porter basket. We have to drop it on the first approach.'

"I said 'Drop!'

"You would not believe! They did built a shithouse about this big and that basket went right into the shithouse. Then the second and the third was okay, so at least they got some medicine afterwards."

We flew on, and Emil talked about a subject that has always fascinated him, yetis.

"South of Chamlang, west of the Arun, there are many lakes. This is at about 14,000 feet. There are a lot of yeti stories from Britishers in early times that come from this area. Yetis struggling over the tents, making spoors and killing yaks. No bullshit!

"Once when a Japanese professor booked a flight near Chamlang, I told him first I want to see those lakes. It was winter; there was lots of snow. Only in the white snow you can see the spoors. We went down and there were four spoors nicely seen. The professor said there must be an explanation, this cannot be from a yeti. So from then on I decided to take a small camera so that I could photograph the yeti spoor and maybe a yeti."

He never succeeded in photographing a yeti spoor, and neither has anyone else.

His voice trailed off into the sound of the engine, and before we reached Kathmandu I mused: in a few years, the air travel Captain Wick pioneered here will be routinized. Equipment will be the latest, the navigation aids will be improved, and by Nepali standards at least, everything will be squeaky clean and done by the book. Then Captain Wick will go back to Switzerland. His job will be done. His former students will be the new captains. The era will be over.

L egends of the yeti can be found in Tibetan literature dating back hundreds of years. But it was not until the late 1800s that a British army officer, a Colonel Waddell, first brought the creatures to the attention of the Western world. Waddell, exploring in the Everest region, came across strange, five-toed footprints in an area where there was no human habitation. His Sherpa porters fearfully told him that the prints were those of the Metah Kangmi, *or sour-smelling man of the snows. Returning to India, Waddell wrote a story for the Calcutta* Statesman *describing his finds and calling the* Metah Kangmi *the "abominably smelling man of the snows" from whence came the name, the Abominable Snowman.*

—Peter Byrne,
"The Abominable Ones"

That's the way it happened, too. Emil left Royal Nepal Airlines and Nepal in 1985 and returned to Switzerland to work at the Pilatus factory. In Nepal, everyone has heard of Captain Wick and he still returns periodically. But on a visit in February, 1995, he dropped in on the Royal Nepal Airlines Corporation office and didn't know anyone there. Until word got around the office, he was just some old guy with grey hair.

His beloved Pilatus Porter, "Alpha Bravo Charlie," was long ago cannibalized for parts. It sits alone in an unmarked field near the airport, forlorn and forgotten.

It is now more than 40 years since the country was opened to the West, at first tentatively, even grudgingly, ultimately whole-heartedly. Today Kathmandu struggles with pollution, garbage and traffic. More than five hundred people have climbed Everest. The magic of the mountains endures, but the magical era is over. The men whose dreams and exploits made them famous—Boris, Freddie, Emil—all gone. There will be no more like them in these parts ever again.

Only the legend remains.

Stan Armington has been organizing and leading treks in Nepal since 1971, when characters like Emil Wick sat around telling tall tales in Boris Lessanivich's Yak & Yeti bar. He now runs Malla Treks, a trekking company in Kathmandu. He is a director of the American Himalayan Foundation, which is working to improve health care and education, and preserve culture and the environment. He is the author of the Lonely Planet book Trekking in the Nepal Himalaya *and is working on a guidebook to Bhutan.*

★

आगो ताप्नु मूढाको
कुरा सुन्नु बूढाको

By the fire of a log, get warm
and listen to the stories of an old man.

—Nepali saying

PART TWO

SOME THINGS TO DO

* * *

A Walk in the Annapurnas

An American aama *discovers*
the joy of walking.

ON A STEEP RISE NEAR LUMLE A NEPALI WOMAN PASSES ME, A *DOKO* loaded with twigs straining against her forehead. She reaches out, grabs my hands in hers, and cries, "*Namaste*, Mother!"

My Nepali sister prays that I will make it up the hill. Dismayed, I suck in my stomach and try to look strong. Soon I realize that, at 62, I am a novelty traveling up the Kali Gandaki River gorge with my banner of white hair.

Some quick research on my fellow travelers—the Western ones—leads me to discover that they're from every country, with an age range from 18 to 30. Half are on their college break, while the other half have just ditched their first careers to reappraise their futures in an affordable Third World place. I was the only one with blue rinse in my duffel.

If this had been the route to the Everest Base Camp, a dearth of senior citizens would have been no surprise, but this is a moderate trek, mostly under 10,000 feet—hardly a thin-air ordeal. It's about 60 miles from Pokhara to Jomsom, another 15 to the medieval town of Kagbeni (9,200 feet) and eastwards up to Muktinath at 12,475 feet. My plan is to go as far as I can, but I have serious doubts about that last, steep climb. At Jomsom, I know there's an

> *We joined the other pilgrims and bathed our faces in the frigid waters spouting from the 108 sacred fountains. I couldn't enter the Hindu shrine but Raj, our leader and by far the most enlightened of our lot, carried my prayers inside while I basked in the light of the sun. Later, we took a short walk to the Buddhist gompa and followed the lead of our Sherpa sardar in doing prostrations before a Buddhist deity, then got down on our knees to observe the eternal flame behind a curtain pulled back by an attendant. As we left we made a small donation. Muktinath is sacred to both Hindus and Buddhists, and welcoming to heathens like me.*
>
> —Larry Habegger,
> "Pilgrimage to Muktinath"

airstrip and a choice of flying out instead of returning by the same route.

The Pokhara-Jomsom trail follows an ancient trade route where there have always been inns for the traveler in almost every town. Reservations (unless you're with a group) are unnecessary; so is hauling in a tent, a camp stove, or dehydrated noodles. This trail is in fact the classic choice for what has come to be called teahouse trekking, or—sometimes—soft trekking. It is also known for the spectacular variety of its people and its landscape. Anyone who enjoys walking a few miles a day can do it—anyone, that is, who is willing to accept the sudden turn of the weather in the mountains and the jolt of another culture. Crucial for wimps and the unconditioned, however, is the porter system.

Let's face it: plenty of people, at any age, never consider the idea of trekking because the sight of a backpack gives them a headache. They don't want to carry an ounce, the body being enough of a cumbersome burden, especially climbing uphill. The porter system solves all that. At first I worried about exploiting them because porters are paid so little; then I felt guilty because I could use only one at a time.

My first porter found me at Lake Phewa in Pokhara, and I found my second, his replacement, in a lodge at Ghorepani, five days on the trail. Both were soft, foothill Hindus of the Chetri caste, not as prepared as they thought for the high country.

Purna, 28 and married, with good English, had much charm but got homesick. Five days from the lake was like five years to him, and the great festival of Dasain was coming up. He wanted to be home.

Ram Chandra, 21 and unattached, was waiting in the wings. He was thrilled to travel north and practice his English, but he didn't tell me that the shorts and sandals he had on were his only clothes, till we got to 9,000 feet and the goose-bumps appeared.

To both I was Mother, an antique of uncertain durability who had to be protected. Purna liked to walk ahead and call back, "Watch out for that loose stone!" and Ram got me over the trembling log bridges by pulling me across with both hands, while I walked forward and he walked backward. When they needed money they came to me (I bought the long pants), and when I needed muscle I went to them. When we had simultaneous blisters, we split the moleskin.

For me, the essential issue was to set my own pace. I knew I wanted to walk, at most, five or six hours a day. I wanted to browse. "No problem!" said Purna—until, out on the trail, his patience was tried as he waited for me to record flute music, watch millet being ground by a foot-hammer and photograph the work-dance of men twisting dried grass into skeins—all, to him, the dull occurrences of daily life.

Along this major path between Nepal and Tibet, we know that both men and animals have been moving goods since ancient times. Salt and wool came south; rice, sugar and kerosene, north. The traveler today still spends a lot of time leaping sideways as he hears the warning donkey bells, then watches the plumes of red-dyed horsehair bob past. Animals in upper-crust pack trains wear Tibetan carpet bridles over their noses—and blankets you would proudly hang on the wall. Other beastly hazards are the sleek, black water buffalo, who, it is rumored, enjoy lunging at tourists. (They can tell.) Skittish hordes of goats, their silky, long hair brushed with fuchsia and ochre markings, traffic-jammed the trail more than once.

By the side of the trail, hair is cut, teeth are pulled, people sleep, cook, visit, work, and pass the news. On their way to school, two sisters climb a while with me up a winding stone staircase. "One, two, three, four, five—rest—and pant!" I repeat as we ascend together. They giggle hysterically, and memorize my strange words in minutes.

An old, toothless man with the legs of a runner shoots past me barefoot and windless, toting a bulky, lopsided bundle held together with rags, bouncing from shoulder to shoulder. At the top of the ridge, where I stop to gasp audibly, he looks at me in my hiking boots, and has the grace to say sympathetically to my porter, "Tell her not to go so fast!"

It was bliss to arrive at the inns in the evening. In the first, at Nagdanda, we were sitting at a trail-side table sipping the hot, sweet, spicy "milk tea" from a glass when an old woman grabbed my mending from me and finished the chore. In the last, at Kagbeni, our rooms overlooked the stable where the grandfather of the house spent all morning sharpening a stick of soft wood to a fine point. About lunch time he tethered his bullock to a post and pierced the nose of the howling animal. Next morning he led it out to work by its new iron ring.

Filthy and unshaven from the trail, the sign in Phokara advertising "Hair Drashing" was as beguiling as the thought of a cold beer. And though the beer we enjoyed lakeside had been as good as beer can be, the Drashing had to wait until we returned to Kathmandu, where we eagerly took turns in a tiny neighborhood shop. This Drasher was his own best advertisement, sporting a tall head of extravagant black hair, and his offering—a shave, haircut, shoulder, neck, and head massage—cost less than half a dollar. One of the better bargains on all seven continents.

—James O'Reilly, "Stairway to Heaven"

The innkeepers lived on the ground floor. Bedrooms, added on for guests, were wooden cubicles on the second floor, often with a window that offered a panoramic view of the Himalayan peaks. Somewhere near was a tap of cold running water; hot water arrived in a big bucket, on request. Toilets were a slit in a dirt floor or porcelain set into the floor.

The best thing about the inn food was that it was all fresh, cooked to order. Someone was always chopping veggies in the corner of a Nepali kitchen, while some form of *chapati* bread puffed in the outdoor oven. Purna and Ram ate *dal-bhat* twice a day, but my favorite was Swiss *rosti*, a potato pancake stuffed with diced onions, carrots, celery and cabbage. I found that the inns often looked poor and shabby from a distance, but were clean, orderly and comfortable when you entered. I never went to bed hungry, cold, or dirty.

Even better than the food and warm bed was the chance to enter the world of our hosts, to sit on a mat by the light of a kerosene lamp and talk.

"Has she been married?"

"Has she children?"

"Is she alone?"

Purna and Ram answered these questions for me every night by the kitchen fire, as we compared notes about our homes, children, and the role of women.

In all its elements, the constant on the trail is change. Its surface can be mud, or gravel, or pine needles, or rocks or a stream bed. At the start, just north of Pokhara, we begin at 2,600 feet in a lush, green, steamy land where banana and pipal trees flourish.

On the second day we push up 4,000 feet to Ulleri, then down again, all the next day, my hot knees shaking. At Tatopani we pick up the Kali Gandaki River and, from now on, we will never be far from its wild flow—muddy and frothing in the fall after the monsoon rains.

As we move steadily upward, tourists thin out and, when I least expect it, I start catching up with Ram. He keeps looking back to find me matching his stride. It's easy now to stay high, sniffing conifers in the crisp air, even as the majestic Dhaulagiri—at more than 26,000 feet—looms over my left shoulder.

Many hill tribes pass us as we climb, the women a gallery of vivid beauty, smashing in their burgundy velvet jackets and baroque gold nose-rings, their necks and chests covered with luxuriant strands of yellow, red, and orange beads. As they glide past in their long wrap skirts, the colors knock you out, and the faces look you steadily in the eye, full of pride and curiosity.

From Marpha (8,750 feet) onwards, the barren hills, prayer

flags, and faces are pure Tibetan. Jomsom is gray and somber, perched on the edge of an alluvial plain. A horseman in a fur hat with the features of a Tartar crosses the wide river bed, and boys sell ammonite fossils by the road, relics of a time when this region was an ocean floor. The imprint caught in the ebony stone is a prawn-like mollusk—and revered locally as "the mark of the gods."

I arrived in Nepal after having spent two years in Japan and was startled at how men and women both boldly looked me in the eye, unlike the Japanese who avoid eye contact with strangers.

—Julia Hendrickson, "Notes from Nepal"

Kagbeni, as far north as we go, is a stark place. My hat is pulled down against the fierce wind, and Ram has made himself a turban from my wool scarf. We're on our tenth day, but it's an age away from the muggy sensuality of Pokhara.

In the end I take a day trip on a balky white horse up to Muktinath where I feel light-headed, but not too weak to pull my nag.

We fly out of Jomsom the next day, Ram turning his head ever so cautiously (for fear he might tip the plane over too far) to look down on the thin white ribbon of river as we whiz back to Pokhara in half an hour. In all their moods—hidden, peeking out, exposed in the dawn at Poon Hill—the mountains never disappoint me, and the effort of getting up into them has paid off in an exquisite euphoria. Coming down after two weeks on the trails, my pants are loose and my mind is calm. I know I will be back.

Virginia Barton Brownback is a freelance writer and photographer residing in Inverness, California. She has spent over ten years reporting mostly from Asia, usually with a focus on the older woman traveling independently. She is still moving, but now prefers pedicabs and river barges.

★

"I thought up this mountain travel thing, which I called trekking. Trekking, of course, is a common word now, but then people didn't know. A Dutch word, really. Came from the Boers in South Africa. Just moving from one place to the other and stopping for the night. In those days trekking was the word commonly used for going to the base camp in an expedition. My feelings then were very different from adventure tourism, trekking tourism, nowadays. My idea was to attract the people who read all the books, you know, read Lord Hunt on Everest and what we did and things like that and thought, 'Oh God, I wish I could go there myself and have this sort of adventure.' And so I said, 'Here we are, we'll lay it on for you.' And of course I modeled the whole thing on what I knew first hand. I was on the British Everest expedition in 1953 as a sort of kitchen boy, and then was a full-fledged member of the American expedition in 1963. In 1950 I was the first Englishman in Pokhara and in 1956 made the first ascent by a foreigner of the Annapurna Sanctuary. Now you read about crowds of 200, 300 people going up. I suppose I was partly responsible for that."

—Colonel Jimmy Roberts, interviewed in Pokhara by Rajendra S. Khadka, Larry Habegger, and James O'Reilly

* * *

Tiger's Lair

Answering the call of the wild
can rattle your soul.

NEARLY AN HOUR AFTER WE LANDED IN MEGHAULI AIRPORT, having crossed another river by boat and walked perhaps half a mile through the jungle, we enter the tented camp. Designed along the lines of similar establishments in East Africa, this is the fanciest tented camp in Nepal—simple enough to give clients the illusion that they are roughing it a bit, luxurious enough for them to leave the illusion behind when the mood warrants. There are solar-heated showers, immaculate pit toilets, and a full bar, not to mention an open-air circular roofed dining area, which commands a panoramic view of the river. Devi, my Nepali colleague, assigns us to our tents, tells everyone that dinner will be served at five o'clock, and makes a point of asking everyone not to walk beyond the confines of the camp without a guide. "It is not the tiger but the rhinoceros that is most dangerous here," he says. "If you wish to walk on your own during your stay, a guide will be assigned to you. By the way, walking at night is strictly against the rules. That's all."

The clients disperse, nervous chuckles and jokes about man-eating tigers and mad rhinos erupting here and there, and head off toward their tents. The great red bulge of the sun, poised just over the tops of the trees on the opposite side of the river, sheds a golden light so rich that I cannot bear the thought of going inside.

Instead I sidle up to the bar. I am no sooner seated than Bess, a client from Mobile, Alabama, suddenly appears from around the corner, hair combed, lipstick freshly applied.

Bess has been on a trip with me before, and we have become friends. I like her very much and find her about a hundred times more interesting than most women who turn up on these tours. Like a few other southern women I have known, she enjoys pretending that she is some sort of good ol' gal, as though her favorite pastime were sitting on the stoop and sipping corn liquor from a Mason jar. In fact she holds a master's degree in English from Yale and has told me that the reason she signed up for another trip with me was that unlike most members of my profession, I give the impression of "having a mind"—which I take as a compliment.

The next morning Rajiv and I set off through a mile or so of swamp to a small pond surrounded by trees and filled with rhinos happily blowing bubbles at each other.

They were pretty far away and I asked if we could get a better view. So we headed into the woods.

"Look," Rajiv said, "rhino tracks. We should be able to get a good look right over here!"

We turned right and Rajiv parted the branches in front of him. There, not more than a foot in front of Rajiv's nose, swished the tail of the Great Indian Rhinoceros. Rajiv quietly replaced the branches, turned to me and whispered, "I think we're too close."

—Eric Lurio, "Buddha is Italian"

She has quite a mind herself. An autodidact of extraordinary ambition, she has laid plans to read all the great books of the Western world in the original languages. On the last trip, I noticed that she was plowing through *Tristram Shandy*, reading a few pages aloud to herself at bedtime. This time she has brought along *À l'Ombre des jeunes filles en fleurs,* and is working her way through it with the aid of a paperback French-English dictionary. None of which, oddly enough, prevents her from calling people she is fond of "Bubba."

"So, Bubba," she says, taking the stool next to me with a smile, "from that hangdog look of yours, I'd say you might be gettin' the least bit tired of this Hemingway shit."

"Could be."

"Gangrene got ya? Hyenas circlin' your tent?"

"Could be."

"That bad? Hey, what's the matter? Got woman trouble? You look like you could use a drink." Spinning around on the stool and facing the bar, she says, "Name your poison. I'm buyin'."

"No bartender."

"Where the hell is he?"

"Beats me."

"Well, gotta be patient, I guess." Giving me an appraising look, she asks, "When this little episode is done, what exotic destination you off to next?"

"Dunno. Bulgaria might be nice."

"Jesus, you *are* depressed."

Just then another client appears from around the corner of the bar—the CPA from Phoenix, decked out in a shopping-mall safari outfit. This would not be so bad in itself, if it did not serve to accentuate the fact that he is a nonstop grinner, the sort of guy who plays handball during his lunch hour and thinks of himself as a hard-ass.

"Disturbing something?" he asks.

"Not yet," Bess says, throwing me a wink.

"Just wanted to ask you, Richard. About seeing a tiger—how would you rate our chances? Good? Great? Inevitable?"

"Good."

"Just good?"

"Here you have as good a chance as you would anywhere—on short notice, that is."

"God, I hope so. I booked this tour months ago. You know, all my friends told me that I ought to go to Africa. But Africa has been...you know...*done*. Anyway, none of my friends have been to Nepal or India. So I thought I'd give it a shot."

"I don't think you'll be disappointed. But it is possible to miss even here."

"Well," he says, "guess I'll just have to keep my fingers crossed. All right if I take a little walk down to the river?"

"No problem as long as you stay in sight. Just watch out for the muggers."

"Muggers?" he says, his expression darkening.

"Crocodiles."

"Ah," he says, "I thought you..." But the explanation trails off with a sigh. "Well," he says, "hope we do see a tiger. Expensive trip to go home empty-handed."

"Chances are good."

"Okay. Well...guess I'll leave you two young lovers to yourselves." With a wave, he strides across the dining area to the head of the trail that leads down the bank. Bess watches him go, and as soon as he is out of earshot, she says, "Nothing wrong with that boy. Just your ordinary, run-of-the-mill, Oedipally-complexed, anal-retentive, sadomasochistic, manic-depressive, all-American ass-hole. I know about ten thousand guys just like him." She adds, "but hey, I don't want to talk about him. How's that book coming along?"

"Gone the way of the dodo."

"How come?"

"Long story."

"Well now, that's too bad. Sort've had the idea you might turn out to be a pretty good writer." She sits quietly for a moment, then says, "Hey, there's something I wanted to ask you about. You know that little guardhouse we passed drivin' in here?"

"Yeah."

"What's that for? They got soldiers guardin' this place?"

"Sure."

"What're they protecting?"

"The park."

"From what?"

"People who live around it."

The history of national parks in Nepal is fraught with controversial issues. The greatest tragedy caused by the creation of a national park occurred in the Jumla district where two villages overlooking Lake Rara were forcibly evacuated and demolished.

The larger of these villages had been inhabited by a prosperous community of Thakuris, who had settled there in the 18th century. At Rara at an altitude close to 10,000 feet, they were successful in making a living by agriculture and animal husbandry. They did not interfere with the wildlife nor encroach inordinately on the resources of the environment. The department responsible for wildlife preservation and national parks nevertheless insisted on their expulsion and they were moved to the tarai where, after several generations spent at high altitude, they experienced great difficulty in surviving in the hot and malarious climate.

—Christoph von Fürer-Haimendorf, *The Sherpas Transformed: Social Change in a Buddhist Society of Nepal*

"The farmers?"

"Yes."

"They don't let the farmers come into the park?"

"Once a year. They let them come in to cut grass for fodder and building material."

"Not otherwise?"

"Not otherwise."

"Doesn't sound too democratic to me."

"I don't think we're talking democracy here."

"Bet they sneak in and cut grass anyway."

"Sure they do. Devi told me the last time I was here, about an old woman who had just been killed at the edge of the park. She waded across the river in the morning, found a quiet spot, and began to cut grass for fodder with her hand scythe. She worked all morning and managed to clear a considerable area. When she had almost finished she took a last swath and a tiger that had been lying up watching her all morning sprang out and killed her."

"Hold on here—how could they *know* that? How could they know the tiger was waiting for her all that time?"

"The grass was all mashed down where it had been lying. It was just a few feet from where she'd been working."

"Wow," Bess says, obviously impressed. "Now *that* story gives me the willies. I don't know about you, but I need a drink. Where's that bartender?"

Later, at dinner, I notice a young man dressed in green khaki— one of the camp staff—appear from the shadows. Approaching Devi hesitantly, he gets his attention, then walks over to him and whispers something in his ear. Devi nods, takes a last bite of curry, wipes his mouth with his napkin, and rises and walks over to me. "Richard," he says quietly, "there is a tiger at the bait. We'd better go now."

Rising from my seat, I pass the word to my clients, and they are all on their feet in seconds. They gather round Devi, who announces that they have three minutes to fetch their jackets, empty their bladders, or do whatever else they need to do before meeting back here. Responding to his instructions, they hustle off.

Three minutes later they are back, the CPA at the head of the line. I groan inwardly when I see him. He has more photographic equipment hung around his neck than the average paparazzo. In one hand he is holding a huge flash attachment. Devi gazes at him and says in a tone of genuine regret, "Sorry, no flash photography is allowed. The flash would frighten away the tiger."

The CPA looks at Devi. He blinks. "You mean..." But he doesn't finish the sentence. Turning to me, his perpetual grin now a rictus of anger, he says, "Why didn't you tell me that, Richard?"

"Didn't know you were interested in taking nighttime pictures."

He gawks, his expression that of a bullied schoolboy about to rush off to speak to the "proper authorities." But Devi is the proper authority here, and there is no court of appeal. At last, looking infinitely disgusted and mumbling something unpleasant under his breath, the CPA turns on his heel and strides toward his tent. Devi looks at me. I look back. But there is really nothing to say.

The moon is shattered silver through the black branches of the trees. As we walk along the sandy path, nightjars are calling all around us, their calls uncannily like the sound of a dull axe striking a hollow log: *Choink! Choink! Choink!* Devi leads the way, flashlight probing the darkness. A small furry creature with ruby-red eyes appears on the trail and pauses for a moment before slinking off into the underbrush.

"What was that?" somebody behind me whispers.

"A mongoose," I whisper back.

After about five minutes, Devi pauses next to a low wooden shelf that someone has placed next to the trail. Turning to face us, he whispers that we must remove our shoes, explaining that the hide, the place from which we will view the tiger, is not far off, and that from this point on we must maintain absolute silence. When all the shoes have been removed and placed on the shelf, we walk on, the sand cool against the soles of our feet.

Within a minute or two we arrive at the long thatched corridor that is the entrance to the hide. Flashlight pointed to the ground, Devi leads us in. At the end of the dark corridor, where it opens out into an even darker room, he takes each of us by the arm and escorts us one by one to an opening in the wall. There are perhaps eight such openings, each a window without glass, beyond which nothing is visible in the darkness.

Moving back and forth behind us, Devi takes perhaps three minutes to be satisfied that everyone is well situated. Then, taking up his customary position at the opening in the wall farthest to the right, he aims his flashlight into the blackness and switches it on.

About ten yards away, on a small area of swept earth, a dead bullock lies on its side, mouth open, squarish teeth exposed, head unnaturally twisted, the length of rope that held it fast at the moment of its death taut about its neck. Dead eyes reflect the light like brilliant topazes. Its belly has been sliced open; the blue intestines have been dragged out in a pile. A large portion of its rump is missing, as if blown away by some small but efficient explosive device. The pink crater of exposed flesh is licked clean like meat in a butcher-shop window. Reclining at the foot of her kill, the tigress gazes unperturbed into the beam of the flashlight. It poses no threat. She has seen it dozens and dozens of times before, even on the darkest nights.

I raise my binoculars to take a look. In the weak, diffused, yellowish glow of the flashlight, the view is astonishing. Her muzzle is soaked with blood. Fat droplets of it cling to the tips of her whiskers. She turns her head, looks directly at me. I can feel her eyes. I stare back at her. Suddenly I have the overwhelming impression that she is looking not *at* me but *through* me. I stare into her eyes, and the walls seem to melt away. Not expecting it, I begin to tremble.

Then I realize that the person standing next to me is trembling as well. Peering into the darkness, I know somehow that it is the CPA. Releasing a sigh or perhaps a quiet moan, he turns away from the window and gropes toward the passageway. I hesitate for several seconds, unable to decide whether I should follow him. Then it crosses my mind that here, in this place, he cannot be left alone. I follow him.

The tiger lay supine, chin down on the ground and absolutely motionless. But its eyes were not. They were wide open and they stared right at me, full of fire and life. There is gold in a tiger's eyes and the glowing, golden light that I now saw, enhanced as it was by the morning sun—the very light of life itself—seemed to burn from great depths. I felt, looking into those eyes, that I was looking into another world, a world mysterious and unreachable, untouchable, a world which held the beginnings of life itself.

—Peter Byrne, *Tula Hatti: The Last Great Elephant*

No more than half a minute later, I find him standing at the edge of the trail in the mottled moonlight, peering into the darkness of the forest. Walking up behind him, clearing my voice quietly so that he will not be startled, I ask, "Are you all right?"

Whirling to face me and holding out a stiffened hand as though to ward me off, he says, "Leave me alone." He turns away. As though struck by an invisible hand, his jaw juts forward, he groans, and a wad of vomit arches from his mouth.

He stands gasping, slightly bent over, hands braced on his knees, staring at the ground. His body is gripped by a spasm, and another wad erupts. I stand there, waiting and watching, not knowing what I ought to do or say. At last he straightens up and turns to face me, a drooping, silvery thread of saliva suspended between the tip of his nose and his cheek. Wiping it away with the back of his hand, he says in a trembling voice, "It's weird.... I didn't think it was going to be like that." His eyes are bright.

For an instant, I almost succumb to the impulse to put my arm around his shoulder to comfort him. Then I become aware of an equally powerful sensation of revulsion. And to my shame, I cannot bring myself to touch him.

Richard Ives has spent most of his adult life touring and living outside the United States. He has led tours in India, Nepal, Burma, Thailand, Malaysia, Borneo, and Indonesia. When not traveling he resides in Paris with his wife and two children.

✦

Asked about his legendary ride on a rhinoceros, he said that a bet with friends was what had led him to undertake such a foolhardy act. The bet was for five rupees, at the time a great deal of money for the 24-year-old Mallu—and all the more so given that the *Tharus* had just begun to learn how to handle money.

His plan was to jump on a rhinoceros that was cooling off in the river. Thus he stalked up to the riverbank, hidden by the tall elephant grass. Steadying himself on a rock platform in the slope, he sprang onto the animal, which had no idea of what was going on. Rhinoceroses see very poorly, but their sense of smell is all the better for it, though in this case that didn't help. Terrified, the rhinoceros ran in the direction of the jungle with Mallu on its back. Afraid that the animal could throw him, he saved himself by a sideward jump into the bush and escaped into the nearest tree. "As a reward," he said laughingly, "I had the five rupees and the pride at having done such a thing." He then showed us a number of larger and smaller scars he had got during fights with bears.

—Susanne von der Heide and Ganesh Sakya, "Mallu the Magnificent"

PETER BYRNE

* * *

The Birds of Rani Taal

*Hundreds of species flock together
in this small piece of paradise.*

ONCE UPON A TIME, IN A FARAWAY LAND CALLED NEPAL, THERE
lived a noble prince, a *raja*, with his beautiful wife, the *rani*. The
raja's name was Singpal and his wife's name was Sangita. Together
they ruled from a walled fort deep in the *tarai* jungles of southwest
Nepal in what is now the *Sukila Phanta*—White Grass Plains—
Wildlife Reserve. The *raja* was a warrior prince and his ancestors
who built the massive fort, a square kilometer in area, came from
Rajputana in India. Apart from that, very little is known about him
and in particular what happened to him, his *rani*, and what must
have been several hundred retainers. We know that he was still living in the fortress in 1898 because in that year Lord Baden Powell
(founder of the Boy Scouts), hunting tiger in the area with British
army friends from India, mentioned him in his journal. Sometime
after this he and his *rani* disappeared and the fort was deserted.
Soon the forest closed in and today all that remains of their jungle
dynasty are the faint outlines of the massive walls of the compound
in which the fort stood. That and the beautiful little lake of Rani
Taal, the lake that bears the name of the long-ago queen of Singpal
who, legend says, used to love to sit at the water's edge in the

117

evening with her ladies in waiting, meditating and watching the sun go down.

Rani Taal lies in the central eastern forests of the White Grass Plains and is composed of two and a half square kilometers of crystal clear water that is home to thousands of water birds. It also provides a habitat for a dozen big mugger crocodiles, and it is regularly used as a watering hole by the reserve's elephant herd and many other animals, including the endangered swamp deer, a herd of 2,000 which lives in the reserve's central grasslands.

I first saw Rani Taal in the summer of 1953 on an exploratory trip through the *tarai* and I remember being astounded at the variety of birds that used its waters and reed beds as a habitat. Purple gallinules waddled across the green water lily leaves, vying for food with white-breasted waterhens. Flights of silver teal and mergansers arched through the warm air of the *tarai* summer while dozens of cormorants and coots bobbed and dived in the weeds. Adjutant storks plodded slowly through the shallow waters along the lake's edge, bills snapping up wriggling fish and frogs. Against the twenty-foot-high wall of dark green elephant grass that composed the southern edge of the lake, small groups of cattle egrets slowly winged their way to feeding grounds, and single sentinel birds stood alone in the shallow waters at the edge of the lake: purple herons, grey herons, greater egrets, white storks, black storks, black-necked storks, white-necked storks, and that most beautifully and delicately colored of the aquatic birds, the painted stork.

Once I watched a flight of 40 spoonbills, a rare bird in Nepal, come arching down out of a

Nepal is one of the most biodiverse countries on earth. Eight hundred species of birds, a tenth of the world's total, live here on much less than one percent of its land surface. Six hundred fourteen species of butterfly have been identified. Many of these life forms have become rare because their habitats have been destroyed by clear-cutting of the forests or alteration of the forests' structure due to trampling of the understory by livestock or the cutting of plants for fodder. The lowland species are especially at risk.

—Alex Shoumatoff,
"The Mountain is Rising,"
Los Angeles Times

dark blue winter sky, dipping their wings in perfect unison, level-ling out, flaring and dipping again, and then planing in to land al-most as a single entity. On another occasion I was delighted to find an equally rare species, the common crane; a hundred of them stood together in blue-grey morning mist on the long mud bank that spills out from the mouth of the Hagania, the little stream that is the main source of the lake's water supply.

Predator birds roost in the trees that line the lake on the north and west, and on any day one can see fish eagles, brahminy kites, and long-legged buteos watching with a wary eye for the halt and the lame. Some of the dead trees provide perches for common cor-morants, black ibis, and the darter, that extraordinary, snake-headed bird that is the nemesis of unwary fish.

Sad to say, in recent years the lake almost disappeared and would have if not for the work of a dedicated few. The cause of its near demise began in 1975 when the *Tharu* villagers of Singpur—a village that stood near the old fort and that was once called Singpal—needed extra water for their rice fields and dug a canal from the lake. When the reserve was expanded in the early '90s, the villagers of Singpur were relocated and the canal, unno-ticed, began to drain the lake. At first its flow equalled that of the intake of the Hagania. Then it began to erode the lake's bank at its exit and a 6-foot gap slowly widened to over 400 feet. When this happened the lake began to dry up and by the winter of 1994 all the water had drained out and the lake was effectively dead. My heart sank when I visited the lake that winter and saw the dust blowing across its desiccated bed, the vegetation withered and dying.

The situation was desperate. I returned to the U.S. and spent many hours on the phone and at the computer—and in the nick of time obtained a grant from the American Himalayan Foundation in San Francisco. Funds in hand, I went back to Nepal and worked to save the lake with a small local group called the Institute for Nature Conservation and Rural Development headed by a stalwart former Nepal Army environmentalist, one Colonel Hikmat Bahadur Bisht.

We built a 400-foot earthworks using local labor—*Tharu* men, women, and children with shovels and baskets—and at the end of the 1995 monsoon, the lake was back to normal. By 1996, the water birds, the fish, and the crocodiles had returned and the lake had been rejuvenated. A single rhino took up residence and once again the elephants made it their watering hole. As an example of the biodiversity that has been restored, at night one may hear the rumble of a hunting tiger coming across the water, to be countered by the cough of a leopard, echoed in turn by the grotesque cackling of hyena and the wailing cries of foraging jackal.

Since 1979, the American Himalayan Foundation (AHF) has been working in the Everest region to improve conditions of its people and protect the fragile Himalayan environment. The AHF works hand-in-hand with Sir Edmund Hillary's Himalayan Trust to build schools and hospitals and operate clinics in Nepal. Besides restoring Rani Taal, it has helped reforest the Khumbu region and contributes to cultural preservation efforts such as the restoration of centuries-old monasteries.

—RK

In more than 40 winters spent in Nepal, I have traveled all across the *tarai*, from the little one-time riverbank town of Bramadeo Mundi in the far west to Kakarbhitta in the east. I have been spiritually uplifted countless times by the sights and sounds of many beautiful places. But for sheer primitive serenity, I find Rani Taal unequalled. Whenever I am there, comfortable in an old canvas chair in the sal trees at the water's edge, entranced by the clamor of the birds and the endless whirring of wings and splashing of the waters, I think of the *rani* and her ladies, sitting at the lake in the evening, with the dark red orb of the sun sinking through the trees and the night slowly emerging. If in life she was as beautiful as the lake she enjoyed so much—the legacy that she has left us—then indeed she must have been an exquisite woman.

Peter Byrne is an explorer, author, lecturer, white water river runner, conservationist and adventurer. He is a member of the Explorers Club and was made a Fellow of England's prestigious Royal Geographical Society for the discovery of a new route to Mount Everest. He is the author of The Search for Bigfoot *and* Tula Hatti: The Last Great Elephant.

✶

Across the dry valley, two lammergeier condors floated between gleaming, snow-covered peaks. It was a ringing blue Himalayan day, clear as a bell. After a few moments I took a silver coin out of my pocket and aimlessly began a simple sleight-of-hand exercise, rolling the coin over the knuckles of my right hand. I had taken to practicing this somewhat monotonous exercise in response to the endless flicking of prayer-beads by the old Sherpas, a practice usually accompanied by a repetitively chanted prayer: "*Om Mani Padme Hum.*" But there was no prayer accompanying my revolving coin, aside from my quiet breathing and the dazzling sunlight. I noticed that one of the two condors in the distance had swerved away from its partner and was now floating over the valley, wings outstretched. As I watched it grow larger, I realized, with some delight, that it was heading in my general direction; I stopped rolling the coin and stared. Yet just then the lammergeier halted in its flight, motionless for a moment against the peaks, then swerved around and headed back toward its partner in the distance. Disappointed, I took up the coin and began rolling it along my knuckles once again, its silver surface catching the sunlight as it turned, reflecting the rays back into the sky. Instantly, the condor swung out from its path and began soaring back in a wide arc. Once again, I watched its shape grow larger. As the great size of the bird became apparent, I felt my skin begin to crawl and come alive, like a swarm of bees all in motion, and a humming grew loud in my ears. The coin continued rolling along my fingers. The creature loomed larger, and larger still, until, suddenly, it was there—an immense silhouette hovering just above my head, huge wing feathers rustling ever so slightly as they mastered the breeze. My fingers were frozen, unable to move, the coin dropped out of my hand and then I felt myself stripped naked by an alien gaze infinitely more lucid and precise than my own. I do not know for how long I was transfixed, only that I felt the air streaming past naked knees and heard the wind whispering in my feathers long after the Visitor had departed.

—David Abram, *The Spell of the Sensuous: Perception and Language
in a More-Than-Human World*

✦ ✷ ✦

Curry in a Hurry

They ate everything but the bleat.

AKAAL BAHADUR AND JEET BAHADUR HAD SPENT MUCH OF THE day bargaining. Finally, they arranged to buy a small goat for 200 rupees. A runt, the goat was missing an eye and unable to forage for food as well as the others. The owner was pleased to be rid of it. Now came the time to slaughter it, and we brought the animal down into the house.

While the porters made preparations, I held the little animal. I wondered how this species had managed to survive. They seemed defenseless, with horns too short to gore anything. Perhaps they survived by running away from danger. Yet, when I stood him up and pushed against the front of his head, his knobby head pushed back. I repeated my push, he repeated his. I realized then that if I stood there for half an hour pushing, he would continue pushing back. Maybe they didn't run away. I smiled at his cute antics and his spunk, and then a twinge of remorse hit me. We were famished and he was to be our dinner.

While Jeet Bahadur carefully sharpened his *khukuri*, Akaal Bahadur picked the goat up by its hind legs and suspended it over a wash basin. Jeet Bahadur motioned for me to hold the goat's mouth shut with the neck extended downwards. As soon as I did this, he took his *khukuri* and sliced into the underside of the throat. Blood spurted from both carotid arteries and splashed into the wash basin. There was no noise but a sucking sound as Jeet Bahadur cut through the windpipe. The goat showed no sign of pain, nor did it struggle as we waited for it to lose consciousness. Soon its eye closed. Jeet Bahadur, with a few swift strokes, severed the head and it fell into my hands. The jaw and neck muscles twitched as I held the still-warm cranium. I felt a sudden queasiness, and I looked around for a clean place to put the thing down. Finding nowhere, I continued holding it upside down in the palm of my hand as I watched the rest of the butchering.

Jeet Bahadur stuck the knife in the underside and with one quick stroke sliced the goat up the belly, through the sternum and chest. Quickly locating the heart, he hacked it free and set it aside, waiting for the carcass to clear of blood. When the flow of blood eased, Akaal Bahadur lowered the body and the butchering began in earnest.

First the organs were removed, the lungs, liver, spleen, stomach, small intestine, kidneys, pancreas all placed in a large bowl. The only item discarded was the large intestine. Next Jeet Bahadur removed the limbs. He pulled the skin back from the joint, then with a few sharp blows severed the front and hind legs at hip and shoulder. The limbless carcass was laid on its back. As Akaal Bahadur grabbed the ribs and pried them open, Jeet Bahadur sliced them free from the skin from the inside. The skin remained attached to the rest of the body. The tenderloins were removed from just near the spine. Finally the rest of the carcass was hacked into small pieces with a few rapid *khukuri* blows. Total elapsed time: four minutes.

Akaal Bahadur now cut the lower spindly portion of the legs from the upper meaty portion. He relieved me of the head, which I still held, and with the legs, he placed it just above the hearth to smoke. I couldn't imagine what Akaal Bahadur thought he was going to do with a smoked head and the bony lower legs.

Auri Bahadur picked up the bowl of innards and disappeared up the ladder. He returned a half hour later with everything washed thoroughly. The small intestine had been sliced lengthwise and chopped into small pieces. The other organs also had been washed and hacked into chunks. Mixed together the pieces no longer were identifiable as heart, liver, intestine, or other innards. Each part of the animal had been set aside, including the blood, for the upcoming feast.

If someone is offered rakshi as a toast, he must take either one or three glasses, but not two. To drink only two glasses of rakshi is bad luck.

If someone should accidentally receive the head portion of a chicken or a duck in a curry during a feast, he will receive good luck.

—Karna Sakya and Linda Griffith, *Tales of Kathmandu: Folktales from the Himalayan Kingdom of Nepal*

The owner of the house came around to offer us some of his *rakshi*, much of which he obviously had imbibed already. I had tasted it the night before and now politely declined. It reeked of kerosene. I decided to hold out for more of his wife's tasty, thick *chang*. Earlier I had felt the rumblings that preceded the intestinal ailments to which I had become so prone in Nepal. Perhaps it would have been better to drink the *rakshi*; I knew that it was distilled, whereas they made the *chang* with whatever water they had available. I decided it didn't matter, I would drink the *chang* and worry about the consequences tomorrow.

Our host lurched from side to side as he meandered into the next room where he slumped down against a pile of old blankets. He would probably sleep the rest of the afternoon away, as he did most days. A tall man, apparently of pure Tibetan stock, he possessed one gold tooth which he showed us repeatedly with generous smiles. A great piece of coral dangled from one ear.

I felt it unkind to note that his wife, now off tending the goats and yaks, was homely as sin, with eyes that seemed painfully closed. But what she lacked in beauty, she compensated for by a generous heart and boundless energy. At five o'clock when she returned, she scurried about tending the fire, making food, fetching water, blithely stepping around her drunken husband. I doubt she complained about her condition, as most of the village men appeared to be plastered by mid afternoon every day. The women missed this dissipated lifestyle since they all left for the pastures early each morning.

As I watched the domestic comings and goings of the household, I heard giggling. Looking up, I saw six heads outlined against the sky through the hole. A smile creased my face and I felt warmed by the sight before me. Beside me, Prem stirred, and I saw him smiling too.

The girls sat around the chimney hole and on the ladder, whispering quietly to each other, multicolored homespun blankets wrapped around them like shawls. Their babies made no sound; we were aware of them only as bulges on each girl's back. Akaal Bahadur and Jeet Bahadur began to sing Tamang folk songs. The girls responded by singing two songs in Tibetan. As the porters launched into another song, Prem leaned over to me. "Parker *Sahib*. This is a marriage song. First the men sing and then the women sing."

The porters had finished the men's part and started to sing the women's part, when the Tibetan girls picked up the melody and sang with them. Astonished, Akaal Bahadur and Jeet Bahadur stopped. Pleased with themselves, the girls finished the female part with a flourish as the men picked up the next verse. Prem and I laughed with amazement as the Tamang porters sang their part in Tamang and the Tibetan women sang their part in Tibetan. The end of the song brought smiles and laughter from all.

After an hour, the Sangdak girls placed the palms of their hands together in front of their faces and drifted off without a word. Hastily, Akaal Bahadur, Jeet Bahadur, and I clambered up the ladder and watched them disappear into their houses. They looked back at us several times, coyly laughing.

Wistfully, with bittersweet smiles, we watched them go. We had truly enjoyed their company. The women of Sangdak clearly were much more interesting and full of life than the men. Our judgment may have been prejudiced from being on the trail for two months, but the presence of these simple girls had certainly changed our demeanor. That day in Sangdak, they seemed to me the most enchanting women in the world.

The porters climbed back down into the house to prepare our feast. I stood on the rooftop in the twilight, the halo of happiness left by the singing girls still warm around me. I missed Clara. It would be only a few weeks now before I would see her again. Her shining black hair, those exquisitely shaped, expressive eyes. Her shy smile and her whispered words of good-bye when I had left. *Soon.*

Our feast began with a mixture of fiery chilies, garlic, liver, heart, kidney, and lungs. Our hostess offered no *chang*, so we washed it down with the kerosene-flavored *rakshi* firewater. For the next course we ate the small intestine fried in blood. Finally we ate the meat with fried potatoes. We ate until we nearly burst and drank *rakshi* until we passed out.

Dawn found me desperately searching for a "toilet."

Parker Antin is a research biologist at the University of Arizona at Tucson and is a fellow of the Explorers Club. His hobbies include photography, skiing, and rock climbing and he holds a black belt in judo.

Phyllis Wachob Weiss is a travel writer and photographer whose work has appeared in The Washington Post, Walking *magazine, the* San Francisco Examiner, *and* Westways.

★

The *rakshi* flowed and tantalizing *Thakali* tribal finger food followed. I didn't want to know what the ingredients were, but Ramesh insisted on giving me a running commentary,

> "...and this is the small intestine, Jono, cooked in *ghee* and its own stomach juices with lots of black pepper.... And this is kidney diced fine and fried with tons of chili and green onions, pancake style...."

Somehow I didn't think that the International House of Pancakes would be serving that one on special.

I thought that I was suffering this banquet of tripe and sweetbreads quite well when the *piece de résistance* arrived—raw kidneys. Yep, the uncooked internal organs of the goat I'd seen eating shit on the street just two hours before. My mind churned, pondering all the long-named diseases I could inflict on myself by downing the quivering cubes of congealed blood. The *Thakali* men were anxious for me to join the kidney club and stared at me with expectant eyes. The *rakshi* was doing its job, so I closed my nose and held my stare at the blank wall while downing the sickly sweet squares. The guys let out a cheer and slapped me on the back. "Jono, you're a real *Thakali*."

—Jono Lineen, "Annapurna Quickly"

★ ★ ★

The Call of Kala Patthar

Trekking in the Everest region is a
challenge for even the most fit.

IN LOBUJE SOME OF US SQUEEZED INTO THE TINY KITCHEN OF THE hostel proprietor and tried to thaw out in the smoky interior. Cold and wet as we were, our spirits were low. For me, it wasn't the same without Rosalynn who had turned back because she was showing symptoms of altitude sickness. When we found that one of the rooms was completely vacant, we decided to spend the night indoors instead of in our tents. P.K., our Sherpa host, produced a can of charcoal from somewhere which generated enough heat to warm and partially dry our wet boots. After treating them with waterproofing solution, we ate supper and planned our goals for the next day.

We would leave before daybreak, hike to *Gorak Shep* (which means "dead crow") near the Everest base camp, and—if possible—attempt to climb up to *Kala Patthar* peak, or "black pinnacle." At best, this would take six hours of steady hiking. We all knew that the trail would be less traveled, the snow deeper, the air thinner, and the climbing steeper than what we had already seen. Furthermore, we had absolutely no time to waste; successful or not, we would have to begin our return journey no later than noon, moving much more rapidly downhill in order to reach Pheriche before it was too dark to see the path.

There was not much enthusiasm or confidence about the next day—a lot of silence, none of the usual bantering among us as we crawled into our sleeping bags, all crowded together on narrow shelves, one above another. Still completely clothed, I shivered for several hours before warming enough to go to sleep. After that, the loud snores from all around awakened me frequently during the night. I was in an uncharacteristically bad mood, declaring to myself that I would rather have been in my tent where it was quiet!

We got up at 4:20 a.m. to eat our standard breakfast of hot tea, cookies, and rice porridge laced with granola and raisins, and were on the narrow, frozen trail by 5:15 a.m. The sky was the most beautiful I had seen in the 30 years since I had left the navy. The Milky Way and constellations from Ursa Major to Orion stood out with surprising brilliance, each star clear and distinct. The almost-full moon had just set and it was quite dark, but after half an hour dawn began to break and we were able to see well enough to walk without our flashlights.

We were traveling on a moraine of dirt and rocks atop the Khumbu glacier, which extended from high on the slopes of Everest and Lhotse down past Lobuje and halfway to Dughla. The snow varied from one to four feet deep; in most places the trail was no wider than a footprint. One behind another, we stumbled forward. Using a single ski pole, I was able to balance well enough to minimize the number of times I fell. Slowly, the scenery unfolded ahead of us. After two hours we got a clear glimpse of Everest, hidden the previous three days by the nearer Nuptse and Lhotse peaks. Now, as we climbed, more and more of the world's highest mountain became visible, surrounded by its mighty neighbors. The atmosphere was crystalline. Perhaps for the first time, we could understand what the word "breathtaking" meant.

By the time we reached Gorak Shep, Ang Tsering and I were several hundred yards ahead of P.K., Dick, and Stan. We decided to go almost straight up the westward cliff toward Kala Patthar. As we neared the top, the *sardar* put his hand on my elbow. He pointed

ahead and we saw nine Himalayan snow cocks sitting just above us
on a horizontal ledge. They flew back out of our sight as we

> *I n the clearness of this
> Himalayan air, moun-
> tains draw near, and in such splen-
> dor, tears come quietly to my eyes
> and cool on my sunburned cheeks.
> This is not mere soft-mindedness,
> nor am I all that silly with the al-
> titude. My head has cleared in
> these weeks free of intrusions—
> mail, telephones, people and their
> needs—and I respond to things
> spontaneously, without defensive or
> self-conscious screens. Still, all this
> feeling is astonishing: not so long
> ago I could say truthfully that I
> had not shed a tear in twenty
> years.*
>
> —Peter Matthiessen,
> *The Snow Leopard*

moved forward, but after a few
minutes sailed down past us toward the small lake between
Gorak Shep and the Everest base
camp. It was a beautiful and eerie
sight. The brown, white, and
gray birds seemed to have a
bluish tinge against the bright
white snow as they flashed by.

We climbed over some very
difficult terrain and finally arrived at the top, well ahead of
most members of our group. We
were exhausted, but proud and
greatly relieved that our climbing was over. As we sat down to
catch our breath and look over at
Everest and the other mountains,
we could also see far below us

the red and yellow tents of the Indian and Japanese expeditions arrayed at the base camp. After a few moments, Ang Tsering said,
"This is really not the top. Most people stop here, but the top peak
of Kala Patthar is several hundred feet above us." He pointed farther to the west; we could barely see a tiny point of rock far above.
Shocked to know that there was more climbing to do to reach our
goal, I didn't know whether to faint or throw up. However, we
resolved to go for it, and so began a slow and extremely dangerous climb upward. It was one of the most foolish decisions I've
ever made.

Knowing nothing about the technical aspects of mountain
climbing, I was extremely uncomfortable as we clung to the large
and often loose rocks with our fingers, thighs, and toes. On our left
was a precipitous drop of several hundred feet. We were not
equipped with crampons or even a rope, and the snow and coat-

ing of newly frozen ice made each foothold uncertain. At that altitude the temperature was almost always below freezing, but in the midday sun some of the snow would melt in small patches on the south side of rocks, then freeze hard as soon as the sun set below the western mountaintops. These sheets of ice made firm footing and handholds impossible. I could not imagine how I had ever gotten myself into such a predicament.

Halfway up we discerned two people on the peak, which gave me some encouragement. Still, it took us two hours to climb the short distance. At first I was more angry with my lack of judgment than pleased with our accomplishment when we reached the pinnacle. We were at 5,630 meters, or almost exactly 18,500 feet above sea level. At that moment I had taxed my maximum endurance and ability and felt no desire to climb any higher—ever!

Far below us we saw P.K. coming our way, alone, the others in our party having wisely decided to remain on the lower peak. We now had a magnificent view of Everest, including the south col, where the Indian climbers were still encamped. The two people we had seen at the top of Kala Patthar were part of the same expedition. One of them was making observations and photographs across the intervening chasm with a celestial-type telescope, and the other was manning a motion picture camera and a radio.

The Indians recognized me with amazement and urged me to speak to the new expedition leader on the south col. Radio fidelity was excellent. I expressed my condolences about the loss of their five men, my admiration for the Indians' courage in continuing the effort to reach the peak, and my best wishes during their final assault scheduled for the next day. I didn't envy them. We had no time to lose; our daylight hours, during which we could traverse the steep mountainside with safety, were waning. We decided to descend by a circuitous but much safer route through the snow. After I picked up a few small stones for souvenirs for my grandchildren, we began our journey back down to Gorak Shep. The trail was not very steep but quite treacherous, and all of us fell more than once into the deep snow that surrounded us. At the base of the cliff I lay down to rest and thought I would never be able to get up again, but after some hot lemon tea, a piece of bread, and a bowl of soup, we were on our way back down the way we had come.

It was soon dark. One of our party was quite ill, and so we put him in front, with a lantern on his head so he could see the trail. He moved slowly, taking only a few steps at a time between periods of rest, but we knew it might be fatal for him if he fell without our seeing him or was inadvertently left behind. While we crossed the many small streams by stepping carefully from one rock to another, he waded straight through, often knee-deep in the icy water. He was obviously disoriented, not knowing what he was doing other than plodding spasmodically ahead.

The Himalayas, more than any other place, inspire in me a profound longing for my wife and children. On a recent trek in the Annapurna region, the only thing that assuaged this ache was the knowledge that each step took me back to them. They were sleeping as I was walking, walking, walking, under the terrible beauty of Dhaulagiri—this beauty which smites me with a sense of mortality even in a photograph—and it comforted me to imagine myself walking through their dreams.

—James O'Reilly,
"Stairway to Heaven"

We arrived in Pheriche at about 9:00 p.m., all totally exhausted. What a relief to have our sick companion under a doctor's care! After receiving some medication and oxygen, he felt much better, recovering rapidly at the lower altitude. Rosalynn, feeling fine, had already flown to Kathmandu. I drank some hot tea, climbed into my sleeping bag without supper, and slept soundly through the night.

When I woke up next morning I was surprised to find that my fingernails were split, my hands were bleeding, both shins were skinned, and I had bruises inside my thighs and on my buttocks. I bathed in a tin pan of hot water, shaved, put on clean clothes, and waited for the helicopter to take us to Kathmandu. When we heard it coming we told everyone good-bye and hurried out to the landing spot.

We had an emotional exchange of *katas* and *namaste* with our Sherpas and the medical staff. The helicopter, however, flew past us and landed a few hundred yards away in the middle of the valley. Two or three people emerged whom P.K. recognized. "Those are two Italian women," he told us. "A number of years ago both their husbands died here from altitude sickness on the same day and are buried in that place. Every two years their wives come to place a wreath on the graves and then return to Italy." After a few minutes the women re-entered the helicopter, which soon disappeared toward the south.

When our small Alouette helicopter came, we had to leave our Sherpas and porters, who would have a long and difficult two-day trek back to their homes in Namche Bazaar. We left Pheriche at 8:45 a.m. and landed at the airport above Namche at 8:53. In those eight minutes we had flashed over Pangboche, Tengboche, Khumjung, and Kunde, distances it had taken us three days to cover on foot. Trekking in the high Himalayas had been an incredibly exciting and gratifying experience, testing all of us to the maximum of our abilities. We had set a formidable goal and reached it.

Jimmy Carter was the 39th president of the United States of America. He is the author of ten books.

＊

We were going to be getting close to the pass and I didn't want to take any chances of dying. So just before we headed out of camp I popped the cap and swallowed a Diamox. As I started to put the container away I discovered that I had taken a Decadron by mistake. The label read "use only with symptoms." "Uh, oh," I thought, "now what?" I laughed one of those nervous laughs when you don't know what's happening and popped the Diamox, just in case. Then we headed out along the trail.

About twenty minutes later I had to piss. Then twenty minutes later. Then twenty minutes later. Every twenty minutes, like clock-work, I peed, for the entire day. No mountain sickness, though.

—Sudhir Dass, "Altitude Sickness"

* *⭐* *

Best Price Buddha

Buy now, pray later.

THERE WAS NEVER ANY DOUBT THAT I WANTED TO BUY A BUDDHA, first and foremost. That doesn't mean I wasn't willing to poke around for other deities; by this point, having convinced myself that Nepali art was both a sound investment and a useful tool for self-improvement, I entertained the thought of going home with as many sculptures as I could possibly carry.

So, while combing through Kathmandu's seemingly endless array of galleries, shops, and street stalls in search of the perfect Buddha, I took ample time to acquaint myself with some of the other popular gods and goddesses who fill out the ranks of what I, irreversibly conditioned by years of Hebrew school, must very respectfully refer to as the Lower Arcana. Because as much as I loved them, and as irresistibly as I was drawn to worship them, these other characters are not merely enlightened gurus, but full-fledged *gods*. Idols! Graven images! The closer I got to them, the closer I skirted to the steep and guilty edges of the Golden Calf Syndrome: a common affliction among Jews in Asia.

But after all was said and done, nothing in the world could keep me from admiring, appraising and, yes, embracing these imaginative, voluptuous deities.

I was prepared to spend a couple of hundred dollars for one of these gods. I wanted as much for my money as possible. Wisdom. Compassion. Protection. Peace of mind! And for sheer devotional value, ounce for ounce, nothing beats a Buddha.

A Buddha is not a simple thing to shop for. He comes in infinite sizes, a full spectrum of colors, and a daunting variety of postures and poses. The postures—standing, walking, reclining, or sitting in meditative bliss—are called *asanas*. Then, to complicate matters even further, there are the *mudras*: hand positions. Sometimes the Buddha's fingers are intricately linked in the tongue-wrestling pose of *dharmachakrapravartanamudra*: "Turning the Wheel of the Law." Or with his right palm raised: "Fear Not." Both hands up, palms facing outward: "Calming the Ocean." Once, at a temple in Thailand, I think I saw a gesture called "Forbidding His Relatives to Fight with One Another."

Fortunately, I knew from the very beginning which *asana* and *mudra* I wanted. The pose is sometimes called "Subduing Mara," but the more familiar title, which I prefer, is *bhumisparsamudra*: "Calling the Earth to Witness."

That pose seemed to embody the state of mind that would fix me up once and for all—it spoke of an approach to life and to work that I needed to be reminded of constantly.

So what does one look for in a statue of the Buddha? What makes a work of figurative art a Buddha and not, say, a Rambo doll or a clay bust of Elvis?

According to Matricheta, an Indian poet who lived fourteen centuries ago, the figure of a Buddha "blazes with immutable signs and marks." The people of ancient India, in fact, went so far as to catalog the 32 major (and 80 minor!) traits that positively identify a Buddha.

During the next few weeks, alone in Nepal, my life took on a frighteningly narrow focus. The only exercise I got was shopping for Buddhas; cycling maniacally downtown, zipping along recently paved and unnaturally broad roads and into the half-dozen shops that had become my veritable opium dens for the daily Buddha fix.

It was truly aerobic. My heart rate and adrenaline skyrocketed every time I threw back a curtain and walked into one of those dimly lit back rooms, hoping beyond hope that today, today, I'd find it—the Buddha of my Dreams, reasonably priced, beatific, of a decent size, with none of the galling flaws that seemed to crop up in Buddha after Buddha. Because even though I might agree to buy a filing cabinet with a few surface scratches, or take a discount on an irregular pair of sneakers, I somehow could not reconcile the thought of buying a seriously flawed Buddha— even for ten percent off list. The whole concept seemed a loathsome compromise of the goal I had in mind: spending money generously and without regret for an object that had no real use in the occidental scheme of things.

In the serenity of the image of the Buddha or of the god of compassion, Avalokiteschvara, of Padmapani and of Tara, man finds at last the conviction that prayer will not be rejected. He will no longer bow down, abject and terrified, but will pray that the divine and compassionate grace will respond to his plea. If we do not understand the implications of this art it will always remain remote and inaccessible to us.

—Giuseppe Tucci, *Nepal: The Discovery of the Malla*

For once in my life, I was going to buy retail.

And so, at last, I decided to try the best. I stopped in at the finest, most expensive art gallery in Kathmandu: the Oriental Art Emporium, owned by a black-eyed and cerebral young man named Babukaji.

To enter Babukaji's shop was to step into a world utterly removed from the familiar chaos of the ambient street scene. The impudent orchestra of New Road—shouting, honking, whistling, and mooing—faded into oblivion as I closed the door behind me. It was almost as if the interior of the gallery created a zone of silence around itself. I blinked, waiting for my brain to adjust to this subdued new esthetic.

Babukaji sat behind a wide desk cluttered with bills and letters. He was on the phone, speaking in imperative whispers, and nod-

ded briefly to acknowledge my presence. It was impossible to guess
his age; he could have been anywhere from 21 to 45.

Babukaji's shop seemed to combine the best qualities of both
gallery and shrine. The artworks, displayed in polished and well-lit
showcases, were extraordinary. I found my materialistic frenzy
loosening, dissolving into puddles of reverence and supplication. I
began to suspect what it would mean—in terms of *responsibility*—
to own a truly potent work of devotional art.

There were yogic saints and dancing Ganeshas; singing brass
bowls and Tibetan bells made from long-forgotten alloys; prayer
beads carved from human bones; ritual daggers with demonic faces
engraved on their hilts.

There was everything anyone could possibly wish for, except a
statue of the Buddha.

"How may I help you?"

Babukaji had ended his conversation and crept up silently behind me, catlike, catching me off guard. In a lame attempt to sound
casual, I began to prattle uncontrollably.

"Well—gee, I don't know. You've got some beautiful stuff here,
no doubt about it, but I'm frankly sort of disappointed by the selection. I mean, aren't you a bit short on Buddhas? After all, this is
Nepal, Buddha was *born* here, so I guess I figured you'd have at least
a couple of really topnotch statues; nothing sloppy, mind you, but
a really sweet little—"

"Wait." Babukaji raised his palm, and I screeched to a halt.
"Allow me to show you something."

He walked behind a low display case, parted a maroon curtain,
and vanished into a back room. I heard a drawer squeaking open;
the jangle of keys; the snap of a lock; another creak. Then Babukaji
reappeared, carrying a small parcel completely mummified in rice
paper and tied with string—like a Nepali Maltese Falcon. He set
it down on a countertop and removed the wrappings.

The chemistry was immediate, complete, and devastating.

For several minutes I could not speak. My ears were ringing; the
shop seemed to go soft-focus around me. I felt like a kid at

Christmas time, staring through a frosted windowpane at the Flexible Flyer of his dreams. Images of coasting fearlessly across the thin ice of this particular lifetime, my new Buddha by my side, danced giddily in my head. I dreamed of the ease and speed with which we would sleigh, the Buddha steering, around the stumps and moguls of *samsara*—illusion and suffering—that lay all along life's twisting path.

"I'll take it," I said.

There was a brief, strained silence. I turned around to face Babukaji and repeated my claim.

"I'm so sorry," the shopkeeper folded his hands and seemed to bow slightly, "but that particular Buddha is not for sale. It is by the hand of Sidhi Raj himself and is being held in reserve for a very important Japanese collector. Besides," he added gently, eyes glancing down at my tattered tennies, "I think maybe this one is a little too expensive for you."

This was the very moment that I'd been waiting for: the chance to cast off an entire childhood of operant conditioning with a single, devil-may-care gesture. A little smile crossed my lips. "Ah, c'mon, tell me. You might be surprised. How much?"

Babukaji smiled as well. "Fifteen thousand rupees," he said evenly.

My mouth dropped open. I barked out a laugh; there had to be a mistake. Numbers, I knew, were always a point of confusion for non-native speakers.

"Write it down," I insisted. And he did, slowly and carefully: a one, a five, a comma, and three zeroes.

"Fifteen thousand rupees," he repeated.

I whipped out my pocket calculator and divided by the going exchange rate.

"But—but—that comes to $666.66666! I'd have to be sick to spend that much money on a Buddha! Whew! Hey!" I slapped my forehead, feeling much like the fall guy in some dumb situation comedy. "You've got to be kidding!"

I paced around the shop as Babukaji rewrapped the statue, dividing the figures again and again in the hope that I had made some grievous error with the math. But no—that devilish row of sixes continued to display itself, with an impassivity that was itself almost Buddhalike, in the tiny liquid crystal display.

"Heh!" I croaked. The wisest thing to do, without a doubt, was to put this insane temptation behind me as quickly as possible.

But not quite yet.

"Listen," I muttered imploringly. "Let me just have one last look."

Babukaji did not blink an eye; he calmly unwrapped the Buddha once more and placed it in my hands. Although barely nine inches high it was, truly, a marvelous work of art. Babukaji knew; he knew that I knew. At one point I took a breath, right on the verge of bargaining. But when our eyes met, Babukaji gave his head the merest shake. It was sufficient; I said nothing.

The Nepalis have such beautiful features: so refined. So *sculpted*. After spending a month looking at statues, you realize that everyone you see on the street resembles one of them. The university co-ed sitting sidesaddle on the back of her brother's motorcycle must have been the model for the Tara I'd passed up a couple of days ago; that rotund fellow lounging in the glass bead necklace stall could only be Ganesh; that little boy ringing the bell on his father's bicycle was the baby Krishna....

Late at night, when I went to bed, I closed my eyes and still saw all those faces. But one face in particular kept creeping into my consciousness, insinuating itself into my dreams. It was the face of Babukaji's Buddha—all $666.66 worth.

And a damned good thing, I thought to myself miserably, that it wasn't for sale.

I returned to Babukaji's every day for a week, hoping he might get something else in, something even remotely comparable—and half the price—of the superb copper Buddha. Every day I asked to look at it again, and every day he patiently took it out of the back room, unwrapped it, and let me gaze at its perfect features.

One afternoon Babukaji said, "I must tell you something. I have learned, just yesterday, that this Japanese dealer has left town. He did not leave word with me, so I must assume he is abandoning this deal. And so I ask you: Do you wish to buy this Buddha?"

I wheezed; I gulped; I asked the price, hoping beyond hope that Babukaji would have pity on the poor dollar. No chance; the price was fixed. By now, though, the rupee had slightly devalued. The Buddha would cost me $650, if I changed money on the black market.

"I gotta think about it," I pleaded.

"Yes," said Babukaji. "I will sell it to no one else until you have decided."

I strolled down toward the Bagmati River, desperately confused. What to do? I was completely in love with that Buddha in Babukaji's shop—but $650! It was a mind-numbing figure. My car cost less than that!

> *Nepal has three religions: Hinduism, Buddhism, and Tourism.*
>
> —A popular Nepali saying

My face felt pale and wan. When was the last time I spent $50 for a nice shirt? I mean, okay, $300 is an exercise, a deep breath that you have to take. A plunge. And it's true, this Buddha represented a small fortune. It cost far more than I earned during some of my leaner months as a writer.

Down at the river, the usual activities were in progress. People were bathing, washing their clothes, watering their buffaloes. I was just about to cross over the bridge to the other side when I saw something going on at a little temple by the bank. A man in a white breechcloth was sweeping, sweeping, sweeping the ashes off a circular pedestal, or *ghat*, upon which a cremation had just been completed.

At that moment I remembered something.

Months ago, while Karen was still visiting, we woke up early one morning and took a taxi out to Pashupatinath, a very important Shiva temple just east of the city. The temple grounds are bisected by the Bagmati River, which manifests directly from Shiva's scalp up in the western Himalayas. It follows a twisting course across the Tibetan Plateau, down into Nepal and south to India, where it joins the holy Ganges.

A half-naked priest raked through the embers of a smoking cremation ghat. We watched from a distance as he poked at something black and egg-shaped. When we came closer to investigate, I saw that it was a human head—and the black, roasted remains of a torso, tiny and twisted. The head seemed to be thrown back in a gesture that was both agonized and inspired. There was something triumphant and ultimate about it, like a face contorted during childbirth.

"Where is that soul now?" Karen wondered. I knew the local answer. The spirit, blind and helpless, would have begun its passage through the Rivers of Fire, clinging to the tail of a sacred cow. Ah, the imagination that goes into creating what comes next! And the aching sigh of mortality: our smooth, warm bodies crackling into ash, skulls bursting with a pop, limbs falling away. We stood still and silent and watched the head in the flames, teeth grimacing at the sky.

"An inevitable turn of events, I'm afraid," I muttered.

And then I realized that, if you take away the words "I'm afraid," what I'd said was essentially Buddha's primary teaching: death is inevitable. The whole trick lies in somehow coming to terms with that fear.

What, I asked myself, is $650 if it can help me sizzle those two words—"I'm afraid"—out of my life? What price enlightenment? Is it a bargain basement commodity, or do you get it when and where you can, damn the expense?

I hailed a taxi and rushed back to the Oriental Art Emporium, full of conviction.

Jeff Greenwald is a contributing editor for Wired *magazine and the author of* Mr. Raja's Neighborhood, The Size of the World: Once Around Without Leaving the Ground, *and* Shopping for Buddhas, *from which this story was excerpted.*

✳

"I'd like you to meet an artist," the girl said, filling my glass with *chang* for the umpteenth time.

"Lovely," I said. I had no special plans.

"He's from Dolpo," she said.

"How did he get here?"

"He walked."

Of course. "That must have taken a while."

"Three weeks."

"Alone?"

"Oh, no," she laughed. "He is a very famous artist in the Dolpo. Two hundred of his followers came with him."

"Why did he come?"

"He was invited to paint a series of *thankas* for the temple here."

The smiling artist said something in a soft singsong voice.

"He's asking if you'd like to see one of his *thankas*."

"Yes, I would, very much."

The elfin fellow nodded, opened up the wooden chest in the corner of his cell, and carefully lifted out a rectangle of stretched canvas, about four feet high and three feet wide.

Slowly, almost shyly, he turned the canvas toward us.

It exploded with color—bright emerald green mountains, golden-edged clouds, pink and sapphire-blue lotus blossoms, curling traceries of leaves, haloed gods, some black and fierce, some with elephant's faces, others with huge mouths and horns and a welter of gracefully waving arms, some almost transparent with long-fingered upraised palms and gentle almond-shaped eyes, and all clad in meticulously detailed robes. There were scores of separate images, each one tingling with symbolic gestures that I couldn't begin to comprehend.

The girl asked how long the *thanka* had taken to paint.

"He says about three months—three months of twelve-hour days."

"And he's painting more?

"Yes, he'll paint more *thankas*. This is his whole life."

—David Yeadon, *The Back of Beyond: Travels to the Wild Places of the Earth*

CAROLYN CARVAJAL

⋆ ⋆ ⋆

Trial by Trisuli

River rafting, a popular activity in Nepal,
is not without its perils.

"OTHERS CALL THEM *ROCKY 1, ROCKY 2,* AND *THE TERMINATOR*,
but I like the name *The Good, The Bad,* and *The Ugly*," says Kumar,
our rafting guide, who describes to us in Hollywood terms the sequence of rapids we are about to challenge on the Trisuli River,
the most popular rafting destination in Nepal. In his broken
English, Kumar explains that the river is like a moody person:
sometimes he is angry, sometimes quiet, but usually friendly. With
widened eyes, he emphasizes, "In October, when river high, he get
very angry." Thus, the names reflect the personalities of each rapid.
Bemused and skeptical, I perceive Kumar to be exaggerating just
a little, for his claim contradicts my reliable guidebook, which describes rafting the Trisuli as "wild enough to be fun, but nothing
to be frightened of." Admittedly though, his warning has
intimidated me.

I am the only Canadian in the group that includes people
from England, Colombia, Australia and the United States. There
are eleven of us in total, including Kumar and his assistant
Ramesh. Short and lean, both are attractive young men, about
twenty years old.

Despite his limited English, Kumar is quite talkative, a charm-

143

ing extrovert who quickly develops a rapport with the clients; Ramesh, on the other hand, prefers to stay in the background. While Ramesh loads the equipment, we stand by the riverbank listening intently to Kumar's instructions—a crash course on whitewater rafting. "When I say paddle, just paddle!" he shouts. "I say paddle left, we go left. Right, we go right." Perhaps, having uttered this string of phrases a thousand times before, he recites them to us with perfect pronunciation and intonation, without a trace of a Nepali accent. Understanding the simple rule, we nod our heads enthusiastically, like eager children about to play with a new toy.

Wearing lifejackets and armed with paddles, we board the raft. I sit at the bow beside Claire, a cartoonist from England. I notice straps attached to the floor for passengers to anchor their feet in case of a rough ride. I try one on, but the fit is loose and makes me feel uneasy. I ask and gesture to Kumar if we can tighten these straps, but he says, "no," pointing to them to show they are not adjustable. Under my breath I comfort my distress, reminding myself repeatedly, "Relax, you're not rafting the Colorado River."

Off we go. For a long time, we float slowly past the scenery and there is little talking amongst us. Everyone seems immersed in the tranquillity of our surroundings: chirping birds, whispering currents, fresh air, but occasionally the serenity is disturbed by distant sounds of honking buses and trucks. This stretch of the Trisuli River is not located in an exotic, remote area of Nepal but runs parallel to two busy highways that connect Kathmandu with Narayanghat and Pokhara.

Only when this presence of mechanical civilization is hundreds of meters above the river do we begin to feel nestled between two imposing structures of nature. As we slither into seemingly unexplored territory—deep gorges to our left, towering mountains to our right—I look up in awe, imagining a pair of invisible eyes looking down on us.

What sounds like a loud murmuring brook is actually the first rapid—*The Good.* Amazingly, we pass through it with playful ease, riding the fast current continuously, up and down, up and down, like a giant slide, with several bumps. We get a spray and scream in unison. Possessing predictability, *The Good* embodies its name and yields a rollicking fun ride. Effortlessly, we paddle to reach the quiet side of the Trisuli, but this peaceful drift doesn't last long— only long enough for us to exchange comments about *The Good*: cool, awesome, fantastic.

I hear echoes of rushing water like a chorus beckoning us to come near. We have no choice. We are pulled into the next rapid where for the first time my body learns the true sensation of white-water rafting. It's as if our raft is afloat in a gigantic washing machine—dancing rapids agitate our raft and make it difficult to keep our balance. I focus on two things simultaneously: paddling and pressing my heels down. I flex my feet under the straps to resist slipping. Sharp tingles course throughout my body, from my fingers to my toes, and finally I scream. By now I am thoroughly convinced the water can hear us and knows we love getting deluged. Happily drenched, we are exhilarated.

"That was sensational, man, just sensational!" cries out Efren, the Colombian fellow. "Is the next one better?"

"Why not?" answers Kumar.

"*Terminator* is bad—difficult," Ramesh says, his first words all morning.

"You mean *Ugly*. Yeah, *Ugly's* water very good," Kumar interjects.

"Are we going to have lunch soon?" Anita asks.

"Why not?" Kumar replies again.

My friend Stella and I chuckle. We have observed by now Kumar's penchant for answering every other question with the phrase "Why not?"

Thankfully, the drive to Chitwan was interrupted by a refreshing raft adventure down the Trisuli River. The rapids of the Trisuli were running a mild Class I in early March. The trip, which takes only a few hours when the river is raging at Class IV level, took two lazy days. At night, the Nepali rafting company set up a tent camp on a sandy beach. They prepared an astonishing feast over an open fire, serving huge pots of vegetable curries, roast chicken, fried rice and fruit cake, topped off by rum tea. Breakfast produced an equally amazing array, including banana pancakes and omelets.

—Ginger Dingus,
"Adventure by Elephant"

Before arriving at what we think is the final obstacle, we are again gliding along the watery highway, now lit up by the hot sun. All morning the sun has been playing hide-and-seek with us, but now it has completely surrendered itself, warming us up.

As we approach *The Terminator*, Kumar, like the captain of his ship, is at the bow of the rubber boat and looking ahead to assess the situation. His squinting eyes and crinkled forehead denote trouble. Then he yells, "Paddle left! Go left, left!" We paddle furiously and make it beyond the entrance of the rapids, when suddenly, water is attacking us from all sides.

Kumar's earlier assertion of the Trisuli's changing moods is ringing in my head—apparently this part of the river is not having a good day. It is no longer a playground. The only way to resist, it seems, is not with paddles but with the ability to ride out the tumultuous waters. Our upper bodies become contorted, as if we are rodeo cowboys riding wild horses. Kumar's command of "Paddle! Paddle!" is muffled by the ear-splitting shrills of unequivocal fear. Because I'm afraid to lose my balance, I cannot concentrate solely on paddling. Consequently, I end up paddling sporadically, always keeping my heels pressed onto the floor and clutching tightly to the rope attached around the inner rim of the raft.

From behind, I hear an anxious, "Oh no!" Stella has dropped her paddle. I watch it disappear into a whirlpool. The raft is spinning. Ramesh and Kumar urge us to paddle harder. I continue to contribute to an unsynchronized effort that is going backwards and forwards. Finally the chaotic paddling yields results. We extricate ourselves from the hungry whirlpool. The women cheer and the men whistle.

"That was a charming little whirlpool," Anita says sarcastically. "It got me a bit worried."

"How many more, Kumar?" Stella whines. "I think I've had enough rafting for today."

"Is this the last one?" I ask.

"Yes—this one we call *The Pinball Machine*."

Judging from the intensity of the previous rapids, I imagine the last one to be the most difficult. At this point, Kumar is wise not

to embellish on it. He only says, "*Pinball* the same as *Terminator.*"
Great. At least we know what to anticipate.

Entering *The Pinball Machine* zone, we are greeted by a shroud
of mist. The thin fog is wafting towards us as if to reveal the mysterious waters beyond. However, this dreamy float is brief: the mist
only covers the entrance to the rapids, and beyond it, the visibility
is clear. Unlike the other rapids, *The Pinball Machine* possesses a
definite shape—rectangular—and so far the biggest in area. There
are several rocks scattered about, requiring more maneuvering on
our part. I begin to understand why it merits such a name. At the
exact moment we are jostled around by the first rock, a big wave
pushes our raft upwards like a seesaw. We are suspended in midair
for a split second. When gravity pulls us down, I perform a magnificent backflip into the rushing water.

The instant I plunge into the water, my world is reduced to the
beat of my racing heart, and tears in my eyes. I can't see anything.
I can't breathe. I can't swim. Panic has bound me up so tightly I
am unable to move. I wish to explode and free myself of this overwhelming fear. Am I drowning? Am I having a near-death
experience?

An unknown length of time passes. When I recover from this
state of disorientation, I suddenly realize that my head is above
water. My lifejacket, which I forgot I had on, has kept me afloat. I
feel as if I'm caught in an ocean storm, for torrential water is slapping my face. Through this wet and muddled vision, I catch a
glimpse of an orange object—our raft—which appears close to
me. Instinctively I reach out and grasp the rope that is attached to
the outer part of the raft. It drags me haphazardly in a way a new-
lywed's getaway car would drag a bunch of tin cans. I cry, "Help
me!" and they shout, "Hang on, hang on!" The thought of
whirlpools waiting to engulf me gives my arm the strength to hold
on even tighter. The friction between my fingers and the rope
stings. I stretch my left arm to meet Claire's hand. As soon as she
has a tight hold I feel my upper body being lifted. I push myself
up, bring my right leg over the rim of the raft and struggle aboard.
I plunk down on the floor like a prized hundred-pound fish. I'm

out of breath. My throat is sore. I hear a barrage of concerned voices. "Are you okay? Are you all right?" Still in shock, I nod and continue to hold Claire's hand.

"Thank you for saving my life," I say softly and embrace her. Of all the million times I have uttered the words "thank you," this moment is undeniably the most sincere and meaningful. Amidst all this, fast rapids continue to strike us, so I kneel on the raft's floor, gripping tightly on the nylon strap and watch everyone paddle hard. Halfway through we pass more pockets of whirlpools, which fortunately, we manage to avoid.

Once we reach the end of *The Pinball Machine*, there is an unspoken sigh of relief. We are as silent as the river which carries us to its banks where we are scheduled to eat lunch. My silence speaks of an unwarranted embarrassment. Blame it on human nature. Though my fall was an accident beyond anybody's control, I cannot help but feel as if I'm the most feeble in our group because I lacked the physical strength to stop myself from falling. The need to talk about this frightening experience is as basic as my need to sleep, eat, or go to the bathroom, but I don't want to be perceived as wimpy by a bunch of strangers who might not understand. So I hold it in. Feelings of anxiety all too familiar begin to bother me like tiny aching pelvic throbs when there is absolutely nowhere to urinate. In the same way, I have nowhere to go. I have no one to really turn to because I'm ultimately surrounded by an assortment of casual acquaintances I've known for half a day. Only in the face of an ordeal does a solo traveler (though physically surrounded by other travelers) like myself realize the sheer isolation of being emotionally alone. Inside, I scream for my mother. Outside, I act cool, not expressing any residual fear and shock which only I know is lingering between the linings of my gurgling stomach, my clammy hands and feet, and my fast heartbeat. My companions' silence? I can only surmise. I wonder if they are thinking, "That could have been me in the water. Lucky it wasn't me." The wordless drift ceases when Anita comments: "Carolyn, you should have seen your face, you were white as a sheet."

"Yeah, you looked really scared. Soooo scared," Chris adds.

"That's easy for you guys to say. You're not the ones who nearly drowned," I respond defensively.

"Don't worry," Kumar says. "Many people fall in the water. No problem. They are okay. But you—you're lucky. You know, two years ago, a guide fall in *The Pinball Machine.* He has lifejacket. He good swimmer, but whirlpool gets him. He is dead," Kumar says matter-of-factly.

His unnerving story reminds me again of how close I might have been to death and how lucky I am to be alive.

As we approach the riverbank, we hear boisterous laugh-

I had learned, over the years, that it is possible to walk the tarai *forests from end to end in complete safety. Walk. Not swim. Not wade. Swimming or wading in the* tarai *jungle rivers or lakes puts one into the territory of the one animal that holds not to the jungle law, the one creature to which all living things are, simply, food. The animal that Kipling called "the belly that runs on four legs." The Mugger crocodile.*

—Peter Byrne, *Tula Hatti: The Last Great Elephant*

ter behind us. A group of young Israeli men, wearing orange life-jackets, are hollering and waving red buckets to catch our attention. Paddling vigorously, they catch up to us and throw buckets of water, provoking a friendly water fight which we engage in willingly. I observe they are wearing helmets and sitting on a raft that looks brand new. We are not.

I strike up a conversation with one of them and ask about the cost of their rafting package. I learn that they paid double the amount we paid. I wonder how many varying prices there are for the same trip. But then again, Stella and I did not exactly shop around nor did we ask for recommendations from other travelers who had gone rafting. The fact that on the morning of our departure there was no van to take us to the campsite as promised should have indicated that something was amiss. Instead, the travel agent who sold us the tickets sent us off on a crowded public bus to Mugling where we were let out in the middle of a deserted highway. Of course at the precise moment when we started to wonder if we'd been had, we heard a voice say, "Canada?" "England?" It was Kumar, with a big smile, ready to pick up his customers. After the incident at *The Pinball Machine* I start to question whether safety and emergency procedures are practiced by rafting companies.

The rafting is over. We are sitting on a pebbly riverbank waiting for Kumar and Ramesh to open the water-proof barrels so we can be reunited with our precious belongings. Everything seems intact and dry—daypacks, cameras, money belts, and neck pouches—except for our lunch. Impatient and hungry, we tolerate slightly soggy cheese sandwiches and soft bananas, though washing down this terrible lunch is divine. The icy cans of soda appease us, changing our sour faces into thirst-quenched smiles. After lunch, Stella and I decide to stay at the campsite for the night, while the rest of our companions return to Pokhara that evening. We say good-bye along the dusty highway amidst a crowd of gawking Nepali children. For the last time, I squeeze Claire's hand and impart a warm smile to the woman who saved my life.

That night, under the watchful gaze of a luminous half-moon and a million stars, we sit around the campfire drinking tepid beer. I relish the cold air tickling my cheeks and nose. I take pleasure in scratching the itchy area surrounding a mosquito bite on my wrist. I am lucky to feel, smell, listen, taste, and see all that is around me. After all, there is a reason to celebrate. I am alive.

Carolyn Carvajal is a traveler and teacher from Vancouver, Canada. When not wandering she devotes her time to photography and pottery.

★

Traditional river navigation in the Himalaya consists of crossings by dugout canoes at the spots between rapids. Usually neither the crew nor passengers can swim. The dugout is towed upstream to the foot of the rapids above. Passengers, perhaps a goat, maybe some chickens, all snuggle in. With gunnels inches above the water, one person in the bow and one in the stern, the crew of two pushes off and immediately starts to paddle furiously for the opposite bank before the current sucks them into the rapids below.

—Daniel Taylor-Ide, *Something Hidden Behind the Ranges*

MEG LUKENS NOONAN

* * *

Zen and the Art
of Mountain Biking

What is the sound of two wheels turning?

AFTER LUNCH WE HAD AN EARTHQUAKE. NO ONE SEEMED TO mind. Eight of us had been pedaling the rocky footpaths in the terraced highlands above Kathmandu, and when we stopped to rest, we felt a prolonged lurch. "Ground's moving," someone pointed out. We all took a couple of long pulls from our water bottles, tightened our helmets, then got back on our bikes to head down the trail toward the chaotic, hazy city. A mid-size earthquake doesn't seem all that interesting after a week of riding mountain bikes through the strange and wonderful kingdom of Nepal. Here, you can count on being moved by things a lot more amazing than that just around the next bend. Magic swirls in the dust, music on the wind. So, the earth moves. You keep on riding.

But that was near the end of our trip. It began a week earlier in Kathmandu, when I was fresh off a plane and in the company of new acquaintances.

We leave the Kathmandu Guest House on a chilly, sparkling morning in mid-October and ride the bus to Naubise, a scruffy hillside village about fifteen miles from Kathmandu. The country's most celebrated holiday, the Dasain festival of early autumn, is in full swing. Like all the other machinery in town, the bus that is to accompany us throughout the trip has been splattered with sacrificial blood and flower petals to keep its occupants safe—sort of Nepal's version of AAA.

The sun is up over the high Himalayan peaks to the north when we all ride out of Naubise heading for the small settlement of Daman, about 30 miles and 4,600 feet above us. We pedal up the old Tribhuvan Rajpath, once the only road linking India and Nepal. The Rajpath is prime mountain-biking territory; the funky hand-hewn road offers a bounty of switchbacks, precipices, ravines, rushing rivers, mud-hut villages, terraced rice fields, and glorious long views of the far-off Himalayas.

We pedal up for three hours, have lunch by a stream, and continue to climb. There are stretches where the grade is punishing, short runs that get us up out of the saddles, stomping hard, trying to maintain some shred of momentum. Then the road flattens and, although we're still ascending, the pedals turn with startling ease. I stop to watch a woman wrapped in red as she plays on a huge bamboo swing that flings her out over the deep, green valley, reels her back in, then tosses her out again.

As we climb, the terrain gets drier, less hospitable. Rampant deforestation and unchecked erosion are stripping the middle hills of their precious topsoil. For now, the fields are planted and the villagers are fed, but the future is uncertain.

The yellow slopes give way slowly to dark stands of pine, and with the altitude, the temperature drops. By dusk we have coasted down into a fragrant valley and are facing another five miles—straight up. One contingent of "Damn or die" riders pushes on. Another contingent (mine) catches the bus to the top of the pass, where we will make camp.

We wait for the others under a hanging lantern in a dirt-floor teahouse and order coconut biscuits, jasmine tea, and, just to take the chill off, a bottle of the local rum. It turns out to be an inspired combination—one that leads to all kinds of revelations. For instance, there are three Atlanta debutantes among us, and a certain doyenne of etiquette and style named Miss Clemens helped guide them all down the rocky road of adolescence. This kicks off a rash of Southern debs-on-wheels jokes and exaggerated drawls that will stick the entire week. We walk to the campsite for dinner— rice and lentils, *chapatis*, cauliflower, and potatoes—and chow down with all the grace of maximum-security prisoners. "Miss Clemens would be shocked, y'all," Catherine says.

Before dawn I wake to a jet-lag-fueled rush of adrenaline and look outside. The stars that had punched through the blue-black evening sky have vanished in a low screen of gray. The wind has dropped and the air is warmer. A rooster crows and sets off the village dogs, who howl straight through to sunup. Out there, reaching through the clouds, are the mountains in all their raging beauty: Annapurna, Dhaulagiri, Kangchenjunga, Manaslu, Lhotse, Makalu, Cho Oyu, Everest. Eight of the world's ten tallest peaks would soon be visible in one mind-blowing sweep of the horizon from above the campsite. There's no going back to sleep with all that rock and drama looming over me, so I wait.

So peaceful were they in their daytime slumber, I could hardly believe they would become Hounds of Hell in the dead of night. "They" were the Curs of Kathmandu, and they deranged me nightly with an astounding range of baying, yapping and howling which penetrated even earplugs and whiskey fog. The torment became too personal; after a while I could have sworn they were barking jamesjamesjames jamesjamessss.

—James O'Reilly, "Stairway to Heaven"

After breakfast we make the final push over the pass and from here on we're heading downhill to the sweet green lowlands of the vast *tarai*. And what a ride. We bank a hairpin turn and see lambent snowy spires soaring above the bamboo. Around the next turn is a back-lit temple floating in the low clouds. Endless folds of blue-fogged valleys collapse onto themselves toward India. We barrel down the road, out of the cold pines and cracked soil, and into a fragrant wet jungle that resonates bird sounds and drips with blooms. Below, the road snakes in infinite S-curves and the small orange helmets of my friends ahead communicate the distances we are covering. It is exhilarating to coast on a bicycle for hours—some 7,000 vertical feet down roads with no guardrails—dropping a shoulder into each swinging corner, letting the speed build, checking it, then letting it build again.

This is probably not the place to try out my newly-learned Zen spin on life, but I do it anyway. "Be Here Now," I say to myself, trying to feel intensely each fleeing moment. "Be Here Now." But really, there is no Here here. It's all going by in a hallucinatory rush. How about "Be There In A Second, Y'all." That works better.

In late afternoon, we finally roll out of the Mahabharat Lekh hills to the flatter terrain of Hetauda, glad to get off the brakes. Everything has changed. In the crowded town there is a feeling of tropical decay—rank heaps of garbage shrinking in the heat, stagnant brown water in the roadside ditches, and barefoot families squatting in the filth. And yet there is beauty and bounty too. Plumeria trees litter the ground with their fragrant blossoms, mango trees bend with fruit, and the rich alluvial fields are shiny with rice and jute.

We pedal the last six miles west, straight into the setting sun, a wavering red ball that melts into the shallow Karra River. The children in the roadside settlements run from the fields when they see us coming and shout "bye-bye"—apparently their only English—from every doorway. I yell "*namaste,*" my only Nepali. We park on the bank of the slow-moving river, and local kids sit silently on a rock through the night watching us set up camp, cook, eat, talk, laugh, and finally sleep in their backyard.

Although the climate is sub-tropical, a reassuring crispness bites the air when our bus, trailing the bikes, pulls into Pokhara, the gateway for trekkers on the Annapurna circuit. But on this clear, pink evening it seems the gateway to something even higher.

In the morning we ride dirt roads to Begnas Tal, a green lake below the soaring peak of Machhapuchare, just nineteen miles away. Later, we pedal to Tashiling, a Tibetan refugee camp, where a small, beatific man leads us into his small house and offers to sell silver jewelry and chunks of turquoise as big as tangerines.

This is our last night in Pokhara, our last on the road. We spent the day cruising the great roads above the town and gathered in the dark to ride in for dinner. Although the moon is full, it has yet to climb above the peaks, so we are pedaling nearly blind through the quiet streets. We linger over dinner, eavesdrop on the German tourists eating strudel at the next table, and poke around a tiny shop before hopping on our bikes and heading back to the hotel.

The moon is high and the grand peaks are washed in hard silver. Machhapuchare, Annapurna, Manaslu—the names ring out with such clarity, such song. We fly down luminescent streets and pass sleeping cows, slow-moving buffalo, snarling dogs. A man is lying by the side of the road. In the shadow of these regal mountains, on the shores of these cold, perfect lakes, it seems there are things that ought to be considered. Like Who am I? and How did I get here? and What does it all mean? Well...maybe I'll think about that stuff tomorrow, because I am Here Now and my legs are strong and the bike feels good. There is enough light to find the way home. The earth moves once more and we keep on riding.

When I went to Pok-hara, I discovered two cities with the same name located a few miles apart. One is Nepali Pokhara, and the other is "Disney" Pokhara where we politically-correct ecotourists are faced with a bit of a dilemma. We detest the blatant Western invasion of this beautiful culture, but we love the good restaurants that play Eric Clapton and German bakeries that make delicious brownies. Everyone comments on how synthetic the town is, yet no one bashes it too much because we all know that if we really didn't like it we could easily pick up and move a few miles to the real Pokhara. And who wants to do that?

—Doug Lansky, "Trekking the Himalayas Is Fun, Remember?"

Meg Lukens Noonan is a correspondent for Outside *magazine and co-author of* Albatross: The True Story of a Woman's Survival at Sea. *She lives in New Hampshire with her husband and two small children.*

★

The road carried us through villages and farm fields as it climbed higher and higher towards the rim of the valley. The mustard fields glowed iridescent yellow against a background of emerald green rice paddies. Huffing and puffing, we were no doubt a curious sight to behold in the eyes of the average villager. Two women, unescorted, dressed in t-shirts and colorful local-style baggy pants (little did they know we had our specialized bike shorts on underneath!), eyes hidden behind dark glasses, heads adorned with some sort of plastic bonnet, sweating and grinding up a steep hill when everybody in their right mind walks, and slowly at that.

As we stopped for a breather at the top of a particularly steep pitch, a wizened, barefoot farmer of indeterminate age appeared from nowhere. He walked right up to us and assessed us from head to foot from behind thick glasses.

"Long suffering?" he asked us in most polite English. It wasn't really a question, it was more of a statement. Wendy and I immediately understood the metaphysical implications of his pronouncement.

"Yes, yes!" we heartily agreed, giddy from the intense physical exertion and the comic clarity of coming face-to-face with a universal truth.

—Maureen DeCoursey, "Mountain Biking with Wendy"

RAJENDRA S. KHADKA

✦ ✹ ✦

In Buddha's Backyard

Return of the native.

ONE SUNNY, WINTER MORNING, I TOOK THE NINE A.M. MINIBUS
from the ratty border town of Bhairawa to Lumbini, the birthplace
of Siddartha Gautam, better known throughout the world as
"Buddha," the Enlightened One. My aunt had assured me that since
it was a *pukka,* paved, road to Lumbini, I'd be there "in no time."
She also asked me to bring back some *peda,* a sweet snack shaped
like a round cracker. I learned later that among the locals, Lumbini
was once as famous for its *peda* as the birthplace of Buddha.

Despite the *pukka* road, the bus, a tinny box rolling on bald
wheels, took two hours to cover the twenty kilometer distance.
After all, it was a cold winter morning; the driver took frequent
tea-pee-and-cigarette breaks whenever he pulled up at roadside tea
shops which also were the informal bus stops.

As the minibus approached Lumbini, I was startled by the sight
of a brilliantly white-washed, single-story mosque squatting in
the middle of the flat, fallow farmland that is the monotonous feature of the *tarai.* It was the cleanest thing I had seen since the sub-
way stations of Singapore. My first thought was: Saudi money
here too? Ignoring the dazzling mosque, I scanned for the land-

marks that had always greeted me on my previous visits: the ancient, sandstone Ashoka pillar leaning just so slightly; the sturdy, sacred Bodhi tree which spread its branches protectively over the Mayadevi temple, which too had once been brushed white, but the ravages of monsoon rains and hot, dusty winters had marked the temple with permanent blotches of gray and black, like an ugly skin disease. I had asked the bus driver to alert me when we reached Lumbini. When the bus stopped at another chaotic bazaar, he nodded at me.

When the Buddhist Emperor Askoa [274-232 B.C.] of ancient India visited Lumbini, he had a sandstone pillar erected to commemorate his visit. The following words inscribed upon it:

Twenty years after his coronation, King Priyadarsi [Asoka], Beloved of the Gods, visited this place in person and worshiped here because the Buddha, the Sage of the Sakyas, was born here.

—V. B. Singh,
"Travels in Taulihawa"

I got off—and felt temporarily lost in the melange of shops, bicycles, pedestrians, motor vehicles, bullock-carts and street-vendors. I found my true north when I noticed a billboard advertising "Lumbini Village Lodge," and at its bottom, fading block letters declared: THE BIRTH PLACE OF LORD BUDHA JUST 5 MINUTE WALK FROM HERE. An arrow indicated the direction to take.

Off the paved road, a tree-lined dirt path led into the ancient Lumbini Garden which I finally recognized. I had an appointment with a Nepali archaeologist, Mr. Bidari, who had been living and working in Lumbini for over a decade. I apologized for being late and told him I was briefly lost because I no longer recognized Lumbini.

"So much activity, the whole landscape has changed," I said.

"Well, surely you know about the Lumbini Master Plan?" he responded.

Yes, I did. It had been uttered like a mantra by every official I had met at the Lumbini Development Trust headquarters in Kathmandu. They would spread out rolls of blueprint on their desks, point to scale models with blunt, stubby pencils, recite impressive statistics, and hand me brochures as I prepared to leave.

When I had mentioned this Master Plan to my father, he had snorted skeptically. "They are trying to hide decades of corruption. So much foreign money has been given in the past twenty, almost thirty, years. And what do they have to show for development in Lumbini? Nothing! Did anyone show you a budget or a financial report?"

"No."

"Of course not! All these years, the bureaucrats developed themselves instead of Lumbini, and now, to fool the public, they declare a Master Plan. I'll believe them when I see Lumbini again. They all lie and cheat. There is so much corruption that even Lord Buddha would have a hard time forgiving them!"

Strong words, but my father had once been a government employee; the experience had disillusioned him. Besides, our family had a proprietorial attitude about Lumbini. My parents' family lived in Taulihawa, the modern name of Kapilvastu, the ancient kingdom of Buddha's father, King Suddhodhan. My parents were born there, and so was I. During winter holidays when I visited my grandparents, I recalled local poets declaiming about "Child Siddartha/who rolled in the sacred dust of our Kapilvastu..."; when young men became despondent, families became worried that he too would follow Gautam's path of exile and liberation. Gloomy intellectuals would comment with dense despair, "Now if Jesus Christ had been born in Lumbini, do you think Christians and Americans would allow such neglect? Oh no, no sir! Lumbini would be a paradise! It

> *It all began with a Buddhist from Burma named U Thant. As UN Secretary General, he made a pilgrimage to Lumbini in 1967 and reportedly wept at seeing the sorry condition of the Buddha's birthplace. His heartache woke Nepalis up to the fact that the preservation of what was clearly an international heritage was an urgent responsibility.*
>
> —Rachana Pathak, "Lumbini as Disneyland," *Himal South Asia*

would have paved roads, buses, airport, hotels, rest-houses and other amenities for the weary pilgrim, but alas! Buddha was born in poor Nepal and Lumbini remains a backwater." We felt the pain when Lumbini remained neglected.

In his office, Mr. Bidari proceeded to give me a detailed explanation of the Master Plan. It was designed by the Japanese architect Kenzo Tange, a winner of the Pritzker Architecture Prize. It covered three square miles divided into four distinct areas: 1) the new Lumbini village with accommodations for pilgrims, scholars, and tourists; 2) a cultural zone where a library, museum, auditorium, and research facilities would be built; 3) a monastic zone where every major Buddhist nation had leased a plot and many had started to build their monasteries; and finally, 4) the renovated Lumbini Garden where the Mayadevi temple, its sacred pond, and the Ashoka pillar have attracted visitors for millennia. An ornamental canal, fed by the Telar River, was also part of the plan. Meanwhile, Mr. Bidari continued, in 770 hectares of land, 650,000 plants and trees of more than 40 species had been planted.

He then invited me to step out of his rather dark office into the bright sunshine. We faced north, towards the Himalayas which were veiled by the dust rising from the vast Gangetic plain that lay to our south in India. Mr. Bidari stretched out his hand and made a grand sweep. He said, "There is a purity of vision in Mr. Tange's design. As visitors arrive, they first enter the worldly domain of Lumbini. Food and accommodations that satisfy the basic, daily requirements of humans. After the physical necessities are satisfied, they move into the intellectual world of books, libraries, museums, seminars, conferences, lectures, and so on; then they enter the religious realm to meet monks and worship at monasteries, in preparation to enter the sacred zone—the ancient tree under which Mayadevi gave birth to Siddartha, the pond where he was first bathed, the temple itself, and Emperor Ashoka's pillar. Now you will notice that beyond all this, the Himalayas beckon, the final destination for those brave enough to renounce this world of *Maya,* of illusion, and pursue the path of enlightenment—and thus become a Buddha. After all, the historical Buddha of Lumbini was

one of many. There were others before him, and others to come."
Mr. Bidari looked at me and smiled sweetly.

"Can you tell me something about that mosque I saw just before we arrived in Lumbini?" I asked.

"Well, it makes perfect sense when you consider that sixty percent of the population in the Lumbini region are Muslims, not
Hindus, and very few Buddhists!"

When I discreetly brought up the topic of my father's rage—
corruption—he did not dodge it as others had.

"Again, we must keep in mind that there were people living in
this area before. Seven villages had to be resettled. There were no
facilities—no roads, electricity, telephone, or piped water. So whoever was in charge of Lumbini's development, whether the Trust
or the government, it could not just come in and start 'development.' It takes a lot of time and money to convince people to leave
their homes, and just as long to set up modern facilities. This is not
to say that things couldn't have moved more quickly in the past or
that there were some dishonest officials."

It was time to leave, and I thanked Mr. Bidari. I was planning to
visit Tilaurakot, the site of ancient Kapilvastu. A friend in Lumbini
had offered me his motorcycle for the day. Before meeting him, I
decided to wander around this emerging "new" Lumbini of the
Master Plan. Mr. Bidari's office building was within the Sacred
Garden area. And all around there was ceaseless activity which unsettled me. I felt crowded, not the quiet, isolated serenity I had experienced during my previous visits when I would sit and gaze at
the mountains beyond.

The Mayadevi temple was wrapped in bright yellow tarp because it was being renovated with the assistance of the Japan
Buddhist Federation. A sign in English said: NO PHOTOGRAPHY.
Devotees entered an ugly, single-story building with a tin roof that
temporarily housed a replica of the original *Child Buddha, Mother,
and Attendants* nativity statue that was in the Mayadevi temple. The
original was somewhere for safe-keeping, but no one seemed to
know exactly where. There had also been an uproar when the sacred Bodhi tree was cut down because its ancient roots were dam-

aging the temple building. The sacred pond's stagnant water was murky but the stone steps around it were neatly swept. At nearby Ashoka pillar, tattered prayer flags fluttered weakly around the shoulder-high iron fence that protected the pillar. These were the ancient icons that had once identified the open, seemingly empty land as the birthplace of the Buddha. Even a casual visit here had produced serenity if not, however briefly, a tug towards religiosity.

In the first few centuries after the Buddha's death he was never shown iconographically; hence the empty niches in early chaityas. At most he was represented by a pair of footprints.

—Michael Hutt,
Nepal: A Guide to the Art and Architecture of the Kathmandu Valley

Before there had been silence and stillness, but now noise and purposeful activity. There were skinny, dark-skinned laborers digging or chipping around archaeological sites. They carried loads on their heads or in clattering wheelbarrows; squatting women hammered rocks into pieces as their babies crawled around them; managers of the Master Plan warmed themselves in sunny porches and open courtyards of their office buildings, smoking cigarettes and talking loudly, no doubt discussing the intricacies of implementing the grand plan. Pious but impatient pilgrims jostled each other as they entered the various temples to worship.

In a shady grove, a family was enjoying a picnic. As I walked past them towards an old pilgrim's rest house, I slipped on an abandoned plastic bag that had been camouflaged by fallen leaves. The entire grove was full of discarded papers and plastic bags.

Above the entrance to an old stucco rest house, yet another notice in three languages (Nepali, Hindi, and English): KILLING BEAST AND DRINKING WINE ALCOHAL IS STRICTLY PROHIBITED. In Nepali and Hindi, the sign also forbade the consumption of fish and any kind of narcotics, including marijuana.

Beyond the ancient landmarks, new construction littered the landscape. The ornamental canal was partially dug up, bordered by brittle green bush; stagnant pools of water collected at haphazard intervals, challenging the mind to imagine a serenely flowing waterway. Sturdy cement and brick structures with intriguing tubular shapes loomed above dry greenery. When I passed the site of the Eternal Flame, I was actually surprised to find it lit. It flickered from within a black, circular container that rested upon a square platform of white marble. This is when I decided I had enough. It was time to pick up the motorcycle and ride to Tilaurakot.

I headed directly west, another twenty kilometers, on rough, bouldery road. Now that I was beyond the tourist-and-pilgrim area, the landscape was truly rural. Except for an occasional public bus or a tractor, bullock carts and bicycles ruled the road; but most walked, and their bare feet had shaped their own smooth "sidewalk."

I passed villages and bustling bazaar towns where I was forced to walk my motorcycle to navigate among vast gatherings of bullock carts, and it was suicidal to assert the power of the machine when women, children, dogs, horses, and cattle darted around. Yellow mustard fields and golden ripening wheat broke the monotony of the flat agricultural land. Sometimes, an entire family was at work. Young children bent over as they cut the stalk with a scythe, the mother gathered the cut crop and handed it to the father who loaded it into the bullock cart.

Tilaurakot was the perfect antidote to the grand activity of Lumbini; it was quiet, wooded—and empty. A flimsy wire fence enclosed the archaeological site, and at the entrance, a billboard identified the area as "the remains of ancient Kapilvastu, the Shakya capital." A man in khaki dress, claiming he was the guard, attached himself to me as I entered the forested enclave. He started to act officious, but stopped short when I spoke to him in the local dialect. I told him my grandparents lived in nearby Taulihawa and that I had visited this site since the early 1960s when a group of Japanese university students had arrived to dig up the ruins. The guard became quiet and followed me as I wandered around.

I first visited the temple devoted to a local goddess. An ancient *pipal* tree grew behind it and its roots and branches had penetrated the crumbling brick walls of the square structure; it had no roof and a narrow opening for an entrance. Nothing had changed in this temple since my childhood visits. Even its process of collapse had been arrested, it seemed, and despite its dilapidation, there was something ineffable and dignified about it, commanding reverence and awe that one reserves for one's aging but redoubtable relatives. No doubt, I thought, when and if development descended upon Tilaurakot, there would be a bright yellow tarp around the temple and the venerable tree would be chopped up for firewood.

Archaeological finds were scattered about in clearings—low brick walls around shallow rectangular spaces that suggested rooms of buildings; low, round mounds that were the remains of stupas perhaps. Incongruously bright cherry-red bricks had recently been added on top of the older ruins. These sites were well-tended; the grass that grew in the open enclosures had been cut and the exposed walls were free of weeds. Next to another carefully pre-served site, a signboard declared in English and Nepali that it was the remains of the "EASTERN GATEWAY...FROM WHICH LORD BUDDHA LEFT HIS WORLDLY LIFE..." Objects such as coins, bangles, beads, a seal, and "shards of some polished wares" had also been discovered here. Digs had unearthed a moat, defense walls, the western gate, terra-cotta human and animal figurines, and pottery dating as far back as the 8th century B.C.

While the ruins were important, it was the natural surroundings that enchanted me. The trees of this forest were thick and sturdy, their branches heavy with glossy leaves. Birds called out and invis-ible forest creatures scurried about. Away from the carefully-tended ruins, nature was left to take its own course.

It was not a large enclosure. One could traverse its widest point in a few minutes. Its attraction was its state of benign neglect, its isolation from pilgrims, scholars, and tourists. During my half-hour stroll, only one person had entered the site, and he had come to worship at the temple.

I asked the guard if the government or any foreigners were con-tinuing to work there. He said no because there was no money in the "budget."

As I prepared to depart, I noticed a cluster of peasants' fragile mud-and-thatch huts nearby. I paused and looked at it carefully, and it occurred to me that this settlement could have easily existed from the days of Buddha himself. Bony cattle were tied by rough rope to a low wooden stake; the villagers' cooking fuel, a patty of cow dung mixed with straw, were stuck to the mud walls to dry. Papaya and banana trees towered over the low huts, and round pumpkins rested on thatched roofs like abandoned soccer balls. Both the men and women were lean and dark; the children wore ragged clothing, and the babies were plump but naked. I thought: take away the paved road, the distant electric pole and its wires fragmenting the sky, the occasional motorized vehicle, and should the Buddha return right now, he would feel at home instantly. To me, it was now Tilaurakot much more than Lumbini that genuinely evoked the life and times of the Buddha.

Before I headed back to Lumbini, I had one final destination. I had to visit an aunt of mine who lived in Taulihawa. My mother had told me to drop in ("even if you don't have time for a cup of tea") because my aunt had fallen into hard times lately.

She had grown even stouter—and she had always been teased for being fat. Her hair was gray and stringy, her skin wrinkled, and her eyes, dull and lifeless. Her house was a squat, square cement structure of the "bungalow" style. Nobody else was there, so it felt hollow, cold and lonely. She cheered up briefly when I said, to tease her, that she appeared quite thin. Since I had declined her invitation to have dinner, she insisted that I have tea. As she struggled with a banged up primus stove, I poured water from a plastic bucket into a blackened kettle. As we waited for the water to boil, I carefully inquired about her husband, her son, and his wife. She laughed heartily and said, "Surely your mother has told you about us..." and did not elaborate.

Yes, my mother had, and thus my visit. The son had quarreled with the parents over their extensive land holdings. Eventually, he had forced his parents out of the farm and the large rambling house they lived in. Now that he was the *zamindar*, the landlord, he would modernize the farm and make it profitable. So here was my aunt, in a town full of relatives who gossiped, without servants or farm hands to fulfill her whims. All alone. Her husband, meanwhile, dabbled in politics and was always away visiting "his people," the future voters.

As the tea steeped, she quickly cracked an egg in a pan and presented me with tea *and* fried egg. She had always been accused of being indolent, insensitive to the needs of her husband and children. Now I marveled at how quickly and efficiently she had prepared this meal for me. But I had seen enough and had nothing more to say. It was getting late, and pleading the arrival of winter's early darkness, I departed hurriedly, guiltily.

I felt better once I was back on the empty dirt road. It was just before sunset, perhaps the loveliest moment in the *tarai*. The sun was a flaming orange ball on the horizon, bathing the entire landscape in a warm pink and crimson glow. A cool breeze fanned my face. Occasionally, I'd pass cattle and goats kicking up a fine cloud of dust as they were herded home.

I thought about my aunt and how events in her life exemplified Buddha's message of the wheel of life. Of all her sisters, she had been married into the wealthiest family. And for many years, she lived a rich, idyllic family life. An then slowly, inexorably, it had begun to fall apart. The source of her misery was her son's greed. But this is nothing new, of course; it is the eternal human drama, that impermanence of our human condition brought about by our ceaseless desires which in turn produce boundless suffering. And as the motorcycle purred on the road back to Lumbini, the words and life of Buddha felt more immediate than ever.

In Lumbini, I inquired about the *pedas*, but was told that Bhairawa had better *pedas* these days.

Rajendra S. Khadka was born and raised in Nepal. He lives in Berkeley, California, and is a staff member of Travelers' Tales.

*

Minutes later, I heard an incongruous honking. I opened my eyes and saw through the open doors of the Lumbini temple that the noise was coming from a beeping black minibus. The panel door opened and out streamed fourteen Japanese Zen monks wearing billowing black robes. Around each neck hung a camera. They fluttered into the temple hall like a flock of crows, clicking their lenses at everything that glittered—the statues, the banners, the frescos, pillars, butter offerings. One of them discovered me, flashed a bulb and brought the others, back robes flapping, as if I were carrion. For a moment, I dwelt at the center of a lightning storm. Then, as one, they flew out of the temple to rob the sparse images of the Theravada hall as well. With equal thoroughness they photographed the pillar and every reconstructed wall of the pseudo-site. In 40 minutes, start to finish, they were back in their minibus, and roaring down the road. Like good Zen monks, they had grasped the essence of Lumbini far more profoundly than I: it is all emptiness; that is why one venerates it.

—Tim Ward, *Arousing the Goddess*

* * *

A Simple Gift

Sometimes East and West do meet.

IT WAS ALMOST WINTER, AND NEARING THE END OF MY STAY IN Nepal, much of my time was occupied with saying good-bye. I had gotten to know many new people on this particular visit, but those persons whom I most actively sought out were those whom I had gotten to know the least.

They were waiters, merchants, black-market money changers; they were little children and old women who sold single cigarettes and matches along damp, narrow streets. I certainly did not know these people as one knows a friend or even an acquaintance, but for the past several months they had been my landmarks along countless streets and in innumerable restaurants, and they were by now as familiar to me as any back home. It was this collection of faces, brief greetings and equally brief conversations that always endeared Nepal to me.

Upon finding one of these persons prior to my departure, I rarely would actually say good-bye. Instead, I found that all I really wanted to do was just look at them once more; to memorize them in their world, perhaps foolishly thinking that the moment could later be recalled with the same life and clarity as the original.

Sometimes, in my marginal Nepali, I would say that I am returning to my own country. Most often the reply was simply a smile, accompanied by the characteristic little sideways nod of the head which in Nepal means understanding. And that was all.

One person with whom I did speak was an old man I used to see almost every day. He seemed to spend most of his time just sitting in the sun on a small, raised wooden platform next to an outdoor marketplace where aggressive women with clumps of wrinkled and faded rupees in their fists deftly negotiated the cacophonous buying and selling of fruits and vegetables.

The first time I saw him he smiled at me. He said nothing, nor did I stop to speak with him. I recall giving him a rather cursory smile in return, and then continued on my way without another thought. A few days later I saw him again, still seated in the same place. As I passed him he smiled at me again just as he had before. I was taken by how sincere this man's expression was, and also how peaceful he seemed to be. I smiled back and offered the traditional *namaste*, which he returned. I could not quite explain why, but it was that ingenuous smile of his that many times made me detour just to see him and say hello.

Eventually I found that he spoke a few words of English, and sometimes we would have a cigarette together and exchange pleasantries. Sometimes, after dinner, I would walk through the silent streets that were now only sporadically lit by the weak light filtering through greasy restaurant windows. Then I would come upon him, still seated in the same place. He would be sitting quietly, smoking, and sometimes drinking tea out of the ubiquitous glass tumbler that someone had probably bought for him.

One evening, on my way back to my room after dinner, I saw him in his usual spot, and I stopped to say hello. For the first time since I had known him, I glimpsed his feet protruding from under the rough woolen blanket that always covered him. They were severely misshapen and deeply ulcerated, and the toes were unusually short and seemed strangely small for his feet. I remembered having seen similar symptoms during a brief stint of clinical work I had done several years earlier. No doubt it was very difficult for this man to walk, and it was now apparent why so much of his time was spent sitting. He had leprosy.

Some time after this I again stopped to greet him. He smiled and appeared glad to see me. We spoke easily now; he in his broken English, and I in my fractured Nepali. Out of respect I now called him *daju,* or "older brother," as is the custom. The first time I addressed him as *daju* his expression did not change, but from then on he called me *bhai,* or "younger brother," as though he had been doing so for years.

I cannot explain the feeling, but there has always been something exquisitely heartwarming about being referred to as "*bhai*" or "*daju*" by the Nepalis. Perhaps these words were intended to convey nothing more than simple courtesy to a foreigner, but countless times I have been struck by the intimacy these words implied, and the genuine affection with which they were spoken.

We talked for a few more minutes, and when I left I gave him a couple of cigarettes wrapped in a five-rupee note. He accepted this graciously and with dignity. I said good-bye, but resolved to continue to see him until I had to leave.

This I did, and in the course of my last few days in Kathmandu we would talk frequently. I would do as much as I could manage in Nepali, but we usually relied considerably more on English. We sometimes had a glass of tea together in the pale afternoon sun, limiting our conversation to superficial things, but enjoying it nevertheless.

It gets cold at night in November, and prior to leaving I wanted to bring the old man a pair of heavy woolen socks that I had brought for use in the mountains. On my last night in Nepal, I found him sitting in his usual place. It was a very cold night. I approached him and said that tomorrow I was leaving. I then said that I wished to give him my socks. He said nothing. I felt awkward, and as gently as I could I lifted the blanket that covered his legs. I put the socks on what remained of his feet and tried to explain that I would be pleased if he would keep them.

For a long moment he did not speak. I feared that I might have made him uncomfortable, but then he looked at me with marvelous compassion in his eyes and said, "God bless you, *bhai*. No one has touched me in a very long time."

Robert Matthews's first trip to Nepal was a logical extension of his lifelong interest in climbing and hiking. However, it was the rich character and spirit of the Nepali people that was responsible for his subsequent visits. He continues to write and teach mathematics in San Francisco where he lives with his cat, and is sustained by an uninterrupted supply of French bread.

✳

The perfume of sandalwood,
Rosebay or jasmine
Cannot travel against the wind.
But the fragrance of virtue
Travels even against the wind,
As far as the ends of the world
and rises to the heavens.

—*The Dhammapada*

PART THREE

GOING YOUR OWN WAY

PETER MATTHIESSEN

* * *

Shey Monastery

A sacred spot renews the spirit.

THIS BLACK POND CAMP, THOUGH WELL BELOW THE KANG PASS, lies at an altitude of 17,000 feet, and an hour after the sun sinks behind the peaks, my wet boots have turned to blocks of ice. GS's thermometer registers –20 degrees Centigrade (4 degrees below zero Fahrenheit) and though I wear everything I have, I quake with cold all night. Dawn comes at last, but making hot water from a pot of ice is difficult at this altitude, and it is past nine before boots are thawed and we are under way.

The snow bowl is the head of an ice river that descends a deep canyon to Shey. In the canyon we meet Jang-bu and Phu-Tsering, on their way up to fetch some food and pots: Dawa, they say, is down again with acute snow blindness.

Sherpa tracks in the frozen shadows follow the glassy boulders of the stream edge, and somewhere along the way I slip, losing the hoopoe feather that adorned my cap. The river falls steeply, for Shey lies 3,000 feet below Kang La, and in the deep snow, the going is so treacherous that the sherpas have made no path; each man flounders through the drifts as best he can. Eventually, from a high corner of the canyon, rough red-brown lumps of human habitation come in view. The monastery stands like a small fort on

175

a bluff where another river flows in from the east; a mile below, the rivers vanish into a deep and dark ravine. Excepting the lower slopes of the mountainside behind the monastery, which is open to the south, most of this treeless waste lies under snow, broken here and there by calligraphic patterns of bare rock, in an atmosphere so wild and desolate as to overwhelm the small huddle of dwellings.

High to the west, a white pyramid sails on the sky—the Crystal Mountain. In summer, this monument of rock is a shrine for pilgrims from all over Dolpo and beyond, who come here to make a prescribed circle around the Crystal Mountain and attend a holy festival at Shey. What is stirring about this peak, in snow time, is its powerful shape, which even today, with no clouds passing, makes it appear to be forging through the blue. "The power of such a mountain is so great and yet so subtle that, without compulsion, people are drawn to it from near and far, as if by the force of some invisible magnet; and they will undergo untold hardships and privations in their inexplicable urge to approach and to worship the centre of this sacred power.... This worshipful or religious attitude is not impressed by scientific facts, like figures of altitude, which are foremost in the mind of modern man. Nor is it motivated by the urge to 'conquer' the mountain...." [Lama Angarika Govinda in *The Way of the White Clouds.*]

> *Whether Machapuchare is indeed a sacred mountain is anybody's guess, but when I saw a poster of it in a friend's Berkeley apartment, my knees buckled, and I knew I had to go back to Nepal. Beholding the mountain itself, in a pink Pokhara dawn, completed a journey that had in fact begun on paper, and yet I could not gaze on it enough, as though it slaked an unending thirst.*
>
> —James O'Reilly,
> "Stairway to Heaven"

A gravel island under Shey is reached by crossing ice and stones of a shallow channel. At the island's lower end are prayer walls and a stone stockade for animals; farther on, small conduits divert a flow of river water to a group of prayer mills in the form of waterwheels, each one housed separately in its own stone shrine. The conduits are frozen and the wheels are still. On top of the small stupas are offerings of white quartz crystals, presumably taken from the Crystal Mountain in the summer, when the five wheels spin five ancient prayer drums, sending OM MANI PADME HUM down the cold canyon.

On the far side of a plank bridge, a path climbs the bank to two big red-and-white entrance stupas on the bluff: I go up slowly. Prayer flags snap thinly on the wind, and a wind-bell has a wooden wing in the shape of a half-moon that moves the clapper; over the glacial rumble on the river stones, the wistful ring on the light wind is the first sound that is heard here at Shey Gompa.

The cluster of a half-dozen stone houses is stained red, in sign that Shey is a monastery, not a village. Another group of five small houses sits higher up the mountain; above this hamlet, a band of blue sheep may be seen with the naked eye. Across the river to the north, stuck on a cliff face at the portals of the canyon, is a red hermitage. Otherwise, except for prayer walls and the stone corrals, there are only the mighty rock formations and dry treeless mountainside where snow has melted, and the snow and sky.

I move on slowly, dull in mind and body. Gazing back up the Black River toward the rampart of icy cornices, I understand that we have come over the Kanjirobas to the mountain deserts of the Tibetan Plateau: we have crossed the Himalaya from south to north. But not until I had to climb this short steep path from the wintry river to the bluffs did I realize how tired I was after 35 days of hard trekking. And here I am, on this first day of November, standing before the Crystal Monastery, with its strange stones and flags and bells under the snows.

The monastery temple with its attached houses forms a sort of open court facing the south. Two women and two infants, sitting in the sun, make no sign of welcome. The younger woman is weaving a rough cloth on an ancient loom. When I say, "*Namaste!*" she repeats it, as if trying the word out. Three scraggy *dzos* and an old black nanny goat excepted, these are the only sentient beings left at Shey, which its inhabitants call *Somdo,* or "Confluence," because of the meeting of rivers beneath its bluff—the *Kangju,*

"Snow Waters" (the one I think of as Black River, because of the black pond at its head, and the black eagle, and the black patterns of its stones and ice in the dark canyon), and the *Yeju,* "Low Waters" (which I shall call White River, because it comes down from the eastern snows).

For cooking hut and storeroom, Jang-bu has appropriated the only unlocked dwelling. Like all the rest, it has a flat roof of clay and saplings piled on top with brushwood, a small wooden door into the single room, and a tiny window in the western wall to catch afternoon light. The solitary ray of light, as in a medieval painting, illumines the smoke-blackened posts that support the roof, which is so low that GS and I must bend half-over. The earth floor is bare, except for a clay oven built-up in three points to hold a pot, with a hole near the floor to blow life into the smoky fire of dung and brushwood. Jang-bu and Phu-Tsering's tent is just outside the door, while Dawa will sleep inside with supplies. GS pitches his blue tent just uphill from the hut, while I place mine some distance away, facing east up the White River toward the sunrise.

The cooking hut is the sometime dwelling of the brother of the younger woman, Tasi Chanjun, whom the sherpas call Namu, meaning hostess. (Among Tibetans as among native Americans, it is often rude to address people by their formal name.) Her little boy, aged about four, is Karma Chambel, and her daughter, perhaps two, is Nyima Poti. *Nyima* means "sun" or "sunny"—Sunny Poti! The old woman's name is Sonam: her husband, Chang Rapke, and her daughter Karima Poti have gone away to winter in Saldang, and Sonam lives alone in the abandoned hamlet up the mountain. Namu says that before the snows there were 40 people here, including twenty-odd monks and two lamas: all are gone across the mountains to Saldang, from where—is this a warning to outlandish men who come here without women?—her husband will return in a few days. Namu's husband has the key to the Crystal Monastery, or so she says, and will doubtless bring it with him when he comes to visit in four or five days, or in twenty. Namu is perhaps 30 years old and pretty in a sturdy way, and self-dependent. She speaks familiarly of B'od but not Nepal; even Ring-mo is a foreign land, far away across Kang La.

That the Lama is gone is very disappointing. Nevertheless, we are extremely happy to be here, all the more so since it often seemed that we would never arrive at all. Now we can wake up in the morning without having to put on wet boots, break camp, get people moving; and there is home to return to in the evening. There are no porters harassing our days, and we are sheltered, more or less, from evil weather. The high pass between Shey and the outside world lies in the snow peaks, ghostly now in the light of the cold stars. "God, I'm glad I'm not up there tonight," GS exclaims, as we emerge from the smoky hut, our bellies warm with lentil soup. We know how fortunate it was that the Kang Pass was crossed in this fine, windless weather, and wonder how long fair skies will hold, and if Tukten and Gyaltsen will appear. It is November now, and everything depends upon the snows.

At almost 15,000 feet, Shey is as high as the Jang Pass. It is located in what has been described as Inner Dolpo, which is walled off from eastern Dolpo by a surrounding crescent of high peaks, and must be one of the highest inhabited areas on earth. Its people are of pure Tibetan stock, with a way of life that cannot differ much from that of the Ch'ang Tarters out of Central Asia who are thought to have been the original Tibetans, and their speech echoes the tongue of nomads who may have arrived 2,000 years ago. Dolpo was formerly a part of western Tibet, and it is certain that some form of Buddhism came here early. Beyond the Karnali River, to the north and west, the Tibetan Plateau rises to Kailas, the holy "Mount Sumeru" or "Meru" of Hindus and Buddhists, home of Shiva and the Center of the world; from Mount Kailas, four great rivers—the Karnali, the Indus, the Sutlej, and the Brahmaputra—flow down in a great mandala to the Indian seas.

Shey Gompa (in Tibetan, Shel dgon-pa) is a monastery of the Kagyu sect, which was established in the 11th century as a departure from the Kalachakra Tantrism of the Old Sect, or Nyingma…. The Lama of Shey is a notable *tulku*, or incarnate

lama, revered throughout the Land of Dolpo as the present reincarnation of the Lama Marpa. On my way here, I entertained visions of myself in monkish garb attending the Lama in his ancient
mysteries, and getting to light the butter lamps into the bargain; I
suppose I had hoped he would be my teacher. That the *gompa* is
locked and the Lama gone away might be read as a karmic repri-
mand to spiritual ambition, a silent teaching to this ego that still
insists upon itself, like the poor bleat of a goat on the north wind.

Last night, the temperature sank to -13 degrees Centigrade and
a strong east wind rattled my tent: this morning I move the tent
into the stockyard of an empty house. On the corral walls lie some
excellent stone carvings, one of them portraying Tara (in Tibetan,
Dölma), born of the compassionate tear of Avalokita (Chen-resigs)
and the embodiment of the Bodhisattva spirit. As the feminine aspect of Chen-resigs, Dölma is the great "Protectress" of Tibet, and
so I am pleased to find her on my wall.

The temple is distinguished from the buildings that abut it on
both sides by the ceremonial raised entrance under a roofed porch
and the abundant ornaments upon the roof, which include prayer
flags, tritons, the great horns of an argali, and the gigantic antlers
of a Sikkim stag, a creature of northern Bhutan and southeastern
Tibet. (Since neither animal is supposed to occur here, GS is fascinated by the origins of these horns and antlers, especially since the
Sikkim stag is said to be extinct.)

Although the *gompa* is locked tight, the two large stupas on the
bluff over the river bridge give a clue to the iconography within.
Perhaps thirty feet high, they have the typical square red base and
red-garlanded white dome, with a tapering cone topped by a lunar
crown and solar disc. On the four sides of the base are crude clay
frescoes of symbolic creatures—elephants on the east face, horses
south, peacocks west, and on the north face the *garuda*, or mythical hawk, here represented as a man with wings bearing what appears to be the sun and moon. The *garuda*, like the swastikas inside
the stupa, is a pre-Buddhist symbol, and so is the ying-yang sym-

bol on the door, which is thought to antedate the early Taoism of
3,000 years ago in China.

In the small chamber inside
one stupa are two rows of ancient prayer wheels, five to a row,
set up in such a way that ten
rounds of OM MANI PADME HUM
may be turned simultaneously by
visitors; each wheel represents
the Wheel of Dharma, first set in
motion by the Buddha, and also
the rotation of the Universe. On
walls and ceilings are bright-
painted mandalas and Buddhas,
including Samantabhadra and
Padma Sambhava, he who
scourged the demoness at
Phoksumdo Lake, depicted here
in his fierce Kalachakra "Tiger-
God" aspect, as a protector of the
Dharma. A benign presence with
four hands, bearing a string of pearls, a lotus, and the blue orb or
mani that signifies compassion, is Avalokita, or Chen-resigs.
Presiding over all is Dorje-Chang, Holder of the *Dorje*, or "thun-
derbolt," the adamantine diamond, symbol of cosmic energy distilled. Dorje-Chang (Vajradhara) is the primordial Buddha of
Tibet, who transmitted the Dharma to the great Indian sage
Tilopa, and thus began a celebrated succession of reincarnations—
from Tilopa to Naropa to Lama Marpa the Translator to Milarepa,
and so forth, to the present day. He also appears outside on a dome
fresco with the Pleiades and black sickle moon over his shoulder;
his sky-blue color signifies his eternal nature, and he carries a bell
that represents the perfect sound of voiceless wisdom. Beside the
dome perches a wind-bell, and its very small clear song, in shifts of
air, seems to deepen the vast silence of this place.

*The base of a stupa, also
called* chaitya *or*
chorten, *represents the earth, the
dome symbolizes water and the
tapering spire, fire. The square
structure on top of the dome where
the "Buddha eyes" are painted is
known as the* harmika. *On a
larger, more elaborate stupa such
as Swyambhu in Kathmandu, the
tower-like midsection has thirteen
rings or steps and they represent
thirteen steps of perfection. On
top of it, the sun (representing
space) rests on a crescent moon
(representing air). The crowning
touch is a parasol, symbolizing
royalty.*

—RK

The second stupa is of like size and character, and between these stupas and the monastery houses, heaped up into a platform five feet high, is a whole field of carved slabs, thousands upon thousands, by far the greatest assemblage of prayer stones that I have ever seen, before or since. OM MANI PADME HUM is the commonest inscription, but there are also wheels of life, carved Buddhas, and quotations from liturgical texts, heap upon heap. The stones vary in weight from ten pounds to several hundred; some are recent, while on others, the inscriptions are worn to shadow by the elements, and all of these conceal the masses more that lie beneath. In addition, a great wall of these stones nearly encircles the monastery and its adjoining houses as well as a group of smaller stupas on the northern side, and there are extensive prayer-stone walls on the river island and along the paths as well. The prayer stones at the bottom of these walls must be many centuries old. Though nobody seems to know who lived here when the first of them were made, the great accumulation of old stones in the Shey region supports the idea that the Crystal Mountain is a very ancient shrine of Tibetan Buddhism, and perhaps B'on before it. Samling Monastery, not far north of this mountain, is an old redoubt of B'on and the repository of B'on's most ancient texts, and I like to imagine that this archaic kingdom might be none other than the Kingdom of Sh'ang-Sh'ung that the B'on-pos claim as the home of their religion. That Sh'ang-Sh'ung is deemed "mythical" may be discounted: the Land of Dolpo is not found in the geographies, and it seems mythical even to such people as myself, who like to imagine they have been here....

There is so much that enchants me in this spare, silent place that I move softly so as not to break a spell. Because the taking of life has been forbidden by the Lama of Shey, bharal and wolves alike draw near the monastery. On the hills and in the stone beds of the river are fossils from blue ancient days when all this soaring rock lay beneath the sea. And all about are the prayer stones, prayer flags, prayer wheels, and prayer mills in the torrent, calling on all the elements in nature to join in celebration of the One. What I hear from my tent is a delicate wind-bell and the river from the east, in this easterly wind that may bring a change in the weather. At day-break, two great ravens come, their long toes scratching on the prayer walls.

The sun refracts from the white glaze of the mountains, chills the air. Old Sonam, who lives alone in the hamlet up the hill, was on the mountain before day, gathering the summer's dung to dry and store as cooking fuel; what I took for lumpish matter straightens on the sky as the sun rises, setting her gaunt silhouette afire.

Eleven sheep are visible on the Somdo slope above the monastery, six rams together and a group of ewes and young; though the bands begin to draw near to one another and sniff urine traces, there is no real sign of rut. From our lookout above Sonam's house, three more groups—six, fourteen, and twenty-six—can be seen on the westward slopes, across Black River.

Unable to hold the scope on the restless animals, GS calls out to me to shift the binoculars from the band of fourteen to the group of six sheep, directly across the river from our lookout. "Why are those sheep run-

In 1820 a Mr. Brian Hodgson was appointed assistant to the [British] resident. His diplomatic coups, if any, have long since been forgotten, but his name lives on as a naturalist. Not permitted to leave Kathmandu Valley, he sent native collectors into the hills, and among a number of new species brought back by them are some which now bear Hodgson's name—including a redstart, a tree pipit, and a hawk cuckoo. In 1833 Hodgson first described the peculiar blue sheep, a species whose behavior I was to study 140 years later.

—George B. Schaller, *Stones of Silence: Journeys in the Himalaya*

ning?" he demands, and a moment later hollers, "Wolves!" All six sheep are springing for the cliffs, but a pair of wolves coming straight downhill are cutting off the rearmost animal as it bounds across a stretch of snow toward the ledges. In the hard light, the blue-gray creature seems far too swift to catch, yet the streaming wolves gain ground on the hard snow. Then they are whisking through the matted juniper and down over steepening rocks, and it appears that the *bharal* will be cut off and bowled over, down the mountain, but at the last moment it scoots free and gains a narrow ledge where no wolf can follow.

In the frozen air, the whole mountain is taut; the silence rings. The sheep's flanks quake, and the wolves are panting; otherwise, all is still, as if the arrangement of pale shapes held the world together. Then I breathe, and the mountain breathes, setting the world in motion once again.

Briefly, the wolves gaze about, then make their way up the mountainside in the unhurried gait that may carry them fifty miles in a single day. Two pack mates join them, and in high yak pasture the four pause to romp and roll in dung. Two of these were not among the five seen yesterday, and we recall that the old woman had seen seven. Then they trot onward, disappearing behind a ridge of snow. The band of fourteen sheep high on this ridge gives a brief run of alarm, then forms a line on a high point to stare down at the wolves and watch them go. Before long, all are browsing once again, including the six that were chased onto the precipice.

Turning to speak, we just shake our heads and grin. "It was worth walking five weeks just to see that," GS sighs at last. "That was the most exciting wolf hunt I ever saw...."

Condemned by cold to spend twelve hours in my sleeping bag each night, I find myself inclined to my Zen practice. Each morning before daybreak, I drag my down parka into my sleeping bag, to warm it, then sit up in meditation posture and perform a *sutra* chanting service for perhaps 45 minutes, including the *sutra* dedicated to Kannon or Avalokita, and the Heart Sutra (the "heart" of the mighty Prajna Paramita Sutra that lies at the base of Mahayana Buddhism). This morning service is lent dignity by a clay *ts'a ts'a* Buddha taken from the piles of these small icons that litter the stupas at Ring-mo—that it may be "B'on" seems of small importance. I place the figure outside the tent on an altar of flat stone, where it will receive the first of the eastern light, down the White River, and I sit bundled up just inside the flap, for at this hour the temperature is never more than -12 degrees Centigrade. Sometimes I am joined for morning service by a hardy little bird that dwells in the brush piles on the roof of the pink stone house behind the tent. With flicking tail, it hunts among the dung chips near the Buddha; the bill is slim in a pale-gray head, and it has a rufous breast and a white belly. This is the robin accentor (*Prunella*)....

For the first time since September, GS is entirely happy. Like myself, he is stunned by Shey, which has more than repaid the long, hard journey; he scribbles his data even while he eats. I keep thinking, How extraordinary!—knowing that this adjective is inadequate and somehow inaccurate, as well....

The nights at Shey are rigid, under rigid stars; the fall of a wolf pad on the frozen path might be heard up and down the canyon. But a hard wind comes before the dawn to rattle the tent canvas, and this morning it is clear again, and colder. At daybreak, the White River, just below, is sheathed in ice, with scarcely a murmur from the stream beneath.

The two ravens come to tritons on the *gompa* roof. *Gorawk, gorawk*, they croak, and this is the name given to them by the sherpas. Amidst the prayer flags and great horns of Tibetan argali, the gorawks greet first light with an odd musical double note—*a-ho*—that emerges as if by miracle from those ragged throats. Before sunrise every day, the great black birds are gone, like the last tatters of departing night.

The sun rising at the head of the White River brings a suffused glow to the tent canvas, and the robin accentor flits away across the frozen yard. At seven, there is breakfast in the cook hut—tea and porridge—and after breakfast on most days I watch sheep with GS, parting company with him after a while, when the sheep lie down, to go off on some expedition of my own. Often I scan the caves and ledges on the far side of Black River in the hope of [snow] leopard; I am alert for fossils, wolves, and birds. Sometimes I observe the sky and mountains, and sometimes I sit in meditation, doing my best to empty out my mind, to attain that state in which everything is "at rest, free, and immortal.... All things abided eternally as they were in their proper places...something infinite behind everything appeared." (No Buddhist said this, but a 17th-century Briton.) And soon all sounds, and all one sees and feels, take on imminence, an immanence, as if the Universe were coming to attention, a Universe of which one is the center, a Universe that is not the same and yet not different from oneself, even from a scientific point of view: within man as within mountains there are many parts of hydrogen and oxygen, of calcium, phosphorus, potassium, and other elements. "You never enjoy the world aright, till the Sea itself flows in your veins, till you are clothed with the heavens, and crowned with the stars: and perceive yourself to be the sole heir of the whole world, and more than so, because men are in it who are every one sole heirs as well as you." [Thomas Traherne in *Centuries of Meditation*.]

Never ending beauty
Everlasting drama
Promise
Always waiting
Listen to the secrets of the wind.

—Anna O'Reilly, age 12

I have a meditation place on Somdo mountain, a broken rock outcrop like an altar set in the hillside, protected from all but the south wind by shards of granite and dense thorn. In the full sun it is warm, and its rock crannies give shelter to small stunted plants that cling to this desert mountainside—dead red-brown stalks of a wild buckwheat (*Polygonum*), some shrubby cinquefoil, pale edelweiss, and everlasting, and even a few poor wisps of *cannabis*. I arrange a rude rock seat as a lookout on the world, set out binoculars in case wild creatures should happen into view, then cross my legs and regulate my breath, until I scarcely breathe at all.

Now the mountains all around me take on life; the Crystal Mountain moves. Soon there comes the murmur of the torrent, from far away below under the ice: it seems impossible that I can hear this sound. Even in windlessness, the sound of rivers comes and goes and falls and rises, like the wind itself. An instinct comes to open outward by letting all life in, just as a flower fills with sun. To burst forth from this old husk and cast one's energy abroad, to fly....

Although I am not conscious of emotion, the mind-opening brings a soft mist to my eyes. Then the mist passes, the cold wind clears my head, and body-mind comes and goes on the light air. A sun-filled Buddha. One day I shall meditate in falling snow.

I lower my gaze from the snow peaks to the glistening thorns, the snow patches, the lichens. Though I am blind to it, the Truth is near, in the reality of what I sit on—rocks. These hard rocks instruct my bones in what my brain could never grasp in the Heart Sutra, that "form is emptiness, and emptiness is form"—the Void, the emptiness of blue-black space, contained in everything. Sometimes when I meditate, the big rocks dance.

The secret of the mountains is that the mountains simply exist, as I do myself: the mountains exist simply, which I do not. The mountains have no "meaning," they are meaning; the mountains are. The sun is round. I ring with life, and the mountains ring, and when I can hear it, there is a ringing that we share. I understand all this, not in my mind but in my heart, knowing how meaningless it is to try to capture what cannot be expressed, knowing that mere words will remain when I read it all again, another day.

"Regard as one, this life, the next life, and the life between," wrote Milarepa. And sometimes I wonder into which life I have wandered, so still are the long nights here, and so cold.

Peter Matthiessen's travels have taken him to remote regions of all five continents, from the Amazon jungles to Nepal. A former commercial fisherman and charter-boat captain, he has always been interested in marine biology and participated in the search for the great white shark that culminated in his book, Blue Meridian. *He is the author of other fiction and non-fiction works including* At Play in the Fields of the Lord, Far Tortuga, *and* The Snow Leopard, *from which this story was excerpted.*

When in ~~Saldang~~ NEPAL I heard again of Shey ~~Tulku~~ *LAMA, this man people would talk about as if he was a living saint. He was in retreat for something like fifteen years in a monastery on the foot of Shey, the Crystal Mountain.

The ~~Tulku~~ LAMA was in solitary meditation—but I asked a monk if I could see him. The monk disappeared and we heard voices. He came back and said that I could not see him, but if I wanted to talk to him, I could sit by the entrance.

The sun was reflecting against the façade of the monastery and the stone courtyard, making it almost like an oven. While waiting I drifted to sleep.

"You want to talk to me?"

The voice woke me up. I opened my eyes onto the closed door behind which the ~~Tulku~~ LAMA was talking. I communicated through the younger monk.

"I came a long way to see you. I SAID I have already been here two years ago, but that time you would not talk to anyone. I would like to ask your advice. You see, I have an important choice to make and I do not know in which direction to go."

I started to explain the details, but the voice behind THE DOOR interrupted me.

"Details are of no importance. When facing two trails, if you are strong enough, always choose the hardest one. The one which will squeeze the best out of you."

—Eric Valli and Diane Summers, *Caravans of the Himalayas*

JEFF HERSCH

⋆ ⋆ ⋆

Jamuna

A new water system taps a village's long history.

THE WATER BUBBLED UP BETWEEN ROCKS AND FERNS IN THE FOR-
est above the village. From a storage tank built the year before, into
a pipe buried two feet underground, it began its seven-mile journey from the forest through the village. Across ridge tops it ran,
through bamboo groves, under trails pounded hard by shepherds
and their goats, past clusters of white and ocher houses with their
thatched roofs and water buffalo pens, around terraces cut deep
into the mountainsides, luxuriant now in late spring with young
rice shoots glowing a green so intense they seemed fields of sap-
phire in the sun. Then it continued past the school and across a
small valley that held the fog in the early morning. Down, always
down, to the bazaar, to the cloth shops and tea stalls, to the spice
and fruit vendors with their pots of yellow turmeric, piles of tangerines, finger-sized bananas, and midget, golden-skinned potatoes. On blankets spread upon the ground lay the stuff of daily life:
combs, hand mirrors, and red-tasseled braids to be wound into
women's thick black hair. Khaki-colored cones of *bidis* rolled by
nimble fingers in Biratnagar waited to be smoked; alongside were
stacked towers of match boxes, containing matches so brittle they'd
snap in two unless struck with just the right motion. Once you

could light your *bidi* with the first match, you felt like a veteran, a Nepal-wallah.

Behind the shops, great dusty burlap sacks, each containing 50 kilos of cardamom harvested from the cloud forest above the village, waited to be carried on porters backs down to the blistering *tarai*, and then trucked to Calcutta and the sea. Merchants squatted next to their wares, wearing *lungis* and blankets, nodding and gesticulating and sipping endless cups of sweet milk tea as the day wore on. This was the business end of Jamuna, and here is where my trouble began.

It was my second year as a Peace Corps volunteer in a small mixed-caste village in the middle hills of far eastern Nepal. Jamuna was four days' walk from Kanchenjunga, the third highest peak in the world, and a day's walk across the border from the ex-British hill station of Darjeeling in India.

I had come to supervise the design and construction of a gravity-flow water system, from a spring high above the village, via underground pipes, to taps that were to be located at strategic points. The village itself was really clusters of houses draped over the sides of hills like so many thatch polka dots on a green-brown background cascading down to the bazaar and river valley.

I had already built six taps and laid miles of plastic pipe through the upper portions of the village. This was the area inhabited by rice-farming Rais and Limbus, descendants of animist Mongoloid peoples who cut their terraces into the hillsides many centuries ago, using the same tool, the *kodalo*, that farmers use today. In exchange for water taps and pipeline, the farmers dug trenches for the pipe and cut stone for the tap stand; local masons then shaped the stone and built *chautaras*, massive stone benches and walls around the tap where people came to bathe and collect water and where porters could rest their loads and cool themselves. Instead of building ugly cement tap stands, I had chosen to use the cement money for stonemasons' wages. I wanted the *chautaras* to be beautiful and to last.

In the higher, poorer areas, the trade worked remarkably well. For each tap, the farmers who would use it put in weeks of hard work. Masons chipped and mortared rock, pipe was joined and buried, and we dropped lower and lower down the hills leaving taps in our wake. Finally we reached the bazaar, an area inhabited largely by Newars, Brahmins, and Chetris, businessmen who ran shops and rented out their land to tenant farmers. When asked to donate their labor for a tap, they responded: "We are too old *sahib*, too infirm. We must run our shops. Our sons are in school. *Ke garne?*" What to do? I explained that if this were the case, they could hire laborers to do their work for them, a solution greeted with the usual nods and head wagging—meaning anything from seeming acquiescence to "I'll just let this stupidity pass through my ears." For four straight days I made the three-hour round trip to the bazaar, only to be greeted with shrugs. "The workers we hired didn't show up. The workers are asking for too many rupees. *Ke garne*, sahib. You must build the tap some other way."

Everything seemed clear in my mind, absolute. The poor farmers had done their share; now these guys were trying to pull a fast one. I gave them an ultimatum: "Tomorrow I'll come back for the last time. No laborers, no taps, so long. The pipeline will pass you by." I remember turning around and heading back uphill, self-consciously taking the high stone steps of the bazaar and feeling all eyes on me as they repeated my stern edict with disbelief. I felt right. I felt powerful. And I felt a knife blade of doubt. I kept walking.

I put a lock on the storage

Most development and the rising standard of living had been attained through the heavy infusion of external aid. The beneficiaries have not always been those who actually contribute to growth and production. But the irony is that those who enjoy the benefits continue to be increasingly unhappy and ask for more without contributing to the process of development.

—Dor Bahadur Bista,
Fatalism and Development:
Nepal's Struggle for Modernization

tank's main valve and made plans to continue the pipeline lower down. But now people were too busy to dig trenches. Next day was "*haat* bazaar," market day, when people from surrounding villages hours away came to buy and sell their produce, and to celebrate—the women proud and beautiful in their maroon velvet blouses and adorned with ponderous gold earrings and nose rings. In the bazaar tea shop, I sat alone; none of the usual conversation or bawdy jokes were directed my way. I sipped my scalding tea quickly and trudged back home. In the dense fog along the forest I felt like Gary Cooper in *High Noon*, only no Grace Kelly awaited me upon my return.

I thought my stand would at least make me some kind of popular hero among the poorer farmers, but I received no showers of praise or support. They seemed as much against my decision as the businessmen.

Someone broke into the tank and tried to turn the valve. But I stubbornly clung to my decision. The tension climbed up the hills to the house which I shared with Omkarnath (O.K.) Bhattrai and his family. Eating *dal-bhat*, boiled rice and lentil soup, around the evening fire, O.K. also opposed my decision, and offered to lend the bazaar merchants enough money to hire laborers. We both knew it was more a gift than a loan. I thought it a terrible precedent to set, rewarding those who contributed nothing. I refused O.K.'s offer. "You came here to build a water system, not to decide what is right or wrong," he said. "Take the money and finish the system."

I went back to my room above the rice storage bins and fell asleep in my sleeping bag with O.K.'s statement filling my brain like a headache.

The Bhattrai family went back many generations in Jamuna. O.K. had been its mayor and was an eminently respected and benevolent landlord to whom villagers came to settle their quarrels. He demonstrated his generosity on many occasions, giving food to the needy and lending his oxen to use as draft animals. I knew of no other villager whose sense of responsibility extended so far beyond his family, and I believed his offer to be in the same spirit.

From the time I first arrived alone and unannounced in Jamuna, with my survey instruments and barely comprehensible Nepali, O.K. had been the project's driving force. Although the taps came nowhere near his house, he helped organize the labor, smoothed over squabbles and prodded men to work when their enthusiasm flagged after two years of construction. Without such help, I knew what village politics could do.

Another volunteer, a friend, had landed in the middle of political and caste feuds while trying to build a water system. Fighting erupted over tap locations, ten feet closer to this house or that. Men crept out at night, hacked the pipe, and tore down tap stands, destroying the previous day's work. After centuries of carrying their water from polluted streams, they were willing to lose everything because a tap was too close to their neighbor. Finally my friend packed his things and left in frustration.

O.K. had been there to prevent such a mess. He wanted the system completed without problems reported back to UNICEF or the water development branch of the Nepal government.

The next morning I awoke as always to a rhythmic *"ka-thump-ing"* reverberating through the clay floor on which my pallet lay. I groped my way out of my room, dark even in daylight, bending over like an old man to avoid cracking my skull on the heavy ceiling beams built forehead high.

In the rice room a woman held onto a leather strap hanging from the rafters to support standing on one leg as the other leg operated the *dhikki*, a heavy, see-saw-like contraption, that on each downward smack into the floor, would smash the hulls off the tan kernels of rice. *Thulo Aama*, or Elderly Mother, my nickname for O.K.'s wife, squatted, swiftly scooping newly hulled rice out of the depression in the floor, and just narrowly avoiding getting her hand flattened, while simultaneously pushing a new mound of rice under the bit of the pounding *dhikki*. All this was done in one smooth movement that bespoke a lifetime's practice, like the grooved swing of a professional golfer.

The women gave me a glass of scalding buffalo milk tea, teasing me about my solitary sleeping habits and O.K.'s loan offer: "Hey Jepp, you'd better stop fooling around and take that money or you'll cause lots of *dukkha*. I'll stop giving you your favorite radish *achar*."

Thulo Aama could always make me smile, even when facing a

plate of *dal-bhat* at seven in the morning. Some of my fondest memories are of sitting near the fire in late afternoon while Thulo Aama chopped vegetables, her glass bracelets tinkling on her wrist like tiny bells. That sound will always bring me back to that cool, dark kitchen and the conversations we had in it—at least everything my Nepali would permit. We talked of our families, America, Nepal, her childhood, and how she came to Jamuna. She was the only person who would talk to me about Madhu, O.K.'s sister-in-law, who had been widowed as a young bride when her husband died in a jeep accident on the Indian border. She was now cared for by O.K.'s family, and though vibrant, intelligent, and still beautiful, she was, by Brahmin tradition, prohibited from remarrying. Sometimes I had daydreams of marrying Madhu and taking her to America, but, of course, this never happened.

At breakfast my reception from O.K. was somewhat cooler than Thulo Aama's, and from the rest of the village, it was downright icy. O.K. informed me that a big town meeting would be held at the school to decide what to do about the water system before I made any reports. Fine, I thought, maybe I'll get some support from the people I've stood up for.

The day of the meeting arrived and I walked with O.K. to the school. Men were streaming in from every direction and the schoolroom was soon overflowing with faces familiar from work, and many unknown. The meeting started slowly—comprehensible and predictable. O.K. presided: "This man was sent by His Majesty's government to build a water system in our village. It's very important and something all of you want for your families. Now, there is a problem in the bazaar; if it isn't solved we might never get any projects for years to come."

I sat on a bench in the middle of the crowd, listening and going over what I would say if asked, so my Nepali would come out smoothly and with some presence. Soon, men were standing up and yelling, others joined in, and within a short time I was the only one sitting. I could see the brown muscular legs of the farmers as they jumped up and down on the bench in front of me, the veins of their calves ropy and distended.

The intensity increased. I could pick up only snatches of what was being shouted, but I could feel the anger of their grievances. It was no longer just about the water system, it went everywhere—crops, irrigation, water, loans, land, cardamom, caste, marriages, deaths. It was the history of Jamuna down to its roots. I felt out of my place, out of my depth. I slipped out the door unnoticed and into the quiet of the trail leading home, stopping at a secluded place where I often sat to watch the cloud banks glide up the valley like old clipper ships under full sail. In the mornings they would silently sail out, and majestically return in the evening. Their predictability usually made me feel better. But not now. How could I ever have thought I could make the decisions I had made? I barely knew the surface of 1,000 years of history here. I was an idiot. O.K. was right: my job was to build the system.

I watched a hawk wheeling and turning, gliding effortlessly in the valley below me. From above I saw him adjust every feather on his wings separately, like the fingers of my hand. With a few powerful strokes of his wings, he flew toward the set of ridges leading south from Jamuna. What took me two days walking, the hawk reached in an instant and was gone.

That night I accepted O.K.'s loan. I completed the bazaar tap several weeks later and left Jamuna soon after. O.K. threw a big party for me and the workers and served *rakshi* to everyone, even though as a Brahmin he never drank or had it in his house. I got very drunk, and when pushed into performing a traditional Nepali dance with hands on hips, moved like a clumsy performing bear. The workers rolled on the floor with laughter.

When I left, O.K. told me what a good job he thought I'd done. But only one person outside O.K.'s family, someone I'd never been very friendly with, said thank you for bringing them

*D*o not expect to be given thanks for doing what is required of you by your dharma, *religious duties. What you are required to do in this life is all pre-determined by what you did in your past life. Your responsibility is to simply perform the tasks well, for that will determine in what position you will be reborn.*

—Barbara J. Scot, *The Violet Shyness of Their Eyes: Notes from Nepal* water. But then Nepalis are never so profuse in verbal thanks. I did get the satisfaction of seeing women and children filling their brass *goggaries* and washing at the *chautara* taps as I walked the trail out of Jamuna for the last time as engineer-*sahib*.

Two years later I slipped from India over the Nepal border and stopped at the upper reaches of Jamuna at Jaubari, a cold, misty bunch of houses and potato fields under the shadow of Kanchenjunga. At a tea shop, as a Sherpa woman prepared hot millet *tongba*, local liquor, in a wooden mug, I asked how the water system down below was working. "It worked well in the beginning, so they stopped paying the man trained to maintain it," she said, as she wiped a bowl clean on the edge of her skirt. "Now some of it is working and some not. Goat herders cut holes in the pipe to water their goats and save walking to the river. Children swung on the faucets. Mud got in the pipes and sometimes the water stops."

"Do you know who built that system?" I asked.

"I think it was a foreigner, an old, old man with a white beard."

Maybe if I return in twenty years, they'll remember me.

Jeff Hersch is a freelance photographer and journalist. He spent three years in Nepal as a Peace Corps volunteer. He has traveled in Europe and Southeast Asia and has written for various U.S. and European publications. When he is in the U.S. he lives in Denver, Colorado.

★

The missionaries had told me the story of a Peace Corps volunteer who had brought vegetables into the area a few years ago. He had taught the people how to grow them, and also how to prepare seeds for the following year. Just before the harvest, however, his father became ill and he returned to the U.S. When he returned to Nepal a month later, the people had harvested and eaten all the vegetables, saving nothing for seed. When he asked them why, they replied that it was too much trouble. They had lived without vegetables for many years, and could do so again. Such attitudes would take many years to change. Could one Peace Corps volunteer really expect to do much in a year or two?

—Parker Antin with Phyllis Wachob Weiss, *Himalayan Odyssey:*
The Perilous Trek to Western Nepal

MONICA CONNELL

* * *

Ritual Sisters

*An anthropologist in western Nepal discovers
that love, medicine, and a little luck
can work wonders.*

THE DAY THAT JAKALI AND I WERE TO BECOME *MITINIS* SHE HAD
prepared a feast. Her husband filled the bronze bowls with yellow
barley beer and we sat around the fire sipping it, while she ground
the salt and chili and the spices and put the final touches to the
meal. When everything was ready she filled up little pots with
water and put them down for us to wash our hands, and before she
served the meal she threw a few grains of rice into the fire for the
household gods. There was always something special to eat at
Jakali's—roasted amaranthus seeds, popped corn, green tomato
chutney—and today, to celebrate, she produced some honey. It had
been gathered in the autumn and stored away in a clay pot sealed
with birch-bark and cow-dung. Inside, the honey was the colour
of autumn leaves. Shards of wax and dead bees floated in it like the
debris caught in a river eddy. That night, between us all, we de-
voured the entire pot.

"This is for life," said Jakali. "From now on my home will be
your home and my children will be your children." We marked
each other's foreheads with red *tikas* and then Jakali went round,
bending down to each person in the room including her baby who
was sleeping by the fire, until we all had the same vermilion stain

between our eyes. Then she gave the bowl of *tika* mixture to her children and they played with it, daubing it on each other's hands and legs, duplicating the tikas on their foreheads until they spread from ear to ear like warpaint. After the *tikas* we gave each other gifts. Jakali went into the inner room and fetched a necklace intricately woven from many different-coloured tiny beads, and I gave her five red glass bracelets and a hair ornament that I'd bought in Kathmandu.

W hen a woman decides to become a mitini *with a girlfriend, they both exchange bangles, needle and thread, pote (a beaded necklace), sari, blouse, and some jewelry, if they can afford it. The clothes and the accessories should be red because it's the auspicious color. Sometimes the women will conduct this* mitini *ceremony at a temple with the god or goddess as the "witness." Some will go so far as to consult an astrologer to make sure that they are of suitable temperament and not break up this* mitini *relationship in the future.*

—Madhuri Banskota, "Nepali Customs and Rituals"

Jakali's children came to see me almost every day, making themselves at home whatever I was doing. Sometimes all five girls came trooping in together; sometimes just the younger ones would come, telling me proudly that Ram Chobar had gone to school—that she was the only girl in the village who went to school—and that Banchu was grazing the cows. Banchu, the eldest, was beginning to take an interest in her appearance and always came with her face washed and oiled and her hair tidily plaited, showing me bits of jewellery and hairslides. The others never said a lot; they immersed themselves silently in my world, passing the time while their mother worked in the fields. One of them always brought the baby, wrapped in a shawl on her back, and sometimes they'd play with her, squeezing and tickling her, and feeding her imaginary mice to make her laugh. Jakali hadn't named the baby yet; she said she'd wait until she grew to be a girl and let the name suggest itself.

One autumn, when Jakali's husband had gone on a trading trip to the south, the two of us harvested her millet crop. We spent five days wading through the sea of grain, slicing heavy brown heads from their flimsy stalks with sickles and tossing them into baskets on our backs. Another time, in early summer, I helped her pick the purple *dantelo* berries that she used for making oil. The *dantelo* bushes grew wild around the village, between the fields and all along the river banks, and we wandered from one clump to another, scratching the backs of our hands on thorns as we rummaged for berries among the thick green foliage. When our baskets were full we took them to the stream and trod the mass of berries underwater so the fleshy pulp was washed away. Two of Jakali's daughters came rushing over when they saw what we were doing. She took off their clothes so they could play naked and they shrieked with delight as they flopped and splashed in the swirling purple water.

During the monsoon I didn't see Jakali for several weeks. She and her family had left the village, locking up their house with its beautiful carved window frame, and taking their cows, dogs and chickens to the monsoon settlements on the south-facing slopes of Jimale. Then one evening, when the rain had stopped for the first time since morning and the wind had swept the sky with watery blue and orange, she came to see me. I knew at once that there was something wrong; her face was strained and she was breathing hard as though she'd hurried. She sat down and carefully unwound the shawl that held the baby on her back. I gasped—the baby's head was covered in blisters; in places the film of skin had peeled away and the flesh beneath was red and angry.

"What happened?" I asked her. She told me that Ram Chobar had been looking after the baby while she and her husband were weeding. They were playing together and the baby had fallen into the fire. I looked from Jakali to the baby—both of them seemed in a state of shock, their eyes dry, their faces empty of expression, as though pain and tears had been temporarily suspended.

"We'll take her to the hospital in the morning," I said, trying to sound encouraging. "I'll come with you."

But Jakali shook her head: the baby was too weak to survive the journey—it was dangerous to take her outside the village where evil spirits would enter her body through the open wound on her head. I tried to persuade her in every way I knew, but she was adamant. "We'll take care of her together," she said. "Between us we can make her better."

I put a pan of water on the fire to boil and fetched some iodine solution, cotton wool and lint, a jar of Vaseline and a bandage from the small medicine box that I kept. The baby was lying across Jakali's lap, firmly clasped in the crook of her arm and half-heartedly sucking her breast. I waited for the water to cool. As soon as I touched the wound she cried and thrashed out, shocked at being hurt within the safe orbit of her mother's body.

The wound was already dirty where fluff, hair and bits of grit had lodged themselves in the soft raw flesh. It was impossible to get them all out, impossible to persevere against the baby's pain and distress. Jakali said it might be easier if she cleaned it up herself, so I passed her the cotton wool and the bowl of water, but the baby struggled almost as much. In the end all we could do was sluice the wound down, hoping that the iodine would prevent infection. When it had dried I covered it with a sheet of lint that I'd smeared with Vaseline, and wound a bandage as best I could around the baby's head. Jakali left almost as soon as I'd finished, anxious to be back with her family on Jimale before it was dark.

Three days later I went, as I had said I would, to change the bandage. It was raining; the path up the hillside was steep and slippery, covered in places with tangled, waterlogged weeds, and the silence of the surrounding forest was broken only by the regular, ominous dripping of trees.

Jakali had told me that her shack was in the first clearing that you came to, only about half-way up the hillside, and I was glad when I left the dark forest and came out into the clear light of day. The upland wheat had already been harvested and cattle were grazing the stubble. I walked across the rough, stony ground towards the nearest of the three wooden huts. I knew that it was the right one when I saw one of Jakali's daughters rushing naked through the open doorway shouting. "*Mitini ama ayo.*" (*Mitini* mother is here.") Then she came running up to meet me.

Inside, a fire was burning in the central hearth. Jakali was sitting on the pine-needle floor, tapping out the dough for *rotis* between her palms and tossing the finished discs onto a heavy iron pan. The baby was lying across her lap, asleep. The bandage hadn't come undone, but it was very dirty and had slipped askew hanging down over one ear and half of an eye. Jakali smiled at me as she turned over a *roti* and, when it puffed up, removed it from the pan, standing it close to the embers to cook right through. She said that the baby seemed all right, but that she cried a lot, especially at night.

I didn't feel hungry but Jakali insisted, as she always did, that I eat. So Ram Chobar fetched me a pot of water to wash my hands and Jakali put two of the warm wheat *rotis* on a plate and ladled out some curd from the wooden container. The swarm of flies that had been buzzing around aimlessly homed in immediately on the food, and I waved them away as I ate.

Again the baby screamed and struggled when I went to touch her head. But this time Jakali was firm, talking soothingly, yet holding down her thrashing arms and legs. The dressing hadn't stuck, as I had feared it might, but underneath the wound was wet with blood and, in one small patch, with pus. I told Jakali that unless we took her to the hospital she might well die. But Jakali refused—she was too frightened for her.

I felt the baby's glands and they were slightly swollen, but she didn't seem to have a fever. So we boiled some water and washed the wound in iodine solution as before. When we'd finished, the baby looked much happier. We'd washed her face as well and the skin on her cheeks was soft and tawny beneath the crisp white bandage. Jakali too seemed pleased and optimistic.

My own heart was weighted down with fear and sadness at their misplaced confidence. I told Jakali once again that I wasn't trained in medicine, that I didn't know how to save her baby. But when, moments later, I produced a bottle of ampicillin as a last resort, I merely reaffirmed her trust. Ram Chobar was delighted with the blue-and-yellow capsules, proud and thrilled that her little sister was to have this perfect, fail-safe medicine. I read the directions on the back of the bottle, tore up a piece of paper, and divided the contents of the capsules into four, parcelling each in a little twist of paper. We emptied one of them into some milk in a bowl and gave it to the baby there and then. She coughed a bit and swallowed. I told Jakali to give her one of these four times every day.

On the way back down through the forest I worried. Maybe I hadn't explained the instructions carefully enough—Jakali might give her too much or too little and either could be dangerous: maybe the baby was allergic to penicillin and Jakali wouldn't know to stop giving it to her if she developed a rash or had trouble breathing: maybe it would give her diarrhea and, if she was weak anyway, she could lose her vital strength and die. I suddenly noticed that the light drizzle had become a teeming downpour. Raindrops hummed on the leaves and branches overhead and mingled with the pervasive whirring sound of crickets. The entire forest seemed to seethe with life.

When I returned to Jimale three days later, I was feeling calmer. Circumstances would have already taken their course and there was nothing to be done now but witness the results. On the way I met Ram Chobar in the forest picking wild raspberries with some other girls and she told me that her mother was out collecting pine-needles and would be back soon. She gave me a handful of raspberries to eat, and I savoured the fleshy orange pulp as I walked along. Soon afterwards I spotted Jakali on the path ahead, stooping under the weight of an enormous load of pine-needles. I called out to her and she waited for me, so we entered the clearing and approached the hut together.

The baby was lying face down on a shawl in the sun, kicking her feet in the air while her two sisters played with sticks in a patch of mud nearby. The bandage was even dirtier than it had been before and it had slipped down to cover almost both her eyes; but she raised her head, peering out with difficulty, and smiled. Jakali put down her load of pine-needles and reached out her arms to pick her up. When she'd carried her inside she gave the baby her breast and after a while produced a little purse from her waistband, from which she took and carefully unravelled one of the paper twists of ampicillin.

This time the baby hardly cried at all when I started to unwind the bandage. Jakali said she thought she must be getting better: she almost never cried at night and sometimes, in the mornings, she'd clown around and make them laugh, as she always used to do. I unwrapped the last section of the bandage, and still apprehensive, eased off the lint dressing. Underneath, the baby's head was dry; a clean protective scab had formed over most of the wound and the patch of infection that I'd feared would spread had gone.

Jakali was thrilled. She squeezed the baby and hugged her, saying it was all right now, she was going to be all right. Feeling equally pleased and relieved, I dressed the wound again and bandaged it and gave Jakali some more of the paper twists of ampicillin.

The following day Jakali and her family abandoned their settlement on Jimale and moved back down to the village. They arrived in the evening, driving the cows, with the dogs following behind, the chickens packed up in one basket, and blankets and cooking pots crammed into another.

That autumn we saw a lot of one another. The baby's head slowly got better. Gradually the scab peeled off and was replaced by a layer of delicate pinkish skin. Jakali was worried that the hair would never grow, that she'd always be bald where the burn had been. But in time one or two straggly tufts pushed through. She kept the bandage on for a long time: at first because she was afraid of the baby scratching the itchy scab and then later because, until the wound was perfectly healed, she was frightened of evil spirits.

When Jakali came to see me now she nearly always brought a little gift—some eggs or potatoes, a plateful of maize flour—and at festivals and other special occasions she always invited me to her house to eat.

One evening we were sitting by Jakali's fire, carding wool. Banchu and Ram Chobar were out somewhere and the three younger girls were asleep. We'd been silent for some time, concentrating on the wool, when Jakali suddenly said that her husband was going to take a second wife.

"Why?" I asked, shocked.

Jakali didn't lift her eyes from the matted greasy wool that she was deftly teasing into a soft white froth. She said that she'd only given him daughters and he wanted a son.

I thought for a minute about what she was saying. I knew that some people who didn't have sons married their daughters at home rather than sending them to live in their husband's villages. "Couldn't Banchu's husband come and live here with you after they're married?" I asked. "That way there'd be somebody to help with the land and to look after you both when you're old."

"My husband's far too proud for that," she said. "And anyway, only a real son who's flesh and blood can perform his funeral rites."

Jakali had been married before—an arranged marriage to a man in Chaura. When she met her present husband they'd fallen in love; he'd paid adultery money to her first husband and she'd run away to live with him. I could tell from her voice and the sadness in her face that she loved him still. The real tragedy, however, was that, in her first marriage, she'd given birth to two sons, but their father had kept them both. Now, she wasn't sure she could conceive again.

"What are you going to do?" I asked, concerned for her.

"Learn to live with her, I suppose." A few moments passed and she looked up from her cloud of wool. "Sometimes we'll laugh and sometimes we'll cry."

> *Tilen came back last winter to visit us. One evening, after Diane went to read a story to Camille, he sat comfortably in an armchair beside me. He was much better, still thin but his spark was back.*
>
> *I could feel that he wanted to say something so I stayed quiet.*
>
> *First, looking at me with a smile, he put his hand on my knees.*
>
> *"You know, when you came the first time in Dolpo, asking all those stupid questions, I got really annoyed. Then, you came back, you came back, and I understood. Now that I see you in your house with your wife and kids...we are the same."*
>
> —Eric Valli and Diane Summers, "The Dutch Doctor"

Monica Connell grew up in Northern Ireland. She studied sociology at London University and social anthropology at Oxford. She is the author of Gathering Carrogeen *and* Against a Peacock Sky, *from which this story was excerpted. Now living in Bristol, she is writing a novel.*

✳

I may here observe that in Nepal, as I found out afterwards, the word friend conveys a much deeper meaning, probably, than in any other country. To be a friend here means practically the same thing as being a brother, and the natives have a curious custom of observing a special ceremony when any two of them tie the knot of friendship between them.

—Ekai Kawaguchi, *Three Years in Tibet*

MANJUSHREE THAPA

✦ ✦ ✦

Meanderings in Mustang

Visit Lo—and behold the clash of cultures.

Lo APPEARED VIBRANTLY, INCREDIBLY, LIKE A MIRAGE, AND changed my impression of Mustang as a land of deprivation. When we crossed a cairn on a rock-and-dust hilltop, Bikas and I found ourselves looking down onto an expanse of red and ochre crags, pink buckwheat fields, and a sparkling blue-green river. In the center of this valley was a settlement of neat white houses with enamel-painted windows that heralded the arrival of another, more Tibetan, world. Eagles were circling the vast blue sky.

The first village, Ghemi, had wide, cobbled lanes that echoed every sound. Wheat fields rustled, sand shifted, and voices drifted in from far away. The path led up to an earth-red *chorten*. Just as we reached it, we heard the clip-clopping of hooves, and a pale, stately man in slacks and a striped Oxford shirt rode into view on a chestnut horse. He smiled handsomely and galloped on, then disappeared into the silence: a princely apparition.

The man who opened the door of the house where we went to eat was just as fanciful. He had taut, Tibetan features and pale, soft skin that signaled privilege. His hair was braided around his head and he wore turquoise on one ear. But his clothes came from another place: straight-leg jeans, brown spurred boots, and a blue cashmere pullover. A carved silver knife hung from his leather belt. Instead of greeting us or asking us questions or inviting us in, as others had, this man folded his hands and stared at us silently, with composure.

Lo was always surprising; its ancient land—blood-red hills made of demons' lungs and *mani* walls of their entrails—was speckled with savvy, self-possessed, upper-class men with Hindu names like Rajendra, Gyanendra, Surendra, or—because cultural imperialism coexisted with cultural reclamation—sometimes not. They wore windbreakers, boots, Ray Bans, even Stetsons, and certainly base-ball caps. The women were more traditional and wore *bukkhoos* of spotless silks and satins and variegated rayons.

It took me a while to find out that these multicultural people were the nobles of Lo, members of the elite Kudak class and rela-tives of the Raja of Mustang. They equated themselves with Nepal's ruling Thakuri clan and adopted the Hindu name Bista.

Theirs was a bustling world of possibilities, with horses to travel around Mustang, plane tickets to take them beyond, land to over-see, villages to direct, festivals to organize and preside over, relatives to visit, and connections to maintain and build on. They upheld the mythic grandeur of the old kingdom.

The other Lobas led more common lives.

The local Gurung women had none of the waxen preciousness of the Bistas. We met them in *bhattis* or on the road as they headed home from a day in the fields, or from a month of farm work, or from a trip to Jomosom for timber. Most had dusty, dark robes hitched up to their calves, and they wore polyester or flannel shirts and well-worn sneakers. Their faces were brown from the sun and their lips were so cracked they looked like dead, dried skin.

Once they got over their hesitation to use unfamiliar Nepali words, they asked us for cigarettes and swapped views and gossip. "Electricity's too costly," one woman told us, and another said, "Our men all marry *Rongbas* nowadays." One woman said, point-edly, "Gyaltsen has a *bhirdi-yo*," meaning video, or television.

Gyaltsen was a Bista, the brother-in-law of the Raja of Mustang, and off-and-on village head of Tsarang. He was a big man who moved slowly, with dignity. Because Bikas had official connections with his family, we were allowed to stay at his house, which stood prominently in the middle of the village. His court-yard was filled not with goats and cows, but with sleek, well groomed horses. The walls of his home were decorated with Buddhist landscapes, conch shells and lotuses. Precious logs from the far south were stacked on the roof.

> *We spoke of his family and of his first jour-ney through Nepal to India, where he was now going with his uncle to sell woolens. His little sister had died two years before, when he was six. He was too busy looking after the sheep to go to school. He knew of my home—Hong Kong—since a cousin had been there to trade. But geographically he lumped it with all the other strange places beyond the borders of his homeland.*
>
> —Edward Peters, "The Forgotten Kingdom," *Los Angeles Times*

I soaked in the small comforts of his house. The clean earthen rooms were decorated with col-orful rugs and strips of cut linoleum. The walls had bright enamel paint and a few posters of Swiss chalets. A cheerful red cloth stretched over the ceiling and protected us from bits of wood and dirt that fell when people walked on the balcony above. In this house, fragments from all over the world appeared out of the blue: Chinese biscuits, Rara noodles, board games, an electrical cooker, an indoor toilet (a hole in the floor that opened onto a manure room underneath), pressure cookers, cupboards stacked with cups and extra flasks, and of course, electricity.

I glanced around furtively for signs of Gyaltsen's *bhirdi-yo*, but I couldn't find any. But clearly, the richest Bista families lived better than most Gurung families. Kalpana, Gyaltsen Bista's daughter, ex-uded the self-confidence that came from economic security. She was educated, and she took care of family affairs as well as public responsibilities like the administration of the electrical scheme. She was the only woman I saw in Lo who wore a *kurtha-sural* in the fashion of urban Nepali women. Her brother divided his time be-tween Kathmandu and Mustang. He was also educated, suave, and self-assured; he cut a dashing figure when he galloped up the dusty hills on a horse, overseeing family responsibilities. The two of them were impeccably turned out during religious festivals. This was what it meant to be well off in Mustang: having modern amenities like electricity, health care, and education, maybe even a television to ease harsh rural conditions, and having tradition to mask this modernity.

It wasn't an extravagant life, but it felt that way in context.

The walled city of Lo Monthang jutted out of a green valley that was surrounded by a horizon of barren hills. The "city" looked dismally tiny from a distance, but as we approached it I saw that it was teeming with life. Two hundred-odd houses, their inhabitants and their animals were tightly packed into an enclosure small enough to walk through in fifteen minutes. The wall that encased the settlement was punctuated, in places, by the windows and doors of the houses on the other side.

The lodge we stayed in was tucked away in an alley behind the palace. It was run single-handedly by a woman named Dolma Gurung, and even the Bistas came there to relax, chat, gamble, drink themselves silly and sometimes pass out for the night.

The guys—Mustang-elite, Kathmandu-exposed, world-weary Rabindra, Jamyang, and Krishna Bista—sat in a circle and played a dice game which made them whoop, cry, shout, curse, hiss, and smack each other on the knee. Each player chose a number and yelled it out loud as he slapped the dice onto a leather pad. Then the player lifted his hands and everyone screamed and yelled about the result. The room thundered with excitement.

Jamyang turned to us every so often to make a wry remark. "Development?" he said once, raising an eyebrow. "With people like this, there's no fear of that in Mustang."

The other men roared with laughter, but Jamyang kept a straight face.

"Keep a dog's tail in a bamboo pipe," Krishna said, from across the room, "keep it there for twelve years, and still, at the end, it'll be curly. These people are like that." He smirked and let his hair fall over his eyes. But only a few people laughed. Krishna lacked

Gyaltsen's finesse; he was too young, too cocksure. He said, "Even Indra's father Chandra couldn't develop this place." He repeated the popular Nepali saying, "Indra's father Chandra."

Rabindra sat apart from them. He was older, around 38 he said, though he looked 20. His eyes were quick, he was more observant, and he was quieter.

When someone claims to perform an especially absurd or impossible task, the Nepalis say that not even Chandra, the father of god Indra who is the king of all gods, can perform such a task (so how can this mere mortal?).

—RK

He said to us, "I've arranged horses for you to go to the border tomorrow. You have to leave early, otherwise the river'll be too high to cross when you return in the afternoon. I'll come at six to wake you."

"Six? Aaack!" Krishna said. "Six!" He shivered with mock horror and looked around for support.

Jamyang grinned. "We," he said, "we Bhotias don't wake up until nine."

Bikas said, "I saw you early this morning on a small horse, with your feet dangling all the way to the ground. Remember?"

He shrugged. "Yeah, I had to let the animals out. But then I went back to sleep."

After some time, Dolma walked into the room and said something loudly in Tibetan. The gamblers groaned and stood up slowly and straggled out. Jamyang gulped down the last of his *chang* and left with the other men without bothering to say goodnight.

"I told them there was a woman among my guests, and that they should leave," Dolma explained, "otherwise they'd play all night."

Our room looked out on the gate of the walled city. Early in the morning, women gathered at the two taps in front of the wall to fill their jerry cans with water. Then they went home to cook a meal. In a while the men led the cows and goats to grazing lands outside the city wall. The women headed to the fields with empty baskets on their backs and the day's rations—*tsampa* and a flask of tea. The alley in front of the city gate bustled with traffic then, and rang with cries and laughter. During the day, when everyone was away, everything was quiet again. A few aged men and women with thick eye glasses and dark, heavy clothes shuffled by with prayer wheels or beads in their hands. Some children played in the dirt. One or two *Rongbas*—school teachers, border guards, health post attendants—passed by on the way to work, and monks shuttled from *gompa* to *gompa*. At dusk, men gathered by the gate and gossiped, some working their spindles to make wool, others rocking toddlers on their laps. There was a sudden commotion when the children swarmed out of school, and again when the women came back from the fields with the animals. The kids ran in motley groups that fought and tussled with each other. Teenagers gathered in boys' and girls' groups, eyed each other, and launched sudden, fierce attacks to push and shove and flirt. The women exchanged jokes and reproaches with the men as the cows, still hungry after a full day of grazing, nipped viciously at the greenery in their baskets.

The Raja's palace stood directly in front of the city gate: a four-story, whitewashed clay structure with prayer flags on top, endless dusty glass-paned windows, and a dismal wood-carved entrance.

Since I had an assignment to investigate the possibility of repairing two of the *gompas* of Lo Monthang, I was able to go inside the palace. A rickety wooden staircase led to a dark landing that was decorated with a stuffed Tibetan mastiff. A live one was also tied up there. Farther up the stairs was an outdoor landing where a retinue of servants cooked rice at a wood-fire stove. Up another stairway was a verandah lined with prayer wheels and painted with Buddhist landscapes. Some of the rooms along the verandah were empty and unused. The inhabited ones were closed.

The Raja met visitors in a room with linoleum floors, a striped linen ceiling, and carved wood furniture mixed with folding metal chairs. A cabinet to the side displayed china and thermos flasks. Opposite, a row of stately Bista men, Rabindra and Gyaltsen among them, sat on mud benches. Both men smiled at us, but they didn't break rank to talk to us. The Raja and Rani sat across from their relatives.

The Raja was a graceful, stout man with unhurried movements and carefully chosen words. He wore a beige jacket over a wool sweater, and his legs were covered by a wool blanket. He talked to us in Tibetan and let his secretary, a Thakali man dressed in spotless Western clothes, translate for him. The Rani, a frail-looking woman with watchful eyes, knitted in demure silence.

I entered the ancient walled city of Lo Manthang, capital of the Kingdom of Lo, known today as Mustang, a remote area of Nepal protruding onto the Tibetan plateau beyond the Himalayas. I had arranged for a meeting with the King of Lo, Jigme Palbar Bista, and thanks to a colleague in Kathmandu, came prepared with silk scarves (given as a gesture of respect) and a bottle of Johnny Walker Black Label.

The king liked the scarves. His face lit up at the sight of the scotch. Buttery salted Tibetan-style tea was served and we talked about the opening of his kingdom to the outside world.

—Brian K. Weirum,
"Trekking Nepal"

During our conversation about electricity and *gompa* repair, a relative taking leave from town placed a *khata* on a table beside the Raja. Then he took out a rupee from his *chuba* and placed it beside the *khata*. He poured butter tea from a flask into the Raja's silver tea bowl. The Raja lifted the bowl and sipped from it without so much as a glance at the man. When he returned the bowl to its stand, the relative filled the cup again. He moved towards the Rani and repeated the same gesture. Then he walked backwards out of the room, scratching his head in reverence.

The Raja's informal authority extended to only a few villages other than Lo Monthang, but even that was shrinking. With more and more people exposed to the Nepali government's regulations, and to leftist and populist rhetoric from the political parties, quite a few traditional customs were eroding.

I found out later from our inn-keeper Dolma that only relatives and those with a vested interest observed the elaborate protocol followed by the man we had seen in the palace. The electrical power house operator of Chhonhup, for instance, also offered a *khata* and money when he arrived to talk about the plant. His job depended on the Raja's goodwill.

When other Lobas had an audience with the Raja they listened silently, scratched their head in humility, and occasionally assented with, "*Kanou, kanou.*"

"And if they passed him on the streets of Lo Monthang?" I asked Dolma. They didn't have to, but if they wanted to they could scratch their heads and smile at him and respond politely if he addressed them.

"Don't you have to stick out your tongue?"

Dolma stared at me with wide, shocked eyes. "Nowadays only villagers do that," she said gravely. "Those of us from the city just scratch our heads."

If you weren't a Loba, you could do anything; the hierarchy observed by insiders wasn't expected of others. For *Rongbas* like us, a "*Namaste*" and the superlative form of address, "*Hajoor,*" sufficed.

Much of the village life revolved around the *gompas*, and it seemed like monks were always conducting prayers at one *gompa* or another, with almost the whole village participating. Every time I entered a *gompa* I saw worshippers.

Once, when I was examining the frescos of Thugchen *Lakhang*, a young man burst into the hall and strode up to the base of the Avalokitesvara. He muttered something under his breath, then flung himself on the ground with such ardor I thought he might hurt himself. He remained prostrate for a long time. I looked away, embarrassed by his fervor, and by my own lack of faith. But I couldn't help looking over again. The man had stood up, folded his hands, and he was chanting. Then he flung himself down again, and stood up, and repeated this motion again and again.

Another day, in Thugchen *Lakhang*, Bikas and I found ourselves surrounded by a mass of teenage girls. They were all dressed identically in black *bukkhoos* and formal black shawls, with their hair done up in braids. Among them was one who was taller than the rest, who stood out because her dress was like a Chinese doll's, with an iridescent, puff-sleeved pink shirt and a billowing satin skirt. She wore coral on her ears and neck. Her hair was done in two buns at the back. She had white, milky skin, flashing black eyes, and rouged cheeks.

She moved towards us slowly and displayed none of the childish inquisitiveness of the other girls. Softly, but with authority, she asked us where we came from. She nodded at our reply and seemed to want to ask more, but she held back in dignity. Then she offered to take us to the *gompa* she was visiting next. "There's a prayer going on there," she said with a gracious smile. We declined politely. Her eyes lingered on us. But perhaps it would have been improper to say much more; she gathered the other girls and led them away. I found out later that she was the daughter of an important lama.

The deep religiosity of the entire community was apparent. When I spoke to the villagers about the possibility of repairing Thugchen and Jamba *Lakhang*, they all responded warmly. Even those youths whose leftist politics made them skeptical of outside intervention raised no voice of protest. "That will be *dharma*," one elderly man said, and the others murmured in agreement.

Some days later a revered Sakya Rinpoche, who was also the Rani's uncle, flew off to Kathmandu in a chartered helicopter paid for by some Japanese Buddhists in Kathmandu.

When the helicopter arrived in the morning, the entire village poured out of the city gate and watched it land in a cloud of dust on a plateau outside the walls. Its blades slowed down and the dust settled. The pilot stepped out in a glitter of dark glasses and neon windbreaker. The co-pilot had plainer clothes but he sported the same movie-star mustache. The local children stared at the men in awe and stole behind the helicopter to finger the sleek machine. Men, women, monks, and *Rongba* employees milled around, peeked inside the helicopter, and commented on the pilots. The neon pilot responded by striding to the edge of the plateau, where he lit an imported cigarette and took in the vista. The other, who agreed to take a message to my family in Kathmandu, spoke only English with me. Rabindra Bista and a school teacher asked me to take a snapshot of themselves in front of the helicopter. Gyaltsen crept up behind them and hammed a sporting smile.

From the Chhoedhe Gompa, there was a low blare of horns. Then a crowd of Bistas dressed in traditional and modern fineries came through the city's gates. The old Sakya Rinpoche, dressed in orange robes and a ceremonial yellow hat, sat on top of a slow-moving horse. He dismounted near the helicopter, and the Raja escorted him to his seat. The Bistas crowded to the helicopter to offer the Rinpoche *khata* and *durkho*—hard cheese—and colorful Chinese candy. Some people pushed and shoved to get near the Rinpoche while others chanted and prayed from afar.

Then the pilots stepped into the clear glass front of the helicopter. The doors closed, the blades swished, and the crowd scattered with laughter and shrieks. The neon pilot, smug and other-worldly with earphones clamped to his head, steered the helicopter away in a storm of dust.

Lo Monthang was like that: in the middle of hardship appeared a spark of stunning wealth, in the middle of tradition, change. The society was ruptured by objects and values from all over the world. I couldn't understand everything, but I could see the evidence of change. I read what I saw like a book in a language I only partially understood; I deciphered familiar signs in a jumble of others.

I saw from these disjunctions that the policy of restriction had not kept upper Mustang beyond the reach of the modern world. Instead it had forced people out. No new sources of income had entered the area, nor had traditional occupations found means to grow. The history-book economic cycle—of farming in the spring, tending to the animals in the summer, and trading in the winter—had remained the same for centuries; it had stagnated.

So seasonal migration, the only lucrative option left, had become more of a necessity than a choice. Almost every able-bodied person went south in the winter—either to the middle hills of

Nepal or to cities like Pokhara and Kathmandu, or to India, and some on to Hong Kong or Taiwan. In southern Nepal they sold *jimbu*, an herb used for cooking, and wool and Chinese consumer goods to *Rongba*. They also sold little somethings—trinkets and crafts—to tourists, and operated restaurants along well-traveled routes. In India, they bought and sold acrylic sweaters. Those who journeyed to the Far East traded in radios, televisions, kitchen appliances, ready-made clothes.

When China occupied Tibet in 1959 and sealed off the border, the traditional trade between the mountain peoples of Nepal and Tibet came to a sudden halt, forcing them to find other methods of income. The situation in Mustang was further complicated because the Tibetan Khampas used this region as a base to make guerrilla raids into Tibet. The Khampas, who had been supported by the CIA, were forced to surrender to the Nepali army when President Nixon visited China and the U.S. government abruptly withdrew its support of the Khampas.

—Larry Habegger and James O'Reilly, "World Travel Watch"

People had gone the way of money, and whether that Hinduized them or Westernized them or Nepalized them didn't matter much. Their exposure brought back into the restricted area fragments of the world beyond: transistor radios, smokeless stoves, electricity, running shoes, windbreakers, and new languages—Nepali, Hindi, some English. And through these imports, even those who remained in Mustang all year long took leave of their traditional way of life.

I understood this impulse to venture out. This was the path all of Nepal took in the 1950's: the one leading out, to prosperity. This was the path my own family took, generations ago.

Manjushree Thapa writes fiction and non-fiction about contemporary Nepal. Her published work includes Mustang Bhot in Fragments, *a documentary account of an ethnically Tibetan community in northern Nepal where she lived and worked for two years. She did her undergraduate studies at the Rhode Island School of Design, and received a Fulbright scholarship for a Creative Writing MFA at the University of Washington, Seattle. She is based in Kathmandu.*

*

"I would very much like to take just one photograph," I said.

"I will ask. Doorkeeper, is it permitted to take photographs?"

"It is not permitted."

"This gentleman is a very distinguished professor. He has travelled all over India, China, and Japan, and now he has come all the way to Nepal. Perhaps he could take just one photograph?"

The doorkeeper shrugged uncomfortably, not quite believing. "From the top of the steps, then, it may perhaps be permitted."

I sympathized with him, but I took my photograph. I returned to the top, feeling guilty of a misdemeanour as the two of them watched me solemnly. Thus and thus, one by one, the forbidden secrets of Nepal are probed, peered at, dragged to the light of day. First the outer frontiers are penetrated, then the inner ones. The foreigner has money, wins helpers, influences people. He drags the curtain aside, infiltrates, treads unharmed where the native-born himself fears to tread, enters first the courtyard, then the sanctuary, then the holy of holies, and bares all the ancient mysteries for the sake of a story to take home.

—Duncan Forbes, *The Heart of Nepal*

JAMLING TENZING WITH RAJENDRA S. KHADKA

✦ ✦ ✦

In My Father's Footsteps

Many are called, few are chosen.

MY FATHER, TENZING NORGAY SHERPA, DISCOURAGED HIS CHIL-
dren from becoming mountaineers because it was dangerous. He
knew, since he and Edmund Hillary were the first men to reach
the top of Mt. Everest in 1953.

My father told us he had become a mountaineer so we would-
n't have to. He encouraged us instead to pursue other careers, so I
did not become a professional mountaineer. However, I did study
at the Himalayan Institute in Darjeeling and became a fully-trained
climber. I love being among the mountains. I enjoy hiking, ice and
rock climbing, and even scaled Himalayan peaks over 20,000 feet
with my father in Sikkim. Later, when I was studying in the
United States, I taught rock climbing during my vacations.

Despite my father's caution about mountaineering, and for reasons I myself do not fully understand, I had dreamed about climbing Mt. Everest ever since I was six years old. But it remained a
dream because it is very expensive to climb Everest. An expedition
member must come up with a minimum of $35,000, excluding
personal expenses such as travel and hotel accommodations. I
couldn't go as a "Sherpa," portering loads for an expedition, because I'd be dishonoring my father.

218

In 1995, it looked as if my dream might come true. The American Sagarmatha Expedition invited me to join their team. It was a group of friends who were professional climbers. Each member was responsible for his own finances. I joined them but couldn't go beyond the Base Camp (17,500 feet) because I just couldn't come up with the money.

My luck changed a year later. David Breashears, the leader of Mt. Everest IMAX Expedition 1996, was making a documentary about the Everest region, and he offered me a central role in it; I was also the deputy leader of this six-person (two women, four men) expedition. On May 8th, we planned to film our actual ascent to the summit of Mt. Everest. All six members—Araceli Segarra, Sumiyo Tsuzuki, Ed Viesturs, Robert Schauer, David, and I—would try to reach the top. Finally, after years of dreaming, training, and planning, I hoped to achieve my goal.

Once we were in the mountains, things quickly began to go wrong. On the day we were preparing to ascend to Camp IV (also known as the South Col at 26,500 feet) from Camp III (24,000 feet), we noticed that there was a whole crowd of climbers, about 35 people, ahead of us, also on their way to Camp IV. There were two commercial expeditions led by American Scott Fisher and New Zealander Rob Hall, a South African group, and a Taiwanese team, and everyone decided to go up that same day. David said we couldn't join this crowd because our plan was to film when only two or three climbers were on the ridge as they made their way to the top. He didn't want to shoot with that crowd crawling up. The weather, too, was turning ugly. Thus, instead of going to Camp IV, we actually descended to Camp II (21,500 feet).

The next morning, there was more bad news. At ten o'clock, a Taiwanese climber at Camp III slipped and fell 60 feet into a crevasse. When the team leader, who was already climbing towards Camp IV, was informed of this, he told his Sherpas to rescue the climber and take him down to the lower camp to recuperate. The leader then continued his climb. Some of our Sherpas who happened to be coming down the mountain helped rescue the injured climber, but he died later that evening. This incident was a portentous prologue to the great series of tragedies that was to follow.

The following day, May 10th, still at Camp II, around one o'clock, we observed through our binoculars the crowd of climbers making their way towards the summit, and we became uneasy be-cause they were very slow. We calculated that a route that would take us three hours to negotiate would take them six. So we an-ticipated problems, meaning that they wouldn't get to the summit or that there wouldn't be enough oxygen left for them to make a safe descent. Without oxygen, a climber becomes disoriented, de-hydrated, hypothermic, and can die very quickly.

inding climbers with the right mental and physical qualifications was ex-tremely important. For many climbers the initial glamour of ex-peditionary climbing soon fades, and the actual experience can be wearisome, disappointing, even devastating. The determination needed to keep melting snow for water and cooking can ultimately be more valuable than the skill to climb steep ice. Mental toughness and physical endurance, rather than muscular strength, are the essential qualities of successful high-altitude climbers.

—Arlene Blum, *Annapurna: A Woman's Place*

Around three in the after-noon, we heard over the radio that everyone was finally on top. But this was not good news. The rule of thumb on Everest is that you do not attempt to summit after one-thirty in the afternoon. You must descend. On this day, why the guides and expedition leaders pushed past that deadline, none of us knew.

Like a deadly avalanche, bad news began to roll in. Sherpas at Camp IV on the South Col radioed to say that only one or two climbers had returned from the summit and that many were miss-ing. We became very concerned when we were informed that ex-pedition leader Rob Hall was still on the South Summit, which is 28,700 feet, with one of his clients, Doug Hanson. To make mat-ters worse, higher on the mountain where the climbers were floundering, a fierce blizzard had developed. Winds howling at 60-80 miles per hour would quickly reduce visibility to a few yards, where the climber would see nothing but wind-churned snow.

At our camp, it was chaotic and frustrating. I was translating messages being radioed by Sherpas about missing mountaineers, but because it was already dark and the weather terrible, we were helpless. There was nothing we could do for the rest of the night except wait—and hope and pray that somehow the missing mountaineers would either find their way back to their tents or survive the night outside, an awful prospect.

Naturally, sleep was out of the question. Even under normal conditions, you don't sleep very well when you are in the high mountains. At three or four in the morning, we started getting calls again. Many climbers were still missing—or dead. The blizzard had died down, so four of our members, Ed, Robert, Araceli, and David, headed up to Camp III to establish emergency relief. David had also sent a message saying that anyone at Camp IV was free to take our oxygen bottles, food, and other supplies we had stored in our tent for our own climb. Sumiyo and I stayed behind to organize our own rescue work. Again, I was busy doing translations and interpretations as simultaneous calls came in from Sherpas and foreigners. I sent our Sherpas to gather medical supplies and other necessities from other expeditions, and as survivors were brought down to our camp, we gave them soup and tea, massaged them and gave them medicines. Frankly, I don't recall the next two days because we were so busy with the rescue work. We were no longer climbers but emergency medical personnel. Near Camp I at 19,500 feet, on top of the Khumbu Icefall, members of our expedition flattened out a helipad, pouring Kool-Aid into the shape of a cross to mark the landing spot. At Base Camp ten different expeditions merged into one huge rescue station. In those 48 hours, we helped many survive their ordeal, but not all.

After the helicopter flew out with the casualties, we assembled at Base Camp to recuperate and make preparations for our own attempt on the summit. Even though our supplies had been used up, we gathered what we required from other expeditions since, of the ten expedition teams, two-thirds decided not to continue. But we remained optimistic, and five days later, we once again headed for Everest.

On the South Col, at Camp IV, our final rest before the climb to the top, after five hours of sleep, I woke up at eleven at night. I had some *tsampa* (roasted barley dough) and dried meat, washed down with Ramen soup. Next, I packed my equipment: oxygen bottles first, tea in a flask, M&Ms and candy bars; extra goggles, gloves, socks, and batteries for the lamp. This fifteen-pound pack was the only thing I would carry. I adjusted my oxygen mask and harness, clipped on my crampons, put on my hat and switched on the headlamp. Then I grabbed my ice ax and stepped out into a clear, cold night.

As if to make up for its part in the recent tragedy, the weather appeared ideal. The wind, which can be the curse of climbing, was gentle, like a refreshing breeze; it was calm and quiet all around. I felt this mild weather was a good omen.

Ed, David, and a few Sherpas had left an hour before and had broken the trail. Sumiyo's health had deteriorated and she remained at the camp, the only one who would not go to the top.

The first half hour was a gradual climb on rocky, icy, crevasse-splintered terrain, but this gentle sloping ended abruptly at a steep, straight ascent. The easy part was over. And for the next eight to ten hours, I was going to have to use every resource I had, every trick I had learned as a climber; this was the final test of all my years of learning. It was going to be climb, crawl, clutch, trudge a few steps, pant for breath and rest for a few seconds, and then start

A time long before I had even heard the name of Everest, many times as a child I saw Mt. Everest, of course, rising high in the sky to the north above the tops of the nearer mountains. But it was not Everest then. It was Chomolungma. Usually Chomolungma is said to mean "Goddess Mother of the World." Sometimes "Goddess Mother of the Wind." But it did not mean either of these when I was boy in Solo Khumbu. Then it meant "The Mountain So High No Bird Can Fly Over It." That is what all Sherpa mothers used to tell their children—what my own mother told me—and it is the name I still like best for this mountain that I love.

—Tenzing Norgay quoted in *Tiger of the Snows: The Autobiography of Tenzing of Everest* by James Ramsey Ullman

all over again using hands, feet, ropes, ax—everything at my disposal to go up and not crawl back down.

As I climbed, especially when it was still dark, every step I took,
I took with care; everything I did, I did deliberately. Among these
massive mountains, I was nothing. A splinter that could be blown
away by a whiff of breeze. And I said my prayers, especially when
I suddenly came upon the dead body of Scott Fisher below the
South-East Ridge (27,500 feet). It was perhaps three in the morning. It was still dark, and my headlamp first picked out some ropes
and clothes. I thought I had stumbled upon the remains of a previous camp. Then I noticed a pair of boots with the feet in them.
Immediately I knew it was Scott's dead body, even though I did
not look at it directly. A few steps beyond, there was another dead
body, but it had been there for much longer, perhaps for two or
three years already. For the first
time, I became very scared. It
was the only moment during my
climb that I was caught by surprise and became unexpectedly
frightened. In the Sherpa culture, it's very bad luck to come
upon or touch a dead body. That

*Twelve climbers died on
Mt. Everest in May,
1996. It was the highest number
of deaths in one season in the history of Everest mountaineering.*

—RK

is why I did not "look" at the bodies. I hurried past them, if you
can "hurry" in such a situation, murmuring the "*Om Mani Padme
Hum*" prayer many, many times.

David and Ed were waiting on the South-East Ridge for the
Sherpas who were carrying the camera equipment. Resting on the
ridge, we witnessed a gorgeous sunrise and spent the next two
hours filming and fortifying ourselves with water, tea, and chocolate bars. My next extended rest was going to be the South
Summit, a steep, three-hour ascent over deep snow.

Throughout the climb, I felt strong and confident. It was the
strongest I had ever felt in my life. I thought of my father, of
course. He had been on this mountain 43 years ago. I felt his spirit
and his support. That is why I knew in my heart, "This is it! I will
be on top too!" Once the sun was out, during most of the climb,

I had my oxygen mask off my face because it was uncomfortable. I knew I was doing well, yet at the same time, I felt anxious. I just wanted to be on top. But I told myself to be careful. You look to one side, you see Tibet, and on the other side, you see Nepal, and each a scary, sheer drop of 8,000 feet. I got a little unsettled looking down, looking around. So I just looked up, waiting to see the summit, but it's not there! You climb, cross a ridge, climb some more—and there is another ridge. When I arrived at the South Summit, I was just 300 feet from the top, but I still couldn't see it. I then negotiated the treacherous traverse to get to the Hillary Step, a very precarious spot because you are totally exposed to the elements. I took care of that one too, and I began to think, well, yes, I've now seen and climbed these landmarks I'd heard so much about. But where was the top? There were two more ridges I had to get over. Just when I thought I'd never get to the top, I saw Ed coming down, and he said, "Hey, it's right there." We hugged and congratulated each other. With renewed strength and spirit, I continued.

I realized I was on the summit when I saw the prayer flags, left there by Sherpas before me. I saw David and gave him a hug. I thanked him because he had made it possible for me to fulfill my childhood dream. Then I cried, I was so happy. I was now the ninth person in our family to summt Everest.

I thought about my parents and prayed. I scattered some rice grains in the air and did *puja*. I left a prayer flag, a *khata*, pictures of my parents and His Holiness the Dalai Lama. Then I raised the flags of the United Nations, India, Nepal, USA—and Tibet. It was the first time since 1959 the national flag of Tibet had been unfurled on its own soil without fear of persecution, and I felt very proud. Finally, I left a small toy of my daughter's, just as my father had done.

I looked around. The summit sloped gently. You could fit twenty people comfortably. The view was stunning. I felt I could see everything everywhere stretched out far, far away and far down below—little puffs of clouds and gleaming Himalayan peaks, all beneath my gaze. I had my oxygen mask off but I had no trouble breathing. I only wore the thin polypropylene gloves. Even on top of Mt. Everest, there was little wind. We stayed almost two hours photographing and filming, savoring our success.

I called Base Camp and asked to be connected to my wife in Kathmandu. I told her, "Hey, I'm on top of the world!" She too was excited, but told me to be careful coming down because more people get hurt or killed descending. Well, there I was, flooded with a great sense of personal accomplishment, yet I also felt truly humble and grateful. I said *"thu chi chay"* (thank you) to the Goddess Chomolungma and asked her to get me down safely.

For me and the Sherpas, climbing a mountain is a pilgrimage because the mountains are sacred to us. A foreigner sees a mountain and wants to climb it because it is the highest or the most difficult. He wants to conquer it, subdue it. But for us, there is too much culture attached to these mountains to merely look upon them as something simply to climb and conquer, as if mountains can be subdued by us humans. That was why I felt humbled, and that was why I cried. Goddess Chomolungma had granted my lifelong wish. I was very happy. My family was even happier. I had promised my wife that after I climbed Mt. Everest, I would never climb another mountain again.

I will not break my word.

Jamling Tenzing, son of Tenzing Norgay Sherpa, lives in Darjeeling with his wife Soyang and their young daughter. A graduate of Northland College in Wisconsin, he operates an adventure travel company called Tenzing Norgay Adventures. He is featured in the forthcoming IMAX documentary Everest, *to be released in February 1998.*

Rajendra S. Khadka also contributed "In Buddha's Backyard" in Part Two.

✳

To my right a slender snow ridge climbed up to a snowy dome about 40 feet above our heads. But all the way along the ridge the thought had haunted me that the summit might be the crest of a cornice. It was too late to take risks now. I asked Tenzing to belay me strongly and I started cutting a cautious line of steps up the ridge. I waved Tenzing up to me.

A few more whacks of the ice ax, a few very weary steps and we were on the summit of Everest.

My first sensation was one of relief—relief that the long grind was over; that the summit had been reached, that in the end the mountain had been kind to us. But mixed with the relief was a vague sense of astonishment that I should have been the lucky one to attain the ambition of so many brave and determined climbers. It seemed difficult at first to grasp that we'd got there. I was too tired and too conscious of the long way down to safety really to feel any great elation. But as the fact of our success thrust itself more clearly into my mind I felt a quiet glow of satisfaction spread through my body—a satisfaction less vociferous but more powerful than I had ever felt on a mountaintop before. I turned and looked at Tenzing. Even beneath his oxygen mask and the icicles hanging from his hair I could see his infectious grin of sheer delight. I held out my hand and in silence we shook in good Anglo-Saxon fashion. But this was not enough for Tenzing and impulsively he threw his arm around my shoulders and we thumped each other on the back in mutual congratulations.

—Sir Edmund Hillary, *High Adventure*

$*\,^*_*\,*$

Honey Hunters

The old man and the bees.

OUR MEETING WITH THE OLD MAN STARTED BADLY. FOR OVER A year we had been searching for a honey hunter, and now having at last found one of the few who remain, it looked dangerously as if the acquaintance was to be short-lived.

"Why do you want to come with me into the forest? If it's honey that you want, I'll bring it back for you."

This strange quest to find a honey hunter began fours years before when by chance we discovered an old ladder coiled over the hearth of a villager's house. Woven from bamboo fiber, it was obviously the long and patient work of craftsmen. Wooden rungs had been carefully inserted at neat intervals between plaits of bamboo. Judging from the ladder's bulkiness, it looked about 50 meters long. We were curious—what could possibly be its purpose?

"It belonged to my father," our host told us. "He died fifteen years ago. He was a honey hunter."

He spoke with obvious pride; I was intrigued. Honey hunter...honey hunter...how does one hunt honey? The son had not followed the tradition of his father. But one day he took us to the foot of a tall cliff in the forest.

"Look up there," he said, pointing. "Those are the nests of wild bees."

At first I could only make out a black medallion tucked under the overhang of the cliff. It looked no different from the rest of the rock face until suddenly a wave rippled across its surface. It was alive with bees.

"My father climbed down the cliff on the ladder. He cut down the hive with two long bamboos. That's how he got the honey."

> "*With many of the city jobs now, you earn money at someone else's loss, sometimes by unfair means or trickery.*
>
> *Children don't learn this in school, but they study there for ten years, and then lose their appetite for farm work. They move to the city, then learn how to make money. But you can't eat money— who knows if it will be worth anything tomorrow?*"
>
> —Aama quoted by Broughton Coburn in *Nepali Aama: Life Lessons of a Himalayan Woman*

I tried to imagine the honey hunter dangling over the 60-meter void in a furious buzzing cloud of bees. How was it humanly possible? Who would risk their lives for honey? It sounded like a bizarre nightmare and even his own people had not found a successor.

"No one will go down the ladder," the young man told us. "There are no more honey hunters in this valley."

He explained that the tradition was a very ancient one with its own rituals; only those initiated in its ways could become hunters. The profession was usually passed down from father to son, but it was dangerous work and most young men did not want to risk their lives. Strangely it was in England that we next heard of the honey hunters. In an apiculturist's review, "Bee World," we discovered prehistoric cave paintings from Spain, Africa, and India illustrating the honey gathering: a man on a ladder with a basket secured by a rope dangling beside him; it was exactly as the young Nepali man had described his father. The paintings dated back as far as 12,000 years to the Paleolithic period. Could we find anyone today practicing this ancient craft?

In a valley deep in the Himalayan foothills and several days' walk from the nearest road, we came to a village for a full moon festival. There we met a villager who told us that one day's walk away lived an old man called Mani Lal. He had inherited the honey hunting tradition from his father. The next day we crossed the mountain torrent and climbed the gorge to the house of the honey hunter.

Despite his 64 years of age, Mani Lal was lithe and supple. He sat cross-legged on the verandah of his mud-brick house and lit a *hookah* of tobacco. The water gurgled as he inhaled deeply. Slowly he released a stream of smoke. His slight build hid his strength. He was strong and sinewy. His almond-shaped eyes, high cheekbones, and slightly flattened nose revealed the Mongoloid origins of his tribe.

When young, he had tried to join the Gorkha regiment of the British army, like many young men of the region, but failed the fitness test. He returned home and, following the tradition of his forefathers, became a hunter of game and honey. "Since my childhood," Mani Lal explained, "I've preferred running in the forest to mixing dung with earth. And so I became a hunter, a man of the forests, like my ancestors."

Mani Lal was gruff and suspicious of us, the only Westerners he had ever seen. He thought that we had come to buy honey from him. The idea of people who actually wanted to accompany him on the hunt was incomprehensible.

Sensing that this was our only chance I put all my passion into persuading him to allow us to come with him. I had to make him understand that we had come here not out of idle curiosity but to learn from him.

"People in the valley tell me that you are the last honey hunter. Your sons do not want to follow your work. When you die, your craft will disappear. There will be no one who can talk to the gods of the forest. No one to hunt the wild honey. The knowledge that has been passed down for centuries will disappear. We want to follow you and learn about your craft, not because we want to collect honey, but because we want to make a book about you. That way the honey hunters will never be forgotten."

Mani Lal looked thoughtful. I had struck a chord with him. After a moment's silence he nodded his head.

"Come to my house when the sun rises tomorrow. We leave for the hunt."

The next morning we were awake before the sun touched the ridges. By his hearth, Mani Lal was wiping the remains of millet porridge from his plate when we arrived. A man of few words, he silently put a handful of dried chilies, a small bag of flour, tobacco and his *hookah* into a shoulder bag and took down an old musket from the wall.

"*Jaane.* Let's go," the old man said.

The sun was just rising, chasing away the blue shadows of dawn as we left. Barefooted, Mani Lal walked quickly down a path winding between terraced fields of corn. There are no roads in these mountainous regions. Everything has to be carried on the backs of porters. Beyond Mani Lal's village, the hazy blue lines of thickly-forested gorges mark the domain of the jungle gods. An icy mountain soars 26,000 feet into a deep blue sky, omnipotent over the valley.

Before crossing the first river, Mani Lal waits for his companions to arrive. Sri Lal, his younger brother by eight years, is the first to join him. He is responsible for filtering the honey and processing the wax. He lights a cigarette and, holding it in his clenched fist, draws deeply before passing it to Mani Lal. Bal Bahadur, who at 47 is the youngest brother, is the next to arrive. He wears shoes bought in Kathmandu. He is the only one who is literate. As the group's accountant, he measures the honey yield and calculates the share of each hunter. The rest—Akam, Krishna, Man Bahadur, Nanda Lal, Amarjang and Purke—arrive together. Each carries a *doko* containing cooking pots, small bags of flour and tin jerrycans for the honey. One of them carries a live chicken. The animal will be sacrificed tomorrow.

"We leave for twenty suns," says Mani Lal.

In the world of the honey hunters his word is law. He decides the dates of the hunt, distributes the tasks and decides each man's share of the honey. It is he who guides the hunters on the secret trails that criss-cross the forest. He is the only one able to speak to the gods and descend the bamboo ladder which Man Bahadur carries in heavy coils on his back.

Mani Lal's village is the last habitation before the forest begins. The river marks the border separating the cultivated valleys and the sacred territory of Pholo, the god of the jungle, the cliffs, and the hunt. In a low voice, Mani Lal recites mantras of protection and taps each of the hunters on the shoulder with a bundle of branches.

Ahead, faint trails wind deep into the forest. Mani Lal leads the way. Behind him is Krishna, the smallest of the group, who climbs the narrow cliff ledges to light the faggots of leaves that are hoisted close to the bees' nests to smoke them out. Next comes Nanda Lal, who wears the black waistcoat of a city shopkeeper and canvas shoes bought on a trip to "Nepal," as the Gurung villagers call Kathmandu. He is followed by Amar Jang, aged 38, the youngest of the hunters. His task is the most difficult, after the old man's. He is Mani Lal's assistant on the cliffs, maneuvering on dizzy ledges without the security of a rope. Next is Purke, the oldest. He has now retired from the hunt but still lends a hand around the camp. And finally, Man Bahadur, bent under the weight of the ladder.

Like creatures of the forest, the men blend in with their surroundings. Their woolen capes, known as *bokkus*, are the colour of dead leaves. They walk quickly and assuredly over trackless undergrowth. Their bare feet grip the earth like roots. Unhesitatingly, they leap from stone to stone across a torrent. From time to time they stop to pick leeches from between their toes. The old man spits tobacco juice onto his feet to repel the bloodsuckers.

It is difficult to keep up with the hunters. If we don't walk at their pace, they will vanish from our sight. But at the same time we have to watch our own feet. The ground is wet and slippery and the rocks covered in moss. As well as carrying heavy photo equipment, we are much heavier and clumsier than the agile Gurungs.

"If I wore shoes like you," Mani says, "I would fall flat on my face."

We walk all day and make camp under the shelter of an over-hanging rock. I sit by the fire and peel off my socks bloody with leeches. I flick each of the vile creatures into the fire, taking pleasure as they sizzle.

The circle of firelight marks the only human presence in the forest. The night is cold, but the hunters wear only their fine cotton tunics. After eating they make up their beds. One man fills his *bokkus* with dead leaves to use as a mattress, his long cotton waistband worn during the day unravels to become a sheet. The *hookah* is passed around one last time before they fall asleep beside the crackling fire.

Next morning, before the sun's warm fingers have reached into the gorge, Mani Lal is up, shaping an effigy of the jungle-god Pholo out of millet dough. On a stone he places the effigy with offerings: an egg, rice, corn, and juniper. Man Bahadur follows with a chicken in his hands. Squatting on a boulder, Mani Lal murmurs ritual incantations. He sprinkles the corn over the slab and burns the juniper. A sweet, acrid smoke rises and the chicken struggles in Man Bahadur's hands as if sensing its fate. Mani Lal slices the bird's throat with one deft stroke of his curved knife. Rising to his feet, he faces the jungle and addresses the god.

"Pholo, Lord of the Forest, I offer this blood to you. I beg you remember that sacrifice is well made. I beseech you not to take any of our lives. God Pholo, look kindly on our hunt."

The hunters would never begin the hunt until the sacrifice is made. Without it, they believe, misfortune, ill-health, or even death would follow. That is what happened to Mani Lal's father, we were told. He was on the ladder cutting down a nest when he was stung in the eye—it was the day when he did not make an offering to Pholo. The old honey hunter lost the sight in that eye and could not harvest honey again.

Mani Lal tears open the bird's chest with his fingers and pulls out its heart and lungs. He examines them for omens. There are no sinister white veins indicating a man's death. The swelling, shaped like a small head, promises a bountiful hunt.

Sri Lal cooks the rest of the bird in a curry sauce. Those parts used in the divination are fried separately and when barely cooked, passed around as a delicacy.

Mani Lal is insistent that we eat.

"*Khanus, Khanus!* Eat!"

We try to refuse politely.

Pleasantly but firmly, the old man makes sure that we take our share. If we are to be with the group, the safety of them all depends on us playing a full part of the ceremonies to the gods.

We leave for Kyumro Bhir, which means a stepped cliff of rocks and hives. All of the cliffs have names: *Samsar Bhir* (the cliff of 100 hives); *Kirlu* (from a small hive comes a lot of honey); and *Sabro* (scattered hives). Purke, too old for the difficult trail ahead, stays at the camp, watching the line of brown-hooded figures disappearing into the forest.

Soon the path climbs steeply up the wall of the gorge, and Mani Lal swings up and over an overhanging branch to reach a higher trail. We try to follow, but not even the other hunters can follow the old man. They cut a trail through the undergrowth with their sickles.

At a meeting of two trails, a party of boys and men await. All wear *bokkus* as protection against the bees and carry a variety of containers in anticipation of the harvest to come. Some are buffalo herders who have come to trade yogurt and milk for honey.

Mani Lal leads on, for he is the only one who knows the way to the cliffs.

At the foot of the cliff, Mani Lal and Amarjang climb first. The loads are passed from hand to hand to the cliff top. The men work together in silence. They do not need to talk. Each man knows his task. Each of them respects the other. One hunter slips. Another helps him to his feet.

"Like the fibres of a rope, our forces are united to allow us to go where one man could not travel alone," Mani Lal says, clenching his hands together. "But the bees are a better example of solidarity than man."

Mani Lal signals for us to be quiet. He points to a large black crescent on the cliff face.

"Be quiet, otherwise the bees will know that we're here and will attack."

Apis laboriosa are the largest honeybees known. They are twice the size of European honeybees and known for their aggressiveness. They are also among the hairiest honeybees in the world, perhaps an adaptation to the cold of high altitudes; they are found between 4,000 and 13,000 feet in Nepal and the Yunnan province in China.

The bees' most striking features, however, is that they are the only honeybees to spend winter without a honeycomb. In the winter months the bees migrate to lower altitudes and cluster in huge masses on the trees and grass. Thanks to a low metabolic rate and a tolerance for unusually low body temperatures, they can survive on the nutrients stored in their bodies.

At the top of the cliff, Man Bahadur unrolls the ladder into the void. The ladder is gold as honey, having spent the winter over Akam's hearth. The smoke protects it from insects but the fibres dry out, rendering it fragile.

> *Turning a corner, I reached a huge cliff, over 300 feet tall, that blocked my way. I climbed a spur of rock opposite the cliff to get a better view. There on the face of the cliff were several huge beehives; although there were no bees present—probably dormant during this winter season. Each hive was a single exposed sheet of wax hanging down from beneath a rock overhang or ledge; they were pocket-shaped and from a distance looked like a pale beard on a man's face. The largest hive was almost six feet across and four feet long. Others were much smaller. I could easily see the details of larval cells that covered the surface of the hive—a marvelous geometric design that stretched from the top to the bottom.*
>
> —Edward W. Cronin, Jr.,
> *The Arun: A Natural History
> of the World's Deepest Valley*

At the camp the ladder is soaked in water and carefully checked, for Mani Lal's life depends on it.

Eric throws his nylon rope alongside the old man's ladder. Mani Lal looks at it disapprovingly.

"Your rope is too thin—it's not strong enough, you will never be able to go down the cliff with me," he says, rolling the cord between his fingers.

"And its slippery. How are you going to hold it? Look at my ladder, the bamboo ropes are five times the thickness of your cord, and my hand can get a good grip. The wooden rungs permit me to stop or go down wherever I like. Anyway, I am the only one to go down the ladder. No one, not even my own men, have gone down the cliff with me."

To get the photos of the honey hunt, we have to be in the action. Already the smoke of the fires lit at the foot of the cliff is billowing upwards, driving the bees away from the nest.

Mani Lal turns away. He has more important tasks ahead than dealing with this crazy foreigner. He sprinkles grains of rice on a broad leaf and places it at the foot of the tree where the ladder is secured. He begins intoning mantras soliciting the god for protection in a low, murmuring, sing-song prayer, like the hum of insects. A gentle breeze rustles the trees like a whisper. Birds call in the distance. The moment is bewitching.

"What should I do?" Eric thinks out loud. "I am about to risk my life in the same abyss as Mani Lal. Have I anything for the gods?" He feels in his pocket and his fingers close on a block of chocolate. Standing behind the old man, Eric makes his own private offering to Pholo. I hope he likes chocolate.

Now Mani Lal puts on his only protection against the bees: a pair of army pants given to him by a cousin in the Gorkhas, and a cape. Then, without a word to his companions, he starts down the swaying ladder.

The old man descends like a spider spinning on a frail strand of web. His bare feet hook each rung like claws. The slightest error of judgment means death. Amarjang watches from his perch. Gripping the ladder with one hand, he leans away from the cliff into the yawning emptiness.

Eric abseils down the cliff beside Mani Lal until they pass an overhang. He no longer touches the rock face, and turns, dangling in the air. Suddenly he sees the nest just below, stuck to the rock. The colony is bigger than it looked from the ground: four feet high and five feet wide. Mani Lal seems so small and vulnerable in comparison. The surface is a crawling, buzzing mass of bees. Sensing the men's presence, they ripple and hum in an ominous wave across the brown medallion, then fall motionless.

Up to 50,000 bees cover the nest to a thickness of several centimeters. In this way they can regulate the temperature of the nest, vital to the survival of the bee larvae and pupae. If the nest warms up too much, bees will leave, or if it cools, bees will form extra layers.

The wind is blowing the smoke of the fires away from the cliff. Mani Lal gestures an order to Amarjang, not daring to speak lest the bees attack. Amarjang relays the message to the top of the cliff and within minutes a flaming bundle of leaves is lowered for Mani Lal to push under the nest with a bamboo pole. Panic runs over the living surface. The bees buzz furiously and depart in a deafening swarm, unveiling the golden comb.

Now Man Bahadur throws down a short stick tied to a rope. The old man threads it through the lower half of the nest. Nothing distracts him from his task; neither the void below nor the bees crawling over his skin. Again and again he thrusts the pole into the nest, tearing the semi-circle of waxy brood cells away from the honey comb until the golden crescent falls. Secured by the rope, it spins and knocks against Mani Lal. The ladder swings like a pendulum, and he holds on tightly until it steadies.

The scene is fantastic—we are witnessing one of man's ancient rituals; Eric forgets the deafening buzz, forgets that he is hanging 120 feet in midair. He grabs a camera lens out of his jacket pocket, and a sharp pain makes him jerk his hand to his face. It's his first sting. Worse than that, he drops the lens into the void below. For the first time he sees that he's covered with bees. He glances over to the old man. Mani Lal is calm and confident. Despite the dizzying void and stinging insects, he is taking a break. Calmly he lights a cigarette. The sight is reassuring. For him it is just another day's work.

At the base of the cliff, Akam seizes the comb as soon as it is lowered within reach. At the end of the day it will be carried back to camp and melted into blocks of wax. Bees buzz angrily around the hunters and villagers. They huddle under their *bokkus* for protection.

"Now send the basket," shouts Mani Lal. A bamboo basket lined with goatskin is tied to the rope and Man Bahadur hauls it up to the nest. The bees close to the nest are disorientated by the smoke and crawl groggily over Mani Lal's face and into his hood. Calmly he picks them off before starting to cut into the honeycomb.

Every muscle in the old man's body is tensed as he thrusts a second bamboo pole into the upper part of the nest, peeling off slabs of comb heavy with honey to fill the basket. At the foot of the cliff the upturned faces of the villagers are smeared and radiant as they stand with mouths wide open and saucepans outstretched to catch the golden drops.

"It's raining honey!" they cry.

Eric Valli, a former cabinetmaker from France, and Diane Summers, an Australian lawyer, met on a bus in 1984 in Nepal. Living in the Himalaya with their two daughters, they have written seven books on Nepal and their work is regularly featured in National Geographic *and* Geo *magazines. They work in depth with their subjects and take several years to complete each of their stories. Their last book,* Caravans of the Himalaya, *was published by the National Geographic Society in the USA and by Éditions de La Martinière in Paris.*

✳

Outside the screen door was a diminutive man in village attire, grey-brown tunic and shorts.

I went out on the porch. *"Hajur?"* I responded, and he showed me a large plastic jug wrapped in a cloth of questionable sanitation. It took careful inspection to figure out that what he was selling was honey. I was delighted. *"Ekchin,"* one minute, I said. I went back in the kitchen and got a plastic peanut butter jar. *"Kati rupia?"* How many rupees, I asked.

He squinted and held the jar at arm's length. *"Ek saya,"* one hundred, he said.

"Dherai mahango!" Too expensive, I exclaimed. He held out the jar again. Ninety. Well okay, it's not every day a man steps out of *National Geographic* to sell you honey.

—Barbara J. Scot, *The Violet Shyness of Their Eyes: Notes from Nepal*

✦ ✦ ✦

Farewell to Aama

Remembrances and reconciliation come to the author
during the memorial ritual of his Nepali mother.

MY COOK AND HANDYMAN WERE TALKING IN THE KITCHEN OF my house in Kathmandu, rather quietly, it seemed. The house wasn't right, as if there were another presence, or something was missing. I climbed the half flight of stairs to the sitting room, listening, reflecting, feeling a peculiar trepidation. I didn't hear the cook slip behind me up the stairs to the landing.

"You had a phone call," he said from the passageway. His voice startled me. "From some relative of your old Gurung lady. She died. She's dead. Gone." One of her grandnephews posted in Kathmandu with the Nepal Police Band had left a message, and I phoned him. He said that her body had been cremated a few days ago. A relative had called him from the single phone line in the Syangja district and asked him to tell me about it. I had been close to Aama for over fifteen years, after living in the loft of her water buffalo shed for two years in the early '70s. Now she was gone.

It's happening again. My mother had done the same thing, she had died without allowing me a chance to speak to her. My mind was prepared for this, from years earlier, but my emotions were not. There was something left I needed from Aama [with whom he had stayed when he was a Peace Corps volunteer], a further un-

239

derstanding, an ability. And there was something I needed to give her. I needed to tell her that I loved her.

Why did I need to tell her?

Well, because I couldn't, or for some reason didn't, tell my own mother. Maybe she knew that I loved her, anyway. But I should have said so.

No, you can't die now.

Mothers die, I should know well.

Who will preserve me from my wandering mind, from my discursive, malignant, self-indulgent thoughts? Who will be here to remind me to stop taking life too seriously, to relieve me of the burden of my attachments?

Aama had indulged, too. She indulged her memories, and her worries. But all conditions of body and mind are temporary—the lamas and Brahmin priests had said so. And there is a reason for everything.

Sun Maya, Aama's daughter, later told me that during the week preceding her death, Aama had grown even more afraid of falling, and used her cane constantly. She had become forgetful, and her hunger dwindled to nothing. To give the appearance of eating, she squatted as usual on her low stool, the best position for digestion, and ate small amounts. She admitted to a relative that she was merely tasting the food in order to sweeten her mouth and to please her daughter.

Sun Maya knew what was happening. Aama grew weaker, and moved to a straw mat on her veranda. There, she could look out over the hills and terraces and forests she had known since birth.

The Gurung say that at the time of death, all one's ancestors and descendants will parade before them. They must have, Sun Maya told me, for Aama was audibly reciting their names, and Didi's and hers and mine, moments before she breathed her last fistful of air. On the morning of the auspicious full moon of the winter month of *Magh*, Aama quietly passed away.

When Aama's breathing stopped, Sun Maya called the lama.

Inside her house, the lama chanted as he washed her body. A relative tied a piece of women's clothing and some fruit and flowers to the end of a long bamboo pole, the *a-lāa*, and erected it beside the peak of the roof—to identify her home as a place of mourning. Sun Maya broke her glass bracelets and unfastened her hair, in renunciation of adornment. Aama's three nephews, her closest male kin, quietly greeted the other relatives who gathered on Aama's terrace.

In the Gurung community there are two ways of disposing of dead bodies, cremation and burial. By studying the position of the constellations at the moment of death the priest decides the method of disposal of the body. There is a common burial ground for the deceased of a village. If the ground becomes crowded an old grave may be dug up and the bones removes to make room for the new body, but it must be a grave belonging to the same family as the dead person. When a grave is dug some rice grains are scattered before the body is lowered into it. A small piece of gold or silver is put into the mouth of the body and some food and liquor is put on top of the body before the grave is filled with earth.

—Dor Bahadur Bista,
People of Nepal

With exaggerated formality, Sun Maya's husband, Mani Prasad, organized seating for them. He dispatched his daughters to find additional straw mats, bamboo for fashioning a bier, ritual objects, cloth, and matches for lighting the incense and the funeral pyre. His motions looked practiced, as if he had been waiting for the day when he could have the last word about what would happen to Aama, while publicly demonstrating an appreciation for her that he hadn't displayed while she was alive. Partly as a result of the grief of blood relatives, a deceased Gurung's son-in-law traditionally acts as the executor. As usual, Mani Prasad was wearing a hangover conspicuously garnished with a few drinks.

Eldest Nephew presented the lama with a length of hand-spun cotton cloth for covering Aama's body. Then the nephews carried her from the house and placed her on a short bamboo frame positioned in the middle of her terrace. The lama clipped pieces of her fingernails and a lock of hair and placed them in a small bamboo tube, which he hid in the village. Were witches or ghosts to encounter these symbolic body parts, they could use them to interfere with the transmigration of her soul. Both the lama and the shaman will need them later, to guide her spirit on to Siminasa, the final resting place of the souls of the ancestors.

From the front of the funeral procession, Third Eldest Nephew, a shaman like his father, shot arrows in the cardinal directions to ward evil spirits away from the bier, which was carried by the other two nephews. From the woodpile, the party of relatives selected firewood that Aama had cut only a few weeks before. Now it would be used for her own cremation. They joined the procession, a log each on their right shoulders. When the bier approached the peak of the cremation ridge across from the Shiva shrine, the lama blew a distant, melancholy blast on his conch.

Mani Prasad prepared the funeral pyre, a task not assigned to a relative of Aama's lineage. By participating in his mother-in-law's cremation, he could show gratitude for the wife Aama had given him, while reestablishing his link with the wife's lineage.

The lama sat cross-legged on a mat, then untied a stack of woodblock-printed pages wrapped in cloth. His upper body rocked softly as he droned a sequence of prayers, in Tibetan.

*O*n the way from the Khumbu, I had witnessed a funeral that the Tibetans called a "sky burial." A long procession carried the body, flexed into a tight sitting position, to the top of a nearby pass. The last two men in line carried axes. We watched them as they hacked the body to pieces, exposing it to the elements and to the vultures, which would pick the flesh from the bones.

—Parker Antin with Phyllis Wachob Weiss, *Himalayan Odyssey: The Perilous Trek to Western Nepal*

Eldest Nephew placed a cotton wick dipped in mustard oil in Aama's mouth and lit it, then ignited the twigs beneath the pyre. The relatives descended to the village, leaving thorn branches on the trail to keep ghosts from following them, while Mani Prasad and the nephews remained to feed and tend the fire. The sparks that arose from her body carried away, in their flickering traces, her *prana,* her breath of life, the same vital essence that animated the earth from which the Christian God molded mankind. Aama had spoken of what happens next.

"As the body burns, its flesh peels off. Sometimes, by the light of its own flames, the letters that are written on the dead person's forehead become visible. These letters are what defined our destiny, and were recorded there on the day of chainti, *the sixth day after birth. If they are black, it means the person was given a troublesome life, and if red, they had a good life and can expect a good rebirth."*

Sun Maya asked Mani Prasad about the letters on Aama's forehead. He said that he hadn't bothered to look and that he didn't believe in superstition, anyway.

The sunset expired, but the coals from Aama's pyre smoldered on. The nephews silently raked and folded the fire's subsiding form onto itself. By morning, only ashes remained.

After the cremation, the lama was the first to step into Aama's house. The relatives watched as he chanted and shook a ritually empowered dagger, the *gwiyantar*, that amplified the tantric energy that surrounded him like an aura, enabling him to chase out the evil spirits that are attracted by death to take lodging inside.

According to the Gurung, Aama's soul would remain in the house for one day. On the second day, it would move to the veranda, then advance to the courtyard on the third. From there, her soul would move to the neighborhood, the village, the fields and forest, at each stage becoming more aware and mobile, like a precocious child.

On the day before Aama's soul was to leave the terrace, the lamas announced—chanting in a way that she would be able to hear—the date of her *arghaun*, the funerary ceremony in which she will be guided to Siminasa. The *arghaun* would take place after six months, during the summer monsoon. Until the time of this ceremony, however, Aama's soul would wander.

On the day of the *arghaun* I rounded the corner at the point of the ridge. The rhythmic *TUN-a-ku-toe, TUN-a-ku-toe* beat of a tablalike drum sounded from within the village, accompanied by the slow bass of a bigger companion drum, the *dhön-dü*, calling relatives and villagers to Aama's *arghaun*. This was the first time I would see the village when Aama wasn't there.

Her porch and terrace were packed with people, many of whom I didn't know, spilling over into the surrounding houses and buffalo sheds. Sun Maya was inside. At 58, she looked older than Aama did when I first arrived in the village; her cheeks were hollow from fatigue and hardship and recurring sickness. Her hair was unplaited for the *arghaun,* and it hung in loose, gray-flecked tangles. So this was why Aama wanted to see American women pull back their free-flowing hair: Wherever she turned, their loose hair was a reminder of death.

Weary but restless, Sun Maya hovered in the kitchen and in the background, helping her daughters prepare tea, busying herself. She nodded at me to follow her, then pushed through the girls interlocked in sitting, squatting, and kneeling positions on the veranda. The normally open porch was darkened by their line of heads pressed against the inside of the thatched eave. Raindrops inflated and hung like tears from the tips of the dangling tendrils of thatch straw. Wisps of steam from the sweat and monsoon mud enhanced the smell of incense and mustard-seed hair oil.

Sun Maya cleared a place for me to sit in line with the three nephews, the classificatory sons in the absence of Aama's own. Like the other ex-army relatives who were standing outside, two of the nephews wore dark-colored vests and skirts of white cotton cloth wrapped several times about their waists and secured by British Army ammunition belts. They exchanged news, joked loudly, and retold the stories they had saved up for such gatherings.

With both hands, Sun Maya presented me a tumbler of distilled millet spirits. We spoke about her daughters and whether there would be enough rice to feed the nearly two hundred relatives and guests. I asked her where Bujay was, Aama's elderly cousin who lived in the house below. Bujay died one month after Aama. Each one of Aama's other remaining cousins and in-laws had also passed away.

Outside, sonorous chanting and staccato discharges from the lamas' human thighbone trumpets signified that the "*plah,*" Aama's effigy, had been constructed. The nephews adjourned to the terrace and I squeezed onto the veranda.

Instantly upon seeing the effigy, I was transported beyond the crowd and clamor to a morning several years before. Sitting exactly where I now sat, I had watched Aama gaze at the empty courtyard and say that she could see in advance, as clearly as a memory, the people and the colors of her funerary rite.

It will be a tight fit for the lamas and their ritual implements. They will sit on straw mats here at the foot of my veranda, while women with their hair untied circumambulate the plah. *The* plah *will be placed in the middle and toward the back of the plinth—which they may fashion from the wooden bed that I sleep on. The plinth will be decorated with butter lamps, rich foods, incense, cloth and flowers. My relatives will weave through it all to present offerings, and my Gorkha pensioner nephews from distant villages will be there, the ones I haven't seen in years. They will stand to the side much of the time except when they are inside drinking and telling stories, or when the lamas or shamans call them out....*

Aama's prophecy seemed to guide the service unfolding before us. In the center of the plinth, Mani Prasad had fabricated the *plah* from a bamboo frame about two feet high, and stretched a white cloth over it. The pair of spectacles that were fitted in San Francisco perched on the effigy above her gold and coral necklace. The fingernails and lock of hair were fastened inside the *plah*, along with a *jantar*, a folded square of paper inscribed with Aama's name and a consecrated mystical design, the pictorial counterpart of a protective mantra. A symbolic shed roof made of bamboo screens decorated with poinsettia bracts covered the *plah* and plinth. Aama's gray-haired second cousins and nieces continued to lavish it with food that she liked, showing her that they had not forgotten her. Sun Maya added to the pile the eggs and half pint of rum I had brought, but first opened the rum bottle—to allow Aama to drink from it.

The nephews and male relatives, the trunk of her family tree, stood with their backs to the sun, protectively shading Aama's effigy. The women cousins tossed back their heads and cried as they circled the plinth, and sang an asynchronous but melodic plea that Aama's wandering spirit come and accept their offerings, then retreat to and reside forever in Siminasa, never to return to the village as a ghost or spirit. After each circuit, they paused to heat their open palms on the rows of butter lamps and redirect their hands toward the *plah*, transferring to it the lamps' warm votive energy.

Bystanders stalled on the trail to peer over the stone wall and down upon the terrace. Aama's effigy had been concealed from direct view, but they could sense that potentially troublesome spirits were being dealt with. Their silent stares expressed contemplation of their own mortality.

...And my scoundrel son-in-law will be there, too, smoking and drinking and carrying on, waving his arms, masquerading as an ex-army officer, embarrassing my daughter....

Mani Prasad sat disrespectfully on the edge of the plinth, his back to Aama's effigy, chain-smoking cigarettes that were jammed between the first two fingers of his right hand, which was clenched into a ball. The veins on his temple distended as he sucked with a low whistling sound from the spiral of his fist. He let his hand drop as if he had picked up a rock, inspected and then discarded it. His other hand wrapped loosely around an antique glass bottle, now less than half full of alcohol. Taking a deep swig, he jerked his head to the side and flung a straightened arm mock-threateningly at the nearest relatives, children mostly, those talking too loudly or not sitting in the proper place. This theatrical, alcoholic sense of propriety was his way of compensating for a lack of manners, and prompted some relatives to smile sympathetically as they would at a retarded person, one who couldn't help himself. Mani Prasad had become a caricature of himself, and he savored a contrary pleasure in shocking his own kin. A self-satisfied smile sneaked across his lips whenever someone responded to him, even if with defiance.

One of the shamans carefully cracked open a raw egg and poured it into a brass bowl. The unbroken yoke would indicate in which form Aama's soul would return, whether as a bird, mouse, or other animal. The shaman set the bowl on a bamboo mat and spread a dusting of ashes around it, to record footprints. Another shaman suspended a chicken by one foot from a low bamboo archway, to isolate the precise moment when Aama's soul would enter the effigy. He carefully calmed the hen. It hung motionless for several minutes.

Abruptly the hen's wings fluttered vigorously, signifying that Aama's soul had occupied the *plah*. At once, the women wailed. As if melding into a single body, they fell to their knees at the plinth and cast their hands onto the base of the effigy.

Aama was here. She had come to see us in the Land of the Living. My face flushed with shock and bewilderment, which suffused into a glow of awe and affection. She looked as she did sitting next to us on tour in America, quietly watching, ready to speak once she could compose her words or recall a proverb. Her eyes caught me not paying attention, not hearing what she'd been saying. She was happy to be with us.

The relatives may supplicate and attract the soul, but only a shaman can guide her onward. The shamans separated into two groups, and both circled counterclockwise with the *plah* between them. They swung their legs in unison, drumming single beats at one-second intervals. Chanting a ballad called the *shyerga*, they described her destination and named the frontiers and dangerous regions they passed, with her along, making sure she took the correct forks in the trail.

One group of shamans assumed Aama's voice. "*What is happening to me?*" they called in song across the *plah*.

The other group responded in the voice of the shaman guides. "You are dead, you have died."

"*How did I die?*" Aama's side asked.

"Of old age, after a long, fruitful, spiritual life."

"*Why are you doing this* arghaun?"

"You have been taken by the God of Death, but we the living have pulled you from his grip and have cleared the way for you to reach Siminasa. You will remain there with your ancestors, or from there you will be reborn."

Village Hindus and Buddhists believe that only great practitioners are able to pass through the after-death state without succumbing to crushing distraction: The light is blinding, the noise deafening, the smell overwhelming, the taste strong, and the touch enervating. Confusion prevails.

Clearly, the nonpractitioner needs guidance after death. This period is most distressing because the soul does not retire easily. It is grasping anxiously for the life it has lost, or is searching for a new rebirth. Unable to recognize its condition as that of death, the soul can loiter about the village, vulnerable to vagrant spirits, resisting the journey to Siminasa. Only a clever shaman can retrieve such a wandering soul and lead it onward. They say that the soul most onerous to survivors, the one most difficult to escort, is that of a person who has died an untimely death.

The lamas pointed their thighbone trumpets skyward, ballooned their cheeks, and blew convulsing, glottal blasts. Halos of smoke from the incense and butter lamps filled the ritual enclosure of the *plah*, anointing Aama's effigy. Hypnotically, the shamans revolved around the plinth.

There she was. My mother. She had taken a place beside Aama and sat a congenial distance from her on the plinth. They had found the pathway, and the shamans were guiding them. They were together.

My mother fixed me with her wry, charming smile. Her face was framed by ageless blond curls. She looked at ease. *You have found me.*

I wanted to suspend her image there, to bundle up the warmth of her face and secure it in an insulated shrine. I could see myself in her features, and recognized her gestures as part of me, the part of me that was love—the love that had been dormant and reclusive, afraid that, if it were expressed, would be taken away, just as she herself had been. This love was the dangerous and powerful force that occupied, along with my mother, the terrifying rooms I had been unable to enter in my recurring nightmarish dreams.

I glanced at Aama. She returned my look with a glow that said, *Yes. We are who you think. Now you can see, young one, that I am not different from your mother, and she is not different from me. In death, we are all kin.*

Broughton Coburn also contributed "A Nosy Neighbor" in Part One.

*

With intense one-pointed concentration say this inspiration-prayer:

> May the divine *vidyadharas* think of me and with great love lead me on the path. When through intense tendencies I wander in *samsara,* on the luminous light-path of the innate wisdom, may *vidyadharas* and warriors go before me, their consorts the *dakinis* behind me; help me to cross the *bardo's* dangerous pathway and bring me to the Pure Realm of Space.

By saying this inspiration-prayer with deep devotion, he will dissolve into rainbow light in the heart of the divine *vidyadharas*, and be born in the Pure Realm of Space, there is no doubt.

—Guru Rinpoche, *The Tibetan Book of the Dead: The Great Liberation through Hearing in the Bardo*

ALLAN AISTROPE

* * *

Virtue's Children

A new world unfolds when the author
opens up his heart.

I HAD CAREFULLY PLANNED A ONCE-IN-A-LIFETIME SABBATICAL from my overly systemized California routines. A time out, a rest, an adventure, and perhaps even an eye-opener on certain exotic levels. I was going to Nepal. After dramatic farewells to family members and friends, and closing down all visible signs of my life in San Francisco, I boarded the aircraft and made a pledge to myself: to live and mingle with the Nepali people, be open, observe, and learn. I had no illusions of meditative posturing on mountain tops, questing the ultimate trek, or seeking enlightenment at ancient temples or monasteries, but I did want to return to a charming society that three years earlier, as a tourist/trekker, I had briefly gazed on in distant admiration. I hoped to become acquainted with the people of Nepal who had impressed me so much with their strength and grace, and with favor I might even glimpse a revelation or two, if not from the heavens, maybe from the streets.

The first three months of my new life in Nepal were a blend of visitors from home, a memorable trek, language lessons, festivals, endless photo opportunities, and what I came for—friendship with some of the Nepali people. I was also lucky to find a Nepali family who happily (and with some compassion) adopted me. They

have, ever since, provided me with home, love, plentiful food, occasional nursing duty, and always high spirits.

In my fourth month I was giving serious thought to making a
contribution by doing volunteer work in Kathmandu. Volunteers
are badly needed in Nepal, and there are plenty of causes to
choose from. My own considerations ceased abruptly when a
friend asked if I would be interested in teaching English at a local
orphanage. Since I had an unexercised Education minor and an
unbounded affection for Nepali children, it seemed an appropriate choice. Also, I was curious to see what a Kathmandu orphanage looked like.

My first visit to the orphanage was to meet with the director,
and in effect, sign up. The building, which housed Nepal's first orphanage, is a long, two-story, imposing monster of brick, mud,
cracked cement, and faded whitewash, and creeping along the back
side is the Vishnumati River, one of the truly rotten rivers of this
planet, a sewer line for Kathmandu. The orphanage was built in an
area originally considered forbidden and haunted because of the
ancient burning *ghats* for the dead positioned along the river
banks. With time and population explosion this area of temples
and *ghats* had filled in with a school, traditional mud-and-brick
housing, tin-roofed shops, and clumsy roads, all in crumbling,
mildewy, smelly condition.

The orphanage director was gracious. He and the other
founders of the Paropakar orga-
nization had spent time in prison
under the autocratic Rana government as punishment for their
efforts to institute Nepal's first
social service programs.

*In Nepali, "Paropakar"
means philanthropy or
benevolence.*

—RK

I was given a tour of the complex, which consisted of a series
of depressing rooms, the largest of which was to be my classroom.
A light bulb dangled from a disintegrating ceiling, and a small
homemade blackboard hung on the front wall. All in all, I was encouraged. I was surprised that we weren't encountering any of the
children during our wanderings, but as we moved on I became

aware of hushed voices trailing us from other rooms, and occasional flashes of small dark heads bobbing from behind doors and windows. Very flattered, I knew that my arrival must be something of a major event. It was for all of us, as it turned out.

My first English class was also my introduction to the children, but my enthusiasm was compromised by a nagging fear that orphanage inmates would be unruly, and I wasn't sure I could successfully adopt a stern, no-nonsense manner. My classroom reception was, however, humbling. The boys greeted me with a standing welcome, brilliant smiles and a chorus of "*Namaste.*" Heady stuff. I tried to duck the obligatory teacher's title of "Sir," but the boys were respectfully insistent, and officially and otherwise, I became Allan Sir.

Early on I organized my classes into three levels—primary, juniors and seniors—with alternated schedules, and I then proceeded to explore my way to a productive teaching style. As opposed to any memories I have of my own school days, the boys appeared excited to be learning English, and in particular, from an American. They ranged in age from four to seventeen, and when they returned in the early afternoon from their regular schooling across the road, my classes began and ran into the evening. I felt some guilt taking them away from what I was sure was serious play time, so I aimed at something entertaining and developed my classes to be short on grammar, long on spoken English, and heavily dosed with questions, jokes, and good-natured ribbing from all sides. I was impressed with how swiftly their conversational English progressed, with grammar a shade behind.

As time and classes moved along, a genial sociability blossomed, and for most of the boys it was the first time in their lives they experienced a genuine, close friendship with an adult. My position in flock shifted, and I became, with much gratification, a doting, paternal guru of sorts. English classes had their place, but shooting-the-breeze, back-patting, dispensing of advice, dressing wounds, and table tennis (the boys are killers), were claiming a fair portion of our time together.

As my rapport with the boys grew, so did my recognition of

their daily struggle with considerable hardships. Except for meager clothing and a few school supplies, they had no worldly possessions, but with the extremes of poverty and squalor so visible in Kathmandu, they gratefully viewed their bottle as half full, and in good Nepali form celebrated their simple lives without complaint.

In my second month of teaching, these hard-won virtues were exemplified with profound clarity through the deeds of Ishwor, a bright, good-looking ten-year-old, who approached me at the end of class one day to claim his spelling contest prize of one small Kraft caramel. Triumphantly clutching his modest, edible trophy he moved to another room while I packed away my English books. I followed a few minutes later and found Ishwor facing a single line of fifteen or more eager younger "brothers," while he patiently cut his precious candy into paper-thin slices for equal distribution to all. Ishwor radiated in his role of provider, and I was the only one present who found this behavior extraordinary. To the queue of smiling children it was simply life on course, and they would have done the same. I never again offered any rewards that couldn't be shared or divided into fifty-one ample portions.

Some days later I complimented Ishwor on a colorful pair of knitted wool gloves that he was wearing. He grinned with embarrassed pride as he acknowledged that the gloves were a result of his own handiwork. Two days later he presented me with a handsome pair of red and white gloves that he had made for me by taking apart his own sweater. They fit beautifully, but are rarely worn; they're a definite keepsake. Later I found that many of the boys knitted gloves and stockings for winter whenever they could get hold of wool.

The boys' system of mutual support seemed to be their major source of personal encouragement and guidance. Through the years a string of live-in supervisors came and went, some with good intentions, others indifferent and occasionally capable of real nastiness. The boys themselves had had to learn to provide their own standards and leadership, and somehow, for years, all the right commandments had been passed down from brother to brother with unquestioned acceptance.

One afternoon after class, an adorable, newly-orphaned and frightened four-year-old, named Umesh, went one noisy round with Dhani, a well-meaning five-year-old. Before any serious blows landed, two of the seven-year-old boys rushed in and separated the combatants. Lessons in apologies, forgiveness, and friendship were dispensed with tenderness and sympathy, and the scene ended with a climactic, warm embrace by all four boys, and silent, warm awe from their observing English teacher.

As dedicated as I tried to be, as an earnest teacher and applauding father figure, there was never any doubt that I was gaining far more from my experience than I was giving. For me our months together were a sobering, intimate, inspirational insight into the struggles and victories of the innocent, and as my year in Nepal drew to an unwelcome finish, I trusted that my new earthbound awareness would not evaporate outside the Himalayas. I was eager to embrace family, friends, and home, but leaving the boys, their startling realities, and their infectious happiness was the dark side of my departure. The unspoken sadness in all of us manifested at the airport. Through choked-up farewells and much hand clasping, I was piled high with enough marigold garlands to make seeing my way difficult. Then feeling like a deserter, I stumbled towards the terminal, trying to retain what little composure I still had. Inside, a young, friendly American woman stared at me and my conspicuous floral display, and commented, "My, you must really be loved." A bit bewildered, I answered, "I guess I must be," and as I watched the boys waving at me from outside, I knew for sure that *they* were.

I left with no idea of how Nepal, or more specifically, the Paropakar boys, would fit into my future plans. I had not suggested that I would return anytime soon, if ever, since I considered it unlikely. Back in the U.S. I visited family, resettled into my home, cornered old friends with my Nepali stories, and when alone fretted about the family of kids I had left on the opposite side of the globe. Funny, tender, loving letters began arriving almost daily, and as welcome as they were, the effect was not so comforting. They were a reminder of a lost wonderland and a cause unfinished. I was here, my heart was there, my thoughts were all over the place, and who was I kidding? In the middle of my third month back I began organizing and packing for my return to Kathmandu.

I didn't alert Paropakar that I was coming back, because my decision had been so last minute that there hadn't been time for a letter to reach them. Besides, I was nursing a mischievous, inner pleasure plotting a surprise appearance.

After a reception and brief visit with friends at the airport, I beelined it alone into old Kathmandu, down my familiar, twisting, grimy road and reached the orphanage. The moment I was spotted trying to sneak in through the main entrance, word flashed throughout that Allan Sir was back, and instantly 51 bodies poured out of doors and windows and rushed en masse. As group hugs go, this was world-class material. In many ways, I had come home.

My second stay in Kathmandu became far more focused. This time I had a sense of purpose and a determination to find more substantial ways to contribute to the boys' welfare. My classes and attention were guaranteed, but I was trusting that with some effort, more permanent, long-term support could be found.

I had particular concern for four older students who were clever, hard working, and approaching the end of their school days and the sanctuary of the orphanage. Only rarely did a kindly benefactor appear from somewhere to help one of the boys to a better life. Children without family, without resources, living in a poor, caste-ridden society, even with some schooling, can expect little more than a lifetime of menial jobs and the accompanying poverty. There were virtually no options for these boys, only a looming, grey unknown, and their post-orphanage life was a fearful subject that they were reluctant to discuss. College was the forbidden dream that they never dared hope for. My parental concerns intensified, and I wondered where I could find help for all four. Enter Olga Murray.

Only by a chance invitation from a third party did I happen to be introduced to Olga and enjoy an evening's visit with her in one of Kathmandu's tourist restaurants. An attorney from Sausalito,

California, Olga was touring Asia by herself, and had arrived in Nepal for only a three-day stay. She quickly expressed deep interest in the orphanage and my work there, so I immediately suggested a visit the next night to meet all the kids. It was fortunate timing, and our evening at Paropakar was a night of unforgettable children's magic. The weather had turned quite cold, and the electricity had gone out all over Kathmandu. We met in one of the gloomy, frigid rooms, but our gathering and the boys' engaging faces were warmed and brightened by flickering candle light. The excitement of late-evening visitors was compelling, and with bouncing exuberance the boys joked, told stories, sang, danced, played flutes, drums, tambourines, and projected their considerable charm. For a couple of hours our dreary old orphanage was alive with laughter and a silly, spontaneous celebration that enraptured us all. Olga fell in love immediately.

She departed the next morning for Thailand, blessing me as she left with a divine, once-in-a-lifetime mission. I met my senior class that afternoon to joyously and proudly announce to all that Mrs. Murray was going to endow full college scholarships, in Nepal, to each of the four graduating boys.

I was the honored bearer of a lifeline of possibilities, providing these four sixteen-year-olds with an unexpected opportunity to seek a productive life. I braced myself for major whoopla, if not chaos, but my blockbuster news was met with only stunned, doubtful silence. The dawning came, though, with half smiles slowly expressing the realization that, maybe, for the first time in their lives, fate had approached with an upward twist. One or two minutes passed and the settled hush was broken by Babu, one of the scholarship recipients, who softly asked, "Really?"

"Yes, really," I answered, with a lump in my throat.

The ragamuffin condition of all the Paropakar boys was also challenged by Olga, and regretting that she didn't have time to shop herself, she presented me with funds to clothe all of the boys. This time around my announcement produced the expected jubilation, followed by a rush of enthusiastic suggestions for my shopping list, and finally, agreement on sweaters, wool hats, shoes, socks and the deepest, most passionate Paropakar lust—jean pants. For the next six weeks I haunted old bazaars and shopped with the mercenary skills of a hardened flea market entrepreneur, arguing and bargaining to the last rupee. I even found a supply of blue denim and a dubious but willing tailor to make 51 custom-sized pairs of American-style blue jeans. The boys were exceedingly helpful during this shopping binge, guiding, translating, transporting and always steering me clear of the unscrupulous.

When they finally gathered for my camera, and stood elated, handsome and beaming in their snappy, new attire, I mumbled a "Bless you, Olga," and trusted that the photos would serve as an adequate thank-you and testimonial to her welcome gift. For once in their drab lives the boys had reason to be justly proud of their appearance. These had been days of unsurpassed attention and support for all of the kids, and in their plucky style they behaved as if it would go on for-

They were traveling through Nepal, intending to stop no more than a couple of days, for they were intent on trekking. The day they arrived they noticed a group of orphan boys begging. That night they followed the boys and discovered that they lived on the wind-swept roof of an abandoned building. The next day the men rented an apartment. Then, bribing the boys with food, they deloused them, bathed them, and bought them clothes. Discovering that the boys had never been to school, the men rented another apartment for a classroom.

The young men were giving them daily lessons in reading, writing, and math. They were also teaching the boys to make crêpes so they could earn a living. The men vowed that the boys would never beg again.

—Maxine Rose Schur, "Discerning the Landscape of the Heart," *The Christian Science Monitor*

ever, but the inevitable came with time, and again I prepared to depart Nepal. Family matters and business responsibilities were calling me home, but with my feeling of commitment to the boys becoming solid, maybe radical, there was no question that I would return ASAP.

When I met Olga in California, I found her very involved in friendly correspondence and budding friendships with her four scholarship boys, and memories of our evening at the orphanage had heightened her concern for all of the children she had met that night. Approaching her own retirement from law, and looking for a new cause in her life, Olga joined forces with me as an undaunted champion of the Paropakar boys. For twelve years, with encouragement and support from friends, and through occasional periods of intense drum beating, our informal efforts matured to official status as the Nepali Youth Opportunity Foundation. Today, the Foundation provides educational and medical benefits for poor children; it supports two homes for orphaned and disabled boys and girls, and also provides extensive support for blind and deaf children and services for street children of Kathmandu.

There is now a rhythm to my life: a few months in San Francisco, a few months in Nepal. Home and the comforts of American life are highly appreciated and decidedly refreshing after several months in Kathmandu, but there is little to equal the wave of bliss experienced when I exit the Kathmandu airport each September and am greeted by the smiling, loving children gathered there to welcome me. I don't reach my ultimate destination, however, until one more time I find my way down the old road to Paropakar, in all its grungy glory, and can sit for hours in one of the dark rooms, immersed in play and chatter with the boys there. I am eternally grateful for the privilege.

Allan Aistrope spends several months each year helping Olga Murray oversee the operations of the Nepalese Youth Opportunity Foundation (NYOF), which currently supports over 300 Nepali children. The U.S. office address of NYOF is 203 Valley Street, Sausalito, CA 94965.

⋆

We stopped to visit a Buddhist temple. On its east side a small door opened into a room with a prayer wheel in the center. Shaped like a standing barrel with an axle through its top and bottom, it was six or seven feet in diameter and ten feet high, and filled the small space.

Nema, our guide, took hold of the wheel's twisted rope and began walking the worn path. At the completion of one rotation the wheel tripped a bell. After three rotations Nema encouraged me to do the same while making an unselfish wish.

Taking hold of the handle I began walking but found myself unable to focus on a wish, unselfish or otherwise. The wheel was heavy but moved easily; I could feel it creak through the handle. I seemed to have spent a lifetime dreaming of travel and adventure, but finally on such a journey, I found myself wondering why I was here and what I was looking for. *Ding*, the bell signaled my first rotation.

I had known I was coming to Nepal for nearly a year and had read in preparation. Although I did not mean my studies to be judgmental, in retrospect I think it had been easier to focus on cultural differences rather than similarities. *Ding*, the bell signaled my second rotation.

My readings, instead of helping to immerse me into the culture, had made me look at my trek from a factual, detached point of view. This approach reflected what I had done to so much of my life. The wheel groaned with its fullness of unselfish wishes, and impulsively I wished for those wishes to be fulfilled. *Ding*, the bell signaled my third rotation.

Leaving the room and emerging into the full sunlight I found myself deeply moved and deeply changed. Entering the room as a traveler I left it a pilgrim.

—Kirk Grace, "The Prayer Wheel"

* * *

Brothers' Keeper

An ancient tradition offers an
alternative to monogamy.

"YOU MEAN YOU DON'T SLEEP WITH TOM'S BROTHERS?" TSERING
Zangmo paused from cutting buckwheat and turned towards me
incredulously.

"No," I said. "I like Tom's twin brother very much, but it's not
our custom. Tom would be very unhappy if I slept with Bob."

"But don't you play around when Tom goes away?" she asked.
How was I going to answer this? Tom Kelly, a photographer by
profession, is my husband. But here in the district of Humla in the
northwest corner of Nepal, where the practice of fraternal
polyandry (two or more brothers sharing a wife) persists among
the Nyinba people, there are no terms to describe our Western
concept of romantic love.

"I *nying rie* Tom," I explained feebly. "I have a feeling of compassion. I hold Tom dear." For the Buddhist Nyinbas, emotional
attachments are thought to be selfish, greedy vices that give rise
to sorrow.

The Nyinbas inherited their practice of fraternal polyandry
from their Tibetan ancestors, who migrated to the Humla valley
centuries ago from the steppes of the Asian plateau. They also in-

herited a love for trading and herding which, together with culti-
vating the meager soil, make up the traditional Nyinba economy.
Polyandry suits this economy.

"With one or two husbands always away on herding or trading
trips, one husband will always be at home to care for the wife," explains Maila Dai, a trader from the village of Bargaau. He has four
sons: Ringin, Rapten, Maila and Tsering Gyap. "We think
polyandry is just like insurance for the wife. If one husband is no
good or leaves his wife, there's always another brother."

To the Nyinbas, the advantages of polyandry are self-evident.
Both men and women talk about the wealth polyandry provides
and the way it distinguishes them from their poorer Hindu neigh-
bours. Says Maila Dai, "If my sons partition the land, we will become as poor as the Hindu village of Tey."

"All our brothers work together," explains Dawa Takpa, Maila
Dai's elder brother, "so we can be wealthy people. If we all go our
own way, how can we survive? We have to study, do agricultural
work, take care of animals and trade, so we have to work together."

"For me polyandry is fine," says Tsering Zangmo, who at
twenty-one is the wife of three brothers, the youngest of whom is
seven. "If I had only one husband, I would be very poor."
Husbands are expected to do nothing that would cause a rift big
enough to bring about the partitioning of the family land. Younger
brothers have to ask the eldest brother in the morning for permission to sleep with the wife that night, but he would be unwise to
refuse: if a younger brother becomes dissatisfied, he might take a
new wife and settle independently on his share of land.

The ideal polyandrous wife is obedient to all her husbands'
wishes, never shows sexual favoritism and does nothing to cause
conflict among spouses. She should also have at least one child
from each father—otherwise one of the husbands might accuse
her of favoritism. (The mother always pronounces paternity.)

I ask Tsering Zangmo about jealousy. "Do the other husbands
get jealous when you sleep more often with one brother?"

She replies, "But they are brothers. They are never jealous."

I persist. "I don't believe you. I think you say that because you are afraid you might get into trouble with Maila Dai if you admit there are difficulties sometimes."

Her face reddens, she giggles and relents. "Well, they only have a very little jealousy. If you like one husband very much, you have to be secret so the others don't know. We make love in the middle of the night, lying naked in sheepskins. We would never do it just before going to sleep or just before waking up, as the others might hear us."

When Tom and I first visited the Humla village of Yakba, we met Tsering Zangmo and the other inhabitants. We had been invited to the wedding of a 12-year-old girl called Tarilal. Her marriage had been arranged to a family of a wealthy villager who had five sons: Bahadur, aged 26, Gorkha, 22, Sonam, 21, Chime Tsering, 15 and Ngodrup, 5. Tarilal's father and the boys' father, Lobsang, worked together, and Lobsang had calculated that, at 12, Tarilal would suit the large age span of his sons. The marriage was conceived with little Ngodrup in mind.

As Tom photographed the wedding activities, making merry with the feasting male relatives, I insisted on eating with the women. Lobsang couldn't understand why I would want to talk to the bride. She was only a little girl after all and not nearly as important as the village elders. After five rich, full days and nights of feasting and celebrating, during which the wedding parties re-enacted the famous marriage of the 7th-century Tibetan king Srongsten Gampo to the Chinese princess Wen Chen Konjo, it became clear that this was in no way the bride's special occasion.

Nima had a premarital sexual relationship with his wife and he knew that a few other men had also slept with his wife, but now after marriage, he was very strict about his wife's loyalty. He could not even stand for a man to look covetously at her, nor even to think of his wife involved with any other man. I asked Nima how he felt when his wife slept with his brother and he said plainly, "Nothing. I have seen them making love many times and often we all sleep naked in the same room."

—Karna Sakya, Dolpo: The Hidden Paradise—A Journey to the Endangered Sanctuary of the Himalayan Kingdom of Nepal

On the contrary, it was Lobsang's, for it was his chance to display his wealth. It had taken him a generation to accumulate what he needed for this one ceremony, which he hoped would establish his family's long-term status.

Dressed in robes of silk brocade, with a turquoise-studded headdress laden with a dangling curtain of silver and coral (all handed down from generation to generation), Tarilal giggled, covering her mouth as any shy twelve-year-old would, when I asked about her wedding. To her it seemed no big deal—it was just a chance for the men to drink and sing and celebrate. No, she hadn't menstruated yet, and after the ceremony she would go back to her parents' home until she reached puberty. Did she like her husbands? She barely knew them. Later, Tsering Zangmo, whom we also met for the first time, said to me, "We women cannot speak what the heart feels. It is not our custom, we are too shy."

A few years later, Tom and I returned to Humla to find that Tsering Zangmo and Tarilal had both encountered marital problems. Tarilal's husband Sonam (Lobsang's third son) had fallen in love with Tsering Zangmo, who had left her husbands and run away to Kathmandu with Sonam. ("I was unhappy with my husbands. I didn't like my mother-in-law and there was too much work to do.") Six months later, the families rearranged themselves. "I had to convince my brothers and my father that Tsering Zangmo was a much better wife than our other wife, Tarilal," says Sonam. He succeeded, and Tsering Zangmo is now married to him and his four brothers. Lobsang had to pay 25,000 rupees to Tsering Zangmo's former husbands.

*A*mong the Tharus of *Chitwan and some other areas there is also a system of working for a wife. A young man has to work for the parents of a girl of his choice for two or three years before he can get her for a wife.*

—Dor Bahadur Bista, *People of Nepal*

Although she was in love with Sonam, Tsering Zangmo's first night as his wife was not spent with him. "It is our custom for the eldest brother to sleep with the wife on the wedding night,"

Lobsang explained. So, following tradition, it was Bahadur and not Sonam who spent the first night with Tsering Zangmo.

"So, Tsering," I teased her, "which of your new husbands do you like best? Who is best in bed?"

She giggled and said, "But I like all of them the same. Women do not like to make love. It hurts. But I have a choice. If I don't like the brother I can yell. 'No, no, I won't. We work, we work, work so much—we are always tired. I don't feel like making love after so much work.'"

Marital instability is not at all uncommon among the polyandrous Nyinbas. Sometimes a polygamous element is introduced to a polyandrous marriage. For example, Maila Dai and his two brothers all shared a wife. Then his young brother Tashi fell in love with his sister-in-law, Scherzoom, and brought her into the house as well. Now the marriage consists of three brothers and two sisters. Tsering Zangmo disapproves, saying darkly, "Two wives are not good, because women are not like brothers—they will fight for their children to receive the best food, the best clothing."

Then there is infidelity. Sometimes extra-marital affairs are used as a strategy to switch marriages: if a woman senses that her husbands are dissatisfied, she may take a lover so that after her divorce she can remarry immediately. But others take lovers on a more casual basis. "Of course we fool around when our husbands are away," Scherzoom, Maila Dai's wife, explained. "We lie and say we haven't slept with other men. But then men lie to us too."

Men also defend their infidelity. "Of course we fool around," Karma, a Nyinba man, told me. "But the reason there are problems with polyandry is that the wives muck it up by playing husbands off against each other. They gossip about the different brothers and that creates animosity."

Tsering Zangmo was more positive about the system, saying, "In our country some married people play around, some don't. Those who like their husbands don't, because their hearts don't feel like it."

Although common, infidelity is frowned upon. If an affair is proven, both partners suffer heavy penalties. The man agrees to pay a large fine to the woman's husbands, while the woman is publicly beaten or ejected from the house. "I know my husbands play around," says Tsering Zangmo. "There is nothing I can do. I don't get angry. They would beat me. Husbands must beat an unfaithful woman. Then they divorce her and marry someone else."

Some of the younger women grumble. "I want one rich, active husband who is a good trader," said Nomdyol, a 24-year-old unmarried sister-in-law who lives in the same household as Tsering Zangmo. "Polyandry is no good. There's too much work for one woman—it's too hard trying to take care of many husbands equally."

But Lobsang insisted, "Polyandry is our custom and we will continue it as long as possible for as long as it works." Work it does, and work it means, for the Nyinba women in Humla.

An anthropology graduate from Princeton, Carroll Dunham has produced films for PBS, BBC, Discovery and ITV. Her books include The Hidden Himalayas, Mamatoto: A Celebration of Birth, *and* Tibet: Reflections From the Wheel of Life. *She lives in Kathmandu with her photographer husband Thomas Kelly, her two foster children and her son Liam, and her favorite escape is to her teepee nestled among the peach trees of her Nagarkot farm. She is director of Sojourn Nepal, a program in experiential education which she began in 1985.*

※

Kancha also brought a letter to Phu-Tsering from his wife in which she informed him that she was leaving him for another man. With tears streaming down his face, Phu-Tsering mounted a rock cairn in the courtyard of the police station and to an assembled crowd publicly read his wife's letter. Then the others cried too, the constables, shopkeepers, housewives, children, all formed a circle around Phu-Tsering, sobbing loudly in sympathy.

—George B. Schaller, *Stones of Silence: Journey in the Himalaya*

* * *

Brief Encounters

A solitary walk through the middle hills
provides a window onto local life.

AFTER A STEEP TUMBLE DOWN A BRACKEN-FILLED VALLEY, I FOUND
my trail again by a glacial stream. I stripped and swam, rinsing off
the muck and blood in the cold waters, then sat in the sunshine to
dry, while I sewed the torn canvas of my running shoe. I pulled my
shorts on when I heard footsteps. A thin, young man in a dusty
grey suit was coming up the trail carrying an old leather briefcase
as his only burden. He hailed me with a hearty "Good morning to
you, sir." I zipped up my shorts and returned the greeting.

He introduced himself as Dhunbar and said he was a lawyer. He
was on his way home from his office in Kathmandu to visit his
family in Besali. He was delighted that his village was my destination for the evening, and offered me a bed for the night. Dhunbar's
pace proved fast, so conversation was slow at first as I laboured just
to keep my wind. His English was not much better than my Hindi,
so we abused both languages equally. The lawyer quizzed me with
the usual litany of questions, including one I seldom heard:

"What's your caste?"

I chuckled. Dhunbar was incredulous when I told him there
were no castes in Canada. I carefully stressed the difference between out-caste and no-caste, hoping not to lose my new-found

friend and his offer of shelter for the coming night. I thought Dhunbar's naiveté would be hard to find in a genuine lawyer, and must have queried him a little too obviously on his background. He insisted he had his certification papers in his briefcase. He never actually showed them to me. Instead, however, he set me up for a devious series of questions which proved his credentials far better than any diploma.

"You like Nepali woman?" he asked.

"*Sunder hai*. They're beautiful."

"You like sex?"

"Oh, yes."

"Canada women, I think no beautiful."

"No, some are very beautiful!"

"I think no beautiful."

"No, no, some very *sunder hai*," I enthused.

"You not married?"

"No. You married?"

"Yes, yes. Perhaps you marry Nepali woman?"

I laughed.

"Family lives?"

"In Ottawa, Canada."

"How many brother."

"One brother."

"How many sister?"

"One sister."

"You like Nepali boys?"

"What? For friends, yes. Sex, no."

Dhunbar laughed. "But you my friend, yes? You stay my family."

"Of course," I said, a little nervously.

"You give your sister to Nepali boy?"

"What?"

"For marry. You give your sister me?"

"But"—too late, I was trapped—"I thought you said you were married?"

"I lie," the Nepali turned his head around and grinned, showing a silver tooth in his smile.

"Ah well, Canada women not same as Nepali women," I said, backtracking. "I can't give you my sister. She only gives herself."

J was strolling sleepily in Bhaktapur, images washing awareness like waves on a lake shore. Sunlight struck dust in the square ahead, turning motes into gold. I passed fruit vendors sitting by displays, and one woman's eyes caught mine in an incandescent flash. In the next second a volume was spoken across a chasm: I loved her and she loved me, but this moment was all the script allowed. She smiled, I smiled, and I was gone, aglow from the blessing and touch of another being.

—James O'Reilly,
"Stairway to Heaven"

This notion seemed incomprehensible to Dhunbar, who, only half-joking, refused to take no for an answer.

"Dhunbar, I give you my address. You write my sister, send photo, and if she likes you, she'll write back."

This traditional Hindu approach appealed to the lawyer tremendously. He grinned over his shoulder at me, as if he had already won his case. He then pressed me for details as to exactly what he should say in his letter. Also, now that the wedding was virtually decided, he wanted to know what she was like. I turned the tables and asked him more about his work as a lawyer, as if to determine his potential worthiness. Dhunbar said proudly he received 16,150 rupees (then worth about 800 Canadian dollars) for three month's work. Quite a lot by Nepali standards, especially for a man who came from a village a three-day walk from the nearest road.

"Besali," the lawyer announced, just before dusk.

No village here, just a loose cluster of houses and rice paddies spread over the undulating hillside. Dhunbar called out to workers in the paddies by name. I was surprised to see a thin yellow band of rapeseed near the crest of the hill. Dhunbar was equally astounded to learn rapeseed grew in Canada. I told him about the Canadian prairies, where fields of rape and wheat stretched flat across to the horizon and a few farmers harvested with giant machines.

"We are poor country," said Dhunbar, shaking his head. "Hill and mountain. No plain. All these people, they work six months on paddy for one rice crop. Look," he pointed to a pile of rice grains lying on a flat circle of packed earth. "That's what we get from one paddy. Half a bag only."

The labourers worked, backs bent, beating small sheaves of rice against the ground then shaking the ends over the small pile of grain. A small sprinkling of rice dropped from each bundle. They beat and shook each sheave three times in order to dislodge every grain before the stalks were cast aside for use as straw. A woman swept the grain into sacking to be carried back to the house and dried for the winter.

Dhunbar's extended family seemed exceptionally prosperous. They were building a new house. Already its three-storey wooden frame had been completed and fashioned into a rough shelter for about half of the clan's 30-odd members. Dhunbar introduced me to his uncles, aunts, brothers, sisters, and cousins, explaining his relation to each in exact detail. Most of the women kept shyly in the background, except the grandmother, who stared at me with frank curiosity, giving me equal opportunity to admire her in return. A large dirty white turban covered her head. Deep wrinkles creased her face so that it looked like a withered apple-doll. A heavy silver ring hung from her nose and a lifetime of chewing betel-nut had blackened her teeth like wet charcoal.

When communal interest in me at last began to wane, I asked Dhunbar discreetly the way to the toilet. Two nights' worth of *dalbhat* and boiled spinach with chilies still twisted and kicked at my intestines. Unfortunately, the word "toilet" was not in the lawyer's vocabulary. I finally communicated by holding up my roll of paper and pointing at my rear. Dhunbar barked orders to one of the younger boys, who dutifully led me up a slope to the side of the house. Two other boys tagged along for the show, following me to a much-frequented rocky grove which served as the community latrine.

> *We have a rule for health. First thing in the morning, even if you don't have to crap, you should at least go out to the field, squat, take a pull on a cigarette, fart and come back.*
>
> —Broughton Coburn,
> *Nepali Aama: Life Lessons of a Himalayan Woman*

"Okay, thanks," I said to my guide and eager followers, "now get lost."

The boys retreated to a nearby fence. I crouched down behind the largest boulder I could find. My audience perched on top of the fence to get as good a view as possible. When I pulled up my shorts they were all grinning at me. They hung back. I knew, with a vague sense of humiliation, that they would examine the green mess I'd left behind, then make full report to all their cousins and friends.

After dinner Dhunbar led the way up a log ladder to a small private room in the semi-finished section of the house. It held a little wooden bed frame that even had a straw mattress on it, a genuine luxury, though sleep felt all too brief.

At dawn Dhunbar awoke me with a visitor.

"You have medicine for my friend?" the lawyer asked. Gopal was a sturdy looking young farmer about my age with close cropped hair and a pug nose. He wore shorts, a faded plaid shirt and a *topi*. His right eye was blood red and swollen. He gazed down at me, unsmiling, not saying a word. I took out my pocket flashlight and shone it in the young man's face. Looking closely at the eye, I could see its blood vessels had become severely inflamed. The iris had a white glaze across its surface.

"Can you see with it?" I asked.

Gopal shook his head.

"I have no medicine for this. It looks serious though. He should see a doctor."

"There is a health attendant north of here, but he's gone back to his own village these days," said Dhunbar.

"Where's the nearest doctor?"

"Arnghat Bazaar. Half a day's walk south."

"Maybe it will get better," said Gopal, suddenly breaking his silence.

"How long has it been like this?" I asked.

"Three months. Now it really hurts."

I found myself getting angry. In three months he'd never thought to take a half-day hike to the doctor? Arnghat Bazaar was a main town I had hoped to avoid during my trek, but I didn't trust this apathetic man to make it there on his own.

We left directly after breakfast. Gopal led the way back through the rice paddies at a surprisingly relentless pace. Like the trail porters, he walked barefoot. Jagged stones and slick mud slopes did nothing to slow him down. I tried walking one-eyed for a while on the steep hillsides, just to see how he managed. The lack of depth perception made my step unsure and dangerous. Gopal didn't seem perturbed. We walked for three hours through the brush, resting only twice for five minutes each time. Eventually we followed a winding descent from lush forest down to the wide, blue-green shore of the Budi Gandaki river. Wooden houses lined the far

Soon afterwards when we were standing up, about to leave, a man brought a little girl to the front of the crowd and showed her to us. He said she was four years old; she looked about two. I don't know what was the matter with her, apart from malnutrition, but I knew that she was dying. Her father asked if we had any medicine. There was something in the way he held her, in the way her sleeping body nestled in his arms, that made me want to choke. I said we didn't; he'd have to take her to the hospital. He looked at me as though I'd suggested that he take her to the moon.

—Monica Connell,
Against a Peacock Sky

bank. A steel-girdered suspension footbridge spanned the river, leading to the market center where cloth merchants, tailors, watch repairers, sellers of dry goods displayed their wares, all carried in from the distant road on porters' backs. Arnghat Bazaar must have held over a thousand people, and it seemed an unimaginable metropolis after four days in the hills.

The Nepali health officer in town shared his office with the bakery. I bought big, fluffy donuts, fresh and golden-brown from the vat, while we waited for Gopal's turn to be treated. The health officer wore a white cotton jacket that could just as well have come from the bake shop as the clinic. He was young, brusque, and spoke surprisingly good English. He borrowed my flashlight, shone it into Gopal's swollen eye and shook his head.

"Conjunctivitis. I can't do anything. Pupil's dilated and fixed. Another two weeks and it will be permanently blind.

"Well—does it spread?" I asked.

"Oh yes, it's highly infectious. In about eighty percent of the cases, it affects the other eye as well."

"And he'll go totally blind?"

"That's right. Unless he sees a specialist in Kathmandu. That's the only place in the country he can get an operation. It's relatively simple, and free. But most of them never bother to make it to the city until it's too late."

Gopal took the news well. He just asked for something to make the eye stop hurting. Back in the bakery half of the store, he munched on a donut and began to look depressed. I offered to help him get to Kathmandu and cover his expenses. He abruptly declined, saying he had a brother-in-law who lived on the path to Gorkha, an afternoon's walk from Arnghat Bazaar, who was well off and could pay for the operation. Gopal could apparently afford cigarettes and matches, and I began to worry that my offer to help may have embarrassed him. I was also concerned he might head back to Besali and call on his brother-in-law later, which might mean never. No, he assured me, he was ready to go to Kathmandu at once, just as he was, in old cotton shirt, shorts and bare feet. He had his *topi* on, and that apparently gave him all the dignity he needed to feel well dressed. I told him my route also lay on the path to Gorkha, and I'd be glad to accompany him the rest of the way to his relative's house. He looked up at me with his good eye, and seemed grateful.

The rust-coloured trail wound up a cliff and then followed a small river out of town. We walked all afternoon. Blisters had begun forming on my feet. I envied Gopal the human leather on which he walked. Yet after another hour, I found myself able to copy the Nepali's smooth, flowing rhythm. I no longer needed to fix my attention on my feet, but could look up and around and absorb the countryside as we marched. I realized that for four days my vision of Nepal had been mostly the mud and rocks at my feet.

I noticed as we crested each hill, the great Annapurnas rising out of the northwest like solid clouds of snow.

Gradually Gopal pulled ahead of me. He crisscrossed his way up a steep section of rice terracing that dropped several hundred meters down into a valley. I called for him to wait. He grinned when I finally caught up, out of breath and panting heavily. He had half finished a cigarette and offered me one.

"No thanks," I said, wheezing while the Nepali puffed. "Bad for the lungs."

Gopal hailed two men and a boy in a nearby field, then instructed me to stay put while he went to greet his kinfolk, careful not to disturb any of the limp stalks of rice drying in the paddies. From the distance I watched the young man explain his request to his brother-in-law. It was a lot to ask, at harvest time, to have someone from the family accompany him to the city. It would cost vital days in the paddy. Brother-in-law scratched his head. Gopal had obviously made his request simply and straightforwardly. It could not be refused. He signaled me to come and join them, then bent down and lifted a sack of rice stalks twice his size onto his back. The other man was old, obviously the patriarch. He wore only a loin cloth and a turban and looked like a walking skeleton covered with loose leather. I watched in amazement as the old man hefted an equally large sack on his own narrow shoulders. Brother-in-law, in contrast, was brawny, with the tanned, rippling body of a pro boxer. His face was smooth and surprisingly handsome, given the rough work that made up his existence. He greeted me with a small smile, hefted his sack with ease, then led the way to his house, surrounded by banana trees, near the crest of the slope.

The house was much smaller than Dhunbar's: a two-roomed bungalow of mud-brick walls and a thatched roof, partitioned like a duplex. Brother-in-law, wife, four children and grandfather all lived in one room, while a family of four, Brother-in-law's brother's family, lived on the other side. A woven leaf wall divided the porch in half. Gopal and his relatives dropped their loads. He offered his cigarettes. They were refused in favour of hand-carved pipes and yellow tobacco as the family gathered on the earthen porch to hear Gopal's story in detail, including perhaps some explanation as to why he had brought a foreigner along with him. Listening to him talk, I thought Gopal's speech was a little slurred. His lower lip protruded and he seemed on the verge of drooling. His right eye was half closed from the swelling. Brother-in-law listened quietly, then returned to the fields for another load of rice. It was impossible to gauge his response. Gopal put his head on his knee, and gazed at his young niece playing with her baby brother.

The toddler was peeing merrily on the mat I was later asked to sit on during dinner. His sister, about five years old, was the most beautiful, radiant child I had seen in all Nepal. She had black hair that ran wild down the back of her neck like the tendrils of some exotic jungle plant. Her skin was tanned deep brown and a healthy protruding belly stuck out from the bottom of her grey rag of a shirt. She showed a constant flow of smiles, eyes full of mirth and good-natured mischief. She played coy with me, keeping her distance while grinning and laughing whenever she looked in my direction. She exuded delight. Where on this isolated hillside was the source of so much happiness? Her older brother, Shankar, told me he was thirteen, though he looked no bigger than ten. He spoke polite school-book English. Impressed, I encouraged the boy to talk. The wild-haired beauty giggled at the tremendous joke of her brother babbling with the stranger. She hefted her baby brother high so we could all see his tiny nakedness. Dangling in mid-air, he kicked with his legs like a frog, squealing with laughter.

Mother moved in and out from hearth room to porch. She wore a purple patterned sarong and a bright red vest. She seemed surprisingly young, her waist slender, hair long, bare arms smooth muscled from the endless round of household chores. She said little more than a greeting to her brother. Taking the toddler from the mirthful daughter's arms, Mother knelt on the porch and tugged up her vest to offer her breast to the boy. He lunged at it, smacking into her, lips first. He grabbed her breast in both hands and suckled noisily. The force of him rocked her back on her knees. She balanced against the assault, then hollered something to her sister-in-law in the other half of the house, and carried on a noisy conversation over the slurping. She seemed at ease and unperturbed by the white stranger, trying not to look like he was looking at her, barely two meters away on the porch.

She was exquisite. She had borne four children, the eldest thirteen, so she must have been close to thirty, perhaps a little younger. Yet her face was unlined, marred only by two dark windburn patches on each of her high cheekbones. The bright red of her vest and the dancing pattern of her sarong blended with the dark glow of her skin. Her eyes looked clear, yet somehow faraway. Sitting this close to her, I felt her love for her children like the radiant warmth of a cooking fire. She rocked slightly to the rhythm of her son's feeding. When her husband returned at dusk with his final load of rice, I noticed her eyes watching him with a glowing intensity.

The toddler, now satiated, rolled his eyes upwards and dropped off to sleep in her arms. She pulled down her vest. Gopal crossed the porch and spoke to her. I saw her eyes fill with concern. I guessed from the few words I grasped that it was not yet decided if Brother-in-law could go with Gopal to the city. I thought of volunteering to stay through the harvest and help Grandfather with the last of the crops. Idle fantasy: I would be near useless carrying rice across the slippery paddy dikes. And if I were Brother-in-law, I would never leave my wife alone with an uninvited foreigner.

She fed me *dal-bhat* and foul boiled green spinach for dinner on the porch. Only after I had finished did the rest of the family eat, indoors. Looking out from the porch, I watched the light fade from the valley. Stars took form from the twilight, crisp and clear.

> *The little girl's mother came out, buttoning the top of her once-white cardigan sweater that had been snagged and patched many times. In the light her skin had the sheen of a pearl. Face wakeful, black hair braided, long wrap skirt frayed from dragging. I was uncomfortable with this, having no idea what a Western man alone says to a Nepali woman alone except, "Room?"*
>
> —Jeffrey Heiman,
> "Dhampus Walls"

Below, orange flecks of cooking fires studded the black hills. After dinner, Brother-in-law pulled out his pipe again, lit it, then passed it around to Grandfather, Gopal, and Shankar. Next, Mother took a long, thoughtful drag on its bamboo stem. I felt an easy equality between sexes and generations, perhaps borne of the hard life of rice farming. They depended on one another. They were companions.

The old man brought me the pipe, then sat down at my side. He had removed his turban and now wore a coarse white blanket to protect him from the evening chill. His head was shaven, a few stiff white hairs sticking up in a fuzz around his huge wrinkled ears. He looked me in the eye and began speaking an incomprehensible dialect that gurgled out of him like water boiling in a large pot. I struggled to guess at his questions and tried to answer in Hindi. The old man chuckled and grinned and nodded his head, obviously understanding not a word. It didn't seem to matter. He was delighted just to talk. Soon I dropped the Hindi and responded in English, which caused him to smack me on the knee and laugh. For the next half hour we spoke our hearts, delighting in the sounds each other made. Words spilled out into the dark air, no longer tools for communicating daily needs for rice and shelter, they became patterns of sound, playing out a rhythm and rhyme that stroked our ears, tickled, and made us laugh. I told him I admired his family, how honoured I felt to be allowed to share the evening with them, and what it was like to be alone, travelling without family or fields of my own. Grandfather picked up my soft hand and examined it, tracing my lines with his earth-blackened bone-and-leather finger. His eyes danced. He clapped his hands again, held my hand between his own, then smiled, stood stiffly and walked into the house to sleep.

Against the outer wall of the house, Mother held her youngest close to suckle, rocking him gently to sleep in her arms. She rose slowly to her feet, keeping her back bent so as not to pull her nipple from the child's mouth as she carried him towards a rough burlap sack strung into a makeshift hammock between posts of the porch. Slowly she lowered him, then dropped him down into it. A loud "pop" rang across the porch as her nipple slipped out, followed by a quick cry of anguish from the hammock. She rocked him gently, whispering musical sounds. In seconds the wail faded unwillingly to a whimper, then silence.

She pulled her vest back down over her breast, picked up a small sack of rice, crossed in front of me to the corner of the porch and sat on the floor in front of a small hand mill. It had a stone base, flat and smooth with a slightly raised circle in the center. The millstone which she placed over the base had a wooden handle on top. To turn the heavy stone, she had to use both arms, and braced herself against the wall with one leg, while the other was tucked under her so she could sit as close to the mill as possible. She poured a handful of rice in a hole in the center of the stone and began a slow, rhythmic grinding, swinging the stone round and round over the base. Soon white rice flour spilled out over the rim. The rubbing of stone on rice filled the air with a warm throbbing noise. It conjured domestic sounds from another lifetime, sounds that made me feel drowsy and secure when I was a child: my mother's vacuum cleaner, clothes tumbling in the dryer. When the woman stopped grinding to add more rice and scoop the flour into a bag, the silence of the hillside rushed in, deafening.

When her eldest son came over to speak to her, I asked the boy, pointing, and using my Nepali/Hindi, what a millstone was called in his language. She answered instead, turning to look at me directly for the first time. She rested her faraway gaze on me for an instant and smiled, answering what must have seemed an awfully stupid question.

"Millstone," she said. It was the only word she ever spoke to me. Meeting her eyes, I forgot the Nepali word at once.

She swept up the rice flour using the same hand broom she had used earlier to sweep off the porch. Then, before rising, she suddenly stopped, as if breaking the flow of her own rhythm, and stared at the red earthen floor near my hand. Though directed towards the floor, her eyes again seemed fixed on some far distant point. In the dim light of the kerosene lantern, I noticed she looked tired. Her family may have been prosperous by Nepali standards, she had four loveable children and a good-hearted, strong husband who adored her, but still it was a hard existence. Her eyes wandered near to my fingers. For a second felt I could read her thoughts. She was wondering, perhaps for the only moment in her life, what it must be like to belong to that other world where this white hand had come from, free of husband and children and the endless round of cooking, winnowing, cleaning and milling rice.

"Take me with you, to the cities and the land of smooth hands, where I can dance, and there are no millstones that slowly grind out my beauty." As if on a boat, we slowly pull away from the house, with its half-harvested fields, her family watching, silently, from the porch, which becomes a dock. Her eyes fix on the glowing light past the horizon, on freedom she has never known, freedom to be other than mother, lover, grinder of grain. She looks back and sees them, already frozen, a fossil, a memory embedded in amber, unable to separate themselves from each other and their land, uncomprehending. It is as if their very hearts have stopped beating. Suddenly, in one fluid gesture, she stretches out a departing hand, touches the earthen porch, and halts the boat. Her chest heaves. The pulse of it, like a heartbeat, shatters the amber. The family moves once more. Her husband reaches out a strong brown arm, helps her to the dock. There is rhythm once more, to this life she has chosen, a dance that I will never know. The boat sails on with me in it, alone. I watch the red vest, moving rapidly, her lungs sucking great gulps of air as if it has been deprived of oxygen. My last glimpse, as the vision vanishes, is her reaching down to touch the earth.

Her gaze changed, uncluttered by idle daydreams now. She brushed her hair back into place behind her ears with her fingers, then carried the new-ground flour back into the mud-walled house.

At three in the morning, she came out to check on the child sleeping in the crib on the porch. Again I heard the sound of the millstone. Inside the house, someone was popping corn for breakfast. Other mysterious sounds of morning followed—a steady rhythmic thudding, liquids bubbling, the patter of grain being sifted on a wicker platter. The toddler, now awake, began to wail. Once disturbed, he obviously felt he deserved breakfast. Mother

rushed back and forth between him and the kitchen, nearly trampling on me where I still lay in my sleeping bag. The elder daughter, who had stayed inside, out of my view, began sweeping out the
kitchen. Dust flew over me, prompting me to rise just in time to
make way for the delightful daughter, who commenced cleaning
the porch with water and a spongy ball of buffalo dung. The dung
picked up all crumbs and loose dirt the broom had missed. I sat as
far out of the way as possible, and turned my gaze again on the pink
hues appearing through the banana trees to the side of the house.

Porch swept, the daughter hauled her little brother up out of his
hammock to play. Something started him crying. Mother rushed
out, eyes flashing in anger. She reached down to her young son,
blocking my view and then, I couldn't see why, struck savagely at
him. He screamed and toddled out of reach, so she directed several
more blows at the delightful one, striking the child across the chest
and arms until she too started wailing. Mother hit her with such
sudden violence that I almost panicked. Then, just as suddenly, it
ended. Whatever happened was over. Mother went back inside,
brushing loose hair back behind her ear. The girl made comforting coos and cuddled her sniffling brother.

The husband of the other family came over to talk with
Brother-in-law, saying something about an eye specialist in
Pokhara, who might be closer. His voice sounded heavy with resentment. Perhaps the two families shared the harvest, and
Brother-in-law's departure would put an unfair burden on the
other family. The other man had a wide, squat nose. His nostrils
flared angrily as he spoke. The previous night while we smoked, I
had impressed upon Brother-in-law the health official's statement
that Gopal would only get the operation in Kathmandu. Now the
brawny farmer held fast to the plan, despite the obvious opposition. I felt a rush of relief, and at the same time anger at the other
brother's protests.

When Shankar told me to go to the squat-nosed man's half of
the house for breakfast, I did so reluctantly. This man's wife
seemed several years older than he. She was freshly marked with
a red dot on her forehead, indicating that she had already been to

the village temple to offer prayers and receive a blessing. Her two young children were pudgy and ate greedily. The boy peered at me from behind darting, piggy eyes. The girl seemed full of malevolent mischief. They served me breakfast of rice and cabbage curry on their side of the porch, and I felt bad for my harsh judgment of a family that had willingly shared and eaten food with me.

While we ate, a thin, middle-aged man in beard and turban entered the yard with his young son. Each carried a home-made fiddle. After a humble greeting, they began to play a fair version of "Frere Jacque" in unison. I joined in, first in French, then in English, for Shankar's sake, on the other side of the porch. When the concert was finished, Grandfather, dressed only in his white G-string, brought the fiddlers a pan of cooked rice which he emptied into their open food bag. I offered a two rupee note, for which they bowed and thanked me before making their way to the next household along the hill.

After breakfast, I found Gopal crouched on the far corner of the porch. I wanted him to confirm that Brother-in-law was definitely going with him to Kathmandu that day. He shook his head. Gopal would stay two days to help with the harvest. Then they would go together to Gorkha and from there to the capital. I learned with delight that Shankar would be allowed to accompany them. It would be the boy's first trip to the city. I breathed a sigh of relief. Gopal would be two days closer to blindness, but at least he would get his operation in time.

"You need money?"

Gopal shrugged and refused to take the crisp blue fifty I held out to him. I struggled through an elaborate argument that imposing on Brother-in-law's time was bad enough; the man shouldn't have to pay for transportation to the city as well. And, after all, I had imposed on the family's hospitality. I couldn't insult their generosity by offering them money for their kindness. But if Gopal would take some money, we would all be even, except for the gratitude, still owed all around. I was uncertain how much I actually conveyed in my wobbly Nepali, but Gopal seemed to realize I would never relent.

"I take 30 for the bus," he said at last.

"Sorry, no change," I said, tucking the bill in the pocket of his shirt. "In my country, it wouldn't buy two bags of popcorn at the movies."

Shankar was assigned to take me to the edge of the village where the trail to Pokhara continued. Brother-in-law had already left for the fields when it came time to go, and there was no sign of Mother or any of the other children around the house. Besides Gopal, only Grandfather, still in his G-string, washing the family goats, remained to say good-bye. He turned to me, pressed his palms together at his chest in a gesture of good-natured respect, and grinned broadly.

I returned the gesture and the grin, and said to him in English, "It's time to get back in the boat."

Tim Ward is a Canadian journalist who spent six years in the Orient. He is the author of What the Buddha Never Taught, The Great Dragon's Fleas, *and* Arousing the Goddess, *from which this story was adapted. He lives in Maryland.*

✳

I believe that there are a few memories which we carry with us beyond death and from which we shall never be free.... Perhaps it is just a smile or a strand of hair or the smell of warm breath, caught in a chunk of light and time and frozen like a fly in amber. But sometimes there is more than that, a whole world with movement and sound and changing colour.

I will remember for all time the soft, clammy silences in the sacred forest at Baglung and the louder, windy silences among the stunted juniper near Tukuche; the porters' stompy legs laced with veins and the thin legs of young girls with long necks and torn dresses; the wrinkled faces of the old women and the tight brown stomachs of the girls-turned-women near Beni whose breasts were held in velveteen *blousiers*. All of these things I shall remember, and much more besides, and whatever I write now will be nothing compared to the memory of them.

—Charlie Pye-Smith, *Travels in Nepal: A Sequestered Kingdom*

PART FOUR

IN THE SHADOWS

★ ★ ★

A Spotty Friendship

You never know what you're going to get.

PIERRE AND I MET ONLY A WEEK AGO AND DECIDED TO BE TREKKING buddies. We are going to the Annapurna Sanctuary. It should take about two weeks, the guidebooks say. We have acquired just about everything we need: backpacks, down jackets, water bottles, sleeping bags, raincoats, water purification tablets, iodine, first aid stuff, flashlights, toilet paper, sweaters, boots, hats, gloves, windbreakers and windbreaker pants, wool socks, and our cotton pants. Now that our outfits match, we feel almost like brothers.

We are sitting at a popular outdoor restaurant on the lakeside in the evening, three days before we are planning to start. The sky is awash in the brilliant colors of sunset, and across the shimmering lake, the foothills glow in shades of orange, pink, and green.

"Man, this is so amazing!" Pierre says, gesturing to the mountains.

"Yeah," I agree. "Who would have thought I'd be here?" I had been in Japan for a graduate program, and after finishing it, had somewhat spontaneously decided to tour Asia on the way home to the USA.

"Here's to our trek!" Pierre announces, raising his beer to the sunset.

"To our trek!" I toast, raising my cappuccino. We are both satisfied, exhilarated, enjoying that fragile calm before the start of a new adventure. Then, as I tilt my glass to my lips, I notice something strange.

"Holy Cow!" My fingers are covered with scores of tiny pustules. "Look!" I show Pierre.

"Yuck!" he responds, moving away from me. "What *are* they?"

"I don't know! They weren't there this morning!" I feel a rush of adrenaline. Being a Jewish-American Intellectual type, I am also a hypochondriac. "Am I going to die?" I ask, only half-joking. I heard of one traveler who died suddenly after getting blood poisoning from a thorn in his foot. My mind is already hard at work generating horrible scenarios: plague, leprosy, flesh-eating bacteria...

"Let me see," Pierre demands, and takes a closer look at my hand in the candle-light. "Man, that's *gross!*" he concludes.

"Oh great!" I say. "Just what I needed, some exotic Asian disease right before a trek!" It's probably going to get worse, I think to myself; it will spread, eventually covering my whole body, nobody will go near me, I'll be an outcast, a freak; the doctors won't recognize it, they'll take photos, samples; they'll write about it in some obscure journal, I'll be in extreme pain, then the hallucinations will set in, the growths will enlarge, death will come slowly. "Damn, I can't believe it!"

"Don't worry, it's probably nothing," Pierre tries to reassure me.

"What do you mean, 'don't worry,' *look at my fingers!*" I hold them up to the sunset. They look horrible.

"Look, eh, maybe it will just go away, try to forget it," he suggests.

"That's easy for you to say, Mr. Canadian Hockey Player." Everything's easy when you don't have a brain, I think. "I mean, you lose a tooth, no problem; you break a rib, just forget it; you get killed, worry about it tomorrow!"

"Look, you're being paranoid, it's probably nothing," Pierre urges. "Just try to eat and forget about it. Look at the mountains; we're in Nepal, it's cool, eh?"

"OK, I'll try," I agree. I breathe the cool evening air. I try to finish my meal but the problem is that every time I raise my glass or my fork, I have to look at my fingers. I can't eat. I feel sick. I need a doctor.

The next morning the bumps have spread. Now they are all over my hands. At breakfast, while Pierre eats muesli and I stare at my fingers, we discuss what to do. We will have to postpone our trek until I get better, or Pierre can go without me. I don't want to go out into the wilderness with this unknown illness.

The proprietress of the guest house where we are staying in Pokhara is a middle-aged Austrian woman named Sita. She wears a combination of green

athmandu has some of the dirtiest water in the world. From one sip the following effects are possible in one to ninety days: salmonella, toxigenic ecola, shigella, giardia, amoebas, worms, and hepatitis. The average development worker submits thirty-eight stool samples to the medical center on the two-year term of service.

—Barbara J. Scot,
*The Violet Shyness of Their Eyes:
Notes from Nepal*

trekking sneakers, purple spandex tights with leg warmers, an orange sweatshirt with little chunks of amethyst and quartz crystal sewn all over it, and a transparent Nepali silk scarf. When we first checked into her lodge, she proudly informed us that she is an ex-devotee of *both* Rajneesh and Sai Baba. Now she just "lives in the spirit on her own." She comes over to our table and I ask her advice.

"Vell," she says, "it looks strange!"

"Pretty gross, eh?" Pierre adds helpfully between mouthfuls.

"Do you know anyone who can help? Like a doctor?" I ask her.

"Mmm? Perhaps you could see Doctor Yeshe, he is a Tibetan doctor," she suggests.

"A what? Are you kidding?" I imagine some weird ritual with gongs and drums banging while poisonous herbal salves ooze on my skin, curing me only to cause a toxic reaction far worse. "No, I mean a *real* doctor. Isn't there a hospital around here, or a clinic?"

"Mmm? Yes, I think there is a little place about 30 kilometers from here."

"That's practically back in Kathmandu!" I say. "That would take hours. I need a doctor *now*."

"I've heard about that place," Pierre interrupts, "that's the clinic where the cows walk right through your room."

"Isn't there another place?" I ask her.

"Vell, you could go back to Kathmandu to the American clinic."

"Too far," I tell her.

"Vait! I have it, I vill do a heeling vit my crystals." Sita pulls a pouch from between her breasts and pours two shards of quartz onto the table.

"So, how do we find Doctor Yeshe?" I ask her.

"Don't you vant my heeling?" she asks, disappointed.

"No that's not it, it's just that…I want to use the indigenous medicine," I tell her, hoping this will be a graceful way out of her suggestion.

"Goot, goot! You are very right!" she agrees. "Ve can do heeling later!"

Sita gives us directions and we rent bikes in town. They look just like mountain bikes, but they turn out to have only one speed. After a long ride we get to Doctor Yeshe's office, a run-down room on the second floor of an old cement building. A few emaciated Tibetan refugees are sitting around waiting for him, coughing. We sit down next to them and they give us toothy grins.

Eventually, it is our turn and the doctor's wife ushers us into his room. The walls are lined from floor to ceiling with jars of little brown balls of herbal medicine. They look suspiciously like goat droppings.

"Cool!" Pierre says, "I'll go first."

"You?" I ask. "You're not even *sick!*"

"Hey, you don't get to see a Tibetan doctor every day," he answers, pushing me aside and barreling into the examination room ahead of me. I follow him to watch. All the other patients do too.

The doctor examines Pierre for quite a while, taking his pulse, pushing on places in his stomach to feel his organs, and looking at his tongue. He even makes him urinate in a jar, which he then examines in the light, sniffs, and even *tastes*.

It seems like hours go by. Pierre and the Tibetan doctor really hit it off. Pierre keeps asking the doctor to check this and that, and the doctor, who is thrilled to work on such a huge Western oaf, eagerly obliges, demonstrating his techniques in minute detail. Meanwhile, I'm sitting all alone in the corner staring at my hands in a cold sweat.

"Pierre," I urge, "hurry up, you're not even sick. Come on!" The Tibetan patients smile at me, not understanding a word I say, and mistaking it for concern for my friend. One of them nods at me as if to say, "He'll be fine, don't worry."

"Eh? In a minute, this is such a *trip*, man!" Pierre answers as he happily samples the different herbal pills and downs a bag of green powder, to everyone's delight. The doctor and his wife applaud. Pierre grins at them and then motions for the doctor to check his knee.

What about *me*? I think.

It turns out that Pierre's liver and spleen are imbalanced, according to Doctor Yeshe. He receives four large bags of brown pills which he is supposed to take three times a day in various combinations.

"Wow, that was great!" Pierre says, plopping himself on the bench beside me. "You've got to try it."

Finally, it is my turn. "What is the problem?" Doctor Yeshe asks.

"My hand," I answer, showing him my fingers. He raises his eyebrows for a moment in surprise. "Mmmm? What is this?" he says. Then he shakes his head. "I can do nothing," he reports matter-of-factly.

"That's it?" I ask him in disbelief. He hasn't looked at my tongue or pressed my stomach, and he doesn't even read my pulse for a second, not to mention the urine test. "But...but..." I stammer, thinking of Pierre's 45 minute VIP treatment.

"That's it. Very sorry, don't worry," the doctor says, and gestures for me to get up.

"Don't worry!" I exclaim. "What, are you kidding, don't *worry*?
I can't believe it. What am I supposed to do?"

"It will go away," the doctor
says.

"So you know what it is?" I
ask him. "Can you give me some
medicine for it?"

"No." Doctor Yeshe is a man
of few words.

"Then how can you be sure it
will go away?"

"It's nothing," he says, "just a
rash. Thank you, please visit
often," he says, obviously tired of
the subject. Then he gives Pierre
a huge slap on the back and says
something in Tibetan that neither of us understand. The doctor's wife shows us out.

"Oh great!" I tell Pierre as we
leave. "That's just great! We
come all the way out here and
you use up all our time with Doctor Yeshe on yourself and you're
not even sick! Then when it's my turn he's burnt out."

"Hey, man, chill out," Pierre says. "You sound pretty tense."

"Well, what would you be like if it was your hands? I mean it
must be something really exotic if *he's* never seen it before. He's
probably seen just about everything out here. I wonder if it's
fatal…"

"Well, man, maybe it's really bad and he just doesn't want to
scare you," Pierre says, hardly reassuring.

I'm going to die, I just know it! There's nothing quite as awful
as getting some nonspecific illness in a distant land.

The next day, it has spread even more. I go to a little pharmacy
shack where one can get just about any medicine over the counter.
Much of it is made in India, and the quality is often unreliable. A

twelve-year-old girl and her tiny brother are behind the counter. "Ever seen this?" I show her my hands.

"No," she answers. "I'll call my mother." She goes into the back room and comes out with her mother. She looks at my hands and says, "I'll call my husband." A few minutes later, her husband tells me, "I'll call a doctor." Three hours later, an Indian man who claims he is a doctor from "Banaras Medical School" arrives on a moped and looks at my hand in the back room under a naked bulb.

"Hmmm...?" he intones.

"Don't you need a magnifying glass?" I suggest.

"No, no, I can see it just fine, thank you," he tells me.

"What is it?"

"Not good, not good," he says.

My stomach jumps through hoops at his words. "What? What have I got? You can tell me, it's OK, I can handle it."

"I'm afraid you are showing the beginning signs of scabies," he announces.

"SCABIES!" I shout. If there was one fear I had about going to Nepal, scabies was it. The little parasites are transmitted by skin contact with others who have them, usually children in unclean living conditions. They burrow under the skin and reproduce in waves, spreading over the body and producing itchy bumps that form scabs, hence the name. It's not fatal, but quite uncomfortable and ugly. I heard that the disease was prevalent in the mountain villages, owing to the poverty, poor sanitation, and lack of medicines. I should feel relieved, but instead, I feel much worse than before. Death would have been preferable. "I'VE GOT SCABIES!"

"Yes, it is regrettable," the doctor tells me, wiggling his head to show concern.

"But we're supposed to go trekking!"

"Yes, it is regrettable," he repeats.

"Well, what do I do?"

"You must put this on three times a day," he instructs, handing me a bottle of gooey poison.

"Should I cancel my trek?"

"No, no, I think you will be fine, you caught it in the early stages."

Later that afternoon, I return to the hotel and inform Pierre of the verdict. He says, "Wow, scabies! That's gross! Stay away from me, man, OK? I mean at least until you're better, no offense."

"Thanks for your support."

The next day, after three applications of poison, the bumps have stopped spreading. I am feeling much better. Pierre and I are sitting at lunch. He is staring at his large beefy hockey-player fingers. "You know, I have these funny little bumps too."

"Let me see!" I look at his fingers. Sure enough, he's got them too. Oh no, I think, I've given them to him. I really am a wretch. My scabies are becoming a social disease. How embarrassing. I wonder if I also gave it to the woman who runs our guest house. And what about Doctor Yeshe and his wife? I begin to recall all the people I've touched in the last few days. A huge tide of guilt washes through me. "Oh Pierre...I...I don't know what to say, I'm sorry..."

"Yeah, I have them too. But I've had them for months. I thought they were blisters, you know, like from hockey when someone's stick hits your fingers."

"You what!" I explode. "You mean you had those all this time and you didn't even tell me?"

"Well, I mean, I didn't think it was that important."

"After all the stress I was going through?"

"But I thought they were *different*," Pierre tells me shyly.

"Well you could have at least *thought* to consider that they might be *related!*"

"Look, man, I'm sorry, it didn't cross my mind. No hard feelings, OK?"

"What *does* cross your mind, you dumb jock?" It seems that I've selected a modern Typhoid Mary as my trekking companion.

"Hey, man, don't get all upset," he says, "Just relax, it'll be fine."

"Thanks a lot. This is just great, I'm going on a Himalayan excursion with Scabies-Pierre! Are there any other plagues you carry that you would like to tell me about before we entrust our lives to each other in the mountains?"

Pierre tilts his head to one side as if weighing his thoughts, then he tells me, "Well…"

"Well?" I am astonished that he might actually have something else to tell me.

"Well, I also have athlete's foot."

"Oh, brilliant, that's just great." I hold my head in my hands. "You lent me your *socks*, you idiot!"

"Oh," Pierre says guiltily.

"So is there anything else? Rabies, hepatitis, mumps, viral meningitis? Why not just kill me and get it over with?"

The next day we are to embark on our trek. Needless to say, it is not an auspicious beginning. But it's too late to find another partner, so I agree to stick with Pierre, on condition that he puts on the medicine too. We spend the first day of our trek avoiding each other like the plague.

Nova Spivack's trek was an uphill battle that went downhill all the way. Disillusioned, he finally found real peak-experiences at Kopan, a Buddhist Monastery above Kathmandu. Today, he is a co-founder of EarthWeb, Inc., a leading Internet technology company in New York City.

✳

"You see I could cure him," said Labrang Tundup about Sonam Tenzing, "but I am missing some ingredients."

"I can bring them from Kathmandu as before," I offered.

"No, no. It is a very powerful medicine. I have most of the ingredients: heart of hare, of a wolf. Asking around, I could get a heart of a vulture, but nobody has human flesh anymore."

"Yes, maybe it's a bit difficult to get," I said pensively.

—Eric Valli and Diane Summers, *Caravans of the Himalaya*

BRIAN K. WEIRUM

★ ★ ★

Tiger Bones

The fate of the world's most majestic creature
hangs in the balance.

THE MAN NEXT TO ME WAS FLOSSING HIS TEETH WITH A BLUNT, rusty blade which looked like the cutting end of a wine opener. Dirty-faced children were clambering over his shoulder to see what was happening in the cramped room. A lone guard stood near me at the door with a rifle languishing at his side, seemingly unconcerned and oblivious to the crowd that was pressing in. Across the courtyard another guard stood with his back to an open door. He was holding his rifle at arm's length with one hand and reading a magazine held in the other.

I was in a small room on the second floor of a building which was either under construction or falling apart. I suspect a bit of both was true. Rods of steel protruded up from floors to support walls that didn't exist. There were as many bricks and holes visible as white plaster on the crudely white-washed building.

The room was furnished with a bench, a chair, and a lone desk which was empty except for two glass paperweights and a red phone inside a wooden box. Bags of rice and flour lined the floors and flopped over the sides of a single filing cabinet.

Beneath us, inside a central courtyard, scores of men crowded towards the gate to see what was happening in the room above. In a separate enclosure several women were sitting over pots, cooking rice. A lone woman and child were screaming protests in Nepali. The woman was in jail for poisoning her husband to death, and as there was now no one to care for her family, her child was consigned to share her fate.

My shirt was stained dark with sweat. The heat was stifling. There was no breeze. Almost, it seemed, no air. It was May and the monsoon rains had not yet come. I was in the jail in Bharatpur, a small town in the *tarai*.

The *tarai* was once one of the most inhospitable places on earth—being home to the healthiest of malarial mosquitoes. Today it is host to a tenuous relationship between people who have flocked down out of the Himalayan mountains in search of better agricultural land and several large national parks which have been set aside to preserve and protect a vast array of indigenous wildlife—including the Royal Bengal tiger, the Indian one-horned rhinoceros, leopard, gaur, wild elephants, sambar, chital (spotted deer), wild boar, sloth bear, cobra, python, countless other animals and a vast array of bird life.

How I got into this unlikely scene reveals a glimpse of a deadly game that threatens to rid the jungles and forests of Asia, forever, of one of the earth's most magnificent animals.

I had driven the length of Royal Chitwan National Park with Chuck McDougal, longtime friend and resident Nepal tiger expert, to meet with Tika Ram Adhikari, Deputy Warden of the park. Tika Ram, a 36-year-old wildlife worker from Lamjung in central Nepal, was one of several people putting together a very aggressive anti-poaching effort. Chuck spoke very highly of him and we wanted to hear how his work was progressing.

Though there are many problems facing the tiger and other endangered species—loss of habitat, population pressure, economic development, and the lack of resources, or the will of tiger habitat nations to combat the problem aggressively—the most immediate threat facing the tiger is poaching to satisfy the market for traditional Chinese medicine.

Tiger bone wine is thought by millions of people to be an elixir of life. To ingest the tiger is to gain its power and vigor. In the 1980's a factory in Taiwan, an island which has never had an indigenous tiger on its shores, was using 2000 kg. of tiger bones a year to bottle 100,000 bottles of tiger bone wine. That figure accounts for the death of at least 200 tigers annually.

Products from tiger bone are not limited to wine and tonics. Powders, ointments, pills and plasters made from tiger bones are also thought to have medicinal value.

Ancient beliefs and customs threatening the tiger are not, however, limited to bones. Tiger penis soup is seen as an aphrodisiac. Eyeballs rolled into pills supposedly cure convulsions. Whiskers should protect you from bullets. The tail mixed with soap is believed to cure skin disease. The hair when burnt drives away centipedes. Sitting on a tiger skin can prevent fevers caused by evil spirits. Claws worn as a piece of jewelry will give courage and protection from sudden fright. And ribs should at all times be carried as a good luck talisman.

The Royal Bengal tiger, found mainly in India, Nepal, Bangladesh, and Bhutan is being vigorously hunted because the Siberian and South China tiger are too scarce to supply the market demand for tiger products. With the recent changes in the former Soviet Union, the magnificent Siberian, or Amur tiger, has been slaughtered at such a pace to almost preclude its survival. Indeed, of the original eight sub-species of tigers, three have become extinct since the 1960s and two may never see the 21st century.

In 1911, King George V and his hunting party shot 39 tigers in eleven days in the jungles of Chitwan.

—RK

The once-thriving national parks of India and Nepal have become shopping malls to satisfy illicit markets in Vietnam, Taiwan, Korea, Japan, and China. Several renowned tiger reserves in India have suffered catastrophic losses since 1989 and several tiger populations monitored by McDougal in Nepal suffered 40 percent losses in the years between 1989 and 1991 alone. Tiger bones have been found at the airport in Delhi; tiger cubs were found smuggled through the Bangkok airport; and bags of tiger bones were found at a remote postal office in the Humla district of northwest Nepal. In August of 1996, a Tibetan in the town of Taklakot (a small town near the base of Mt. Kailas on the remote Nepal-Tibetan border) told me of a man in jail in the Ngari region town of Ali for trying to barter tiger bones for *shahtoosh*—wool from the endangered Tibetan antelope. Nepal clearly lies on the smuggling route of the tiger's path to extinction.

We met Tika Ram at his office in Saurah on the eastern end of Chitwan National Park. It didn't take long to see that this man was indeed a courageous and dedicated individual. His tale depicted a one-sided war but he was undeterred and spoke with almost mischievous glee about his battle with the poaching organizations. In somewhat broken English he told me over lunch, "I don't care about my life. How to catch tiger and rhino poachers at the site—this is my hobby."

He had a list of 72 suspected individuals who were being monitored by 7 people in his employment. They were paid a small amount to keep tabs on the movements of suspected poachers and traffickers. For example, one man was being paid 500 rupees (about $10) a month to watch a fellow named Som Lal Kami who was known to have killed three rhinos with spears after snaring them in a trap. There was now a tacit agreement between the Nepal army stationed inside the park and the warden's office to seriously detain this Mr. Kami if he ever ventured into the park.

There seemed to be two major smuggling/poaching organizations, one based in Pokhara and the other nearby in Narayanghat. The identity of the ringleaders was known but they were difficult to apprehend. Like everywhere else in the world, bribery, influence peddling, and big money kept those at the top protected.

Tika Ram told us that he himself was under surveillance by a man who allegedly was employed as a cook in a neighboring tea house at Saurah. He had been sent by the Narayanghat poaching ring to keep tabs on the warden's activities. So they were both spying on each other in this rather dangerous game. The stakes were high. Bones for a full grown tiger could get up to $1,000 US and a rhino horn could command as much as $10,000 US in Kathmandu. Rewards had been made commensurate with the profits to be gained. Up to 50,000 rupees ($1,000) were now being offered for information leading to the arrest of those involved in the poaching and trafficking of endangered species. Fines and penalties for killing tigers had now been raised to equal that of the rhino.

After lunch Tika Ram asked us if we wanted to go to the jail in Bharatpur to question two of the arrested poachers. This caught me totally by surprise. Chuck and I realized that this was too great an opportunity to pass up, so off we went in an open Land Rover.

En route to the jail we stopped at a narrow dirt lane. Tika Ram pointed out a white, two-story house on the edge of the forest. This was the home of Chij Kumari, a woman Tika Ram said was known to be the supplier of a poison called *fikum* which, mixed with DDT, was being used to kill tigers by a new and devious method.

Evidently, some villagers who lived on the edge of the park were given free cows and water buffaloes on the understanding that they should allow their animals to stray into the periphery of the park. If any of their animals were killed by a tiger they were to contact a certain person immediately. After a kill, tigers generally drag their larger prey off into the high grass and eat their meals over a period of time. The carcass of the animal would be laced with poison, and the tiger would die when it returned to finish the meal. The tiger would then be buried and its bones dug up at a later time and transported via the smuggling circuit to another destination. The villagers could then keep the remaining animals as their own.

Had we not been eager to get to the jail, I'm sure Tika Ram would have suggested that we pop on over to her house and ask to talk to her. This was his attitude when talking about all the miscreants in this affair. He had no qualms whatsoever about spontaneously confronting these people to let them know he was on their trail. This, indeed, was how the idea of going to the jail had come up.

Our host during this interview was the head jailer, a Mr. Sharma. He was a handsome man with a cleanly-pressed shirt which almost mocked the muggy disarray in which I found myself. He was wearing a colorful *topi*. His attitude varied from bored insouciance to open amusement at some of the questions and answers. The red phone rang a few times and all was still as he briefly conducted his jail business. Then, with a polite nod of the head, he indicated that Tika Ram could continue the interview with Sita Ram and Rom Bahadur Kami.

Sita Ram was dressed in thongs, shorts, and a loose-fitting, multi-colored, striped shirt. His hair was closely cropped, slightly graying, and had a drooping mustache which went well with the sneering scowl permanently etched on his face. My gut told me he was guilty.

Sita Ram had been caught in a sting operation digging up tiger bones at the Park Headquarters in Kasra Durbar. A tiger had been found dead and it was decided to put the carcass to good use. Informants approached Sita Ram and asked if he would dig up the bones and get them to an isolated school yard known to be a meeting place for the poaching trade.

Throughout the interview, he denied this charge, saying he just happened to be there, but did admit to being involved in three previous incidents of bringing bones up from India to that remote school yard. When confronted with the names of heads of known poaching rings, he admitted only to the existence of the organizations and said he had never heard the names of the leaders. Sita Ram had not been formally charged for this crime as yet. If convicted he was facing a possible sentence of fifteen years in prison and a fine of 75,000 rupees ($1,500). He pleaded with Tika Ram for understanding, claiming to have a son that needed his fathering. With primitive plea bargaining, it was suggested that if he provided helpful information about the poaching organization, some understanding could be reached. I've been told that he is now out of prison and a paid informant in the anti-poaching war.

Rom Bahadur Kami was tall and thin. He wore loose-fitting broken sandals, a pair of shorts, and a khaki shirt hung over a dirty white undershirt. He, too, wore a colorful Nepali *topi*. Unlike the unpleasant demeanor of Sita Ram, Rom Bahadur carried himself with a dignified air, and his face, though stern, occasionally offered a kind smile.

Rom Bahadur had been arrested in a raid on a house where forty-four rhino hooves and two horns had been confiscated. That represents eleven dead rhinos. Word had been spread through the local village of Bibinagar that a buyer was interested in rhino hooves. A response came back that there indeed were rhino hooves available but the buyer would also have to purchase an expensive and highly-prized rhino horn. A deal was cut over several days of negotiating.

When the park rangers raided the house, the scene turned into something out of a Keystone Cop film. People and rhino evidence began flying out windows and doors and holes in the roof. Eight people were arrested in this incident. Our talk with Rom Bahadur did not produce any new information.

Two hours later I looked around the room. The novelty of our visit had evidently worn thin. We were alone. No curious and pre-cocious children. No armed guard at the door. I stood near the door, and as Rom Bahadur began to glance outside from time to time, my paranoia had me wondering if I should try to stop him if he made an attempt to flee across the rice fields into the forest. The guard who had been at our door was now down under the shade of a large banyan tree. His rifle was lying on the ground and he was playing caroms with the young children. The other guard across the way had dropped his magazine and was dangerously close to nodding off on top of the bayonet affixed to his rifle. Our visit was now old news. We thanked Mr. Sharma for his hospital-ity, pulled in behind a bullock cart, and ate dust all the way out to the main highway.

On the road back to Saurah we stopped briefly to cross a small stream before entering a massive sal forest. The setting sun was now a huge ball of flame balancing on top of the trees. The intensity of the heat had been mercifully tempered by shade and an occasional breeze. A languar monkey was perched above us cradling a small baby in her arms. A spotted deer drank from the stream. Far off in the forest, an Indian cuckoo was singing its repetitious yet melodious refrain. All was becoming very still. The jungle was preparing for the night.

I asked Tika Ram why he was so dedicated to this often dangerous and thankless task. My question seemed to surprise him and he was quiet for a moment. His arm swept across the horizon gesturing to the smooth flowing Rapti River; the twenty-foot high green and golden brown elephant grass; the dense riverine sal forest; and on to the massive white snows of the Annapurna Himal in the distance.

"The grasses and forest-cover burn and are reborn every year," he said. "I never feel like this is an old area. I am always excited when I see the park as it is always changing. If we don't do something and the tiger and rhino are forever gone from our forests—then what is the meaning of this beautiful place?"

Brian K. Weirum has been leading treks in the high Himalayas for more than twenty years. He is the founder and president of The Fund for the Tiger, a tax-exempt, non-profit organization dedicated to saving the tigers of Nepal and India. The Fund's address is P. O. Box 2, Woodacre, CA 94973.

✳

It was our winter holiday and we were visiting a relative in the *tarai*. Since we were city boys, naturally we wanted to go hunting. Our cousin was a *zamindar* and he indicated that hunting to him was as natural as breathing. So, no problem, he'd take us city kids to hunt in the jungle, which was his backyard.

We woke up at four in the morning; it was very cold and pitch black. A bullock cart waited for us. Our cousin, with his double-barreled gun, my brother, and I got into the cart. The driver tapped the bulls and we were off, and the creaking of the wooden-wheeled cart seemed frightfully loud. A *shikari* walked along the cart, holding a kerosene lamp that illu-minated the rutted path in the forest.

After what seemed like a very long time (despite the damp chill, I had dozed off), the cart halted, the men's murmured chatter stopped. Silence. I heard the *shikari* whisper, "To your left, sir."

Our cousin got up and aimed. I looked in the direction of the pointed gun and there, in the feeble light of the misty dawn, I saw half a dozen deer of various sizes grazing in a clearing. They were astonishingly beau-tiful and delicate—and I suddenly regretted my city boy's glamorous fan-tasies of going hunting.

A loud bang! and the deer scattered. Not one fell. A second bang! but the deer had disappeared. And just as our cousin disappointedly lowered his gun, a deer re-appeared into the clearing, looked around, and grace-fully bounded away. It was a most enchanting sight—and I was glad our cousin was a lousy shot.

I have never gone hunting since.

—RK

ALISON WRIGHT

Democracy Day

A photographer bears witness
to the 1990 revolution.

TRUCKLOADS OF UNIFORMED RIOT POLICE LINED THE EMPTY
streets of Kathmandu. Each brandished a wooden shield resembling hand-carved folk art. Many of the local people had chosen
to stay locked in their homes, fearing the violent skirmishes over
the last few weeks between the police and protesters opposing the
Nepali Panchayat government. The police positioned themselves
along New Road, smoking cigarette after cigarette in anticipation
of further demonstrations. Ignorant of the impending danger, a
bull and a cow, animals considered almost more sacred than humans in this Hindu culture, enjoyed the unusual absence of traffic
and began to mate with unabashed pleasure in the middle of the
street. There I stood with my cameras poised—just the Nepali
police, the mating cows, and me.

I was hopelessly attached to this tiny country which I had come
to visit for a month, and after staying four years, now considered
home. I admired the strength and conviction of the people who
were so determined to fight for democracy in their country, something that I had always taken for granted in my own.

February 25th had been designated "Black Day" and the opposition parties in Kathmandu had encouraged all those who ob-

jected to the recent violent acts of the government to show their
solidarity by wearing black arm bands and waving black flags in
protest. Already more than 1,000 political workers had been arrested throughout the countryside, while others were still missing.

For years there had been talk of a corrupt government and
rumblings of overthrowing the monarchy, and now it appeared that
the time was ripe. When the Nepali people saw the success of the
mass movements in Eastern Europe, they felt encouraged in their
decades-long struggle to establish a democratic institution. While
a tiny percentage of the people had become wealthy from corruption, smuggling, and an immense amount of foreign aid, most of
the people of this agricultural society remained at poverty level.
They had had enough and were finally demanding changes. The
hard-line Communist parties of Nepal and the liberals of the
Nepali Congress had united in their attempts to abolish the
absolute monarchy established by the Shah dynasty over two centuries ago in which the King was considered to be an incarnation
of the Hindu god Vishnu.

All week prior to Black Day, small pockets of the Nepali opposition party had been fighting the government forces and graphic
photos taken from the outer villages were posted around
Kathmandu, showing police who had been brutally flayed alive
and dragged through the streets behind cars. Tensions by angry
protestors rose when the town of Patan announced that the neighboring city of Kathmandu was not being vocal enough in its
protests against the government. In fact, Patan officials had recently
sent a sari and bangles to the representatives of Kathmandu, insinuating that they were acting in a womanly and cowardly fashion.

I was a photographer and every day I had gone out to document the ongoing political strife. Because of this, friends warned
me that my phones were probably tapped. It would take more than
that to make me paranoid, but not much.

On the evening of Black Day, I bent over the light table viewing the slides that I'd shot earlier. Laurie Anderson blasted from my
small stereo speakers, and I had to lift my head to decipher an un-

usual noise in the background. I reached down to lower the volume, and, in an unnerving coincidence, a huge brick flew through my front window and slammed down onto the light table where my head had just been. I hit the floor just as another brick came shooting past my ear and shards of glass sprayed across the room. Terrified, I heard someone breaking through my front door.

"*Didi* (sister), turn the lights off!! There's a blackout and your light table is on." Expecting a swarm of protesters, I was relieved to see only Shanti, my Nepali neighbor, who had risked running up the stairs to warn me.

I squirmed through the broken glass now thoroughly embedded in the grass mats on the floor. The rocks and bricks were flying in fast and furious until I yanked the closest electrical cord. The room was abruptly silenced from Laurie's kinetic voice. Damn, wrong cord. Glass cut through my knees and the palms of my hands as I stretched even farther to the other cord.

O ne feature of the revolution which also took the opposition leaders by surprise was the imagination displayed in some of the protests. Artists sat down outside Trichandra College in Kathmandu with black scarves tied around their mouths in silent protest against the Panchayat government. Such black scarves became the most common symbol of defiance throughout the revolution. A large number of housewives gathered outside the gates of the Padma Kanya College and raised a din by banging pots and pans together. In the eastern city of Biratnagar, dogs, cows, and donkeys decorated with black scarves and anti-government slogans were let loose into the streets. Most remarkable, however, were the voluntary blackouts which began in Narayanghat in the tarai.

—William Raeper and Martin Hoftun, *Spring Awakening: An Account of the 1990 Revolution in Nepal*

Suddenly, darkness. My heart racing, I lay flat on the glass and straw, breathing in the pungent odor of moist grass matting mixed with sweat.

I dared to get up only when I heard the angry mob distance itself, as they made their way up the Hadigau hill. Only then did I notice how dark the rest of the neighborhood was. Later, Shanti told me that the opposition had encouraged the people to switch off their lights in a silent vote for democracy. I gave Shanti a big hug and thanked her. Later, sitting alone in the darkness, I reached for my box of clove cigarettes and with shaking hands drew in the deep sweet smoke.

On April 6, 1990, I was out at dawn, photographing a small group of demonstrators who were already marching through the back streets of Chetrapati and the tourist areas of Thamel. Young men in a youthful frenzy yelled democracy slogans through bandanna-covered mouths while waving the Nepali Congress and Communist hammer-and-sickle flags. Occasionally, familiar people would pass by waving their clenched fists in greeting.

By mid-morning I was on my mountain bike, climbing the hill to Patan, amidst an astonishing crowd of more than 50,000 people marching towards the local police station. After weeks of sporadic violence, the crowd was now demonstrating peacefully and there was a buoyant feeling of camaraderie in the air. Incredibly, as the demonstrators passed the police and military soldiers, all paused to smile and shake hands with one another. It seemed that the weeks of conflict might actually be resolved. I felt witness to history in the making, although, realistically, I knew that very few people outside of Nepal would care about such a small and seemingly in-significant country sandwiched between India and China. By late afternoon I had precariously positioned myself on top of the mosque to photograph the thousands of people who had now congregated across the street in Ratna Park. A wall of police and soldiers protecting the King's palace butted themselves against the growing mass of 200,000 agitated men and women who appeared more determined than ever to yell their slogans directly into the monarch's ears.

Abruptly, something in the air changed. The hands which only moments before had reached out in peace, were now angrily tearing down the metal signs which for so many years had paid homage to the King. A police booth was torn from its roots and rolled through the crowd towards the line of military in Durbar Marg. I didn't like it, yet as the crowd became more enraged, I wanted to get closer to the action. I jumped down from the mosque and ran through the back streets until I came up behind the police barricade.

My friend Ravi caught up with me and saw that I needed to break through the wall of police. He ran in front of the line, distracting them as I dropped down on my hands and knees, crawling between their legs. Looking up I was suddenly confronted by a wall of soldiers in green uniforms and bulletproof vests, their weapons poised. I swung around to photograph a young boy who had managed to climb up the top of the statue of King Mahendra on Durbar Marg in front of the palace. Victoriously he waved the scepter that he had grabbed from the King's iron fist, but his triumph was short-lived. The police immediately shot him to the ground.

This action immediately set off both the police and the demonstrators, and I wanted to escape. The police suddenly charged with *lathis*, batons, and the crowd retaliated by throwing bottles and stones. Pushing my way through the crowd, I felt the force of a heavy stick come down on the back of my head. Biting down hard, I tasted blood. My first reflex was to lean forward to protect my equipment, but I quickly flipped back in fright as a gun went off near my face. It was only tear gas, but at extremely close range, and I was completely incapacitated.

With a head now turned to liquid, I immediately fell to my knees vomiting; snot, tears and blood ran down my face in a steady flow. As far as I was concerned, all hell had officially broken loose. I threw my shirt over my face and ran the other way, my feet barely touching the ground. Once I could breathe again the shirt came down and the camera back up. I turned around and headed back into the throng of people.

I felt almost untouchable, in a protective bubble, as I worked my way back through the crowd, photographing young children pinned in doorways, their small arms raised in terror against the police batons coming down on their heads. Men and women lay on the ground, hands pressed together in *namaste* as they begged for mercy. The enraged police opened fire as people attempted to flee; some were shot in the back as they ran. Briefly, I mused at the absurdity of a profession that obliges one to rush toward an incident that everyone else is fleeing. My eyes felt as though they had been seared with hot pokers.

Suddenly, I felt someone from behind grab my hair and pull me towards the doorway of the Star Hotel near Ratna Park.

"Hide your film, they're after you," whispered a familiar Nepali teenager. I wisely decided to hide myself as well and ducked behind a wooden desk in the lobby. Seconds later, the hotel was overrun with a group of baton-wielding police shattering windows, mirrors and potted plants in their wake. I feared they would hear my heart pounding, yet dared to peek around the corner of the desk. Horrified, I watched them throw open a bathroom door where a young rickshaw driver was urinating. Dragging him by the hair to the middle of the lobby they quickly beat him to a bloody pulp before moving on to another room. Outraged by such arbitrary violence, I ran out to comfort him; his eyes were already swollen on his brutally torn face.

Outside, the quiet was surprising—and disconcerting. The once-immense crowd looked as though it had melted into the ground. Hundreds of shoes and sandals now littered the empty streets.

Cutting across Trichandra College campus, I managed to get back to my mountain bike and drop my film off at a local lab where I knew it would be safe. But the sudden cracking sounds of gunfire were becoming more pronounced as I rode back towards town. Where was it coming from and who was it directed at? I quickly returned to where I had just been in Ratna Park. The folk-art-shield-bearing police had now been replaced by the Nepali army, and they certainly weren't brandishing museum pieces. On bended knee, each soldier braced himself against the impact of his shot. They were no longer firing just tear gas, but real bullets. I knelt down and began photographing them.

"Hey," whispered a small boy in Nepali, calling out from under the metal door of his store front, "don't stay out there!" It was the first time I noticed how totally alone I was. But still, I wondered, who were these soldiers shooting at?

I followed the army towards Bir Hospital. The soldiers were shooting into the crowds trapped by barricades. Fires burned in dumpsters, sending black, acrid smoke billowing into the air. Dozens of bodies lay in the street, and people were frantically carrying the wounded through the hospital doors. Ironically, many were being shot right in front of the hospital.

When I decided to write, others asked me if I were not afraid of being tortured. The point is that fear is the strongest weapon of a dictatorial state. If we give in to fear this early in the game, then we might as well roll over on our backs and surrender all our rights and liberties, including that of free speech.

—Barbara Adams,
"Barbara's Beat," *People's Review*

"We have your friend in here," an older man screamed at me in Nepali, as he dragged me by the arm towards the hospital entrance. I didn't know if I was quite ready for what I knew would be an intensely gruesome scene, but the man was unrelenting. "We have your friend, your friend is here!" I thought of all my friends who were out demonstrating just this morning, laughing with me as they waved their red flags. Oh no, was it one of them?

The scene in the hospital was tragic. A battlefield of bodies lined the floor throughout the lobby, filling the next room. My dirty boots tracked bloody imprints on the floor as I moved from person to person. Crude bandages had been wrapped around various body parts. It was obvious that the small hospital staff had far more patients than it could handle. The man who had led me in tugged on my arm. "Your friend, your friend," he whispered.

Overhearing, a doctor walked over. "Is this a friend of yours?" he asked. I looked down. Oh God, I saw what this was about now. Blue eyes caked with blood stared back at me. A Westerner had been killed, probably a tourist caught in the line of fire. There was a clean bullet hole right in his jugular.

"No. I don't know. I'm not sure." Actually he looked very

familiar, like a friend who was visiting me. Had he worried about me and ventured out of the house? His features were so bloodied it was difficult to tell.

"We need to find out who he is," the doctor looked at me apologetically, "and as you can see we're really quite busy."

The doctor recognized me, since I had interviewed him a couple of days ago when the staff had staged a protest at the hospital. He now encouraged me to photograph as many of the bodies as soon as possible. "Especially the Western guy. Police trucks are gathering the dead bodies from here and in the streets. We don't know where they're taking them. We hear they may be dumping them in a mass grave near Gokarna. We'll never know how many people have really been killed today. Bastards."

In what felt to be a truly sacred act, I knelt down and opened the money belt resting against his bony hips. I delicately rummaged through a typical traveler's stash: a few rupees, Drum tobacco, rolling papers and travel documents. My heart ached as I thought of his poor parents. Pulling out the familiar British passport I shakily read his name and birthdate to the doctor. Only twenty-six years old, a tourist. We were about the same age. He had the stamp of an Australian work visa in his passport, as I had in mine, only now he would never get the chance to use his.

"You idiot," I thought, "what were you doing out in the middle of this mess?" I looked around and asked myself the same question. I took the doctor's advice and photographed what I could in the hospital. I was afraid the tourist's body would disappear. Surely news of a Westerner being shot would be bad for Nepal's tourist industry and I didn't know how far they would go to keep it quiet.

As I made my way through the room, another Westerner was carried in on a stretcher. He worked here in Kathmandu and I recognized him from the bakery near my house where I shopped. He'd been shot in the back and was paralyzed from the waist down.

Yet another tourist caught in crossfire arrived with his leg shattered by a bullet below the knee. This further convinced the doctors that illegal dum-dum bullets were being used, bullets that splinter upon impact and have been banned since 1945.

I ran back out to where I'd stashed my bike and rapidly pedaled back up the street to the lab. Five soldiers blocked the road, pointing their guns at eye level. I knew from what I'd just seen that they weren't kidding.

"There's a curfew, you know, and you shouldn't be on the streets," I was told with severe authority.

"A curfew? Oh, OK." I attempted to sound accommodating. "My hotel is up here though, I'm staying at the Yak 'n Yeti."

As I cycled through town, I kept swinging my long blonde hair with dramatic flair, praying that the lost tourist bit would carry me through the town safely. Binu was surprised to see me at the Associated Press office, but happy to have some black & white film which, unlike color, could be sent out over the news wires.

There was no way I could get through the roadblocks back to my house, so I headed back to Thamel to stay in a hotel, and when I got to the familiar Shambhala Hotel I was just glad to be in a place that served cold beer. The roof garden took on a surreal quality compared to what I had just witnessed. A couple playing backgammon in the corner passed a sweet-smelling joint back and forth. Now stuck in their hotels indefinitely, no one seemed very happy about having their travel plans interrupted by a revolution.

Despite protests from my friends who worked at the hotel, I sneaked out on my mountain bike during the curfew the next morning. Stopping at the hospital, I was amazed to see the hallway empty, and the doctors shared

But Nepal is not Shangri-La. This became quite clear to me one afternoon as I sat in the garden of the Kathmandu Guest House and read through an Amnesty International report entitled Nepal: A Pattern of Human Rights Abuses. *Reading the booklet gave me a nagging sense of disconnection from the immediate environment, which consisted mainly of Western tourists and travelers lounging around on the manicured lawn, drinking fresh lemon sodas, reading travel guides, smoking hashish or Yak cigarettes, and reminiscing about the Hill Tribes of Thailand or the beaches of Goa...*

—Jeff Greenwald,
Shopping for Buddhas

with me the disturbing news that in fact it was the slowest day they'd ever had. Because of the ongoing curfew, no one had been allowed to bring in the injured.

The town was empty except for gun-toting soldiers and the unusual sight of army tanks crawling along Ring Road. Taking a chance I rode my bike at top speed out to the airport where cranky tourists were lined up waiting for nonexistent flights so they could escape this vacation-turned-nightmare. After some serious pleading I convinced a doctor heading to India to carry my film out in his sock. Someone from *Time* magazine would meet him and pick it up.

Later that night television broadcast the King announced that he would meet with the opposition party leaders. He then commanded that the curfew be ended. Tragically, he neglected to inform the police on duty, and as cheering celebrators ran into the streets, they were promptly shot.

On April 9, 1990, the newly approved Democracy Day, thousands took to the streets, this time in joyous revelry to celebrate the prospect of actual change in their country. Men applied red *tika* powder to the foreheads of passersby; truckloads of young boys drove by screaming and waving red flags, while photos of the dead were hung by family members in remembrance of those who had sacrificed their lives for this triumphant moment in history.

Meanwhile, after enjoying my first fresh change of clothes in four days, I headed to Patan Hospital to see how the injured were doing. I settled into the back of a taxi, marveling at the jubilation of the people who continued to pass us on the way.

At one point I berated the taxi driver for driving too fast in such a crowd, and just as I was in mid-sentence, he hit a bicyclist. A spray of glass flew into my open mouth as a young boy crashed through our windshield, blood pouring from a gaping head wound. Feeling these horrific scenes were just never going to end, I screamed at the driver to continue to the hospital as I gave the injured boy first aid in the back seat. In the hospital, he clung to my hand in fright. Just as the doctor was finished, another doctor entered the room, looking for someone who could speak English and Nepali. Handing me a duffel bag, he requested that I search through the belongings of an unconscious Western trekker who had just been brought in by his Sherpa guide. Diagnosed with altitude sickness after being detained in the mountains while the airport was closed, it didn't look like he was going to make it; and in fact he died the following day. Unfortunately, after identifying him and contacting the consulate, we later discovered that the Sherpa had accidentally brought down the wrong bag and we mistakenly reported that the wrong man had died.

Three days later commercial flights resumed and I returned to the mountains for a much needed walk in the mighty Himalayas to clear my head. Yak herders, oblivious to the impassioned demonstrations in Kathmandu, placidly led their lumbering animals through the villages, past stacks of sacred *mani* stones and colorful Buddhist prayer flags flapping in the wind. The serenity of the snow-laden peaks calmed my spirit, even as the stark images of death continued to haunt me. The government-controlled radio and newspapers had suppressed any news of the recent revolution and the Sherpa villagers were astonished by the tales of mayhem that they were only just receiving by word of mouth. Even here, the immense beauty couldn't mask the nation's impatient desire for a better way of life. As I pondered the recent events in this tiny Himalayan kingdom, I realized how far they had yet to go. Only time will tell.

Born to an English airline stewardess who hitch-hiked her way across America, Alison Wright's wanderlust was deep rooted in utero. Her travels and photo assignments have taken her from the outback of Australia to the Amazon Basin. She is a recipient of the Dorothea Lange Award in documentary photography for her work with child labor in Asia. Based both in San Francisco and Nepal, she travels most of the year documenting indigenous cultures and projects of social concern.

*

I am often asked, "Did you like Nepal?"—to which I usually reply, "Yes" and leave it at that. But no one merely "likes" Nepal; Nepal weaves a net

out of splendour and pettiness, squalor and colour, wisdom and inno-
cence, tranquillity and gaiety, complacence and discontent, indolence and
energy, generosity and cunning, freedom and bondage—and in this be-
wildering mesh foreign hearts are trapped, often to their own dismay.

—Dervla Murphy, *The Waiting Land: A Spell in Nepal*

PAT MURPHY

* ✱ ✱

Before and After

Every moment is a miracle.

WE WERE DRIVING TO KATHMANDU FROM THE SMALL TOWN OF Hille, down the winding mountain roads, laughing, Claire and I. That was, of course, before the car went off the road.

"We'll tell people that you must walk in from Jiri and back to Hille to get the total experience," Claire said. "To get a feel for the culture of Nepal, you just have to hike down through the Arun Valley. And cross all those bamboo bridges. If you miss those, you're just a tourist."

I laughed. For the past week, we had been hiking through tiny villages on a trail that criss-crossed the Arun River. To cross the river, you had to balance precariously on an arching span made of a few stalks of bamboo, lashed together with fraying twine. The bamboo shifted and creaked underfoot and the white water rushed beneath your feet. A terrifying experience, but now that they were behind us, those bridges would make fine travel stories.

"Yes, and the food is not so bad, once you get used to it," I said, "*dal-bhat* can really be quite tasty."

"And hiring a car is the best way to get back to Kathmandu," Claire added. "You see so much more of the countryside."

We laughed some more. Back in Kathmandu, when we had

315

arranged for the car to pick us up at the end of the trek, we had considered taking the bus from Hille to Kathmandu.

The bus trip took 24 hours—if you were lucky. Twenty-four hours of swaying down mountain roads at frightening speeds. In the end, we had decided that going by car would give us a chance to see the scenery along the way.

It was already late afternoon, and the sun was setting as we made our way down the mountain, through a series of hairpin turns. It would soon be dark, and we would see nothing of the rivers that the road crossed or the jungle of the *tarai*.

"Oh, yes," I agreed. "The car ride is an essential part of the trip. It's the only way to do it."

We grinned at each other, happy to be in the back seat of a Toyota after more than a month of hiking through tiny villages, far from any road or automobile. Kumar, the guide who had been with us from the start of the trek, glanced back at us and smiled, not certain what had amused us so, but willing to share in the joke. The driver, the driver's younger brother who had come along for the ride, and Kumar were all crammed together in the front seat of the small car.

This was, you know, before the car went off the road.

Claire and I had started in Jiri, a town about six hours northeast of Kathmandu. Kumar had shown us the trail and Kaji, a cheerful young man who spoke more English than he let on, had carried our pack.

We hiked along a well-traveled trekking route to Gokyo, a high-altitude location that provides the most extensive view of Mount Everest. Then we hiked back down to the lowlands along a route less commonly traveled by non-Nepalis, through the Arun Valley to the village of Hille.

All in all, we had walked over 140 miles and climbed over 14,400 meters. (Mount Everest is 8,848 meters at its summit.) Obviously, our hiking involved a lot of ups and downs—we'd climb a pass, then descend into a valley, then climb up out of the valley again.

It had been hard going, some days. Claire had asthma, and the trip had been a personal triumph for her.

Occasionally, we had considered turning back. There was the day we hiked from Kharikhola to Surke, up through what seemed like an endless rhododendron forest. Sometimes, I would see what looked like a crest ahead, but always the trail turned and continued ascending. It was muddy and slippery, and far below us, we could hear the sound of water: the *Dudh Kosi,* or Milk River, named for the whiteness of its rushing water. Late in the morning, Claire stepped on a rock that gave way beneath her foot, sliding off the trail. I was ahead of her, and I heard her say, "Oh, shit!" and I looked back to see her clinging to a stalk of bamboo that grew beside the trail, dangling over the edge.

I grabbed one arm, Kumar grabbed the other, and we hauled her back onto the trail, muddy and scraped.

That evening, in a teahouse in Surke, Claire confessed, "I've decided that I don't like hiking." We talked about flying out of Lukla, the high altitude airport that was near our route. We told ourselves we didn't have to hike for the entire month. We could turn back. But by the time we reached Lukla, the disastrous trail had become an amusing story to tell to fellow trekkers. No need to turn back.

Then there was the day we hiked to Tengboche, a long steep climb up another muddy trail. Kumar and Kaji had gone on ahead, and Claire and I sat by the trail, exhausted. We talked for a while about our *koan*—we had been reading Peter Matthiessen's book, *The Snow Leopard,* in which he goes on at length about his *koan,* which was a poetic and slightly mystical unanswerable question. We decided that our *koan* was somewhat less mystical, but equally unanswerable: "What the fuck are we doing here?"

We were three-quarters of the way up the hill and we did not want to continue. "We could just stay here forever," I suggested.

"Sure," Claire agreed. "We could beg for food from people passing by. And maybe Kaji would bring us *chapatis.*"

"Eventually, we'd make the news," I said. "Two American

women who are halfway up and halfway down. Maybe *Weekly World News* would do a story on us."

"And they'd bring us food," Claire said.

We sat by the trail for a while, and talked about food. Food had, by that time, become a recurring topic of conversation. After a few weeks on the road, we longed for the taste of home: for pasta, for Chinese food, for cheeseburgers, for french fries.

"Tomorrow morning, we can have breakfast at Mike's Place," Claire said.

"Absolutely," I agreed.

Mike's Place was in a garden opposite the police headquarters in Kathmandu. The restaurant had pancakes and waffles and eggs and all sorts of wonderful things—or so some British trekkers had told us. (We were not the only trekkers who had become obsessed with food along the way.)

The sun had set and we had crossed the Tamur Khola and the Sapta Kosi, two rivers spanned by substantial bridges. We had passed through a few towns, marveling at the electric lights. So strange not to have to rely on our flashlights any longer.

"We'll take hot showers," I mused. "And get all our clothes washed."

"Oh, yes."

We lapsed into happy thoughts of food and cleanliness, two commodities that had been in short supply for the last month. We were tanned and thin, hill-hardened and in shape.

"Dinner?" our driver asked as we drove through one town. He was a tall, dark-haired man who seemed to find Claire and me, and our enthusiastic attempts to speak Nepali, infinitely amusing.

We agreed that it was time to have dinner, and we stopped in an open-air restaurant for *dal-bhat*. Then we kept driving, along rough dirt roads that grew worse with each mile. We were crossing the *tarai*, the lowland jungle area of Nepal, near the southern border with India. The air was warm and muggy. Claire and I slept in the back seat, twisting our bodies into unnatural positions and waking when the car jounced over a rock or into a pothole.

At some point I looked out the window at a dirt lot, crowded with buses and trucks, illuminated by headlights and a few distant electric bulbs. My back ached from sleeping curled up in the back of the Toyota.

"Why are we stopping here?" Claire asked the driver.

"Check point," he said, peering out the windshield at a small building in the distance. Then he turned to look back at us. "Fifteen days before," he said in careful English, "a bus was kidnapped by a man on a horse in the jungle. Eight kilometers." He waved a hand at the other vehicles—a few trucks, a few cars. "We wait and go together."

Claire and I nodded, agreeing that we would be happy to wait and travel in safety and avoid equestrian hijackers. Then we grinned at each other. "A bus was kidnapped," Claire said softly. It was an adventure, driving across the southern lowlands of Nepal at night, through a jungle where vehicles caravaned for protection.

We got out of the car then, and went off together in search of a place to pee. In America, it's easy to take restrooms for granted. In Nepal, finding a place to pee is never easy. On our trek, Claire and I had cataloged the toilets along the way, and sent the list to the friend who had supplied us, prior to the trip, with pee funnels. A pee funnel is a device that lets a woman pee standing up like a man. Claire and I had, at the time we wrote the letter, peed by the side of the road, peed out a teahouse window when we were locked in for the night and had no other op-

*S*houts, then running; one person passed us followed by several more. Not, Mohan assured me, a good time to be wandering around looking for latrine ditches.

Indeed. A local villager had apparently decided to take advantage of all those immobile buses filled with tourists to make a bit of cash. He succeeded only in stabbing a passenger in a bus several vehicles ahead of us and making his escape under cover of darkness. With this bit of information, I decided that keeping my bladder under control would be of primary importance, as I didn't want to be literally caught with my pants down.

—Elizabeth Baugh Staphit, "Night Bus to Kathmandu"

tion, peed by the side of the trail, and peed in latrines of all kinds.
Our favorite latrine was in the village of Bung, where the floor
overhung the pig pen and you could hear the pig grunting below.

Claire and I wandered away from the other vehicles. With the
help of the driver, we asked the policeman at the checkpoint if
there was anywhere to pee. He waved a hand into the jungle. You
could pee anywhere you wanted.

There was a stone wall marking some official boundary, and
we followed that for a short distance. There we squatted and peed
together.

We returned to the car and the driver started off. We were in
the jungle proper now; on both sides, trees loomed above the car.
Our headlights reflected from tree trunks. Easy to see how a rider
could appear from the darkness and intercept a bus. Once our
headlights caught a jackal by the side of the road—a thin long-
legged dog with ears upright and alert. The animal watched us approach, then faded into the forest.

I remember that the sun rose. We were out of the jungle then,
and we'd left the flat lands behind. We were back in the mountains,
the road twisting and curving as it climbed around one bend and
then another.

I was drowsy, half asleep, but I opened my eyes and saw three
barrels—metal oil drums—painted white. They served as a primitive highway barrier, marking a sharp curve of the road. I opened
my eyes and saw the barrels marking where the road curved. The
car went straight, through the barrels, over the edge, and into
darkness.

All that was Before. After, I came to consciousness on a bus, an
ordinary Nepali public bus, driving through the mountains and
heading toward Kathmandu. I assumed that the bus was a dream.
I knew that Claire and I were in a Toyota, so how could I be on
a bus?

The bus was crowded and I couldn't see Claire or Kumar or the
driver anywhere. The only one on the bus who looked familiar
was the driver's brother, the smiling young man who had been riding in the front seat of the Toyota with Kumar and the driver. I

tried to ask him, in this dream, what we were doing on the bus. He told me something about an accident. I might have asked him again—where was the car? Where was Claire? Same answer. He didn't speak much English and there didn't seem to be anyone else on the bus who spoke any English at all.

There had been an accident. I was clutching something: the flannel blanket that I had used as a sleeping bag liner while trekking. I didn't know why I had that wrapped around my shoulders; I didn't know why I was on the bus; I didn't know where Claire was. As near as I could guess, in that way that one tries to make sense of a dream world, I figured Claire must have

A side from discomfort on these bus journeys, there could be fear. A week or so earlier a boulder had dropped onto the Kathmandu-Pokhara trunk road, taking out a bus, and could not be levered off until heavy machinery made it over from the city, a day later.

On the trip out from Kathmandu there had been a bus belly-up in a ditch. People shook their heads but from the way they talked you got the idea that these tragedies were part of a series not expected to end.

—Jeffrey Heiman,
"Over the Border"

gone on to Kathmandu by some other means of transportation. If there was an accident and she was hurt, they must have rushed her to a hospital in a car and left me to take the bus.

I faded in and out of consciousness, certain that all this was a dream. There is no time in dreams, but my best guess is that I was on the bus for an hour or so.

When we got to Kathmandu, the bus stopped at the Bir Hospital. I followed the driver's brother, who seemed to know where he was going, to the hospital's emergency room. It was all very fuzzy, still dreamlike.

I remember seeing Kumar on a gurney, with an IV drip in his arm. He wasn't conscious; I couldn't talk to him. He was wrapped in another flannel sleeping bag liner, the one that Claire had used with her sleeping bag, and the flannel was smeared with blood. I kept clutching my own flannel sleeping bag liner because I was cold, so cold. I couldn't get warm.

I remember trying to walk down the hall to the toilet. In my memory it is a very long hall, so long that I had to sit down and rest halfway to the toilet. If I hadn't sat down I would have fainted. After that, I remember being wheeled around in a wheelchair. I remember someone asking me to pay in advance for medical care. All just a dream—though it began feeling a little more real when I was sick to my stomach and vomited on the hospital floor.

I remember, though maybe it was a dream, that the American Embassy called while I was waiting in the emergency room. Someone had told them that there had been an accident and Americans were involved.

I told them that I was OK; I didn't feel too bad. I told them that I was waiting to see Claire, I didn't know where Claire was and I would call them when I found out how she was. I don't know if I made much sense—but then, I don't know if the phone call was real or a dream.

Then doctors started examining the cut on my head and I realized that my shirt and the flannel around my shoulders were smeared with blood. I hadn't realized that I'd been hurt.

They sat me on a table and shaved my head around the cut, then closed the wound with a few big stitches. (Later, the American doctor who removed them marveled at the size of the stitches. "Were they trying to save thread?" she asked.) They x-rayed my skull and found no fracture, then gave me the x-rays to take away with me.

Then a doctor who spoke English told me I should go to my hotel to rest. I refused, of course, saying that I couldn't leave until I saw Claire—I wasn't going to leave her in the hospital alone. Where was she? I thought she'd be in the emergency room too, but I hadn't seen her.

That was when the doctor said, "I don't want to shock you. But Claire is dead."

That made no sense. Claire and I were in a car, coming back to Kathmandu and telling jokes. It made no sense that Claire was dead.

The driver's brother, the young man who had been on the bus with me, helped me catch a taxi and go to the Kathmandu Guest

House. The cab let me out in the courtyard in front of the hotel, a large brick area where there are bicycles to rent and café tables for tourists who want to sit in the sun and have a beer. I went directly to the front desk.

My head was wrapped in gauze. My left cheek was scraped red and raw and my face was decorated with scratches. My shirt was bloody from the scalp wound. My pants, I learned later (though I was unaware of it at the time) had been ripped in the accident, and my underwear was showing. I had no luggage, but I still clutched the bloody, vomit-stained flannel sleeping bag liner. My glasses were broken and I was wearing prescription sunglasses. I had been carrying the sunglasses in my fanny pack which had remained fastened to my body. Somehow, they had not been broken.

I leaned on the counter at the front desk and said, "My name is Pat Murphy. I have a reservation."

While I was standing there, a woman came up beside me and said, "Do you need some help?"

My first thought (and this is the part that made one of my friends howl with painful laughter) was "What a perceptive woman. How ever did she figure out that I could use a hand?"

Debbie Ryan, a tourist from Canada in Kathmandu to go trekking, adopted me for the next few days. She sat me down in her room while they got a room ready for me. She called the American Embassy. She gave me a pair of underwear to wear until my luggage was retrieved from the car. She told me my pants were torn. She threw away the bloody, vomit-stained flannel that I had clutched for so long. That first night, she slept in the extra bed in my room and woke me every now and then. (A person with a concussion, I learned, was not supposed to sleep for more than a few hours at a stretch.) She got me an appointment at the Western clinic and took me there in a cab.

And then, when she went on trek, she appointed an elderly British couple to baby-sit me. Bill and Mary always called to see if I had had dinner. They checked in on me.

I've been trying to piece together what I did in those days between the accident and my return to America. The accident was

on the morning of November 7. My flight, which even the
American Embassy could not manage to change, left Kathmandu
on November 12.

What did I do? I went to the Western clinic. I slept. It was hard
to get out of bed—all the muscles in my back and neck had been
strained, and I had to position myself carefully to get up out of bed,
using the weight of my legs to lift my upper body, so that I did not
have to use the muscles in my back.

The Embassy brought me the luggage from the car. There was
the day pack that I had carried for so many weeks, the pack Claire
had carried, the large backpack we had shared. The Embassy officials brought the stuff to my room and stayed while I sorted
through our possessions, separating my belongings from Claire's. I
kept the bottle of iodine crystals that we had used to purify our
water. It seemed important to keep that. For so long, we had relied
on those crystals to purify our water.

What did I do? I went to Mike's Place and had breakfast in the
garden, sitting alone under the trees and trying not to cry. I was
afraid someone would ask me what had happened, why my head
was wrapped in gauze, and I couldn't tell them without weeping
and then they would sympathize. But there was nothing they
could do, nothing they could say, nothing that would help or
change this After to Before, before when we were happy and
strong and triumphant and everything was right.

The American Embassy called each day to check up on me.
Once they called to tell me that they would be cremating Claire's
body and to ask if the usual Hindu ceremony would be appropriate. I suppose I could have asked to attend the ceremony; they
didn't ask me if I wanted to, but I could have asked. But in some
deep place that I did not want to touch, I was afraid.

I stayed in the hotel, where I could hide from death, from pain,
from myself. Once, a phone call woke me up and I heard a
woman's voice on the other end of the line. "Claire!" I said, so glad
to hear her voice. I knew it was Claire. She was back, she was fine,
it had been a mistake, a misunderstanding.

But the voice was Debbie Ryan's; she was waking me to see if I wanted to have dinner.

My friends in the States called each day to see if I was all right. But everyone was far away, so far away.

One day, I went to the trekking service that had set up the trek for me, and I asked about Kumar, our guide. He was in the hospital, but he would be all right, they said. I left some money to be delivered to Kumar, the traditional tip that trekkers give a guide at the end of a trek.

Later, the American Embassy brought me a box that held Claire's ashes, took me to the airport, and saw me through customs. It was a long trip home. On the plane from Kathmandu to Bangkok, the woman sitting beside me asked what had happened. When I told her, I started crying. She comforted me with chocolate and tissues. When I went through Thai customs, they asked what was in the cardboard box, and I cried as I told them.

Before, just moments before the car went off the cliff, it had been a wonderful trip, a joyous success. The story of the trek was a humorous tale, a prolonged joke.

And then there was After. The two times don't match up; they don't go together. It is impossible to reconcile them.

When people ask me about Nepal, I don't know what to tell them. Should I talk about the triumph of reaching Gokyo, the beauty of the Himalayas, the shared jokes and laughter? Or should I tell them of the sadness and pain and confusion that followed? I don't know. It's all of a piece, one trip, one event. But the two halves don't match.

Before, I used to say "if I die." I remember when I was preparing to go skydiving, I wrote a silly little will, leaving my sparse possessions to various friends. "If I die...," I wrote.

After, I say "when I die." I will die. You will die. We will all die at some point, possibly by surprise, possibly after an adventure, possibly without warning.

I travel to see things and to test myself. To climb impossible passes and test my ability to get by; to learn about bamboo bridges and *dal-bhat* and Buddhist temples. I travel to learn things about myself and my world. I don't always like the lessons.

I want to go back to Kathmandu. I want to walk around Swayambu, the temple that's perched on a hill outside of town. From the tower atop the hill, painted eyes gaze serenely across the valley; brightly-colored prayer flags fly in the wind. I will spin the prayer wheels that send up prayers with each rotation and burn incense and think of Claire. She went trekking to test her limits, and on that car ride home she said, "Now that I've hiked to Everest, I feel like I can do anything."

A few months ago, I dreamed that a mutual friend called me to tell me that she'd heard from Claire. In the dream, I asked how Claire was doing, how it was for her after what happened in Nepal. My friend said that she was doing fine, Claire was traveling now, she was happy.

I was glad when I woke up, so glad. I don't know what happens After; I've never really believed in a Christian heaven. But I'll accept that conclusion: Claire is traveling now and she's happy. Finding new places and people and things and joking and laughing as we go. Those two go together, for Claire and me. Traveling and being happy.

Pat Murphy has written award-winning novels and books about science. Her fourth and latest novel is Nadya: The Wolf Chronicles. *Her latest nonfiction book is* The Color of Nature, *a book about natural colors. Currently she writes for the Exploratorium, San Francisco's museum of science, art, and human perception. She is the recipient of the Nebula and Philip K. Dick awards and has taught science fiction writing at Stanford University and Michigan State University. She has a black belt in kenpo karate.*

★

> Existence is infinite, not to be defined;
> And, though it seem but a bit of wood in your hand,
> to carve as you please.
> It is not to be lightly played with and laid down.
> —Lao Tzu, *The Way of Life*

BRIAN K. WEIRUM

⋆ ⋆ ⋆

Avalanche

*Fear and loathing on Mount Mera
during the storm of 1995.*

"BUNG HO," I CALLED UP INTO THE WHITE VOID. USING THE CLAR-ion call from the hilarious mountaineering satire *Rum Doodle*, I was looking for Base Camp. At the time it seemed humorous to me. Here I was, leading a group of eight clients with a support staff of 14 (not including porters and yaks) to a mountain known as Mera, and I couldn't even find Base Camp.

Mera, 21,247 feet high, is at the cul-de-sac end of the remote Hinku Valley just east of the main route to Mt. Everest. It offers unparalleled summit views of Everest, Kangchenjunga, Lhotse, and Makalu (four of the five highest mountains in the world). It was generally agreed amongst those who had spent a lot of time in the Himalayas, and who did well at high altitude, that climbing Mera was the easiest, least dangerous, least technical way to get that high anywhere in the world. But not always.

The morning had begun 2,000 feet lower at Tang Nag. I had been enjoying the walk along a beautiful stream looking for an auspicious rock to place on the summit of Mera. When the first snow flakes began to fall I commented to Janet and Mike how much I liked to walk in the snow. Now, here we were, stumbling through brush and slippery rocks in a foot of fresh snow, visibil-

ity was about 200 feet, and our tents and camp were nowhere to
be seen.

"BUNG HO," came the retort from above and we worked our
way up the last bit to Khare, the official Base Camp at 15,800 feet

It continued to snow heavily throughout the day and into the
night. I became concerned because I couldn't see where we were
or what was above us. We were in a total whiteout.

Sleep that night was fitful. We had to push or dig the snow away
from our tents continually and all night long we could hear the
sound of tent ceilings being pounded from inside to prevent the
weight of the snow from collapsing the tents on top of us.

At 6:30—later than usual—I decided to make a move and unzipped my tent door. No light. No air. Only snow. I put on my
double boots and kicked my way out into the blizzard. The snow
was relentless. Heavy and wet. The dining tent had completely collapsed. Drifts of snow revealed only the tops of my clients' tents.
Visibility was about 50 feet.

I worked my way over to the Sherpa tent and found them
sleeping like hibernating bears. Ang Tshering, our *sardar* and dear
friend who had trekked with me for 13 years, stuck his head out
of his tent and summed up the situation with one word: "SHIT!"

Ang Tshering and I decided that the best strategy would be to
pack several days worth of bare essentials in our day packs and be
prepared to go down to Tang Nag if the storm did not soon abate.
We could return to dig out later. Sherpas Tarkgay, Sona, and
Gyalgen were working hard to resurrect the dining tent and we
agreed to meet there when we were packed and ready to go.

At 9 a.m., the moment I sat down to eat, I heard Ang Tshering
yell "AVALANCHE!" Before the words registered in my mind I heard
a "swooshing" sound, then was hit from behind and my face was
imbedded in a perfectly good piece of French toast.

For a split second panic set in. I tried to raise my head and
shoulders but couldn't. It was completely dark and the air around
me was very tight. Then panic gave way to common sense. I told
myself to try to breathe calmly, which I realized I could now do in
the rarefied atmosphere. The hit from behind was gentle, but I was

very firmly bent over the dining table at a 90 degree angle. My legs were free to move under the table. It all happened so fast I was more stunned than afraid. What seemed like an eternity was actually only a few seconds and I knew I was OK.

There were eight of us in the tent and we were able by voice contact to assure each other that we were all safe. Within fifteen minutes we were all able to slide down under the table and work our way out a small hole in one corner of the tent. Jeff had been coming down from his tent and witnessed the whole spectacle. Sam had been nearest the tent entrance and got caught chest deep in snow as he tried to flee upon hearing Ang Tshering's warning.

The moment I crawled out I was devastated by the realization of how fortunate we all were. Three of the tents were now buried under six feet of new snow. A matter of moments had meant the difference between life and death for five friends. Had they still been packing inside their tents there would not have been enough time to dig through that much snow to save them.

I fought to control my panic. Fleeing this madness seemed to be the only sensible thing to do, but ten minutes down the trail we saw the obvious folly of this idea. Other climbing groups were also trying to flee below us, and after 30 minutes of digging in waist-deep snow we moved only a few feet.

No one would be getting to Tang Nag this day. There we stood with little food, no sleeping bags, and only the clothes on our backs. Some of us had our day packs. Some didn't. Mine was buried deeply in the recesses of the now totally destroyed dining tent. Luckily, we all had on our double boots and were wearing wind and snow protection.

This was truly a doomsday scenario. As I looked down the narrow trail, visibility was at best 200 feet before disappearing into a white void. It was snowing as heavily as it had been for the last

> *I knew too well that a mountain journey is never a triumphant progression toward a shining goal, but rather a limited quest, a daily struggle to reach the village or campsite just ahead.*
>
> —George B. Schaller, *Stones of Silence: Journey in the Himalaya*

24 hours. Our progress was nil. Avalanches boomed down on all sides of the valley far below. The mountains seemed angry. I said to Jeff, standing nearest to me. "I have a real bad feeling about this."

The trail seemed to grow narrow around us in the continuing blizzard. Our attention more and more turned to what was above us. Sherpas and trekkers alike kept looking up nervously at what we could not see.

The deepening concern on Ang Tshering's face gave me no comfort. This was a man who had survived many Himalayan ordeals; he had summited Mt. Everest with Junko Tabei, the first woman to do so, in 1975.

Earlier that morning, in the dining tent, we had been saved by the fickle finger of fate. A light dusting to remind us of our fragile mortality. But I had known in an instant that I was alive and uninjured.

Now I had the dubious opportunity to stand and contemplate the inevitable. I felt my heart sinking into my stomach as my stomach was trying to escape through my throat. As I looked down into the blurred white funnel where we proposed to go, unseen avalanches continued to roar, and for the first time in my life I thought that I might not live through the day.

But this was about more than just me. I was the leader of a group of people who had come with me to climb Mt. Mera; we had a wonderful support staff of Sherpas and kitchen boys and girls. A quiet voice inside me kept saying, "You're really in over your head on this one."

I can't say how long we stood there. I think it was while looking down at John that the obvious finally dawned on me. He had already turned around and was looking up at me. His head was tilted slightly to the side and his face had a look, though still politely British, of quizzical exasperation as if to say, "I say, old cock, when are your lights going to go on?"

Ang Tshering came up the trail and suggested that we go back up and try to dig out a campsite beneath the protection of one of several large rocks at Khare. We turned around but the trail was already obliterated. Eventually we made it back up to Khare, made a makeshift camp, and successfully reclaimed the day packs and duffel bags from the buried tents. The snow finally ended about 10 o'clock that night after 36 continuous hours.

Crammed into the few remaining tents we barely slept that night. The morning of November 11th revealed a different world. The valley we had walked up the morning of November 9th, a prime yak grazing area of boulders and scrub brush, was now a smooth snow bowl with little definition and no sign of a trail.

The summit of Mera now seemed to mock us in the crystal blue sky. I remember muttering to no one in particular that Mera didn't seem to want us on its slopes. There was now no question of going up the remaining 5,400 feet to the summit in chest-deep snow. We decided to spend the day drying out and counting our blessings. We were, after all, together, alive, and in good shape.

At noon the sky turned ugly again and the jet stream threatened another storm. We packed quickly and fled down-valley like mad dogs.

Sunshine had revealed three climbing groups at Khare and two other groups came swimming down in deep snow from high above on the Mera La. Our procession was very slow down to Tang Nag. Over 100 people arrived there at dark after five hard hours.

That night Ang Tshering and I huddled in a tea house around a radio and began to hear the first sketchy stories about the magnitude of this storm and the deaths throughout Nepal.

A massive rescue operation had been mounted and helicopter reconnaissance flights up all the major glacial valleys were being conducted to see who most needed help. On the morning of November 12th our agent in Lukla, Appa, landed briefly to see if we and the others in the Hinku Valley were OK. He indicated that the trail down was bad, very icy getting up to Chetera, and that to go over the Tsera La, the direct but sometimes treacherous route back to Lukla, was out of the question. Then he took off to assess other trouble spots.

At about noon I heard a thunderous noise and looked up to see an avalanche roaring down the East Face of the 21,000 feet Kusum Kangaru (affectionately nicknamed Gruesome Kangaroo). The mountain was directly above at a distance I couldn't calculate. The ridges coming down from the mountains to the left and right of us leveled out to form a narrow valley leading to Tang Nag, and the avalanche was coming directly at us.

L ooking down the Kali Gandaki Valley from Jomsom I couldn't believe the cloud cover rolling our way. It never rains here in November. But a day later I realized how wrong I was. Luckily we were dropping to lower altitude when the storm hit. The howling wind blew the rain sideways and rubble was dropping from the water-soaked canyon walls. The risk of being blown into the raging Kali Gandaki River below was real. I concentrated on every step, but could only think of the people up higher. Anyone crossing the passes would be in desperate shape. Friends were climbing in the Khumbu at that moment and my stomach was in a knot. I knew people were dying up there.

—Larry Habegger,
"Pilgrimage to Muktinath"

We stood there, mesmerized, and watched the snow, powder, and gas rolling over ridge after ridge towards us. For an instant it seemed to finally run its course and disappear—only to boil up and over another ridge.

I couldn't believe my eyes. Two days before I had been sucker-punched from behind by an avalanche of unknown proportions. Now I was watching this awesome spectacle threatening to devour us all. When the white clouds rolled up and over the last ridge before camp, awe gave way to fear and we started diving off in all directions behind rocks and tea houses as the white clouds dissipated just before hitting the village.

That did it for me. Unnerved but not yet completely unhinged, I walked over to the edge of the camp and stood alone, close to myself, and looked down-valley where we proposed to go. In my gut I suddenly had a very bad feeling about the hike out. The valley was solid white with evidence of new avalanches spilling over the snow-covered trail. The weather was good and would probably hold. I remembered how difficult, rigorous, steep, and exposed the trail out of Lukla had been when dry. Appa had warned me about the main trail out of the Hinku. What would the alternatives be like?

It was a difficult decision. Part of me wanted to finish the trek and walk out but I had to consider the mental and physical condition and the safety of not only myself but everyone in my group. It was time to cut our losses, stop tempting fate, and get out. The mountain gods had spoken.

I found Ang Tshering in the tea house, told him what I was thinking, and he agreed. I called the group together and asked their support for my decision to send a message to Lukla asking for a helicopter evacuation. We met with another climbing group camped next to us and two Sherpas volunteered from each of our group to go to Lukla with the message.

Gyalgen and Sona took off with our cheers and blessings at 3:30 on the afternoon of November 12th. I estimated it would take them two days of careful hiking to get down to Lukla on a trail which had taken us four days to get up to Tang Nag under excellent conditions. As Appa knew we were safe, I expected our evacuation would get a low priority, and mentally prepared for a wait of three to four days.

Our yaks were running out of food and it was extremely difficult for them to get to water over the break-through crust in the snow. Our head yak man, Antari Sherpa, left with the animals to get them down-valley out of the snow. We were now without porters or pack animals. The die had been cast. Time to wait and be patient.

The morning of November 13 was clear and the snow blinding. Much to the amusement of the Sherpas, who were now having fun with my avalanche paranoia, I asked that camp be moved out of the way of the direct valley coming down from Kusum Kangaru. I was certain I saw another crack high up there on a glacier just waiting to give way.

We moved the tents down closer to a spot stamped out in the snow for helicopter landings. I had also asked everyone to go through the boring ritual of packing up completely every morning as if we were leaving on a moment's notice. Hurry up and wait. This was going to be a long several days.

At 11 a.m. I heard a noise down-valley. It couldn't be. Ang Tshering came stumbling out of his tent pulling up his pants yelling "chopper." I assumed it was another recon flight going elsewhere but ran down to the landing spot anyway.

I couldn't believe my eyes when the chopper circled in to land and I saw Appa's face in the window gesturing at me to come on. I turned around and bellowed "Let's go!" to my incredulous group. The next twenty minutes were complete and wonderful chaos. Appa told me to calm down. They were going to commit three flights that day to get everyone out of the Hinku Valley.

Gyalgen and Sona had arrived at Appa's home in Lukla at 4:30 in the morning making the incredible journey in 13 hours nonstop through the night, passing several corpses on the icy descent to Lukla.

As the big Russian helicopter lifted off the ground, I collapsed with joy and relief. Jangbhu, a kitchen boy sitting next to me, had never been in a flying machine before, and the look of wonderment on his face as we zipped across the snow fields made me think he had just been transported to Disneyland. An elder Sherpa sitting across from me had also never been off the ground and his face was frozen in sheer terror. In 20 minutes we were in Lukla. H. G. Welles's time machine had nothing on us.

There was, however, one bit of unfinished business. Our cook, Tsering Tendi, assuming we were stuck at Tang Nag for several days, had left with one assistant early that morning to go down to Kote to retrieve a five-gallon jug of kerosene that we had stashed for the return trip. I told Appa about this and he assured me they would look for him on the last flight.

The moment Tsering Tendi and his assistant heard the noise of the first helicopter they started running back up towards Tang Nag. They had left at 5 a.m. and were all the way down on the Hinku River at Kote. They had to run back up through the snow in rhododendron, birch and pine forests to get out into the open.

On the final rescue flight back to Lukla, a co-operative Russian pilot was skimming low over the snow fields when out of the trees came a screaming Tsering Tendi waving his jacket. The chopper hovered two feet above the snow as Appa pulled the two exhausted and incredulous Sherpas into the helicopter.

As we waited in Lukla a few days for our flight to Kathmandu, keeping tabs on the storm-related news and continuous helicopter rescue activity, a member of the group helped put all this in a proper perspective. Mike had summited several mountains throughout the world and reminded me that "to stand on the summit of a mountain is one thing, but to be part of a human drama such as this, is quite another."

I met our head porter, Bing, and was heartened to hear that all of our porters had made it safely out of the mountains before the storm hit. Yet just a few thousand feet above us was a sad and poignant reminder that we were among the fortunate. The trail we had walked just a week before, and thought to be so very steep, rigorous, but exciting, was now an icy deathtrap holding the exposed remains of four porters who did not make it through their night.

When all was said and done, the storm affected most of Nepal—from Dhaulagiri in the west to Kangchenjunga in the east. Conceived in the Bay of Bengal, it had attained cyclonic proportions by the time it hit the Asian landmass at Orissa.

Sixty-three people died in Nepal and more than 550 people were rescued by helicopter in a five-day period beginning November 11. Local people lost countless numbers of precious livestock as yaks, *zopkios,* and other beasts of burden simply got stuck in the snows and starved to death. Kathmandu, normally dry in November, got 6 inches of rain in 24 hours.

At Bagarchap, a village on the Marsyangdi River along the very popular trekking route around Annapurna, a torrent of water, mud, and rocks came tearing down a gorge killing twelve people and wiping out the New Tibet Guest House.

On the far eastern border of Nepal, a climbing group on Kangchenjunga lost four Sherpas and three Japanese members.

At Gokyo, a picturesque trekkers' destination known for its emerald lakes and wondrous views of four of the world's highest mountains, 3.5 metres of snow were recorded in 36 hours. Trekking groups were stranded for up to five days.

Just three hours below Gokyo the biggest tragedy of all occurred at Pangkar. Twenty-six people died in a massive avalanche. Rescue helicopters flying over could see no sign of tents and only parts of rooftops. Ironically, Pangkar is a place where trekking and climbing groups normally do not camp. It is only a short two hours above Machermo and three hours below Gokyo. People don't even stop there for lunch but continue up into the rocks to a place called Nilibuk. I have no way of knowing if this group was going up and had camped there as a respectful precaution against altitude sickness, or were camped there because of the bad weather. Either way, this presumably prudent decision cost them all their lives.

When a storm of this magnitude strikes, the forces of nature become the common denominator which unites us all. When such a storm joins forces with the world's greatest mountain range, mere mortals receive an instant lesson in humility and respect.

The Hindus and Buddhists consider the Himalaya to be the abode of the gods. When the gods become angry, we are at their mercy. But if we are blessed, the gods will give us another chance to return another time.

Brian K. Weirum also contributed "Tiger Bones" in Part Four.

✳

For years I have known of Khumbila, the spiritual guardian of the Khumbu, but I never understood how he protected his believers. Wondering about recent disasters in the Khumbu Valley, I ask, "How about the giant flood last year? Where was Khumbila then?"

"The flood reminded us to think carefully about our land. Were many people killed in the flood? Very few! The flood was going to happen.

Perhaps Khumbila's influence released the flood on the day everyone went up to a festival in the high yak pastures. Imagine if the flood happened in October when the trails by the river are crowded with Sherpas, porters and foreign trekkers. Khumbila protected us from that disaster."

"And when accidents happen to people?"

"Khumbila can't protect everyone from everything. His protection depends on the person's *karma,* the impending consequences of previous behavior. If your work here was without merit, you may not have been able to see the vision Khumbila offered."

—Frances Klatzell, "Places of Power"

SUSAN VREELAND

* * *

Do Buddhists Cry?

No matter where we go, longing
remains part of our lives.

FROM THE CAST IRON SKILLET, YANGZI LIFTS A PERFECT, FLUFFY
omelet with brown lace edging its pale yellow surface, balances it
across floorboards grimed with years of ash and yak dung, and carries it safely to my plate.

Those floorboards tell that this Sherpa house is more than half
a century old. The planks are wide, hewn when trees were large,
before deforestation of Nepal's Khumbu Himal, when Yangzi's
father-in-law, Dorji, was a boy. Now aged and bent, his face the
hue and texture of cedar bark, he sits next to the stove where
Yangzi feeds the cooking fire with thin birch branches. She ladles
water into the *dal*, her cooking a continuum of bending and stooping. The stove, made of hand hewn rocks with an iron slab over
the top, is only twenty inches high. Without a table, she bends to
cut a purple onion on the floor, grinds garlic and chili in a wooden
mortar and pestle, also on the floor.

Meanwhile, Dorji talks to my trekking partner, Al Burgess, a
veteran climber. Mixing Nepali and Sherpa, they speak of Tibetan
borderlands, of storms and climbs and summits reached and beyond reach, of villages and shared friends. Chuckling, they try to
figure out Dorji's age, somewhere between 65 and 85—he can't be

sure. Only the Dalai Lama's birthday is celebrated here. In the absence of a count of time, how does one measure whether a life is full? By storms and climbs and summits of all types, and shared friends. His gentle smile remolding his features into ridges and valleys as he glances in my direction tells me he now counts me among them.

Yangzi offers me sweet milk tea, then breaks the circle of the cup rim with a smear of grainy *tsampa,* so that demons trapped in the circle can escape and will not enter my mouth to make me sick. A thoughtful gesture. I'd read of it. Now here it is. Dorji says something approving and fatherly to Yangzi and her flat wind-burned cheeks begin to round. She tucks a stray strand into the green cotton kerchief tied perkily at the back of her head, then insists that a heavy narrow chest be pushed close to me in order to leave the central space empty even though that means I must turn my booted feet sideways. The reason for this, like many mysteries in Nepal, baffles me.

Privately, Al shares with me Yangzi's story. She is from Makalu, another Himalayan valley four mountain ranges and four river systems away, with 20,000-foot peaks in between. A two-weeks' walk, one way, in good weather. But summer monsoons prevent travel with small children when school is not in session, and Khumjung School, gift of Sir Edmund Hillary, is too precious to waste. Besides, Dorji and Aama-la, Yangzi's revered mother-in-law, have grown too old to take care of themselves, so she must stay, separated from her people. "Whither thou goest I will go; and where thou lodgest, I will lodge," Ruth, the young widow of the Old Testament says to Naomi, her mother-in-law. And so has Yangzi.

I wonder if the day she left she walked quickly or slowly. Did she weep over the shy periwinkle blue irises, a mere four inches tall, which peer from the shelter of rocky crevices into vast space, lingering until the trail became unfamiliar, the horizon a multitude of new contours, until rocks changed from tan to gray, the language of passersby tinged with different sounds? Did she look back, only to see wet clouds come rolling up the valley in banks of spume to swallow the stone houses and ghostly prayer flags flying from the ochre-painted rafter of the room where she was born?

Walking into the valley in the shadow of Mount Khumbila, Guardian Spirit of the Khumbu, did she stumble, dash her foot against a stone? Did the gouged peak of Ama Dablam, the jagged knife ridge connecting Nupste to Lhotse, with Everest looming behind seem a terrifying landscape? Did she find the blue-white light of bright mornings after a snowfall different here than home? The mountains here more intemperate, uncompromising? The woods sparser? The raven's cry sharper? Was it for her a brave new world? I try to imagine, from her perspective, the lost assurance of the familiar, the ache of knowing her parents will never see her children, the tyranny of homesickness.

To add to that, her husband, Dawa, is away two seasons of the year, guiding Western trekkers. It is the way in Sherpa households, the man having shifted from agriculture to trekking jobs, gaining thereby an ease with foreigners and access to the larger world, the woman staying home, digging the potato patch, doing the wood-cutting, leaf-gathering, cooking, washing, tending the children, the yaks, the sick and aged, transporting on her back foods bought in lower bazaar towns.

At every leavetaking when Dawa serves a trek to Makalu, does she beg him to gather news of family, of childhood friends? While he's gone does she relive moments filling water jugs with neighbors at her village stream, connections which fade at each reliving, becoming more the fruit of invention than memory? The minute he returns, is she crazy with questions, desperate for any shred of home? Maybe that's the reason he struck her once, an impatience at her incessant need for news.

Do Sherpa women wonder to what extent their husbands perform services for Western female trekkers? I think of Yangzi's cold sheets. Oh, there are no sheets. No beds. Only sleeping platforms edging the walls. Perhaps that is well. Their narrowness does not scream loneliness so loudly.

Dawa has sometimes many weeks between jobs, spent she doesn't know where, drinking away his wages. When he does get a trekking job, he comes home dressed as in Hindi movies: flashy clothes, leather shoes, a cowboy hat and Rolex watch. But you can't feed a child with a hat. And when Yangzi gets sick, the village figures out he has brought home to her not income, but syphilis, courtesy of whores in Kathmandu and elsewhere.

Do Buddhists cry? I wonder. In Buddhist thought, it is only human misconception which experiences suffering. In Tantrayana Buddhism, it is not that one leaves one existence to go to nirvana; the realms are essentially the same. "See everything around you as Nirvana; see all beings as Buddha; hear all sounds as mantra," a Tantric Buddhist meditation urges. What does that do to differences between Makalu and Khumbu, invisible to an outsider but keenly felt by

"Have we foreigners coming here destroyed the local peoples' culture?"

"No, not really," Rinpoche answers. "There are outward changes in appearances: some of our dress, houses, occupations, and opportunities. However, our Sherpa ceremonies and traditions—how we name children, honor the dead, get married, and celebrate a year's passage—all this remains the same. What is most important to us remains. Foreign visitors coming to Khumbu have not changed our inside culture."

—Frances Klatzell, "Hearts and Minds: The Inside Culture"

Yangzi? Is the affection and gratitude of Dorji and Aama enough to neutralize the profligacy of their younger son?

At Thyangboche, the mountaintop monastery a day's walk from here, lamas teach the *dharma*, Siddartha's Middle Way to liberation from attachments and desires of the delusory self. Maybe Yangzi's meditation separates her from self and dissolves her ache. And maybe it doesn't. I am projecting, true, but to live, momentarily, in the fiction of her life, deepens mine. It is, I believe, the strongest reason to travel.

It was Al, not Dawa, who made sure she was treated in a Kathmandu clinic. So it is sorrow that softens Yangzi's movements, makes her solicitous in her ministrations toward him, toward me. She says little while she works, serving tea to her Naomi, peeling potatoes hot from the fire for Al and me, trekkers, those very people who drew her husband away. Jolted out of naïveté, I feel like a child relearning life again, remembering the poet Robert Hayden's line, "What did I know, what did I know of love's austere and lonely offices?"

As I watch Yangzi cook, wishing to help but not knowing whether the offer is culturally appropriate, I practice feeling the oneness of the universe myself. In this family half a world away I recognize some semblance of my own, of any: making tea just the way her mother-in-law likes it, trying to make all parts of a meal for guests ready at the same moment, swallowing selfish thoughts to make a home run smoothly. Every few minutes one daughter opens the kitchen window to shout urgent child's play messages to the other daughter outside whose laughter tinkles like monastery bells. For each message, a blast of cold air billows the ash in the open stove and spreads it over everything. Yangzi tells her not to. Just once more, mama. It's important. Yangzi clamps the lid on the pot to protect the dinner just in time for that one last important cloud of ash. We look at each other and smile. I know her exasperation. It has versions in every household the world around.

Al tells me that Yangzi and Dorji had been worried about the rough and spicy food they would feed the *memsahib*, me, but the lentil soup over a white

I'd had almost nothing to eat for eighteen hours and was now out of food. The villages where I had planned to eat were deserted because the residents had taken their stock to lower elevations for the winter. I was exhausted after a long night curled in a cold stone hut. But now the sun was up, and the steep trail rose out of the cold canyon toward the sunshine. I inched closer, every step an ordeal. High above I thought I saw a man sitting on a wall, but I didn't dare allow myself the thought for fear I couldn't handle the disappointment when I discovered the figure was just a rock. But it was a man after all, sitting in the sunshine, who had a fire burning in his hut, who had tea brewing and potatoes cooking. With the care of a saint he gave me food, saved me from my delirium, and made it possible for me to continue on my way. It was the most satisfying meal I have ever had.

—Larry Habegger,
"Into the Khumbu"

mountain of rice is delicious. Still, Yangzi does not stop cooking, and that is when she layers the onion omelet over my half-eaten rice.

Eggs! Two of them! There are no chickens in Khumjung. It is 12,400 feet here. Without enclosures hens would be snatched up by vultures, lammergeiers, and eagles. And in winter they'd freeze without heated hen houses, an impossibility here where every stick of wood is hauled on human backs and rationed for human warmth.

I think of Yangzi carrying the eggs over the 1,600-foot ridge from Namche Bazaar, half a day's walk, the nearest place they could have been purchased, and even then they were carried by traders from villages four or five days below Namche. They're as valuable as fruit brought from the lowlands, and must be purchased with cash, not traded for. That means some of Dawa's trekking money had to be asked for, with the reason that a child was sick or Aama was not well.

In the Khumbu, if a friend has the flu, you can't just bring her flowers. You bring her an egg.

Would Yangzi balance eggs on top of her load of yak butter, lentils, rice, powdered milk, brick tea, and sugar suspended from her tumpline, or cradle them carefully in her hands as she stepped over boulders? Through Al, I ask. She carries them two at a time buried in fine sand in a pot wedged securely into the top of her load. And here, blanketing the rice in a perfect yellow circle on my plate, is all she had. She noticed I had arrived flushed and breathless today, knew I had to walk onward tomorrow.

> *rekking is a man's world in Nepal,"* says Mrs. Yankila Sherpa, owner of Snow Leopard Trek Ltd, in Kathmandu. *"Women own or actively run only two or three trekking companies and we have encountered active resistance from the men."*
>
> Yankila organizes special women's treks, with emphasis on cultural exploration. *"We help trekkers meet village women, translating conversations so the trekkers can understand the realities of life in the village. We visit families on farms at harvest time and attend festivals or weddings."*
>
> —Thalia Zepatos, "Sherpa Women Take the Lead," *Eco Traveler*

Just another story of Sherpa grace, some would say. Trekkers hear countless stories of Sherpa gentility, of their laughter when greeting hardship, their devoted care of Western travelers. Hushed voices in teashops along trekkers' routes repeat stories of Sherpas' ultimate grace, giving one's life in an icy crevasse to save one's climbing client. It is, after all, a profession, this portering and guiding, with a certain image to be preserved. It's good business. But Yangzi is not "on duty." She's not on display for tourists. She's just cooking dinner in her husband's kitchen.

Yangzi's delicate balance of eggs and kindness is, for me, another story of how, during my journey in the Khumbu, I am moved. I can tell it in many versions, with many names: Kumar Puri walking watchfully behind me on the sharp-edged trail, his arm shooting out to catch me when I stumble; Dorji welcoming into his home our Rai porter, a different caste, by calling him *daju*, brother; Chedre Lama giving me a roll of toilet paper; Ching Dolma, Khumjung's community leader, thinking I am too thin and building up her fire with precious sticks to make me mashed potatoes at nine at night. All of them, testimonies to the Metta Sutra: "Even as a mother watches over and protects her only child, so with a boundless mind should one cherish all living beings, radiating friendliness over the entire world." All of them expressive of the energy put into the maintenance and nurturing of the spirit.

Yet to be moved means to be transported from where I was in thought to another dimension and not go back again, to be brought out of self by being mindful of "otherness." To do this, I must declare at once those conditions and simple acts for which I am grateful: not just clean hands, boiled water, the sun on my neck; not just ears open to the winds and ravens, eyes alive to wonder and glory; but wool gloves knit by a Tibetan refugee whose memory of Lhasa grows dim, every greeting of *namaste*, the benediction that moves me two steps farther up the trail; Al's hot buttered rum on a cold afternoon, which includes the woman who carried butter up to Khumjung from the lower bazaar, the Tibetan who milked his yak and churned the butter, and the yak itself.

After dinner, the woodcutter arrives with snow dusting his daily load of sticks like powdered sugar. It's taken him longer today.

Dorji guesses why: each day he has to walk farther to find wood. He's a mere boy, twelve years old, contracted by Dorji from a lower village for the season. His legs and neck are thin, his wrists pitiful sticks. His sharp, elfin features, unravelling sweater, perky woolen cap and wooden flute are something out of a medieval fairy tale. His very life is medieval. Yangzi gives him a bowl of *dal-bhat* and he sits on a wobbly wooden stool no bigger than a bread box. He remembers Al from previous visits, asks him where he's been. Al tells him of a few villages and peaks just several days' walk from here, not half the distance to Makalu. His eyes get wide, admiring. I wish some day I could go there, he says, with the same awe that a Western boy would feel at space travel. Maybe some day you can be a cook's helper, Al tells him, or when you grow some and can carry a load, you can be a porter. I can carry a load now, he says, and stands up puffing out his little chest to show how he carried the wood.

Al asks him to play his flute. The sounds are woodland folk tunes, sprightly and birdlike, and I think of him sitting in a tree where he's climbed to cut branches, taking a break to imitate a bird. Afterwards, he flutters his small hand, dismissing his own efforts, and looks at me as if to say, not good—I wish I could play better. And I wish for him a longer dreamy summertime of childhood in which to play.

Teasing, Yangzi's daughters sing to him the first three lines of a courting song which require him to make up a fourth that rhymes. After a moment for a puckish grin, he sings his line back. They challenge him again, the song more flirtatious this time. He rolls his eyes to the bamboo mat on the ceiling, searching for a line. He plays a few notes to help, then triumphantly, he sings the response. They sing back and forth until he's caught without a rhyme, and the girls, giggling, have him beat. I wonder if Yangzi played this courting game from an open window with Dawa as he passed through Makalu, and if she, like her daughter, won the match.

The girls get the idea to teach me Sherpa dancing, done in a line, our arms around each others' waists. I feel enormous, Gulliver in Lilliput, and stretch down to reach them. Step, stomp, brush and a sideways step, the movements subtle, the rhythm gentle against the wooden floor. I try for their grace and lightness, an impossibility in my hiking boots. Then they teach me again. Connected now, we move around the room, and suddenly it hits me—the need for floorspace. Yangzi knew all along there would be dancing tonight.

One of the cultural icons in Kathmandu is the living goddess, a spoiled child confined in silks within a palace, but discarded the day she reaches puberty—impurity. Here Yangzi's girls in jeans and Chinese plastic tennis shoes are living goddesses of a more substantial kind. They huddle in animated consultation, then perform a Nepali song accompanied by precise gestures about a chamois hunter who, lying in wait in the high mountains, thinks of his true love at his lowland home. For the first time, Yangzi stops her work and sinks against the door frame to watch. It makes my heart turn over.

She catches me looking at her, straightens up, and refills my glass with *chang* she made herself. Does any suggestion that she had made a mistake slide into her thinking at lonely moments when the moon like a swollen silver egg hangs low over Makalu?

Are there songs of women's longings too? I ask through Al.

Yes, of course, she says. Nepali women's songs of pride that their husbands are *lahures*, Gorkha soldiers in the British Army, but those are also songs of loss and loneliness.

The Bible says of Ruth, "Thou hath left thy father and thy mother and the land of thy nativity and art come unto a people which thou knewest not." Knowing now it applies to both of us, I bow my head to drink the liquor of her labor.

Susan Vreeland's first novel, What Love Sees, *was made into a movie and aired by CBS in 1996. Her short fiction has appeared in* CALYX, Dominion Review, *and other publications. She has traveled extensively in Europe and North America and she currently teaches literature and art in San Diego public schools.*

★

I didn't work on the potato harvest every day. Most of the time I stayed at home, reading and writing. On one such day Chola came back from the fields early so she could press some oil to fry the *puris* for Sigarup's departure to Aula in a few days' time. She fetched the paste that she'd made from roasted hemp seeds, and the little wooden gully on which she pressed it, and knelt down, ready to begin. When I went on to the roof to join her she said, "Sister, everything's so easy for you. You have oil and *ghee*; you have spices of every kind; you eat meat and eggs and honey and rice as often as you like; you have medicine, contraceptives, nice clothes, soap to wash with; you don't have to work in the fields all day—you can just sit at home, reading and writing...."

—Monica Connell, *Against a Peacock Sky*

PART FIVE

THE LAST WORD

JAN MORRIS

★ ✦ ★

Chaurikharka

A weary traveler is nurtured
in a simple mountain home.

ALL OF US KNOW PLACES—ASPECTS OF PLACES EVEN—WHOSE memory can trigger in us haunting sensations of happiness, sadness, or plain nostalgia. For me their epitome is Chaurikharka, which is a speckle of small huts, encouched in gardens and potato fields, somewhere in the Himalayan foothills of east Nepal. I can find it on no map, and it appears in none of the travelers' tales because it is not on the way to anywhere in particular, contains nothing very startling, and is inhabited only by quiet Sherpa people. Yet the very name of the place, so exotic, so mellifluous on the tongue and so devilishly hard to spell, summoned up in me a mood of lyrical and slightly mystical serenity.

I was ill when I went there. Trekking down from Namche Bazaar in the company of a Sherpa named Sonam, I was suddenly felled by a combination, I suppose, of fatigue, excitement, altitude sickness, and a somewhat cavalier attitude of hygiene. Sonam immediately invited me to spend a few days in his own home. It was only a few miles off the way, he said, and he and his family would see me through my fever.

Sonam's house in my recollection was darker, smokier, and more mysterious than other homes. This is perhaps because he rolled out my sleeping-bag for me in the room that was also the family temple, with a dozen small images of the Buddha, attended by butter-candles, gleaming at the other end. The room was warm, woody, creaky, smoke-blackened, and through its shadows I could always see those gently smiling images, flickered by their candlelight.

Outside the house everything *steamed*. The monsoon was upon us. The rains fell heavily for several hours each day, and the gardens that surrounded Chaurikharka's houses were all lush and vaporous. My room had no window, but the open door looked out upon the Sonam family plot, and from it there came a fragrance so profoundly blended of the fertile and the rotten, the sweet and the bitter, the emanations of riotous growth and the intimations of inevitable decay, that still, if ever my mind wanders to more sententious subjects, I tend to smell the vegetable gardens of Chaurikharka.

The taste of the potatoes, too, roasted at the family hearth, seemed to me almost philosophically nourishing, while the comfort of the powerful white liquor, *rakshi*, with which the Sonams now and then dosed me, and the merry voices of the children, frequently hushed lest they disturb my convalescence, and the kind wondering faces of the neighbors who occasionally looked through the open door, and the clatter of the rain on the roof and the hiss of it in the leaves outside, and the enigmatic smiles of those small golden figures in their half light at the end of the room—all built up in my mind an impression not just of peace and piquancy, but of holiness.

Mind you, it is all a blur to me. During all my time in Sonam's house I was in a baffled state of mind. This is partly because I was sick, but partly because I did not know then, as I do not know now, precisely where Chaurikharka was. It seemed in my fancy to be somewhere altogether alone in that wide and marvelous wilderness. One of the great Himalayan peaks rose to the north of us, white as Heaven itself, but I never knew which. A little river rushed through the gully below the house, rocky and slate-gray, but I have no idea what its name was, or where it was going. When we left to resume our march to Kathmandu, Sonam took me, still in a kind of daze, back to the wide trail which led from the Sherpa country to the central valley of Kathmandu, but whether we had been to east or west of it, north or south, I was never entirely sure. Chaurikharka might have been an invented place, dreamed up by kindly necromancers to restore me.

Was it? Have I invented it myself? Not, I promise you, in the fact. Chaurikharka exists all right, somewhere out there, and I really did go there with Sonam. Every place, like every experience, is both active and passive. It gives to you, and you also give to it, so that its meaning is specific to you alone. Others might have found in Chaurikharka stimulants, depressants perhaps, of altogether different kinds; it is out of my particular sensibility that my own image of it comes—my need to match its fulfillment, my distress to fit its solace, my sickness to find its cure in that quiet darkened room. So it is that I carry my Chaurikharka wherever I go, frequently sensing the hot steamy damp of its fields as I lean from my window at home, and remembering the silent Buddhas among their candles, when the softer rain of Gwynedd spatters my roof.

Jan Morris has been wandering the world and writing about her experiences for more than 40 years. She is the author of numerous books and her essays on travel are classics of the genre. This story was excepted from Pleasures of a Tangled Life. *She lives in Wales, the only person in her postal code.*

WHAT YOU NEED TO KNOW

*W*HEN TO GO/WEATHER

Fall and Spring are the tourist seasons. Winter months are very cold in the upper elevations and the Himalayan passes are usually closed. However, winter is quite pleasant in the lower valleys and the *tarai* in the south. In the fall, the monsoon-fed swollen rivers make for great white-water rafting, and the valleys and hills are emerald green. Occasionally, lingering monsoon clouds may obscure the mountains, but clear, warm, sunny days are the norm, and the Himalayan panorama will take your breath away. It's a fine time to be in Nepal for mountain photography. One of the great joys of trekking in the spring is to observe the blooming flowers and plants, especially rhododendrons. Since it is getting warmer, it is also considered the best time for viewing wildlife. But as hot, dusty summer approaches, a perpetual haze veils the Himalayan scenery, awaiting the monsoon to clear it all away again.

Monsoon, the rainy season, can start as early as mid-June and is supposed to end in September, but it is not unusual to have rains continue until mid-October. Although this is not the season for Western tourists, and certainly not for trekking (visualize leeches!), packaged tour groups from India descend upon Kathmandu to escape the heat and dust of their homeland's parched plains. During the monsoon months, a fair number of Japanese and Europeans hang out in Pokhara's lakeside resort.

*V*ISAS AND TREKKING PERMITS

Visas

All foreigners, except Indians, are required to have a valid passport and visa to enter Nepal. Tourist visas can be obtained at an overseas Nepalese embassy or consulate. They are also issued at the Kathmandu airport or at the road borders with India and Tibet. You must extend your visa if you stay in Nepal for more than a month.

⁀HE NEXT STEP

You can obtain visas in different categories for varying prices. The longer the visa the more the cost, so try to plan for the amount of time you will actually need.

- 15 days, single entry. Allows one entry to the country.
- 30 days, single entry. Allows one entry to the country.
- 30 days, double entry. Allows you to leave the country and return once within 30 days.
- 60 days, multiple entry. Allows you to leave the country and return more than once within 60 days.

Don't overstay your visa. You must pay a small fine at the airport if you've overstayed less than seven days. If you've overstayed longer, you may be prevented from boarding your departing flight and may have to go back to the immigration office in Kathmandu to settle the situation there. Missing a flight, especially during the busy trekking season, can mean being stranded for several days.

Visa extensions and trekking permits are normally available the same day, but during the busy season you should allow up to three working days for an extension to be processed. Every visa extension or trekking permit requires your passport, money, photos, and an application form. Collect all of these documents before you start waiting in the queue.

At peak times the queues are long and the formalities are tedious. For a certain fee, usually nominal, travel and trekking agencies will stand in line for you.

You are allowed to stay in Nepal for a maximum of 150 days per year (which is counted as January to December) on a tourist visa. If you are traveling from Nepal to India or Tibet and returning to Kathmandu within 30 days you should either buy a double entry visa or get a re-entry permit before you leave Nepal. This is an easy process at the immigration office.

Trekking Permits

A Nepal visa is valid only for the Kathmandu Valley, Pokhara, and those parts of Nepal accessible by road. To travel into the roadless areas you need a trekking permit. Only the immigration offices in Kathmandu or

Pokhara may alter a permit. Permits for restricted areas are issued only to individuals or groups whose trek has been arranged by a trekking company.

A normal trekking permit costs US$5 per week for the first four weeks of trekking and US$10 per week thereafter. The cost of a permit for other areas is different for each region. For example, fees to restricted areas such as Upper Mustang or Inner Dolpo (i.e., Shey Gompa) can cost as much as $700 per person for 10 days and a government liaison officer must accompany the trekking party. Individuals can go to the immigration office and obtain permits themselves, but most companies that organize treks will do the legwork for you if you've booked with them.

*C*USTOMS AND ARRIVAL

Nepal's customs formalities are now less cumbersome because a "green channel" has been introduced. All hand baggage is x-rayed when you enter the customs hall and checked baggage is x-rayed as you pass through the green channel.

Electronic goods attract special attention. If you have a laptop computer and video camera, customs officials often write the details in your passport to ensure that you take them back when you leave the country. Video players and televisions are considered luxuries and require an import license. If you are carrying such items they will be impounded and kept in customs bond until you depart. Excessive amounts of film, 16 mm movie equipment, firearms, or food and gear for mountaineering expeditions are also subject to special restrictions.

The duty-free allowance includes 200 cigarettes, 20 cigars and one bottle of liquor. There is a duty-free shop in the arrival hall of Kathmandu airport. Personal effects, including trekking equipment, are permitted free entry. You may not import Nepali rupees, and only nationals of Nepal and India may import Indian currency. There is no restriction on bringing in either cash or traveler's checks, but the amount taken out at departure should not exceed the amount brought in. The rules say that you should declare cash or traveler's checks in excess of US$2000, or the equivalent.

Baggage is also inspected when you leave the country. Checked baggage is x-rayed and the security check for hand luggage doubles as a customs check.

Getting into the City

There is now a taxi service from the airport into Kathmandu and various hotels. The Airport Taxi Service information booth is located just outside the baggage clearance and customs area. The price is fixed based on your destination. There are no buses or shuttles, but of course there are numerous touts who will try to get your business and may also try to rip you off, so be prepared to bargain if you choose to go this route. Some hotels will send a car for you free of charge if you have booked a room in advance and request such service. Other hotels and some travel agencies will charge you anything from US$5.00 upwards for this service. If traffic is light you can get to Thamel in about 25 minutes; during rush hour it can take an hour.

ℋEALTH

There are no vaccinations required for entry into Nepal, however, responsible preparation and awareness is recommended. If you are planning to trek, prepare yourself physically before you go. Once in Nepal, be aware, as much as possible, of what you eat and drink. Busy restaurants are generally safer because the food is cooked and consumed quickly. It is also a good idea to buy travel insurance in case you need to return home due to unforeseen circumstances.

Some Helpful Tips:

* See a doctor and dentist prior to departure for general health check-ups.
* If you go on a trek you may be far from a hospital or any kind of medical help, so be sure to consult a doctor about recommended immunizations before you leave home. Opinions vary on what is necessary, but it's a good idea to have current immunizations for tetanus, polio, and typhoid, and to consider immunization for hepatitis, menin-

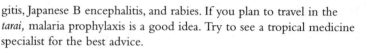

gitis, Japanese B encephalitis, and rabies. If you plan to travel in the *tarai,* malaria prophylaxis is a good idea. Try to see a tropical medicine specialist for the best advice.

- Record all current immunizations on your yellow International Health Certificate and carry it with you.
- Don't drink the water or ice, purify first.
- Peel your fruit and do not eat raw vegetables.
- If you wear prescription glasses, bring an extra pair.
- Rehydrate, rehydrate, rehydrate.

Pack a medical kit which includes: aspirin or acetaminophen, antihistamine, antibiotics, Lomotil or Imodium for diarrhoea, rehydration mixture, antiseptic such as iodine or Betadine, Calamine lotion, bandages, bandaids, tweezers, scissors, thermometer, cold and flu tablets, insect repellent, sunscreen, chapstick, water purification tablets, and possibly even sterile syringes with needles, dressings, and gloves.

Also consider taking a travel kit of basic homeopathic remedies and a homeopathic first aid book. Such remedies can provide rapid relief from common travel ailments including gastrointestinal problems, fevers, and many acute conditions. Books and travel kits are available through your local health food store. If you come home with any serious tropical diseases, including malaria, effective treatment is available from homeopathic medical practitioners.

Emergency Assistance

If you have an unexpected health problem and don't know where to turn, contact the CIWEC Clinic Travel Medicine Center in Kathmandu. The clinic has been providing medical care and advice and doing research on travelers to Nepal since 1984. The clinic is located just off the street called Durbar Marg not far from the Royal Palace. Turn down a lane that offers access to the Yak and Yeti Hotel and the clinic is the first house on the right, well-marked with signs. The clinic is staffed by three doctors—two Americans and one Nepali—and has its own laboratory. Its lab technician is widely recognized as the finest in Nepal.

℃HE NEXT STEP

Travel Insurance and Assistance

Several companies in the U.S. and Europe provide emergency medical assistance for travelers worldwide, including 24-hour help lines, English-
speaking doctors, and air evacuation in extreme cases. Travel agents and
tour companies can recommend policies that can work for you.

℃IME

Nepal is 5 hours 45 minutes ahead of Greenwich Mean Time, and 15 minutes ahead of Indian Standard Time. Thus, when it's noon in Nepal, it's:

10:15 p.m. yesterday in San Francisco
6:15 a.m. today in London
1:15 a.m. today in New York
1:15 p.m. today in Bangkok
2:15 p.m. today in Hong Kong
3:15 p.m. today in Tokyo
4:15 p.m. today in Sydney

ℬUSINESS HOURS

Most government offices in Kathmandu are open from 10 a.m. to 5 p.m.
Sunday through Thursday. Winter hours (usually mid-November to mid-
February) are 9 a.m. to 4 p.m. Businesses close at 3 p.m. on Friday.
Saturday is the weekly holiday and most shops, banks, and offices are
closed. Government offices, businesses, and banks often close during im-
portant religious festivals and holidays.

ℳONEY

In Nepal, the unit of currency is the rupee (Rs). 100 paisa equals one
rupee. A 50 paisa coin is called a *mohar*; a 25 paisa coin is called a *sukaa*;
locally, a hundred rupee note is referred to as a *gaida*, meaning rhinoceros.
Look at the picture on the note and you will see why.

Changing money is not a problem in the main tourist areas, but away from
the major towns, changing a 500 or 1000 rupee note can be difficult. It is

wise to have some of your money in small denominations, even in Kathmandu, where taxi and rickshaw drivers might not have change for the larger notes. In fact, they will often claim not to have loose change and round it off to the nearest rupee.

It's worthwhile to collect bank receipts when you change money in case of a change back to the old rules when you were required to produce bank receipts to prove you had changed US$20 per day for every day of visa extension. This requirement has been dropped and replaced by a US$1 per day fee for visa extensions.

Nepal is very much a cash-oriented society and personal checks and plastic remain largely unknown in daily transactions. Major credit cards are accepted, however, at better hotels, restaurants, and shops. Elsewhere, be sure to carry enough cash or traveler's checks.

Money can be changed at banks or by moneychangers. The procedures are hassle free and most banking hours are from 10 a.m to 2 p.m. Sunday through Thursday, 10 a.m. to noon on Friday, and closed Saturdays. Moneychangers are available seven days a week in main tourist areas.

The Nepali rupee is fixed against the Indian rupee. Rate changes are posted daily in all banks, major hotels and local English newspapers such as *The Rising Nepal* or *The Kathmandu Post*.

*E*LECTRICITY

Nepal's electricity is nominally 220 volts, 50 cycles, but fluctuations are severe and unpredictable. You must use a voltage stabilizer to protect all sensitive electronic equipment. The power supply is inadequate in Nepal, so there is occasional load shedding. During thunderstorms, transformers sometimes blow up and the power goes off for periods of a few minutes to a day or more. Until new generating capacity is provided, the electricity supply will continue to be unstable, but many large hotels now have generators.

There are many kinds of plugs used in Nepal, mostly the Indian round pin variety that come in three sizes and tend to burn out. Rather than carry a collection of plugs, stop in at a local electric shop in Kathmandu and have them make up an adapter that connects whatever plug you have to whatever socket your hotel has. It should cost less than Rs. 50 for a custom-made connector.

There is locally generated electricity in a surprising number of villages throughout the hills. It is mostly in the 220 volt range, but it's unstable and usually on only at night except in the Khumbu region where electricity is abundant and used during the day for cooking. You can charge batteries in many villages for a fee of about Rs. 50 per hour. A good solar charger is a cheaper and more versatile solution if you plan to rely on a battery-powered appliance when trekking.

*M*EDIA: NEWSPAPERS, RADIO, TELEVISION

Several international newspapers and magazines such as *The International Herald Tribune, USA Today, Asian Wall Street Journal, Time,* and *Newsweek* are readily available in Kathmandu. Nepali and especially English-language newspapers & magazines from India that are excellent sources of national and international news include *The Rising Nepal, The Kathmandu Post, The Statesman, The Times of India, India Today,* and *Himal.* The Nepali daily English language newspapers such as *The Rising Nepal* and *The Kathmandu Post* are now available on the worldwide web.

Radio Nepal and Nepal TV, both government organs, broadcast news, cultural programs, and other local fare. They get tough competition from Rupert Murdoch's Star cable TV out of Hong Kong that offers the usual American and English TV programs, including talk shows, soap operas, movies, sports, and the BBC World Service.

*T*OUCHING BASE: PHONE CALLS, FAXES, POSTAGE, EMAIL

Calling home can be expensive. International calls from Nepal range from Rs. 180-230 per minute depending on where in Nepal you're calling from. However, Kathmandu has many "telecommunication offices" with facilities for phone calls and faxes. You can also email, "e-fax" or surf the

net from these offices in Kath mandu and Pokhara. The cost depends upon the size, and surfing starts at around Rs. 30 per minute. When sending a fax you'll be charged by the n nute rather than by the page.

To call Nepal from abroad dial the international code followed by 977, then for the Kathmandu Valley dial 1, for Pokhara dial 61. To reach an operator for international calls, dial 186; for long distance calls in Nepal, dial 180. Directory assistance is 197. And be patient: you're not likely to get a prompt response when you call the operators in Kathmandu.

Letters, souvenirs, and gifts can all be sent home from Kathmandu. Expect it to take ten days minimum for a letter to get to or from Nepal. On the other hand, if you are sending anything other than an innocent aerogramme letter to your friend in Nepal, make sure you send it by registered mail. Packages, checks, and other large items may never reach their intended destinations.

CULTURAL CONSIDERATIONS

*L*OCAL CUSTOMS: DOS AND DON'TS

- *Namaste* is both hello and goodbye. You press your palms together as if praying while you say it.
- Public displays of affection between men and women, even married, are offensive to most Nepalis.
- Clothing is conservative. Women should avoid bare shoulders, halter tops, and shorts. Men should not go bare-chested and shorts should be at least knee-length. Suits and ties are customarily worn at formal occasions such as weddings.
- *Bakshish* is a customary extra payment for service (money, clothing, or anything else), and usually given to porters or laborers at the end of a job. There is no set rate. Observe, listen, and ask locals for advice.
- Cows are sacred in Nepal and wander around freely. Thus, beef is not something you will find prepared in a Hindu home or in a local restaurant.

- Wash your hands before you eat, and eat only with your right hand. It is good manners to ask for seconds, but only accept as much as you can eat. Do not offer leftovers, or anything half eaten, to anyone else because this food is *jutho*, or "ritually polluted." This is really a sanitary precaution rather than a cultural one. However, an indication of strong friendship between two individuals is when each will eat the other's *jutho* food. Among immediate family members, too, *jutho* food may be shared. Proper etiquette is that nobody gets up until everyone has finished eating.

- Drinking water is a test of a person's status. Water can become "polluted" if handled by a person of a lower caste. This polluted water then pollutes anything it touches. If a person touches a water vessel with his mouth, the water becomes *jutho* and the vessel must be emptied and rinsed before it can be filled and used again.

- Feet should never be pointed at anyone. Don't step over anyone, and always move your feet to let people avoid stepping over you.

- Heads are sacred and should be treated with respect. Do not pat children on the head.

- The left hand is used for cleaning oneself after using the toilet. Never use it to pass or accept things, especially food.

- Nepalis don't divide a bill or go "Dutch." Whoever issued the invitation pays.

- Nepalis take their shoes off at the door. Don't ask others to handle your shoes.

- Time is very flexible. People usually arrive late for appointments. But since you are a foreigner, you are expected to be on time.

- Married women wear *sindoor*, a streak of red powder in the parting of their hair. Another symbol of marriage would be a *pote*, a string of glass beads worn as a necklace.

- *Tika*, usually a red mark or dot, is worn in the center of the forehead by men, women and children. Besides having religious (Hindu) significance, a *tika* worn by women can come in all sorts of colors, shapes and sizes, and can be trendy fashion statements.

- Always walk around Hindu or Buddhist temples clockwise, keeping your pure right side to the temple. You walk counter-clockwise only at that rare Bon-po shrine.

- As a foreigner, you will be stared at. Privacy will be scarce as Nepalis will want to look at you, watch what you're doing, and touch your skin. Be prepared for this and try not to lose your temper. Doing so could ruin your visit.
- On a more mundane level, do not accept a friendly stranger's invitation (in Hong Kong, Bangkok, Kathmandu or anywhere) that you join his "import-export" business to dramatically increase your travel budget. Smuggling gold, drugs, and foreign currency in and out of Nepal is illegal.
- Nepal also prohibits the export of antiques. Items that look old should have a certificate from the Department of Archaeology. Other items that may not be taken out of the country are silver, precious stones, wild animals and their skins and horns. The penalties are severe for lawbreakers, informants are everywhere, and the jails in Nepal are dismal places. Forget it!

$\mathcal{E}$VENTS & HOLIDAYS

No matter which month you arrive in Nepal, you will be sure to find Nepalis celebrating a holiday or religious festival. Keep in mind that Nepal's lunar calendar, known as "Vikram Sambat," is 57 years ahead of the Christian calendar (1997 = 2054) and the new year begins on April 13 or 14. The following are some of the major and minor festivals of Nepal (the name of the Nepali month is in brackets):

January–February

(Magh) *Magh Sankranti*, the day of the winter solstice, is a festival which celebrates the end of the coldest winter month. *Basant Panchami*, occurring in late January-early February, marks the beginning of spring and also honors Saraswati, the Hindu goddess of learning. Many school children (and even some college students) visit temples to get their books, pens, and pencils blessed.

February–March

(Faagun) *Losar*, the Tibetan new year, is celebrated on the new moon of February. Go to Boudha in Kathmandu to see the celebration in its full expression.

THE NEXT STEP

Maha Shivaratri celebrates god Shiva's birthday. The place to be is Pashupatinath temple in the evening amidst a chaotic mix of Indian pilgrims and *sadhus*, Western tourists, and local worshippers. The public address system warns of pickpockets when not naming yet another child who has been separated from his or her parents.

Holi is close to the spring water festivals of other Asian countries and falls on the full moon day of the month. On this day, anyone is a target of balloons filled with clear and colored water. Red powder is smeared on faces and clothes. Wear your dirtiest clothes possible and expect to get wet and painted. Don't bother taking a shower in the morning.

March–April

(Chaitra) *Chaitra Dasain,* known as the Small Dasain, is dedicated to the goddess Durga, just like the main *Dasain* that takes place in October. During the celebration of *Seto Machendranath*, a chariot is pulled around Kathmandu for four days; it occurs one month before the more important *Rato Machendranath* festival of Patan.

April–May

(Baisakh) The Nepali new year is celebrated on Baisakh 1, April 13. There are parades and floats galore. In Bhaktapur, the locals celebrate *Bisket Jatra* with processions and a tug-of-war.

Rato Machendranath, Patan's spectacular chariot festival, is also a prayer to abundant rain. Passionate devotees push and pull the swaying, 60-foot chariot through the streets and alleys of Patan.

Buddha Jayanti, Buddha's birthday, is celebrated on the full moon day of Baisakh. Visit Boudha or Swayambhu, light butter lamps, give alms to the poor.

May–June

(Jeth) *Kumar Sasthi*, celebrates the birthday of Kumar or Kartikkaya, the warrior-god who is also a son of Shiva (and the brother of the more popular god Ganesh).

July–August

(Saaun) *Janai Purnima* is the day when high-caste Hindu men change their *janai,* or sacred thread. It is a private family affair.

Gai Jatra, or "cow festival," is a very public celebration. It is dedicated to those who died during the year before. (Cows are supposed to lead the dead to the underworld.) Revelers wear funny costumes and young boys are also dressed up in various cow-like costumes. On this day, local Nepali newspapers and magazines publish parodies and satires ridiculing the rich, famous, and powerful members of Kathmandu society.

August–September

(Bhadra) *Teej* is the Festival of Women, when many fast and bathe in holy rivers to wash away sins.

Krishna Jayanti, also known as *Krishnasthami*, is god Krishna's birthday. Lamps are lit, hymns are sung, and his adventures acted out. Visit the Krishna temple in Patan's Durbar Square on the eve of this celebration, which occurs in late August.

Indra Jatra is a rowdy, colorful, week-long festival. Wearing masks and costumes, and pretending to be gods and demons, people dance in the streets. One of the most important events during this festival is the procession of the Royal Kumari, the living goddess. She is brought out of her palace on a palanquin to bless the crowd. She also places a *tika* on the king of Nepal, thus granting legitimacy to his rule.

September–October

(Ashoj) *Dasain* is Nepal's biggest festival and usually falls around late October. Officially, it lasts ten to fifteen days leading up to the full moon of Ashoj, and celebrates the victory of the goddess Durga over the forces of evil. Families visit elderly relatives to receive blessings; gifts are exchanged. The tourists are especially fascinated by the ritual sacrifice of buffaloes, symbolizing the demon Mahishasura, in one of the open courts in Kathmandu's Durbar Square.

THE NEXT STEP

October–November

(Kartik) *Tihar,* the "Festival of Lights," is also knows as "Diwali," and follows on the heels of *Dasain.* It used to be that the entire country shut
down for almost a month to celebrate *Dasain* and *Tihar.* Among others,
Laxmi the goddess of wealth, who is symbolized by the sacred cow, is honored at this time. During the five-day celebration, crows, dogs, and cows
are worshipped. On the fifth day, sisters invite their brothers for meals and
blessings. During this festival, rooftops, entranceways and even windows
are lit every evening with small, oval-shaped clay lamps, candles, or multi-
colored, blinking electric bulbs. Noisy firecrackers burst in the night;
neighborhood children (or adult singers and dancers) go door-to-door
singing songs and collecting tips. The ban on public gambling is briefly
lifted. It is one of the few occasions when there is indeed "night life" in
Kathmandu and beyond.

November–December

(Mangsir) *Sita Biwaha Panchami* is celebrated in the eastern *tarai* town of
Janakpur. It commemorates the marriage of Sita, the daughter of King
Janak of ancient Janakpur, to Ram, the hero of the Hindu epic the
Ramayana. Pilgrims from all over India and Nepal attend a five-day *mela*
(festival).

Almost directly north in the high Himalayas, the Sherpas celebrate *Mani
Rimdu,* a festival rejoicing Buddhism's victory over the ancient Bon-po
religion. Lasting four days, there are religious *pujas,* mask dances and pan-
tomime, especially those of Thyangboche monastery, another good reason
to go trekking in the Everest region in November.

IMPORTANT CONTACTS

FOREIGN EMBASSIES IN KATHMANDU AND THEIR PHONE NUMBERS

- Australia   (411578; fax 417533)
- Canada   (415193; 415389; fax 410422)

- ◆ China   (411740; fax 41405)
- ◆ France   (412332; fax 419968)
- ◆ Germany   (412786; fax 416899)
- ◆ India   (410900; 414990; fax 413132)
- ◆ Israel   (411811; fax 413920)
- ◆ Italy   (412743; fax 413879)
- ◆ Japan   (231101; fax 228638)
- ◆ Thailand   (213910; fax 226599)
- ◆ UK   (410583; fax 411789)
- ◆ USA   (411179; fax 419963)

TOURIST OFFICES AND THEIR PHONE NUMBERS IN NEPAL:

- ◆ Kathmandu: Government Tourist Office, Ganga Path, (01-220828) Department of Tourism, Babar Mahal, (01-214519)
- ◆ Pokhara: Tourist Office (061-20028)
- ◆ Bhairawa: Tourist Office (071-20304)
- ◆ Janakpur Tourist Office, Bhanu Chowk (041-20755)
- ◆ Kakarbhitta Tourist Office (023-20208)
- ◆ Tribhuvan Airport Tourist Office (410537)

ACTIVITIES

FIFTEEN FUN THINGS TO DO:

- ◆ Tour the current Royal Palace after you tire of the old palaces of Durbar Square. The fee to do so is nominal.
- ◆ Gamble the night away at some of the luxury hotels of Kathmandu such as the Soaltee or the Yak and Yeti. Hotels provide shuttle buses.
- ◆ Get an overview of Kathmandu Valley. Go ballooning.
- ◆ Go to a classical music concert. They are held in Kathmandu once a month near the Royal Palace at Narayanhity. The concerts take place in an open temple and are well attended.

THE NEXT STEP

- Don't have time or inclination to trek but still you want to be among the mountains? Make your reservation on the daily, one-hour "Mountain Flight" operated by several air carriers in Kathmandu. Subject to weather conditions, of course.
- Join the masses in close quarters and sing, laugh, and cry with them as you watch a three-hour-long Indian or Nepali movie in a local theater.
- On a Saturday, bicycle to the village of Godavari in the southeast corner of Kathmandu and observe nature as you meander among families enjoying a picnic in the Botanical Garden. You'll find loud radios, screaming kids, and boisterous adults who will be eating, drinking, and making merry, for tomorrow is Sunday, workday. Along with the urban refugees, you will also get a glimpse of traditional rural life. All this, and you are less than ten miles from the tourist ghetto of Thamel.
- Nepal has over 840 recorded bird species and is considered a paradise for bird-watchers. Contact Bird Conservation Nepal, P.O. Box 12465, Kathmandu (tel. 22-44-87). Every Saturday from May to September the group takes people bird-watching free of charge. It has branch offices in Pokhara, Chitwan, and the Koshi Tapu Conservation Area in southeastern Nepal. Binoculars are essential.
- In the evenings, drop into a local temple or a square, especially around Asan Tole. Hear the devotees singing hymns and songs, as has been done for centuries. Just sit quietly, listen, and soak it in.
- Overnight visits to some of the resort areas around the valley such as Dhulikhel or Nagarkot are quite enchanting, especially for the sunrise and sunset against the backdrop of the Himalayan peaks.
- For an unusual cross-cultural experience, ask about watching a wedding ceremony. The events are festive and people will welcome you if your interest is genuine.
- An "after trek" treat for women is to visit one of the local beauty parlors in Kathmandu's upscale hotels such as Summit or Shangri-la. Go for the works: facial, hot oil hair treatment, body massage, pedicure, manicure. Try an ancient Asian beauty practice called "threading" where they wrap thread like a cat's cradle in their fingers and expertly—and painlessly—remove unwanted body hair.

- When in Pokhara, look into horseback riding.
- Got a problem? If it's physical, emotional, psychological, or social, consider visiting a local shaman. Ask around for recommendations, but try to ask someone you trust.
- No longer a hippie, but still hip? Check out the cyber cafe K@mandu on Kantipath.

*N*ATIONAL PARKS/CONSERVATION AREAS/HUNTING RESERVES

If you trek in the Annapurna region, you will enter the Annapurna Conservation Area and must pay a conservation fee, and if your trek enters a national park, you must pay a national park fee. You can buy a ticket in advance at the national park office or you can just pay the fee when you arrive at the park entrance station. For information, contact:

The Department of National Parks & Wildlife Conservation
P.O. Box 860, Babar Mahal, Kathmandu
(Phone: 01-220912)

Below is a list of the national parks of Nepal:

- Annapurna Conservation Area, including the Annapurna Sanctuary, Annapurna peaks and a good part of the Kali Gandaki Valley, runs from just north of Pokhara to the Tibetan border. The area is run by the Annapurna Conservation Area Project, or ACAP.
- Dhorpatan Hunting Reserve is in the Dhaulagiri Himal in western Nepal.
- Khaptad National Park is a rarely visited park in far western Nepal.
- Koshi Tappu Wildlife Reserve runs north from the Kosi Barrage and the Indian border along the flood plain of the Sapt Kosi in eastern Nepal.
- Langtang National Park, the nearest park to Kathmandu, begins 32 km. north of Kathmandu and extends to the Tibetan border.
- Makalu-Barun National Park & Conservation Area, just to the east of Mt. Everest and containing Makalu, the fifth highest mountain in the world, is marked by the Chomolungma Nature Preserve in Tibet to

the north, the Arun River to the east and the Sagarmatha National Park to the northwest.

- Rara National Park, an important water bird habitat, surrounds the beautiful Rara Lake in little-visited western Nepal.
- Royal Bardia National Park in the western *tarai*, borders the Karnali River, with Chure Hills to the north.
- Royal Chitwan National Park and Parsa Wildlife Reserve are southwest of Kathmandu near the Indian border in the *tarai*. The world-famous Tiger Tops jungle resort is in the Royal Chitwan National Park.
- Royal Sukla Phanta Wildlife Reserve, one of the last strongholds for the endangered swamp deer, is in the far southwestern corner of Nepal on the Indian border.
- Sagarmatha National Park, most known for Mt. Everest, is northeast of Kathmandu and alongside the Tibetan border. It also includes Lhotse and Ama Dablam peaks.
- Shey Phoksundo National Park, the largest park in Nepal, encompasses the Kanjiroba Himal in western Nepal and runs north to the Tibetan border.

ADDITIONAL RESOURCES

⊂*N*EPAL ONLINE

There are numerous Nepal resources on the Internet. Point your browser to the following sites:

- AMAA Network Consultant, Inc.: http://catmando.com/nepal/htm
- Ayo-Gorkhali Nepal Link Page:
  http://www.fiu.edu/~bajracha/pub/nplinks.html
- CIA Worldfactbook:
  http://www.odci.gov/cia/publications/nsolo/factbook/np.htm
- Department of Tourism: http://www.south-asia.com/dotn/index.html
- GORP: http://www.gorp.com/gorp/location/asia/nepal.html
- Himal: http://www.south-asia.com/himal.html

- InfoHub:
  http://www.infohub.com/TRAVEL/TRAVELLER/ASIA/nepal.html
- Introduction to Nepal:
  http://www.interknowledge.com/nepal/index.html
- Kathmandu Post: http://www.south-asia.com/news-ktmpost.html
- Ministry of Tourism: http://www.south-asia.com/visitnepal98/
- Nepal Home Page: http://www.info-nepal.com/
- Nepal Trekking Home Page: http://www.bena.com/nepaltrek/
- Newsgroup: rec.travel.library: http://alpha.remcan.ca/rec-travel/asia/nepal
- Shangri La Home Page:
  http://aleph0.clarku.edu/rajs/Shangri_La.html
- Stego's little FAQ on Nepal:
  http://www.cfn.ist.utl.pt/~stego/NEPAL1/
- Travel Nepal: http://travel-nepal.com
- U.S. State Department travel advisory:
  http://travel.state.gov/nepal.html

🍮IVING BACK

There is a lot to be gained by traveling in Nepal, and many people are moved to support good causes once they've returned home. A few organizations that do good work and could use contributions follow.

The American Himalayan Foundation is a tax exempt, nonprofit organization dedicated to helping the people and protecting the ecology of the Himalayan region. It supports programs in health care, education, environmental conservation, and cultural preservation. *Contact: 909 Montgomery Street, Suite 400, San Francisco, CA 94133, USA; tel: 415-288-7245; fax: 415-434-3130.*

Educate the Children is a non-governmental organization (NGO) striving to educate children and empower impoverished women in Nepal. It started in 1990 by sponsoring three street children in Kathmandu and has grown to benefit over 15,000 people through projects in Kathmandu and the rural villages of Manakamana, Fikuri, Kaule, Valche, and Lahare. *Contact: Box 414, Ithaca, NY 14851-0414; tel: 607-272-1176; fax: 607-275-0932.*

The Fred Hollows Foundation, Inc. is a community-based NGO that has not only brought cheap and effective cataract treatment to thousands of Nepalis, but has established an intra-ocular lens factory in Kathmandu. Its work is complementary to the Seva Foundation listed below. Fred Hollows works in Kathmandu, Seva throughout the country. *Contact: Suite 2, 414 Gardeners Road, Locked Bag 100, Rosebery, NSW 2018 Australia; tel: 61-2-669-5899; fax: 61-2-669-5188; email: hollows@magnet.com.au.*

The Fund for the Tiger is a tax exempt, nonprofit organization dedicated to saving the tigers of Nepal and India. Its funds go directly to people and groups working on the ground in anti-poaching efforts in both countries. *Contact: P.O. Box 2, Woodacre, CA 94973, USA; tel: 415-488-0410; email: jaibagh@aol.com.*

King Mahendra Trust for Nature Conservation is an autonomous nonprofit organization that works for nature and wildlife conservation in Nepal. It has successfully undertaken over 60 projects in the fields of nature conservation, biodiversity protection and sustainable rural development. *Contact: P.O. Box 3712, Jawalakhel Lalitpur, Nepal; tel: 977-1-526571; fax: 977-1-526570.*

The Nepal Community Development Foundation is a Canadian NGO that supports the Namsaling Community Development Project and others like it in Syang, Nayabazaar, and Ilam in eastern Nepal. Through these projects the foundation is helping the villages work to attain self-sufficiency. The foundation focuses on improving education, adult literacy, health, water, and income generation. It is looking for supplies, service, time and monetary donations. *Contact: 152 Carlton Street, P.O. Box 92557, Toronto, Ontario, Canada M5A 4N9; tel: 416-944-3347; or Kha 2-140 Dilli Bazaar, P.O. Box 4903, Kathmandu, Nepal; tel: 977-1-418049; web site: http://www.nepalfriends.com/.*

The Nepalese Youth Opportunity Foundation provides educational and medical benefits for poor children in Nepal as well as support for blind and deaf children and services for street children of Kathmandu. It also supports two homes for orphaned or disabled children. *Contact: 203 Valley Street, Sausalito, CA 94965, USA.*

The Seva Foundation is a tax exempt, nonprofit organization that since 1979 has worked with the government of Nepal, WHO, and other partner organizations to build comprehensive eye-care services throughout Nepal. Prevention of blindness activities include village-based screening and treatment and referral to regional eye hospitals for cataract surgery. On occasion, Seva places volunteers in Nepal to provide training for program staff. *In the U.S. contact: 1786 Fifth Street, Berkeley, CA 94710; tel: 510-845-7382; fax: 510-845-7410; web site: http://www.seva.org; email: admin@seva.org. In Canada contact: Seva Service Society, 200-2678 West Broadway, Vancouver, BC, Z6K 2 G3, Canada; tel: 604-733-4284; fax: 604-733-4292; email: sevacan@axionet.com.*

RECOMMENDED READING

We hope *Travelers' Tales Nepal* has inspired you to read on. A good place to start is the books from which we've made selections, and we have listed them below. Many general guidebooks are also worth reading and the best ones have annotated bibliographies or sections on recommended books and maps.

Aitken, Molly Emma. *Meeting the Buddha: On Pilgrimage in Buddhist India.* New York: Riverhead Books, 1995.

Anderson, Mary M. *The Festivals of Nepal.* Calcutta: Rupa & Co., 1988.

Armington, Stan. *Trekking in the Nepal Himalaya.* Victoria, Australia: Lonely Planet Publications, 1997.

Antin, Parker with Phyllis Wachob Weiss. *Himalayan Odyssey: The Perilous Trek to Western Nepal.* New York: Laurel Books, a division of Bantam Doubleday Dell Publishing, Inc., 1990.

Bernbaum, Edwin. *Sacred Mountains of the World.* San Francisco: Sierra Club Books, 1990.

Bezruchka, Stephen. *Trekking in Nepal: A Traveler's Guide*. Seattle,
    Washington: The Mountaineers, 1997.

Bista, Dor Bahadur. *Fatalism and Development: Nepal's Struggle for
    Modernization*. Calcutta: Orient Longman Limited, 1991.

Bista, Dor Bahadur. *People of Nepal*. Kathmandu: Ratna Pustak Bhandar,
    1987.

Blashford-Snell, John and Rula Lenska. *Mammoth Hunt: In Search of the
    Giant Elephants of Nepal*. London: HarperCollins Publishers, 1996.

Blum, Arlene. *Annapurna: A Woman's Place*. San Francisco: Sierra Club
    Books, 1980.

Breeden, Stanley and Belinda Wright. *Through the Tiger's Eyes: A
    Chronicle of India's Wildlife*. Berkeley, California: Ten Speed Press,
    1996.

Byrne, Peter. *Tula Hatti: The Last Great Elephant*. Boston: Faber and
    Faber, 1990.

Carter, Jimmy. *An Outdoor Journal: Adventures and Reflections.* Fayetteville,
    Arkansas: University of Arkansas Press, 1994.

Coburn, Broughton. *Aama in America: A Pilgrimage of the Heart*. New
    York: Anchor Books, a division of Bantam Doubleday Dell
    Publishing Group, Inc., 1995.

Coburn, Broughton. *Nepali Aama: Life Lessons of a Himalayan Woman*.
    Santa Barbara, California: Ross-Erikson, Inc., Publishers, 1982; New
    York: Anchor Books, a division of Bantam Doubleday Dell
    Publishing Group, Inc., 1995.

Connell, Monica. *Against a Peacock Sky*. London: Penguin Books
    Limited, 1991.

Cronin, Jr., Edward W. *The Arun: A Natural History of the World's Deepest
    Valley*. New York: Houghton Mifflin Company, 1979.

Crossette, Barbara. *So Close to Heaven: The Vanishing Buddhist Kingdoms of
    the Himalayas*. New York: Vintage Departures, a division of Random
    House, Inc., 1996.

Daniélou, Alain. *Gods of Love and Ecstasy: The Traditions of Shiva and
    Dionysus.* Rochester, Vermont: Inner Traditions International, 1992.

Fleming, Robert Sr., et. al. *Birds of Nepal*. Kathmandu: Avalok Publishers,
    1979.

Forbes, Duncan. *The Heart of Nepal.* London: Robert Hale Limited, 1962.

Greenwald, Jeff. *Mister Raja's Neighborhood: Letters from Nepal.* Santa Barbara, California: John Daniel Publisher, 1986.

Greenwald, Jeff. *Shopping for Buddhas.* New York: Harper & Row, Publishers, Inc., 1990; Hawthorne, Victoria, Australia: Lonely Planet Publications, 1996.

Greenwald, Jeff. *The Size of the World: Once Around without Leaving the Ground.* Old Saybrook, Connecticut: Globe Pequot Press, 1996 and New York: Ballantine Books, a division of Random House, Inc., 1997.

Gurung, Harka. *Vignettes of Nepal.* Kathmandu: Sajha Prakashan, 1980.

Herzog, Maurice. *Annapurna: First Conquest of an 8000-Meter Peak.* Translated from the French by Nea Morin and Janet Adam Smith. New York: International Collectors Library, 1952.

Hillary, Sir Edmund. *High Adventure.* New York: E. P. Dutton & Company, Inc., a division of Penguin Books USA, 1955.

Hillary, Sir Edmund. *Nothing Venture, Nothing Win.* New York: Coward, McCann & Geoghegan, Inc., 1975.

Hutt, Michael with David Gellner, et. al. *Nepal: A Guide to the Art and Architecture of the Kathmandu Valley.* Boston: Shambhala Publications, Inc., 1994.

Ives, Richard. *Of Tigers and Men: Entering the Age of Extinction.* New York: Nan A. Talese, a division of Bantam Doubleday Dell Publishing Group, Inc., 1996.

Iyer, Pico. *Tropical Classical: Essays from Several Directions.* New York: Vintage Departures, a division of Random House, Inc., 1997.

Knowles, Peter and Dave Allardace. *White Water Nepal: Rivers Guide Book for Rafting and Kayaking.* London: Rivers Publishing, 1992.

Matthiessen, Peter. *The Snow Leopard.* New York: The Viking Press, a division of Penguin Books USA, Inc., 1978.

Murphy, Dervla. *The Waiting Land: A Spell in Nepal.* New York: The Overlook Press, 1987.

Nepali, Gopal Singh. *The Newars: An Ethno-Sociological Study of a Himalyan Community.* Bombay: Himalayan Booksellers, 1988.

Peissel, Michel. *Tiger for Breakfast: The Story of Boris of Kathmandu*. New
    Delhi: Time Books International, 1990.

Pye-Smith, Charlie. *Travels in Nepal: The Sequestered Kingdom*. London:
    Penguin Books Ltd., 1988.

Raeper, William and Martin Hoftun. *Spring Awakening: An Account of the
    1990 Revolution in Nepal*. New Delhi: Penguin Books India, 1992.

Raj, Prakash A. *Kathmandu and the Kingdom of Nepal*. New York:
    Hippocrene, 1993.

Reed, David. *Nepal: The Rough Guide*. London: The Rough Guides,
    1996.

Sakya, Karna. *Dolpo: The Hidden Paradise—A Journey to the Endangered
    Sanctuary of the Himalayan Kingdom of Nepal*. New Delhi: Nirala
    Publications, 1991.

Sakya, Karna and Linda Griffith, Ph.D. *Tales of Kathmandu: Folktales from
    the Himalayan Kingdom of Nepal*. Brisbane, Australia: House of
    Kathmandu, 1980.

Schaller, George B. *Stones of Silence: Journeys in the Himalaya*. Chicago:
    University of Chicago Press, 1988.

Scot, Barbara J. *The Violet Shyness of Their Eyes: Notes from Nepal*.
    Corvallis, Oregon: CALYX Books, 1993.

Slusser, Mary Shepherd. *Nepal Mandala: A Cultural Study of the
    Kathmandu Valley*. Princeton, New Jersey: Princeton University Press,
    1982.

Snellgrove, David. *Himalayan Pilgrimage: A Study of Tibetan Religion by a
    Traveller through Western Nepal*. Boston: Shambhala, 1989.

Stablein, Marilyn. *The Census Taker: Stories of a Traveler in India and
    Nepal*. Seattle: Black Heron Press, 1985.

Stevenson, Andrew. *Annapurna Circuit: Himalayan Journey*. London:
    Constable and Company Limited, 1997.

Taylor-Ide, Daniel. *Something Hidden Behind the Ranges: A Himalayan
    Quest*. San Francisco: Mercury House, 1995.

Thapa. Manjushree. *Mustang Bhot in Fragments*. Lalitpur, Nepal: Himal
    Books, 1992.

Tucci, Giuseppe, translated by Lovett Edwards. *Nepal: The Discovery of the
    Malla*. New York: E. P. Dutton, a division of Penguin Books USA,
    Inc., 1962.

Ullman, James Ramsey. *Tiger of the Snows: The Autobiography of Tenzing of Everest*. New York: G. P. Putnam's Sons, 1955.

Valli, Eric and Diane Summers. *Caravans of the Himalaya*. Washington, D.C.: National Geographic Society, 1994 and Paris: Éditions de La Martinière, 1994.

Valli, Eric and Diane Summers. *Honey Hunters of Nepal*. New York: Harry N. Abrams, Inc., a Times Mirror Company, 1988.

von Fürer-Haimendorf, Christoph. *The Sherpas Transformed: Social Change in a Buddhist Society of Nepal*. New Delhi: Sterling Publishers Private Limited, 1984.

Yeadon, David. *The Back of Beyond: Travels to the Wild Places of the Earth*. New York: Harper Perennial, a division of HarperCollins Publishers, Inc., 1991.

Glossary

a-lāa	a bamboo pole that is decorated with a piece of women's clothing, fruit, and flowers and erected on the roof of a home to identify it as a place of mourning
achar	spicy side dishes; pickles; salsa
arghaun	a funerary ceremony that occurs six months after death
ashutosh	immediate satisfaction
banjhankri	spirit dwellers of the forest
Bhagavad Gita	a section of the Hindu holy book, *Mahabharata*, in which Krishna delivers a sermon on *dharma* to the warrior Arjuna
bhai	younger brother
bharal	blue sheep found north of the Himalaya
bhattis	tea houses
bhirdi-yo	television
bidi	local cigarette made of tobacco leaf and held together with string
bukkhoos	traditional dress of Tibetan women
chainti	sixth day after birth
chaityas	a Buddhist shrine also known as stupa (*chorten* in Tibetan)
chang	home-made liquor
chapati	unleavened bread
chorten	the Tibetan term for a *stupa* or *chaitya*

chautara	resting stone platform built around a tree
chuba	smock worn by Tibetan men
crore	numerical value equal to ten million
dai	older brother
dal	soup made with a variety of lentils
dal-bhat	lentil soup (*dal*) and boiled rice (*bhat*)
dar-keko	torrential rain
darshan	ritual viewing or worship
dharma	usually translated as "religion" but literally means "that which holds" or "that which one must do"
dhikki	wooden mill found in many Nepali homes
dhotis	traditional loin wrap worn by men
didi	older sister
doko	an upturned conical bamboo basket
dom	a person of the untouchable caste that is responsible for burning dead bodies
dukkha	sorrow; suffering
durkho	a hard cheese
ganja	marijuana or hashish
gara	a blacksmith, the lowest in the social ladder of Tibetan culture
garuda	mythical beast of the Hindu religion that has the upper body of a bird and the lower body of a human
ghat	a stepped platform beside a river, used for bathing and washing, or for cremations
ghee	clarified butter used in cooking
goggaries	large water pots made of metal or clay
gompa	a Tibetan Buddhist monastery
goru	ox

gwiyantar	ritually empowered dagger
haat	weekly or bi-weekly marketplace
hare ram	"Oh God!"
himal, himalaya	the term "*himal*" means snow and "*alaya*" means place; himal, the short form, means "snow-capped mountain"
Jagir	employment, job, service, usually connected with government services
jantar	the pictorial counterpart of a mantra
jimbu	a mountain herb used in cooking
ke garne	what to do
khata	a white ceremonial scarf
khukuri	a Nepali curved knife, made famous world-wide by the Gorkha soldiers
kodalo	a short hand-held tool used for digging
kora	a clockwise circumambulation of a shrine, temple, holy city, or sacred mountain
kumari	a virgin girl
kurtha-sural	a knee-length shirt and loose trousers
lingas	a representation of the generative powers of Shiva, and the most common Shiva icon, usually a smooth egg-shaped stone mounted on a base which represents the *yoni* or vagina
Lakhang	shrine
lakh	the numerical value equal to one hundred thousand
lathis	any long stick or bamboo staff
lingam	a stylized phallus worshipped as a symbol of the god Shiva
lung-gom	literally with "wind" or "air," the vital energy or breath
lungi	a wrap-around tube-like skirt; sarong

madeshi	a native of the *tarai* or "*madesh*"
Manis	wish-fulfilling gems possessed by serpent-like beings
Maya	in Hindu philosophy, illusion (such as the phenomenal world); in everyday use, affection or love.
mitini	ritual sister
momos	steamed dumplings filled with meat or vegetables
mudras	hand gestures; the attitude of a deity's hands, an important element of Hindu and Buddhist iconology
naga	serpentine water deity
naga puja	ritual worship of the *naga*
namaste	term for "hello" as well as "good-bye"
nath	master; lord; supreme
Newari	the language, culture, or tradition associated with Newars, the original inhabitants of Kathmandu valley
om mani padme hom	Hail to the jewel in the lotus
pahari	hill people
pashmina	wool from the underbelly of a Himalayan goat
pashu	animal
pati	husband; lord
peda	sweet snack shaped like a round cracker
plah	effigy of a dead person
prasad	consecrated food
prana	breath of life
puja	ritual worship
pukka	paved (as in road); authentic, genuine
rakshi	local home-made liquor

rani	queen
rimpoche	a Tibetan title accorded to reincarnate lamas.
rishis	holy men; hermits
rotis	unleavened bread
rumali mil	the distance required to dry a handkerchief
Rongbas	people from the lower valleys
sadhu	a holy man, mendicant, or wandering hermit
sahib	an honorific used to show respect when addressing certain people, including foreigners
salwaar kameez	loose trousers (*salwaar*) and knee-length shirt (*kameez*) worn by women
samsara	in Hindu philosophy, the world of phenomenon
sardar	head Sherpa; trail boss
sarki	shoemaker
shikari	local hunter or naturalist
sim-sime	fine, gentle rain; drizzle
stupa	a Buddhist shrine also known as *chaitya* (*chorten* in Tibetan)
sukkha	condition of ease or happiness; opposite of *dukkha*
syako tyako	Newari phrase meaning "the more you kill, the more [material goods] you gain"
Tantric	that which is based on sacred texts called Tantras composed from the 7th century onward, which emphasized the mystical and psycho-sexual aspects of religious practice and iconology
tarai	the lowland belt of southern Nepal that is a part of the Gangetic plain of north India
tempo	a three-wheeled motorized vehicle

Thakali	people who are native to the Thak Khola area in the Gandaki River valley
thanka	Tibetan term for an iconographical painting on cloth
Tharus	people indigenous to the *tarai*
tika	a colorful spot of paint or other material placed on the forehead as a blessing
tongba	type of home-made liquor
topi	a cloth cap worn by men
ts'a ts'a	a bas relief clay impression used as votive offering
tsampa	roasted flour of various grains, usually barley or wheat
tulku	incarnate lama
yoni	a symbolic representation of the vagina
zamindar	landlord

Index

Index of Contributors

389

Acknowledgements

I must begin by thanking Larry Habegger and James O'Reilly, who as series editors achieved what the Jesuits could not: to instill some solid Protestant (Catholic?) work ethic in this rather languorous Hindu scrivener. Without their constant threats and harangues, portions of this book would still be languishing in unmarked files dumped in "milk carton" file organizers. My mother and late father, who put up a brave front even as their wayward son refused offers to "settle down," despite many attractive incentives to do so. Cynthia Collins and Susan Brady, the persistent production managers who slowly but surely transformed a very messy pile of papers into a finished manuscript, and at whose homes, under the pretext of "meetings," I've had some of the best meals in my life. The irrepressible Jennifer Leo, P.R. person par excellence, who has promised me fame *and* fortune. Also, Tim, Wenda, and Sean O'Reilly, Paula Mc Cabe, Linda and Allen Noren, and the design team at O'Reilly & Associates.

Dherai, dherai dhanyabad (many, many thanks) to Usha Lama of Third Eye Travel in Fremont, CA, Govind Shahi of Himalayan Treasures & Travel in Pinole, CA, and Kathy Measure of Thai Airways, San Francisco, for arranging the editors' most recent journey to Nepal.

In Kathmandu, thanks to Stan Armington, Sushil Upadhyaya and the entire staff at Malla Treks. My Nepali friends who turned my "research" into pleasant recreation include Kishor Gurung of House of Music, Captain Binod Puri of Everest Airways, and Rabi Singh, a very busy businessman who nevertheless put his office and car at my disposal.

The expats in Kathmandu, especially Patricia Roberts, whose support, enthusiasm and contributions to the book were invaluable. And I would not dare to return to Kathmandu without acknowledging Kanak Dixit, editor of *Himal South Asia*; my brother, B.K. Singh, who facilitated the entry and exit of the series editors at the Kathmandu airport with unforgettable swiftness and elegance; and my sister Nita who convinced her husband to give up his motorcycle so her editor-brother could use it to do his "research."

Back in the USA, scholars and gentlemen who helped with matters large and small are Robert L. Fleming, Jr., Rattu Lama, Norbu Tenzing of the American Himalayan Foundation, Gautama Vajracharaya of the University of Wisconsin at Madison, and Roger Willaims of Snow Lion Graphics, Berkeley/Hong Kong.

Finally, thanks for years of support and affection to John Gasperini, Narendra and Mira Gurung, Julia Hendrickson, Maria Judson, Paul O'Leary, George Pauly, Jr., David Randolph, Minu Singh, and the Nepali community of the San Francisco Bay Area—all who helped me feel at home abroad.

They resisted the temptation to ask: "So, when will you get a *real* job?"

"Tiger's Lair" by Richard Ives excerpted from *Of Tigers & Men: Entering the Age of Extinction* by Richard Ives. Copyright © 1996 by Richard Ives. Used by permission of Doubleday, a division of Bantam Doubleday Dell Publishing Group, Inc.

"The Birds of Rani Taal" by Peter Byrne published with permission from the author. Copyright © 1990 by Peter Byrne.

"Curry in a Hurry" by Parker Antin and Phyllis Wachob Weiss excerpted from *Himalayan Odyssey: The Perilous Trek to Western Nepal* by Parker Antin with Phyllis Wachob Weiss. Copyright © 1990 by Parker Antin and Phyllis Wachob Weiss. Used by permission of the authors.

"The Call of Kala Patthar" by Jimmy Carter excerpted from *An Outdoor Journal: Adventures and Reflections* by Jimmy Carter. Reprinted by permission of the University of Arkansas Press. Copyright © 1988, 1994 by Jimmy Carter.

"Best Price Buddha" by Jeff Greenwald excerpted from *Shopping for Buddhas* by Jeff Greenwald. Reprinted by permission of the author. Copyright © 1990 by Jeff Greenwald.

"Trial by Trisuli" by Carolyn Carvajal published with permission from the author. Copyright © 1997 by Carolyn Carvajal.

"Zen and the Art of Mountain Biking" by Meg Lukens Noonan reprinted by permission of the author. Copyright © 1989 by Meg Lukens Noonan. This story originally appeared in *Outside* magazine.

"In Buddha's Backyard" by Rajendra S. Khadka published with permission from the author. Copyright © 1997 by Rajendra S. Khadka.

"A Simple Gift" by Robert J. Matthews published with permission from the author. Copyright © 1997 by Robert J. Matthews.

"Shey Monastery" by Peter Matthiessen excerpted from *The Snow Leopard* by Peter Matthiessen, first published in Great Britain by Chatto & Windus 1979. This paperback edition first published in 1989 by Harvill. Copyright © Peter Matthiessen 1978. Used by permission of The Viking Press, a division of Penguin Books USA, Inc. and Harvill Publishers.

"Jamuna" by Jeff Hersch published with permission from the author. Copyright © 1997 by Jeff Hersch.

"Ritual Sisters" by Monica Connell excerpted from *Against a Peacock Sky* by Monica Connell. Copyright © 1991 by Monica Connell. Reprinted by permission of the author.

"Meanderings in Mustang" by Manjushree Thapa excerpted from *Mustang Bhot in Fragments* published by Himal Books. Copyright © 1992 by Manjushree Thapa. Reprinted by permission of the author.

"In My Father's Footsteps" by Jamling Tenzing with Rajendra S. Khadka published with permission from the authors. Copyright © 1997 by Jamling Tenzing and Rajendra S. Khadka.

"Honey Hunters" by Eric Valli and Diane Summers adapted from *Honey Hunters of Nepal* by Eric Valli and Diane Summers reprinted by permission of the authors. Copyright © 1987 by Eric Valley and Diane Summers.

"Farewell to Aama" by Broughton Coburn excerpted from *Aama in America: A Pilgrimage of the Heart* by Broughton Coburn. Copyright © 1995 by

Selections from *The Back of Beyond: Travels to the Wild Places of the Earth* by David Yeadon reprinted by permission of the author. Copyright © 1991 by David Yeadon.

Selection from "Barbara's Beat" by Barbara Adams reprinted from the February 6, 1997 issue of *People's Review*. Reprinted by permission of the author. Copyright © 1997 by Barbara Adams.

Selection from "A Bath for Christmas" by Preb Stritter reprinted by permission of the author. This article first appeared in *North by Northwest*, the magazine of Vermont Public Radio. Copyright © 1986 by Preb Stritter.

Selection from *The Back of Beyond: Travels to the Wild Places of the Earth* by David Yeadon reprinted by permission of the author. Copyright © 1991 by David Yeadon.

Selection from "The Buddha is Italian" by Eric Lurio published with permsision from the author. Copyright © 1997 by Eric Lurio.

Selections from *Caravans of the Himalaya* by Eric Valli and Diane Summers reprinted by permission of the authors. Copyright © 1994 by Eric Valley and Diane Summers.

Selection from *The Census Taker* by Marilyn Stablein reprinted by permission of Black Heron Press. Copyright © 1993 by Marilyn Stablein.

Selection from "Death in the Afternoon, Kirtipur Style" by Robert Peirce published with permission from the author. Copyright © 1997 by Robert Peirce.

Selection from "Dhampus Walls" by Jeffrey Heiman published with permission from the author. Copyright © 1997 by Jeffrey Heiman.

Selection from "Discerning the Landscape of the Heart" by Maxine Rose Schur reprinted from the February 5, 1997 issue of *The Christian Science Monitor* Reprinted by permission of the author. Copyright © 1997 by Maxine Rose Schur.

Selection fom *Dolpo—The Hidden Paradise: A Journey to the Endangered Sanctuary of the Himalayan Kingdom of Nepal* by Karna Sakya published by Nirala Publications. Copyright © 1991 by Nirala Publications. Reprinted by permission of the author.

Selection from "The Dutch Doctor" by Eric Valli and Diane Summers reprinted by permission of the authors. Copyright © 1997 by Eric Valley and Diane Summers.

Selections from "The Fabled Exploits and Recipies of Boris of Kathmandu" by Xenia Lisanevich published with permission from the author. Copyright © 1997 by Xenia Lisanevich.

Selections from *Fatalism and Development: Nepal's struggle for Modernization* by Dor Bahadur Bista reprinted by permission of Orient Longman Limited. Copyright © 1991 by Orient Longman Limited.

Selection from *Gods of Love and Ecstasy: The Traditions of Shiva and Dionysus* by Alain Daniélou published by Inner Traditions International, Rochester, VT 05767. Copyright © 1979 by Libraire Artheme Fayard. Translation copyright © 1982 by East-West Publications. Reprinted by permission.

Selection from "Greatest Human Member" by Maureen DeCoursey published with permission from the author. Copyright © 1997 by Maureen DeCoursey.

Selections from "Nepali Monsoon" by Kunda Dixit published with permission from the author. Copyright © 1997 by Kunda Dixit.

Selection from "Night Bus to Kathmandu" by Elizabeth Baugh Staphit published with permission from the author. Copyright © 1997 by Elizabeth Baugh Staphit.

Selection from "Notes from Nepal" by Julia Hendrickson published with permission from the author. Copyright © 1997 by Julia Hendrickson.

Selection from "Over the Border" by Jeffrey Heiman published with permission from the author. Copyright © 1997 by Jeffrey Heiman.

Selection from *People of Nepal* by Dor Bahadur Bista published by Ratna Pustak Bhandar.

Selections from "Pilgrimage to Muktinath" by Larry Habegger published with permission from the author. Copyright © 1997 by Larry Habegger.

Selection from "Places of Power" by Frances Klatzell published with permission from the author. Copyright © 1997 by Frances Klatzell.

Selection from "The Prayer Wheel" by Kirk Grace published with permission from the author. Copyright © 1997 by Kirk Grace.

Selection from "Sherpa Women Take the Lead" by Thalia Zepatos reprinted from the January/February 1996 issue of *EcoTraveler*. Reprinted by permission of the author. Copyright © 1996 by Thalia Zepatos.

Selection from *The Sherpas Transformed: Social Change in a Buddhist Society of Nepal* by Christoph von Fürer-Haimendorf reprinted by permission of Sterling Publishers Private Limited. Copyright © 1984 Christoph von Fürer-Haimendorf.

Selections from *Shopping for Buddhas* by Jeff Greenwald reprinted by permission of the author. Copyright © 1990 by Jeff Greenwald.

Selection from *The Size of the World: Once Around Without Leaving the Ground* by Jeff Greenwald reprinted by permission of the author. Copyright © 1995 by Jeff Greenwald. Originally published by The Globe Pequot Press.

Selections from *The Snow Leopard* by Peter Matthiessen, first published in Great Britain by Chatto & Windus 1979. This paperback edition first published 1989 by Harvill. Copyright © Peter Matthiessen 1978. Used by permission of The Viking Press, a division of Penguin Books USA, Inc. and Harvill Publishers.

Selection from *So Close to Heaven: The Vanishing Buddhist Kingdoms of the Himalayas* by Barbara Crossette. Copyright © 1995 by Barbara Crossette. Reprinted by permission of Vintage Books, a division of Random House, Inc.

Selection from *Something Hidden Behind the Ranges: A Himalayan Quest,* © 1995 Daniel Taylor-Ide. Published by Mercury House, San Francisco, CA, and reprinted by permission.

Selection from *The Spell of the Senuous: Perception and Language in a More-Than-Human World* by David Abram. Copyright © 1996 by David Abram. Reprinted by permission of Pantheon Books, a division of Random House, Inc.

Selection from *Spring Awakening: An Account of the 1990 Revolution in Nepal* by William Raeper and Martin Hoftun published by Penguin Books India. Copyright © 1992 by the Estate of William Raeper and Martin Hoftun.

About the Editor

Rajendra S. Khadka was born in Kapilvastu, Nepal, the land of the Buddha. Fearing their son might follow in the footsteps of the Enlightened One, his parents put him in a boarding school in Kathmandu run by American Jesuits.

A graduate of Williams College, he has been living and working in Berkeley since 1981. Among other things, he has been a film projectionist, waiter, chef-on-call, travel agent, and freelance writer. His book reviews and essays have appeared in the *San Francisco Chronicle,* the *East Bay Express*, and other publications. He currently works for Travelers' Tales and, according to the staff, has great hair.

NOTES

NOTES

TRAVELERS' TALES

LOOK FOR THESE TITLES IN THE SERIES

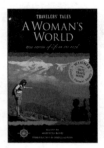

"I loved this book! From the very first story, I had the feeling that I'd been waiting to read these women's tales for years. I also had the sense that I'd met these women before. I hadn't, of course, but as a woman and a traveler I felt an instant connection with them. What a rare pleasure."

—Kimberly Brown, *Travel & Leisure*

TRAVELERS' TALES: A WOMAN'S WORLD
Edited by Marybeth Bond
1st Edition June 1995, ISBN 1-885211-06-6

**A WOMAN'S WORLD and THAILAND,
Winners of the Lowell Thomas Award for
BEST TRAVEL BOOK**
Society of American Travel Writers

"This is the best background reading
I've ever seen on Thailand!"

—Carl Parkes, author of *Thailand Handbook,*
Southeast Asia Handbook by Moon Publications

TRAVELERS' TALES THAILAND
Edited by James O'Reilly & Larry Habegger
1st Edition December 1993, ISBN 1-885211-05-8

"Sterling's themes are nothing less than human universality, passion and necessity, all told in stories straight from the gut."

—Maxine Hong Kingston,
author of *Woman Warrior* and *China Men*

TRAVELERS' TALES FOOD
Edited by Richard Sterling
1st Edition November 1996, ISBN 1-885211-09-0

Check with your local bookstore for these titles or call O'Reilly to order:
800-889-8969 (credit cards only-Weekdays 6 AM -5 PM PST)
707-829-0515, 800-998-9938 (inquiries), or email to: order@ora.com

"If Paris is the main dish, here is a rich and fascinating assortment of hors d'oeuvres. *Bon appetit et bon voyage!*"
—Peter Mayle, author of *A Year in Provence* and *Toujours Provence*

TRAVELERS' TALES PARIS
Edited by James O'Reilly, Larry Habegger & Sean O'Reilly
1st Edition March 1997, ISBN 1-885211-10-4

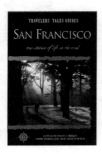

"As glimpsed here through the eyes of beatniks, hippies, surfers, 'lavender cowboys' and talented writers from all walks, San Francisco comes to vivid, complex life."
—*Publishers Weekly*

TRAVELERS' TALES SAN FRANCISCO
Edited by James O'Reilly, Larry Habegger & Sean O'Reilly
1st Edition June 1996, ISBN 1-885211-08-2

"*Travelers' Tales Hong Kong* is a most elegant, entertaining, and reliable way of getting to grips with the conundrum that is Hong Kong."
—Jan Morris, author of *Journeys, Locations,* and *Hong Kong*

TRAVELERS' TALES HONG KONG
Edited by James O'Reilly, Larry Habegger & Sean O'Reilly
1st Edition January 1996, ISBN 1-885211-03-1

"Only the lowest wattage dimbulb would visit Brazil without reading this book."
—Tim Cahill, author of *Jaguars Ripped My Flesh* and *Pecked to Death by Ducks*

TRAVELERS' TALES BRAZIL
Edited by Annette Haddad & Scott Doggett
1st Edition January 1997, ISBN 1-885211-11-2

Packed with instructive and inspiring travel vignettes, *Gutsy Women: Travel Tips and Wisdom for the Road* is a must-have for novice as well as experienced travelers.

TRAVELERS' TALES: GUTSY WOMEN
TRAVEL TIPS AND WISDOM FOR THE ROAD
By Marybeth Bond
1st Edition October 1996, ISBN 1-885211-15-5

"A superb, eclectic collection that reeks wonderfully of gazpacho and paella, and resonates with sounds of heel-clicking and flamenco singing—and makes you feel that you are actually in that amazing state of mind called Iberia."

—Barnaby Conrad, author of *Matador* and *Name Dropping*

TRAVELERS' TALES SPAIN

Edited by Lucy McCauley
1st Edition November 1995, ISBN 1-885211-07-4

"All you always wanted to know about the French but were afraid to ask! Explore the country and its people in a unique and personal way even before getting there. Travelers' Tales: your best passport to France and the French!"

—Anne Sengés, *Journal Français d'Amérique*

TRAVELERS' TALES FRANCE

Edited by James O'Reilly, Larry Habegger & Sean O'Reilly
1st Edition June 1995, ISBN 1-885211-02-3

"The essays are lyrical, magical and evocative: some of the images make you want to rinse your mouth out to clear the dust."

—Karen Troianello, *Yakima Herald-Republic*

TRAVELERS' TALES INDIA

Edited by James O'Reilly & Larry Habegger
1st Edition January 1995, ISBN 1-885211-01-5

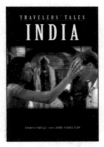

"*Travelers' Tales Mexico* opens a window on the beauties and mysteries of Mexico and the Mexicans. It's entertaining, intriguing, baffling, instructive, insightful, inspiring and hilarious—just like Mexico."

—Tom Brosnahan, co-author of Lonely Planet's *Mexico—a travel survival kit*

TRAVELERS' TALES MEXICO

Edited by James O'Reilly & Larry Habegger
1st Edition September 1994, ISBN 1-885211-00-7

VISIT TRAVELERS' TALES
ON THE INTERNET

READ A STORY. ENTER A CONTEST. PLAN A TRIP.

Way back in 1993, we were the first travel book publisher on the World Wide Web, and our site has been growing ever since. Point your Web browser to **http://www.ora.com/ttales** and you'll discover which books we're working on, how to submit your own story, the latest writing contests you can enter, and the location of the next author event. We offer sample chapters from all of our books, as well as the occasional trip report and photo essay from our hard-working editors. Be sure to take one of our Webtours, an exhaustive list of Internet resources for each of our titles, and begin planning your own journey.

SUBMIT YOUR OWN TRAVEL TALE

Do you have a tale of your own that you would like to submit to Travelers' Tales? We highly recommend that you first read one or more of our books to get a feel for the kind of story we're looking for. For submission guidelines and a list of titles in the works, send a SASE to:

Travelers' Tales Submission Guidelines
101 Morris Street, Sebastopol, CA 95472

or send email to ***ttguidelines@online.ora.com***
or check out our website at **www.ora.com/ttales**

You can send your story to the address above or via email to ***ttsubmit@ora.com***. On the outside of the envelope, ***please indicate what country/topic your story is about***. If your story is selected for one of our titles, we will contact you about rights and payment.

We hope to hear from you. In the meantime, enjoy the stories!

Joyce Dupee